ANGELL, Shirley

ANF
796.522

Pinnacle Club : a history of women climbing
Pinnacle Club
£14.95   0 9513967 0 6
List 51   -17/03/89   Item   2

JOHN MENZIES LIBRARY SERVICES   NOTTINGHAM

PINNACLE

CLUB

A History of Women Climbing

by

Shirley Angell

First President of The Pinnacle Club, Eleanor Winthrop Young. Taken two days before her marriage in 1918. Photo from E. Winthrop Young.

This book is dedicated to
all women climbers
and to all supportive husbands
and families.
Especially my own husband, Ian,
and my family,
Timothy, Adrian and Stephen.

First published in Great Britain in 1988 by
The Pinnacle Club
Copyright © by the Pinnacle Club.

Pinnacle Club
 Pinnacle Club: a history of women climbing.
 1. Great Britain. Women rock climbers. Organisations.
 Pinnacle to 1986.
 I. Title. II. Angell, Shirley. 1930
 796.5'223'06041

ISBN 0 9513967 0 6

Typesetting by Bureau-Graphics Ltd, Glasgow
Graphic Origination by Creative Halftones, Glasgow
Printed by Thomson Litho, East Kilbride
Bound by Hunter & Foulis, Edinburgh
Cover by Arneg, Glasgow

Distributed by Cordee, 3a DeMontfort Street,
Leicester LE1 7HD.

ACKNOWLEDGEMENTS

Many people, clubs and organisations have generously assisted in the production of this book.

My deepest thanks go to all Pinnacle Club members who responded to my pleas for information, those who lent precious diaries and photographs, those who criticised the text and suggested improvements, (Eleanor Winthrop Young, Livia Gollancz, Margaret Darvall and Gwen Moffat), and those who edited the finished text so carefully, (Janet Davies, Angela Soper and Margaret Clennett). If you disagree with my use of capital letters, I take the blame.

Secondly, my thanks to The Fell and Rock Climbing Club of the English Lake District, and in particular to Muriel Files for providing information, the loan of Blanche Eden-Smith's diary, and a photograph of Pat Kelly; to the Alpine Club; the Rucksack Club; and to the British Broadcasting Corporation for permission to publish a letter.

I thank Ken Wilson, Geoff Milburn, Ken Vickers and Peter Hodgkiss for their encouragement and advice. Peter, in particular, told me how to save money, guided me through all the stages of publication and showed his faith in the finished result by buying a copy in advance.

I am grateful to Ian Smith for permission to publish his photographs, and to Douglas McCord for spending long hours getting the best results from some of the older snapshots.

Finally, I must mention my husband, Ian, who said, yes, he had always wanted a computer, but who never complained when I commandeered it. He also took me climbing when I needed a break.

Shirley Angell.

CONTENTS

Foreword *by Gwen Moffat.*   xiii

Introduction.   xiv

Chapter 1. *Founder Members. Len Winthrop Young, Pat Kelly, the Wells sisters, Inaugural Meeting.*   1

Chapter 2. *More Founder Members. E.H. Daniell, Lilian Bray, Dorothy Pilley, Pat Kelly soloing Jones Route, FRCC members, Blanche Eden-Smith, Dr Corbett.*   6

Chapter 3. *'Saas for the Goose is Saas for the Gander'. Wasdale, Saas Fee, Norway, Second Annual Meeting.*   11

Chapter 4. *Emily Kelly dies.*   18

Chapter 5. *"You could pay six shillings if you like". 1922-2. The first journal, first Manchester Dinner. Routes in Britain and the Alps.*   20

Chapter 6. *1924-1927. Paddy Hirst's Presidency. Climbing abroad. First ascents. First Alpine Meet. 'Coming of Age' of the Fell and Rock Climbing Club.*   24

Chapter 7. *1928-1929. Cuillin Ridge, Dent Blanche, Women's Achievements World-wide. Alison Adam, Brenda Ritchie, Evelyn Lowe.*   31

Chapter 8. *"Heaven for a bob a day". 1930 to 1932. A Hut in Wales. More New Members.*   36

Chapter 9. *1933-35. Mabel Barker. Dorothy Pilley as President. Climbing worldwide and more new members. "Climbing Days" published. Meet in High Tatras.*   44

Chapter 10. *1936 to 1939. Mrs Eden-Smith President. A headless corpse. More climbing. Ruth Hale's death. Opening of Brackenclose. Entertainments. Rockfalls. New routes.*   51

Chapter 11. *1939 and the early war years. Travelling to meets. Mabel Jeffrey President. Last pre-war Alpine meets. The Richards in America. Gladys Low's expedition in the Himalayas.*   59

Chapter 12. *War work. A German P.O.W. Camp. The Hut in wartime. 21st Birthday. Start of BMC. Deaths of Nancy Forsyth and Jean Orr Ewing. The war ends.*   65

Chapter 13. *1946-7. Evelyn Leech President. New Members. National Parks. Scottish and Skye meets. Paddy Hirst on Munros.*   72

Chapter 14. *1948-1949. First post war dinner. Meets and members. A post card from Chamonix. A reluctant President. Gwen Moffat. Alpine meet. Freda Rylatt's accident. E.H. Daniell.*   78

Chapter 15. *1950. Menu cards - Marjorie Wood starts a tradition. Hut maintenance. Club badge. Climbs and meets. Sid and Jammy at ODG. Alpine routes. Pat Whinnerah on Kilimanjaro.*   86

Chapter 16. *1952. Gwen Moffat and Morins at the hut. Nea Morin President. An influx of new members. Alpine Climbing Group. Girl Guide Association. London Section. Alpine routes.*   92

Chapter 17. *Bunny Bull meets the Great Ones. Morin family climbs. Alpine Climbing Group. Gwen Moffat first woman guide. Everest climbed.*   99

Chapter 18. *More new members. Maud Godward and the M.A. Manchester University W.M.C. Kay Boucher's experiences. Nea's Pinnacle Club Alpine Meet.*   103

Chapter 19. *1955. Mrs Bryan President. Hard climbs. Margaret Darvall, Denise Shortall. Welsh 3000s. Alpine routes. Hut in disrepair. LSCC Himalayan Expedition 1955.*   111

Chapter 20. *1956-1957. Dinners. The hut. New members. Dorothea Gravina. Eileen Gregory's first Himalayan trip. Deo Tibba. Greenland. Norway. Rie and Denise in the Alps.*   118

Chapter 21. *1957. A winter ascent of Snowdon. Mur y Niwl. Eileen Healey President. 3000s in 9 hours. Alpine Club Centenary. Dolomites Meet.*   125

Chapter 22. *1958. A new Treasurer. Janet Cox. LSCC Jubilee. A festive Christmas. Eileen married. Collapse of a barn wall. Mollie Taplin. Dorothy Lee. In mother's footsteps.*   131

Chapter 23. *1959-1960. Ama Dablam. Cho Oyu. Good routes - hut parties - hut troubles. More new members. Nancy Smith. Jo Scarr on Kaisergebirge Wall. Dauphine Meet. First ascents on Rhum. Midland Spitzbergen Expedition.*   137

Chapter 24. *1961-1962. Winifred Jackson President. An accident. Membership and hut matters. Preparing for the Jagdula Expedition. Alpine routes. Space published. Women's Kulu Expedition. Meets and membership.*   147

Chapter 25. *1962. Jagdula Expedition. Other trips. Anne and Ssylvia at the hut. Froggatt Meet. Reunions and climbs in Wales. An accident and a news bulletin. Tin Trays.*   158

Chapter 26. *1963-1965. Dorothea Gravina's Presidency. Floods in the hut. Members. Meets. Helen Goodburn finds friends in Nea and Denise.*   166

Chapter 27. *1965,1966. Dawa Tensing in Britain. S. Angell's first meet. Matterhorn Centenary. New members.*   177

Chapter 28. *1967-1969. Barbara Spark appointed to MLTB. New members. Meets. Helen and Chris in the Alps. Hard climbs and expeditions at home and abroad. Peuterey Ridge. Janet Rogers President. Mairet and Ruth lost. A less serious accident.*   189

Chapter 29. *Whitsun at Cwm Dyli. Hard routes on Scafell and Pavey. British Women's Himalayan Expedition. Ron and Barbara James in the Dolomites. Barbara leads Cemetary Gates. Baptism of new rainwear.*   200

Chapter 30. *1971. Jubilee Year celebrations and Journal. Alpine Routes. Peru. Dorothea's travels. Evelyn Leech dies.*   205

Chapter 31.*1972 1973. Denise Wilson President. New members. Climbs and meets. A night ascent of Snowdon.*   210

Chapter 32. *1974-1975. Annual Dinner Meets. Cromlech Boulders. Meets and members. Evelyn Leech's memorial. Good routes abroad.*   221

Chapter 33. *1976-1977. Meets. A secretary's post bag. Everest ascent. New members. Meet at High Moss. Scottish skiing meet.*   226

Chapter 34. *1978 and 1979. New members. The duties of a President. Expeditions. Annapurna and death of Alison Chadwick. Caving. Camping.* 232

Chapter 35. *1980 Lahaul Expedition.* 240

Chapter 36. *1981 and 1982. Sixtieth Anniversary Dinner. Skye Ridge. International Climbing Meets. Fiftieth Anniversary of Emily Kelly Hut.* 245

Subscribers 250
Index 251

ILLUSTRATIONS

All illustrations are from the Pinnacle Club Collection. Further acknowledgements are made where possible.

Front Cover. *On the traverse of the Funffingerspitze, 1974. Photo: S. Angell.*
Back Cover. *On the Himalayan Expedition, 1980.*
Frontispiece. *First President of the Pinnacle Club, Eleanor Winthrop Young. Taken two days before her marriage in 1918. Photo from E. Winthrop Young.*
Page 3. *Pat Kelly. (Gift from F&RCC Collection).*
Page 5. *Dorothy Pilley's receipt.*
Page 12. *L Bray, D Pilley and A Wells on the first independent feminine Alpine ascents. Egginergrat, 1921. Portjengrat, 1921. Note the sunbonnet. Photos from L Bray.*
Page 17. *Pat Kelly on The Scoop, Castle Naze.*
Page 30. *Easter Meet, Kiln Howe, Rossthwaite, 1928. Back row: L-R: Dr Taylor, H A Turner, Mrs Isherwood, M S Ashton, Mrs Eastwood, H M Clark, Marjorie Wood. Front row: E M Hobkinson, Lilian Bray, Ella Mann, Hilda Summersgill, Dr Corbett, Madge Scott.*
Page 40. *The Emily Kelly Hut, Cwm Dyli.*
Page 41. *Dr Corbett and her brother at the bonfire.*
Page 42. *L-R: Lowe, Lear, D Seth-Hughes, J Seth-Hughes, Wood, P Seth-Hughes.*
Page 43. *H M Kelly's invitation card.*
Page 45. *Coniston, 1933. L-R: Eden-Smith, Pilley, Corbett, Mrs Humphries, R Hale, Ashton. Front: Annette Wilson, Ursula Lawrie, Alison Adam.*
Page 45. *Coniston, Easter 1934. Back row L-R: Wood, B Ritchie, Arning, Pirie Wilson, Bennett, Adam, ?. Second row: Dawson, Turner, Corbett, Pilley, Bray. Front row: Heys-Jones, Harper, Lowe, Eden-Smith.*
Page 55. *Easter 1938, Penelope Seth-Hughes leading Yellow Slab and Pinnacle.*
Page 62. *Chandra Singh on snowfield, Ghopils in background. Photo: Jean Punnett.*
Page 93. *Gwen Moffat on Milestone Superdirect. Photo: S R G Bray.*
Page 107. *S Long on the Pointe des Ecrins, 1954.*
Page 107. *Le Bez, 1954. 'We all fitted into the taxi'. L-R: D Tharby, P Wild, A Wilson, S Long, N Morin, R Leggett, E Pyatt.*
Page 108. *Top. L-R: A Flew, S Long, N Morin, R Leggett.*
Page 108. *Bottom. On the Aiguille de Sialouse, 1954. Photos from Suzanne Gibson.*
Page 123. *Rie Leggett in 1956.*
Page 141. *Nancy aged 18 on Simian Exit, Murray's Route.*
Page 151. *Greetings card from the Jagdula Expedition. L-R: Barbara Spark, Nancy Smith, Jo Scarr, Denise Evans, Pat Wood, Dorothea Gravina.*
Page 158. *Expedition Christmas Card.*
Page 163. *Froggatt Meet, 1962, and Party Pieces. Nea on The Boulder. Nancy on The Boulder. On Brown's Eliminate. Photos: ˙˚Frances Tanner.*

Page 166. *Cartoon: The Sensible People. Sheila Crispin.*
Page 167. *Cartoon: Digging Drainage Ditches. Sheila Crispin.*
Page 172. *Outside the Dalmazzi Hut, 1964. Nancy Smith, Ian ?, Pat Wood, Joe Brown, Sylvia Yates, Mary Stewart, Tom Patey, Chris Bonington. Photo Frances Tanner.*
Page 173. *L-R. Pat Wood, Sylvia Yates, Nancy Smith. Photo Frances Tanner.*
Page 177. *Dawa Tensing at Cwm Dyli, 1965. L-R: Helen Jones, Annette Wilson, Margaret Darvall, Dawa Tensing, Dorothea Gravina, Dorothy Lee. Timothy and Shirley Angell in front. Photo: Ian Angell.*
Page 183. *Angela Soper on Cave Arch, Stanage. International Women's Meet 1984. Photo Ian Smith.*
Page 187. *Jill Lawrence on Cream. Photo Ian Smith.*
Page 205. *Back and front pages of PC 50th Anniversary Dinner menu card.*
Page 220. *Anniversary Meet 1985. Dorothea Gravina and Gwen Moffat. Photo: Dorothy Wright.*
Page 236. *Stella Adams on Mesach, Tremadoc, 1984. Photo: Ian Smith.*
Page 240. *General area of 1980 Expedition, and of previous expeditions by J-G Low, E Healey, M Darvall & others.*
Page 241. *Area covered by 1980 Expedition.*
Page 242. *1980 Expedition members. Angela Soper standing. L-R. Stella Adams, Jean Drummond, Steph Rowlands, Sheila Crispin, Sheila Cormack, Jay Turner. Photo: Denise Wilson.*
Page 247. *Members of the International Meet at Cwm Dyli. L-R: Mandy Glanville, Rosie Andrews, Nicole Niquille, Christine Jambort. Photo: Ian Smith.*
Page 249. *Mulled Wine by the bonfire. Photo: Dorothy Wright.*

FOREWORD

The members of the Pinnacle Club have other achievements to their credit: in their careers, in parallel activities, but they have been most memorably active in mountains: from the Himalaya to the Sierras, from the Arctic to the New Zealand Alps.

Their base is a hut, Cwm Dyli, under a cliff called Lliwedd in North Wales: a small slate and stone structure which for some may be closer to what they know as home, what they "feel" is home, than any place they will ever know.

But this is more than a group of women and a cottage. When we drink to the Club we stand. We are the Club but it is more than the sum of its members. When it was formed in 1921 the founders knew only in part what they were about. Initially they were creating an environment in which they could lead on their own choice of route and, refuting all suggestions that a woman could lead only with the support of a male second, they led all-woman ropes. From that point we developed.

We do not dislike men. We marry them, we continue to climb with them, but there is always this deep and wondrous sense of security that, in the event of all else failing, we can go back to Cwm Dyli and live, if only for a weekend, as we were wont to live, climb as we should climb, on Lliwedd and Tryfan and all points radiating throughout our world, climb with people we have known and trusted perhaps for decades, whom we may see only at the annual Dinner, and for long spells not even then.

The Club is a tradition, a form of continuity, like children, but posterity does not demand that it should be of one's own blood, although it is supremely important that those who inherit the tradition possess the same spirit. The girls coming in to the Club now, those that will come in the future, will be the same as those of the Twenties in everything that matters.

We have all served in greater or lesser degree, but how many of us feel that we have contributed less than we have derived from our relationship with the Club? Until now the major contributions (apart from superb and glamorous climbs) have been in the mundane but extremely onerous capacities of committee work and maintenance. Now there is another form of achievement: the record.

Shirley Angell has dedicated years to producing this book: researching, selecting, compiling, correlating, until finally the labour of love emerges: a portrait of a club and a celebration of women, past and present, who love rock and high mountains and who, given a focal point for adventurous souls, have discovered that they are not alone. Other women are explorers too, not out there, but in here, in the Pinnacle Club.

Gwen Moffat
Weasel Creek
Bozeman
Montana 1988

INTRODUCTION

The first two women's climbing clubs in Britain were founded because the doors of men's clubs were closed to women.

The Ladies' Alpine Club was founded in 1907 as a sister to the Alpine Club, and the Ladies' Scottish Climbing Club in 1908.

In England, things were a little different; the Fell and Rock Climbing Club, founded in 1906 for exploring the fells and rock-climbs of the English Lake District, was a mixed club which welcomed women members. The need for a women's club became apparent only when women wished to concentrate on their rock-climbing skills and to lead their own expeditions. As regards this, at least one Fell and Rock member, Pat Kelly, found the F&RCC 'very male orientated'. Thus the Pinnacle Club was the first to be formed specifically for women's rock-climbing, and was founded later than the other two women's clubs, in 1921.

This book draws on many sources to outline mountaineering achievements this century, putting into context a history of the Pinnacle Club as a whole. The Club's membership has included many outstanding women, often distinguished in fields other than mountaineering and not always of great rock-climbing ability.

The life-blood of clubs and sports lies in enthusiastic participators; some trying to improve their ability, others using the pastime as relaxation from a demanding career or from the demands of family life; but every now and again a star appears, sometimes with the brief excitement of a shooting star, and sometimes with a steady glow.

The stars have their place, and so do stories of first expeditions, finding a Club hut, the president's dress: major events and those which are trivial but fun and part of Club life. Above all there are stories of past and present members, often from diaries and records of the time. Being by, and about, women, they are enchantingly different from the usual run of mountaineering literature.

Shirley Angell
Largs
Ayrshire 1988

CHAPTER 1

FOUNDER MEMBERS

*"In nineteen hundred and twenty-one
The Pinnacle Club it was begun . . ."*
Len Winthrop Young, Pat Kelly, the Wells sisters, Inaugural Meeting.

The story starts in 1920 when Eleanor Winthrop Young was a very new member of the Fell and Rock Climbing Club. Geoffrey, her husband, had joined the year before and Emily Kelly had been a member for the past two years.

Over sixty years later, at the Pinnacle Club's Diamond Jubilee Dinner, Eleanor, generally known as Len, enthralled her audience with vivid memories of the Club's founder. I was so fascinated by the account that I knew I must write it down, so I called on Len in her small, comfortable home in Marlborough and we sat down at a table and talked. On the wall were many photographs, including one of a beautiful, dark-haired girl. Geoffrey had written her name across it all those years ago.

"But you've written Eleanor Slingsby," she said.

"Yes," he said. "That's who you are."

So I was looking at the past and the present in a quite enchanting way. At 86, Cecil Slingsby's daughter and Geoffrey Winthrop Young's wife, but most of all *herself* was a kind and lovely lady, small and full of life.

"I can tell you exactly what happened," she said. "It was 1920 and Geoffrey and I were sitting in the Sun Hotel, Coniston. We always had our meetings there and the Kellys were sitting there across the room – it wasn't a very big room – and I said: "Mrs Kelly's there: she's looking this way."

"She was very impetuous, something which drew me to her, and she rushed across the room – she never did anything slowly, you know, and said, "Can I have a talk to you about something?" She sat down on the floor and started off about wanting to start a women's club. Geoffrey at once said that it was a splendid idea. He was always keen on it. I think I was a little bit quieter, because I was the baby of the party, rather. So what we said then, I can't remember, but we were very close and very keen indeed.

"While we were talking about it, quite early on I said, 'it seems awfully dull just to say Ladies' Rock Climbing Club. There's Ladies this and Ladies that'. Geoffrey, in a thoughtful way, gave me a key, but I really was responsible for the name. He said, 'You know there was a very nice club - a lucky club - a ladies' club in London when I was young called the Pelican'. We went to bed, we talked no more about it: and from the Pelican we really got the Pinnacle."

Although they had joined the Fell and Rock, the Winthrop Youngs had even stronger connections with North Wales than with the Lake District. Geoffrey Winthrop Young had been a member of the Climbers' Club for many years and Cecil Slingsby was a founder member and past president. In 1911, when their parents were to be abroad, Geoffrey

Winthrop Young invited Len, aged 15, and her brother Lawrence, then 17, to his Pen-y-Pass party. Len did her first Welsh route, Gashed Crag, and soon climbed many other routes. Her father had taken her for walks and climbs as long as she could remember, and she says:

"He wrote in the Norway book he gave me in his wonderful Elizabethan writing: 'First learnt rock climbing' (it meant nothing - a few scrambles) 'Cray Ghyll.' It was Buckden, and we used to go there driving with horses a lot. Then he'd take us to Malham and there I learnt an important lesson from him. It wasn't climbing, but it taught me a lot. At Malham Cove, you've heard of it naturally - a tremendous place and we used to go there often. My brother and I were quite small (I was the youngest; my brother was killed in the First War) and we were fooling about and my father said, 'Now then, children, listen to me' – it's a lesson I've never forgotten – 'Whenever you're on the edge of a cliff like that you must be careful. You never know where it's slippery and if you go down there we are not going to get you back'.

"I don't know if we did very much climbing. We scrambled with father and he was very cross if we dropped stones when we went over those big stone walls. That was shocking; you ought never to do that. I remember sitting on top of one wall when I was a very little girl; I said, 'I can't get down, father'. He said, 'Yes, you can,' and I had to!

"Then, you see, I grew up in the First War and there was nothing doing very much, and I married Geoffrey at the end of the war. It was all very exciting: Geoffrey was determined to get back into climbing and everybody thought it was crazy and mad, and that *I* was. You see, I must explain this. When this famous man of mine lost his leg on the Italian Front he was already 41, and he lost it right up near the top, which is much more difficult than if you keep the knee. I used to drive him to go on. I was the one who said we'd start the parties at the Pen-y-Pass again which he thought we couldn't because everyone who used to come had been killed, either while climbing or in the war. We had tremendously big parties and lots of merriment at them - in 1919, 1920 (I think I was tied up with a baby) and 1921. That year he was very keen because he knew we were starting the Pinnacle Club down at PyG. Lockwood, who was at the Pen-y-Gwryd, was never a great pal of ours, but he was very kind about this and said we could use the billiard room. So there we were."

Long before meeting the Winthrop Youngs in 1920, Emily 'Pat' Kelly had been very busy contacting every person and organisation that might be interested in the proposed ladies' climbing club. Among those who were not connected with the Fell and Rock Climbing Club were the three Wells sisters. I visited Trilby Wells, who at 92 years of age was still extremely active: going to local events, walking every day, full of humour, candid remarks and Yorkshire grit. She told me how they came to join:

"We were walkers, not climbers, and at the beginning, when Mrs Kelly was trying to get things started and get members, I think she got in touch with people who'd been in the Cooperative Holidays Association. Well, my sister met someone who knew Mrs Kelly, and through this friend she met Mrs Kelly, who asked her to join. Of course my sister said that there were two more of us, and that we all walked. We were mountaineers, we'll say, and we'd done quite a lot, but we'd never done any climbing."

By the time of the inaugural meeting, Annie (known as Paddy), the eldest, and Biddy, the youngest, had both started climbing and qualified as full members. Trilby became an associate member and qualified in 1925 by taking a girl called Maisie Gregg up a climb, then leading a man, she can't remember his name, up another route – "And so I qualified."

FOUNDER MEMBERS

Pat Kelly.

She remembers Biddy's first venture, at Laddow:

"We went to Laddow quite a lot. The first time we went Mr Kelly was there and he took Biddy climbing. They climbed everything there was to climb on Laddow - and on the next morning Biddy couldn't get out of bed."

Now that 'Mr Kelly' has been mentioned it seems appropriate to draw on H.M. Kelly's own reminiscences of the years leading up to the club's formation. Entitling them "Founding Days", he first outlined the influence on Pat of the feminist movements in the early 1890s. These ideas, together with Pat's warm disposition and understanding mind, led her firstly to practise and improve her technique as an independent rock climber and secondly to expend endless patience and encouragement on the efforts of her more tentative sister-climbers. When Harry Kelly joined the Rucksack Club she became a member of the Fell and Rock Climbing Club, which, however, she found very male-oriented.

The Kellys' meeting with Annie Wells in Easter 1916 led to others and then to gritstone meets, and gradually more and more women became interested in the sport. The idea of a climbing club for women members only was aired and nurtured: "And by 1920," writes H.M. Kelly, "It was evident that something would have to be done. Pat and I then had a small office at 29 Fountain Street, Manchester, and this became the seat of operations. Unfortunately the building was later pulled down to make room for an extension of an enjoining emporium, otherwise Manchester could do itself proud by putting up a plaque to inform the world that the Pinnacle Club was founded here.

"A letter was written to the *Guardian* (then *Manchester Guardian*) saying that it was proposed to form a club for women rock-climbers and inviting those interested to communicate with the writer (Pat). To our delight, the letter was not only published but was benevolently approved in a short leader by the Editor (C.E. Montague). It was remarkable to have the backing of a paper of such prestige, and it was gratifying to have the sympathetic approval of male climbers such as G.W. Young. Most important though was the response from women."

The inaugural meeting was planned for Easter 1921 and the winter was busy with preparations: proposed rules and an agenda were drafted and Mrs Winthrop Young suggested as president.

Miss Lilian Bray, a very forthright person and experienced alpinist, queried some of the rules, and her intervention caused the Kellys and J.H. Doughty, who was helping them, to re-examine the proposed constitution for possible flaws. They held a mock inaugural meeting with Pat as secretary, H.M. Kelly as chairman and Doughty as possible critic. Nothing which could aid the formation of the club was left to chance.

The Inaugural Meeting proper took place in the billiard room of the Pen y Gwryd Hotel, Llanberis, N. Wales on March 26th, 1921.

Two members came from the Pen y Pass: Mrs Winthrop Young and a musical friend, Ursula Nettleship, who used to go to the Pen y Pass parties. Climbing was not her forte, but she was very keen to give the new club a good send-off. Quite a number of women joined for the same reason, then resigned after a year or two.

Eight members came from Ogwen: Mrs Eden-Smith, Mrs Evans, Mrs Johnson, Mrs Kelly, Miss Michaelson, Miss Rathbone, Miss Stanley and Miss Turner; and seven were already staying at the Pen y Gwryd: Miss Bray, Mrs Burnham Smith, Miss Dutton, Mrs Wallbank, Miss Wells (Paddy), Mrs Wigner and Miss Wild. Some of these names are hardly heard again and others, along with some who were unable to attend the meeting, have become almost a legend. In all, there were 20 full members and 23 associate members plus two who joined later in the first year.

The proposal that Len Winthrop Young would take the chair was welcomed by all, and she came well prepared. She gave a resumé of how the concept of the club arose, pointing out how women could help each other to become more proficient in the art of rock climbing and mountaineering; how they were bound to gain confidence, as one after another they learnt to lead, not necessarily anything very difficult and, little by little, their confidence in each other would develop. One thing every member could attain was to become first rate when climbing second on the rope. Finally she read extracts from a letter to Mrs Kelly written by a great mountaineer – Mrs O'Malley – on what should constitute good leadership. The resolution to form a club was carried unanimously.

The draft rules were now studied and the proposed name amended from "Women's Rock Climbing Club" to "Pinnacle Club". It was decided to wait a year before electing any vice-presidents. Mrs Kelly became honorary secretary and Mrs Eden-Smith recording secretary. Len remembers: "When I came away from that first meeting I told Eden-Smith that she was the Recording Angel and I called her Gabriel". This became her nickname and was later shortened to "G".

The committee comprised Miss Michaelson (Lella Michaelson, Mrs Eden-Smith's sister), Miss D.E. Pilley (famous as Dorothy Pilley and, later, Mrs I.A. Richards), Miss A. Wells (Paddy Hirst, the club's second president) and Miss Ward, who helped to get the club started then resigned in 1925. The final business to be conducted at the Inaugural Meeting was the arrangement of the club's first official climbing meet on Tryfan the next day.

As for the rest of the weekend, we know that most members spent it climbing. Len had to go straight back home for a dress rehearsal as she was a member of an amateur operatic society and had a solo dance in a big production of 'Merrie England'. Still wearing climbing boots, she practised dance steps in the train.

Of the ladies who used their boots for the proper purpose, those at P-y-G merely tell us that climbs were done, but the party from Ogwen listed the climbs done by each member. On March 25th the whole group from Ogwen Cottage climbed on Idwal Slabs, and on the 26th, a short day because of the meeting, they all ascended Milestone Buttress. On the 27th Mrs Kelly, Mrs Evans and Miss Rathbone ascended Central Buttress on Tryfan and descended South Gully. The following day Miss Michaelson and Mrs Eden-Smith joined Mrs Kelly and Mrs Evans on Little Tryfan, probably getting cold and sopping wet in the process. The weather deteriorated during the weekend and became very bad:- torrents of rain, followed by snow. The stamina and spirit of the new Club were already being tested.

Dorothy Pilley's receipt.

CHAPTER 2

MORE FOUNDER MEMBERS
E.H. Daniell, Lilian Bray, Dorothy Pilley, Pat Kelly soloing Jones Route (severe), FRCC members, Blanche Eden-Smith, Dr Corbett.

Several of the women who became founder members already had considerable prestige as climbers or mountaineers and some were famous in other fields as well. Emily Daniell was the novelist E.H. Young and also, on August 14th 1915, had led the first ascent of Hope on the Idwal Slabs.

"It is quite difficult to realise," wrote R.B. Henderson, "that, before she came, those slabs had never been climbed. Moreover several experts, including O.G. Jones, had abandoned them as unclimbable. Emily led straight up what is now called Hope and by so doing opened up the whole cliff with Holly Tree Wall above – and all in boots, remember."

Sympathetic though she was with the aims of the Club, E.H. Daniell was not able to attend many meets. Len remembered:

"One who disappeared almost at once was Mrs Daniell. I wish I could find out more because she made a great impression on me. She was a sister to the actress Gladys Young – I didn't know it till later. She died rather young, but she was a very keen climber and an absolutely charming woman and I always wished I knew more about her. When she died in 1949 I pulled myself together and wrote to the celebrated actress, Gladys Young, not realising who she was, saying how sad we were and she wrote me a charming letter. She said, 'We were very keen on mountains always: it was in my family. I was too until I took this funny job.'"

In E.H. Daniell's memory a complete set of her novels, and mattresses for the bunks, were presented to the Club. R.B. Henderson had been her friend and climbing companion for many years and was appointed her literary executor. He visited the Pinnacle Club Hut to make sure that her wishes were carried out to his satisfaction.

Lilian Bray has already been mentioned as questioning some of the proposed rules for the new club. She was a keen alpinist and had joined the LAC in 1913. In fact, she was the only Ladies' Alpine Club member to join the Pinnacle Club and it is amusing to discover that she resigned from the LAC a few years later over their decision not to publish a journal. She said that a club which did not think its exploits worth recording was not worth belonging to. She was a commanding person with considerable mountaineering experience, already in her forties, and she inspired other members with a mixture of awe and affection. Eleanor Winthrop Young had known her for some years:

"I had a great respect for Bray," she said. (It was trendy and modern to be known by ones surname in the Pinnacle Club, and everyone was known by their surname or a nickname). "I was terrified of her in some ways – she could be very fierce. She belonged to a family of judges – Justice Bray – and I thought she looked a bit like him. They came from Surrey and she lived in a very bleak sort of big ugly house. We lived in Surrey too and quite early on when I was living there and still a young woman I was invited to tea and I remember being petrified. She was very snappy – she couldn't help it and I got to like her tremendously. Oh, she was very good – good value.

"I wish you could have known her. She made a counterpart to Kelly in a way, because Kelly was this spare little lady. To me she looked as if she might be rather delicate. She wasn't at all really. She was very strict about her climbing and very neat; and Bray was rather spare, but none of Kelly's grace. She had no grace, had Bray. Bray would come marching in."

Len was with Bray the first time she saw Dorothy Pilley:

"Pilley I met first in 1920, not knowing much about her. She was at a Fell and Rock meet, I think with Richards. She came up the path and I said, 'Who's that pretty girl with a scarf on?' Bray was with a man called C.F. Holland and she said: 'Oh, that's Dorothy Pilley'. Pilley didn't come a lot to meets, she was so much with Ivor Richards, you see. It was rather like me having to take care of Geoffrey. I was organising our walks and climbing parties and that's why I was really such a bad, absent member."

Despite being so bad and absent, she remembers lively meets in Wasdale and Derbyshire. As for the pretty girl with the scarf, she became joint editor with Bray of the first Pinnacle Club Journal and remained editor until 1948. In 1933 she became 5th president of the club. She has written her own account of the Pinnacle Club in her famous book, *Climbing Days*, and in an article she wrote for the Jubilee edition of the Fell and Rock Journal (1956) we read of her early climbing experiences.

Her first roped climb was with Herbert Carr in 1915, the prelude to a lifetime of enjoyment, despite climbing being generally thought a strange activity for a young woman in those days. She wrote:

"One had really done something drastic by becoming a climber... And it wasn't smiled on either -- not with smiles you like to see. In those days, even up in the Lakes, a girl couldn't walk about a village in climbing clothes without hard stares from the women and sniggers from the louts."

In the same article Pilley quoted a letter from Pat Kelly which gives insight into the latter's skill and emotions when rock climbing:

"Here is a note from a letter of Pat's about her climbing of Jones from Deep Ghyll alone. 'A bite of lunch in Deep Ghyll, some moderate climbing to get warm and to gain confidence, and then the delight which only a rock-climber can appreciate – to stand on a mere inch or so of rock and look down an almost sheer 200 feet: the awesome exhilaration of a delicate, airy, upward step to a toehold on which to balance before grasping a firm bit of rock securely with both hands and so raising oneself on and up to the land of pure delight – out in the sunshine to sit on top of Pisgah and have a view to satisfy all hill lovers. Just across the way was the Pike, with its summit cairn and new War Memorial. Gable, Kirkfell, Yewbarrow, the Screes: the very names will call up a picture to one who knows.' It shows what climbing was to this remarkable personality who was the chief inspirer of the Pinnacle Club."

Dorothy Pilley had joined the Fell and Rock in 1918 and was a very active and enthusiastic member. She helped found the London Section in 1920 and became its first secretary and treasurer. She writes entertainingly of its inauguration in the Fell and Rock Journal for 1921. This issue is a particularly happy and satisfactory one for Pinnacle Club members because they hear from so many of their friends: H.M. Kelly gives an account of climbs in Wasdale; Pat Kelly writes an article about the foundation of the Pinnacle Club, and in his notes the editor, R.S.T. Chorley writes the following:

"To the Pinnacle Club, members of our own Club will extend a particularly hearty welcome, for it is very much bone of our bone and flesh of our flesh."

This was true, for over a third of the new Club's members were already members of the Fell and Rock. Pat Kelly wrote, after giving an outline of the club's activities so far,

"We are glad to have the sympathy and help of our big brother, the F.& R.C.C. I say Brother, but that is not quite enough; to some of us the Lakeland Club is more a Wise Parent, – shall we say Father and Mother in one? May we never disgrace our family and the larger family of Rock Climbers in all the world."

In this same year, 1921, Pat Kelly and Dorothy Pilley, together with Miss E. Harland, another founder member of the Pinnacle Club, became the first three women committee members of the F.& R.C.C. I do not find these circumstances completely unconnected; the independence, energy and initiative required in the formation of the new club were being recognised and appreciated by the parent club.

For interest, I include a list of F.& R.C.C. members, – the year they joined is in brackets – who became founder members of the Pinnacle Club:

Mrs A H Binns (1913), Mrs E H Daniell (1911), Miss L Dutton (1919), Mrs Eden-Smith (1919), Miss E F Harland (later Mrs J C Appleyard, 1913, Miss A Huddleston (1918), Mrs H M Kelly (1918), Miss B L Michaelson (1920), Mrs T C Ormiston Chant (1918), Miss D E Pilley (later Mrs I A Richards, 1918), Miss C Rathbone (1917), Miss H M Todd (1920), Mrs E Winthrop Young (1920), Miss A (Paddy) Wells (later Mrs John Hirst, 1918).

Mrs Blanche Eden-Smith, who never in her life was called Blanche by Pinnacle Club members, but was always known as Gabriel or 'G' or maybe Eden-Smith, was indeed a recording angel. Not only did she keep the club's climbing records but she also kept her own personal climbing diary for many years. In the latter she gave the position of each member of the party on each climb, the weather, often the time taken, where they stayed, the transport they used to get there and where they had tea. This diary was presented to the Fell and Rock Climbing Club in 1981 and is a mine of information for both clubs. The Pinnacle Club is very grateful to the F.& R.C.C. for a photocopy.

She started climbing in 1916 when she went up Scafell from Borrowdale with her husband and two boys, Jock and Waddy, and H and OE Johnson. They went down Broad Stand. By 1918 Gabriel's sister, Lella Michaelson, often joined her climbing and walking expeditions, but Mr Eden-Smith rarely went. He was a complete contrast to his wife, being very neat and much older than she was. Two neat things about Gabriel were her climbing and her handwriting; for the rest, she was a big, happy, outgoing person with short-cropped hair, and, with her climbing clothes on, she looked like a boy. She and her two sons were often taken for three boys together, and, to add to the image, she owned a motor bike and side car.

She and Miss Michaelson, called Mike, used the motor bike to get to the Pinnacle Club inaugural meeting; on Maundy Thursday they went by train to Llandudno Junction, then motor biked to Tal y Waen, Capel Curig. On Good Friday, in torrents of rain, they joined other brave souls at Idwal Slabs and Gabriel climbed first with Miss Turner, then with Bower. Rucksack members had come in force to cheer the new club on. March 26th is a red letter day in her diary, being the meeting for the formation of the Pinnacle Club; then she tells us that March 27th, Easter Sunday and the day for the first official meet on Tryfan, was very wet. She writes:

"Walked down to Tal Llyn, Ogwen, and had tea and supper with Mrs Kelly, H M K, Bower, Doughty, Chorley, & Pritchard." (The men felt themselves to be Rucksack Club on this occasion, though in fact they were also all members of the Fell and Rock Climbing Club).

"March 28th. Savage rain all day. Slab climb on Little Tryfan. Self and B L Michaelson unroped. Tea and supper at Tal Llyn and fine walk back afterwards.

"March 29th. Much snow. Biked to Pen y Pass & walked up Pig Track to see Snowdon. Range magnificent in snow.

"March 30th. Biked to Llandudno Junc: & came home by train, 2.2 p.m."

Len says that Gabriel is one of the people she misses very much:

"When we were together and weren't climbing we used to walk about together, she and I. She used to tell me all her life and she'd had a wonderful time. I think they were an Irish family."

Trilby remembers Miss Turner, whom Gabriel first climbed with on that wet Good Friday:

"She was very small but she was a wonderful little climber, and she was awfully good when we got the hut (in 1932). She could do anything in the hut, you know – provide meals and all that sort of thing."

Turner became treasurer in 1934. Len says:

"She was a darling because she kept all the money things right. She was a quiet little competent person and came from the Manchester area. She was treasurer and kept us on the mark and was so good and so nice.

"I tell you who was a lovely character too – Biddy (Wells). She was quite different to look at, again. She was very powerful and threw me over her shoulder once – for fun, I mean – and she was a very fine climber. Bray, I know, thought a tremendous lot of Trilby, but she and Paddy weren't tall."

Trilby says she climbed with Miss Bray quite a lot: "She liked to have me as her second, then a novice on the end of my rope so that she didn't get any bother at all with the novice; she left that to me. She was a great character, was Miss Bray.

"Olive Minor was tallish and an excellent climber." (Her father, P.S. Minor, was president of the Fell and Rock Climbing Club from 1917 to 1919).

"Dr Corbett had a brother, Rooke Corbett. He would be Fell and Rock and he would be Rucksack, I think. That would be how Dr Corbett got in touch – through her brother and Mr Kelly, and then on to Mrs Kelly. I wouldn't say she was a first class climber, but she was an excellent walker.

"She and her brother had several old aunts and they lived with them. He lived with some old aunts, who gradually died and left him; and she lived with old aunts and she was gradually left. She drove a car, but she had no idea about anything connected with a car. People said she went round corners on two wheels. Biddy and I were once out with her. We were going back to where she lived, near Burnley, and she had a puncture. So she just looked and she said: 'What do we do now?'

"'We'll change the wheel. Where's your jack?'

"She had no idea where the jack was, so Biddy and I had to hunt through the back of the car till we found the jack and then we started taking off the wheel. She had no idea at all.

"In spite of being such a poor driver and not knowing anything about a car, we only heard of one accident. She'd bumped into a confectioner's car and there was confectionary all over the road.

"But she was a very interesting person. I should think she was one of the first ladies to qualify as a doctor. She had run a hospital in Serbia during the First World War, and she had a lot of trouble with Germans coming and then she had to take them into her hospital.

"When we first knew her, she lived at Padiham near Burnley, and she was a medical officer under the education committee. She looked after children in schools. I was a teacher. In the end I had a school for defective children, the Margaret Macmillan school. I retired in 1953. Biddy was my head assistant. We worked together and enjoyed our work very much. In fact one day I heard some of the children discussing us. They called me Big Miss Wells. I wasn't as big as my sister, but I was the Head, you see. They were discussing us and one was saying, 'Oh, I like Big Miss Wells, she's so and so,' and the other, 'Oh, no, I like Little Miss Wells, she's so and so,' and one girl stood up straight. She said, 'I like them both; they're both comical.' It meant we had a sense of humour and enjoyed a joke."

Trilby remembers Dr and Mrs Evans very well. He was the American Vice-Consul for Sheffield and didn't start climbing until he was forty, but he was a very good climber. Dorothy Evans was at the inaugural meeting and joined as an associate member. Her husband often joined her on Club meets and took beginners up routes. In her article 'The Early Days' in the Pinnacle Club Jubilee *Journal*, Trilby recalls one of them:

"She came off quite regularly, making no attempt to attach herself to the rocks. I can see her swinging contentedly and with a pleasant smile looking up to her leader and saying admiringly, 'Oh, isn't Dr Evans a strong man!'" Trilby does not divulge who this person was, but she quotes two lines from John Hirst's poem, written in celebration of the birth of the Club:

And those who can't climb are admitted instead,
On a knowledge of knots and the use of the 'thread'.

John Hirst was a Manchester climber and a member of the Rucksack Club and Fell and Rock. He was a most kind and helpful friend to Pinnacle Club members and, with Herbert Carr, he even found himself on the same route as Paddy, Pilley and Bray in 1921 and, as Bray complained, led them astray down a 'short cut'. Nobody, except perhaps Paddy Wells, realised that he had an ulterior motive. As Len Winthrop Young says,

"Paddy very happily married John Hirst. He used to come and help us a lot on meets. We didn't realise he wanted to be married to Paddy, but he was very kind and very nice. He wrote brilliant rhymes and songs and there was lots of joking going on about rope attachments. Bray and I made rather a silly joke about a rope attachment when John was married to Paddy."

CHAPTER 3

'Saas for the Goose is Saas for the Gander'
Wasdale, Skye, Saas Fee, Norway, Second Annual Meeting

The second meet recorded is on May 17-18th, in Wasdale. It was attended by ten members and the weather was beautiful. Both days were spent on Gable. Mrs Eden-Smith led Dr Corbett up Needle Ridge and Arrowhead, and Mrs Kelly soloed both routes. The next day Mrs Dydynski and Miss Harland led up Eagles' Nest, easy way, and a committee meeting was held on the Dress Circle (a vantage point for watching climbers on Napes Needle). Probably only the leads done by Pinnacle Club members are recorded, because the Wells sisters were there, also Miss Dutton and Miss Minor, all of whom would have wanted to climb, and Pat Kelly would not have been soloing if there had been a lack of leaders. Whitsun had been very wet the year before, and she had led Miss Dutton up Slingsby's Chimney on Scafell rather than do the harder Jones' route with her husband, Morley Wood and Dorothy Pilley. H M Kelly then went on to try for a first ascent despite the rain. Dorothy Pilley writes: 'It was a pity Pat Kelly was not there, but she, as so often, was leading another woman up a neighbouring climb.' On the 1921 meet, Pat may well have been giving encouragement to leaders and checking rope management of seconds. There is evidence that both were necessary.

In June there was a meet in Skye, attended by four members: Kelly, Bell (Ilsa Bell, a Scottish member), Michaelson and Eden-Smith. Len was feeling very frustrated about the Skye meet: 'That was thrown to pieces for me because I was going to go, then my mother-in-law chose to get very ill and I had to rush off to Cuckham.' Mrs Eden-Smith wrote a good account of the meet for the first *Pinnacle Club Journal* and the *Rucksack Journal* recorded it as follows:

"On a scorching day on June last, four members of the (Ladies') Pinnacle Club took two of our members a little jaunt from Glen Brittle. The main ridge of the Cuillins was traversed over fourteen 'tops' from Bruach na Frithe to Sgurr na Banachdich and Glen Brittle was regained at 1.30 a.m. Had it not been for the tins of fruit thoughtfully provided by the ladies, it is feared that the guests must have perished of thirst."

Successful as the Skye meet was, the main triumph of the year was considered to be the Alpine meet in which Bray, Pilley and Paddy Wells took part. Bray wrote about it for the *Journal*, in the delightful style of someone who knows her own character and reputation, and has come to terms with it.

"We had firmly resolved in our minds before we started that we would do some guideless climbing, but we barely mentioned it to one another, and we never even breathed it to anyone else, as it is not usual for ladies to go guideless in the Alps.

"There were three climbs we had in our minds which we hoped to do in the week we were staying in Saas, and the first one was to be an easy ridge, the Egginergrat. We fully discussed the climb the previous day in all its aspects, there being many points to decide.

Above: Taken on guideless ascent of Egginergrat by D. Pilley, L. Bray & A. Wells in 1921

Below: Portjengrat, 1921. Note the sunbonnet. Photos: L. Bray.

Among others we had to settle who should lead it - that is to say, I had to choose who should be the leader, and I naturally chose myself. It so happened that the Egginergrat was much the easiest of the climbs, but it must not be supposed for a moment that that was the reason I chose it. Far from it ...

"We had an early breakfast, at which I criticised my companions' clothes. Miss W. had on very beautiful dark-blue corduroys. They looked much nicer than mine, so I was naturally annoyed and told her they would not stand her style of climbing for long. Miss P. actually wore upon her head a mauve cotton sunbonnet! Now, no one had ever climbed a mountain in a sunbonnet - it simply isn't done, and I told her most severely; but she only laughed at me and even my best language did not prevail upon her to change her headgear."

The climb went so easily that they were on the summit before they realised they had climbed the 'difficult' chimney. They 'strode triumphantly home, having accomplished our first guideless climb.'

"The following day was one of rest. That is another of the joys of Swiss climbing: there are complete off days when you lie out of doors dreaming of what you have done and what you are going to do - and there is generally a good deal more of the latter than the former.

"Our next climb was to be the Portjengrat, another rock ridge, but a very different one to the Egginergrat; I knew there was real climbing on this one, and that it was certainly well above the rank of moderate. The local guides were distinctly annoyed; they were used to the 'Herren' going guideless, but the 'Damen' never, and they prophesied all sorts of terrible things..."

Bray tells us that two men from the hotel were going to tackle the Portjengrat on the same day, and the ladies made it quite clear to them that they would have nothing to do with them on the climb. The two men were H R C Carr and John Hirst. It was the latter's first visit to the Alps and he wrote an account for the Rucksack Club *Journal*. Having descended from the Britannia Hut to Saas Fee he writes:

"Here our party was reinforced by the left wing of the Pinnacle Club, intent on guideless conquest, presumably on the principle that Saas for the goose is Saas for the gander ...

"The Portjengrat defied separate parties of Pinnacles and Rucksackers on a first attempt, and a mixed company beat an ignominious retreat in a thunderstorm, minus a rucksack and much cuticle, but a few days later two undaunted damosels, scorning even the moral support of the mere male, returned to the attack, and departed for Ried with flying colours."

Pilley had now arranged to join the Carrs - Herbert Carr was the person who had introduced her to climbing in the first place - and they traversed the Weissmies together, leaving Paddy and Bray to climb the Portjengrat alone. Bray writes:

"To our joy we had the whole mountain to ourselves. There were no others climbing that day, so we could not be accused of following a guided party as is sometimes done by the guideless. The way was not difficult to find, as like the Egginergrat it was well scratched. There was only one place where we lost all signs of scratches and further progress seemed barred on all sides. We could not make it out, till at last it dawned upon us that we had to make a hand traverse. There were several distinctly difficult pitches, and we had to make one abseil down a bare slab. I must admit that Miss W. led well; not that I could not have done just as well, but I must certainly give her her due as a good leader.

After the most perfect climb we got back to the inn for tea and to our hotel in time for dinner, and I well remember our pride in sauntering past the sullen-looking guides sitting on the wall.

"After this our week was over and we parted to join men and guides."

The other expedition of note during 1921 was that of Len Winthrop Young, who accompanied her father to Norway, where they had five weeks of rain and storm. Her father, who was over 80 and a semi-invalid, had a kind of Royal Progress and Len had a very energetic time. They were interviewed by a reporter on the *Bergen Tidende* and found themselves on the front page of the evening's edition: 'Slingsby, the Veteran Mountaineer, his return after nine years, his young daughter, and the Pinnacle Club which she had the honour to represent.'

Slingsby was considered a very great man in Norwegian climbing circles; he had always enjoyed climbing and exploring there, and living with the people and making friends with them, climbing with Norwegian companions whenever he could. They named him the Father of Norwegian Mountaineering.

His most famous first ascent was that of Skagastölstind in 1896. Naturally, Len wanted to climb it, but the weather made it out of the question. She says that as they left in the evening they caught one momentary glimpse of the mountain, 'and at the sight of this finest of all Norwegian peaks I wondered no more at the glory that had fallen to its solitary first climber.'

Their companions while they were in Norway were Ferdinand Schjelderup and his wife, and Fru Schjelderup applied to become a member of the Pinnacle Club.

Fru Schjelderup's application form, with her address: Vetakollen, Kristiania, Norway, went to Pat Kelly as secretary, and caused her to write the following letter to Len. (Pat had given Len a title of her own invention - Dainty Presidente).

Dear D. Presidente,

Would you mind forwarding the enclosed note to Fru Schjelderup for me, as I do not know if the address she gives on the application form is sufficient to find her. Please read the letter and alter it if you wish.

I am enclosing four more handbooks, and one of these days you had better say what you are out of pocket for stamps, as I think it is customary to set aside Treasurer's expenses.

At the Easter Meet I shall of course get a Balance Sheet for you to submit at the meeting, I wish some kind Godfather would endow us with a fortune sufficient to enable us to get out a really fine Journal, for our No.1 effort. Or perhaps we shall have to borrow, but that is a bad principle, but we simply MUST have a Journal next year even if we don't have another for two or three years. Now, mustn't we? Money is of course the last thing to get, - Articles, illustrations, 'copy' in plenty for Gabriel, and I feel sure the money will be obtained.

It seems as if it might be quite a long time before I see you again, but we must write to each other. I wish you could come along to our Laddow Meet next weekend, I think there will be about 18 of us, including about 6 or 7 Rucksack men.

I have lots of Pinnacle work to do, so must say adieu.

    Yours ever,
    Your G. Sec.

This letter was dated October 21st, 1921, and Pat Kelly's letters to Len from then until the second Annual Meeting give a good picture of the Club and her own character and concern for the Club's welfare. She also describes events in the climbing world:

"Jan 20,/22. We have had Mallory in Manchester, - a delightful lecture. Perhaps you saw the report in the *Manchester Guardian*. There was also a fine article 'The Happy Mountain Climber', unsigned, in the same paper, did you see it? I think it must have been by C.E. Montague.

"We had a good time at P-y-P at Xmas, 3 days out of four on the rocks (Lliwedd). At New Year I found only Doctor Corbett, - two other members were at the Summit Hotel, and the remainder had gone home again. So Dr. C. and I had Lliwedd again, Central Gully and Slanting Buttress. The latter we finished at 2.55, and then had a most exciting rush to catch the afternoon train from Betws. We did it by 2 minutes but the train was five minutes late in leaving! Mr and Mrs Claude Elliott, Porter, and Shadbolt, and a lady whose name I do not know (climber) were at P-y-P, it was nice to meet them. Porter sang some nice little chanties." (The story of the members at the Summit Hotel is recorded in *Climbing Days* and the first P.C. *Journal*).

Four days later she wrote again:

"I have just seen a copy of the Rucksack Journal. Your two pages on 'The Pinnacle Club' are excellent, - far better than what I wrote for the F & R C C which I sent to Chorley last October, and wrote in white heat...

"In regard to Hirst's Song Book, he is taking it for granted that we, the Pinnacle Club, will buy a copy of the Music, price probably £4. It seems a lot for a mere song book, we ought to find at least ten times as much for our own Journal, as other Clubs' songs. I wonder will we? Of course I told Mr Hirst that it would have to be considered by the Committee.

"Our next Meet (and the last until Easter) takes place this week end. Castle Naze on Saturday, and Sunday to Tuesday at Stanage."

Pat Kelly had no reason to be ashamed of her article in the Fell and Rock Climbing Club Journal, it was full of vitality and fun. Len's was more dignified. It appeared in the 1922 Rucksack Club *Journal* and extracts from it appeared in the May 1922 issue of the *Alpine Journal*, not entirely appropriately under the heading "Alpine Notes". The passage in the latter reads:

"The PINNACLE CLUB (FOR LADIES) - This club is the outcome of a steadily growing conviction among many women that it was desirable to have a centre - social, educational and advisory - for women and girl climbers.

"In climbing with men where 'the best must lead', women have little opportunity to master, or to enjoy, the finer points and sensations of the art itself; to learn the business of finding their climbs, of steering a mountaineering course, or of exercising judgement and responsibility in the actual climbing ... The new Club makes a special feature of the training of its beginners, both in route-finding and in technique; and ... it supplies an energetic criticism - free from the polite restrictions imposed by differences of sex - of the methods and the capabilities of all its members."

Pat's letters before Easter show her bubbling enthusiasm and her care for detail. The second Annual General Meeting of the Pinnacle Club was held at Idwal Cottage in the Ogwen Valley on April 15th, 1922 and there were 17 members present.

Len gave a resumé of the Club's activities then, as treasurer, presented the accounts.

There was a balance in the bank of eleven pounds, four shillings. Pat reported that there were now fifty-nine members. A handbook had been issued during the year and this contained a list of members, rules of the Club, list of meets, and guardians of climbing areas. (These were members with a good knowledge of a particular area, who were prepared to take other members climbing there). Ten meets had been arranged during the year and considering how scattered the members of the Club were, these had been well attended.

Two matters were brought up, both very interesting for different reasons.

The first item concerned the name of the Club. Miss Bray proposed that the name should be changed from Pinnacle Club to Women's Rock-climbing Club on the grounds that the name 'Pinnacle Club' led to ridicule. When reminded about this Len said, 'That was Bray all over. I don't remember it, but Bray would always have something to say and I can imagine Bray saying something like that about the Club's name. She'd think it affected.'

The second item was about the Federation of Clubs. "The Hon. Sec. read a letter from the Hon. Sec. to the Advisory Council of British Mountaineering Clubs, inviting the Pinnacle Club to join the Advisory Council. After discussion Miss Bray proposed and Miss Wells seconded that the invitation be accepted. This was carried unanimously." This scheme was dear to the heart of Geoffrey Winthrop Young. In 1920 he had published an open letter to members of mountaineering, climbing and rambling clubs in Great Britain proposing a federation. He wrote:

"Its purpose would be to strengthen the position of the Clubs, individually and collectively, by instituting a simple machinery for taking joint action in matters of public or general mountaineering importance; and for increasing their capacity to offer facilities, to disseminate information, and to encourage climbing, both within and without the Clubs." This was the distant forerunner of the British Mountaineering Council.

A final item was the suggestion, by Miss Wells, that all members of a climbing expedition should provide themselves with a rope, or arrange to share someone else's rope. Neglect of this precaution had led to difficulties on recent expeditions. This was unanimously agreed to. No mention was made of rope management, but Notes on the Use of the Rope were printed in the Handbook for 1922, concluding with the admonition that, 'They should take care (a) when the preceding climber is moving to see that the rope pays out easily and does not become caught in any way; (b) not to begin moving until summoned by the climber above.'

This last injunction reminds me of a splendid joke which happened while Alex White was climbing Eve, a VS on Shepherd's Crag in Borrowdale, on a Pinnacle Club meet in 1981. The climb was well populated as usual, and having allowed the preceding party to get well ahead, she started up the second pitch. A climber below her said: "I should wait a little while, dear; your leader hasn't reached the stance."

Alex replied: "I *am* the leader."

While lying in bed on April 16th, Pat Kelly remembered that the Meet Record Book was now to become the Log Book, and wrote the following note in pencil:

"Our Hon. Recording Secretary says no-one has sent her Reports (except of course the Sec.) & she thinks the office is not necessary. So thought the members at the Annual Meeting especially in view of the fact that a Journal has been decided upon, & our Editor can use the Reports sent in *for* the Journal.

"This book will now be converted into a Log Book.

"Present Custodian: Mrs Isherwood.

"If Custodian not at any Meet, she will ascertain from some members who attended, the names of those present and the list of climbs done."

From Mrs Isherwood's record of this Meet, it is obvious that 'Pinnacles' were swarming all over Milestone, Idwal Slabs, Wrinkled Slab, Central Arête and Gashed Crag; also, that the six men mentioned by Pat Kelly as being of the party had no objection to being led up these routes by the ladies. (They were H.M. Kelly, J H Doughty, F Wallbank, H Coates, J V T Long and R Evans.) No wonder the Pinnacle Club regarded the Rucksack Club with gratitude and affection.

Pat Kelly on The Scoop, Castle Naze.

CHAPTER 4

Pat Kelly Dies.

The last day of the Meet, April 17th, was marred by an accident as inexplicable as it was serious. Three parties were climbing on Wrinkled Slabs, which are on the West Face of Tryfan and give about three hundred feet of slab climbing. They were very popular in the 1920s, though almost unvisited now. Three 'Pinnacles' were leading: H M Kelly and Long were giving practical and moral support to Miss Collins; Dr Corbett was leading H Coates and Miss Turner; Mrs Isherwood led the last rope, with Pat Kelly to second her and Miss Hilton behind. Pat had felt unwell that morning, so decided not to climb, but came along later to see how things were going.

The climbs were all completed and people descended the easy rocks and mixed ground at the side. Perhaps Pat Kelly stayed behind to coil the rope and was thus last down; at any rate, nobody saw what happened. Pat was found, pitched headlong on the ground and with a climbing shoe missing. It was looked for but nobody came across it. Trilby was climbing higher on Tryfan and her party saw the stretcher being taken up, so they went down to find out what had happened. Pat had head injuries and her face was badly cut about. She was taken to Bangor Hospital.

Gabriel Eden-Smith, who had been unable to join the meet at Easter, now came up to Wales. Len Winthrop Young was still at Pen-y-Pass, and Gabriel gathered her up and they went together to Bangor. Len said: "It was tragic, because her (Pat's) head was really very badly hurt. Then I had to go home with Geoffrey and Gabriel kept me posted all the time about 'our little friend' as we called her."

Two letters remain, the first from the British Hotel, Bangor, and dated April 26th, 1922.

Dear President,
I grieve to tell you we have lost our little friend.

She stood an operation well yesterday to open & drain the wounds & a big abcess which was causing terrible swelling in face & neck. Last night she was still unconscious, & Matron said we had better not stay the night with her, as she would be quite quiet & not need us. This morning there was a sudden change for the worse & we were phoned just before 8 a.m. Mr Kelly & I were up there in a quarter of an hour, & were with her when she slipped quietly over just before 9 a.m. She has really not been conscious since Sunday, & we rejoice to think she had no pain latterly.

There is to be an inquest tomorrow afternoon, & on Sat: she will be taken to Manchester for cremation. I am staying on, as otherwise poor H.M.K. is alone & he seems to want me to stay. He is a plucky beggar, President. I can't write about Pat now, but oh! how we shall miss her.

The second letter is written from Gabriel's home, Eggerslack Cottage, Grange Over Sands, on April 30th, 1922.

PAT KELLY DIES

Dear President,

Many thanks for your letter. You are right in saying that the P.C. must be kept going. It is up to us all now to make the club the success Mrs Kelly always hoped & longed for it to be. It was the biggest interest in her life & it would be just waste of all that work, enthusiasm, & pluck of hers for us to let it go down now. I spoke to several of our members at the funeral & found them all very strongly of the same opinion. We hope to have a meeting after you get back to the north & go into matters thoroughly.

I am really glad I went to Bangor. Pat knew me at first & seemed pleased to see me, & when Kelly's two men friends left on Sunday, I was able to take a good share of being with her off his hands. Poor Lad, he had a terrible night with her one night & was about worn out. But he was most awfully nice & made it easy for me to help him by taking things for granted & not repelling my clumsy attempts to be of use.

The day she died seemed as if it ... (The second page is missing, but there is the end of a postscript) ... brick all through & I am glad to have got to know him. He is going to have a hard time now, I fear. Yours ever, Gabriel.

Gabriel wrote in her climbing diary:

"Ap: 26. We lost Pat."

Everybody was stunned. Not only by her death, but by the fact that she had had an accident at all. Loose rock seemed the only possible explanation though even that implied an error of judgement, however slight. However, the accident had happened. The truth was in fact discovered about six months later, but remained hidden for nearly sixty years for fear of causing unnecessary self-condemnation and reopening wounds in those who loved her.

About six months after Pat Kelly's death, Trilby and Biddy Wells were climbing on Tryfan with Dr and Mrs Evans and suddenly realized that they were in the same area on the west side of Tryfan where the accident had happened. Dr Evans insisted that they should remain roped for the descent and the women were safely down when they heard an exclamation behind them. Dr Evans had found a climbing shoe, caught fast in the ground by one of its front nails, and he realized at once that it was the one worn by Mrs Kelly on the day of the accident. It had been searched for at the time but never found.

The shoe told the climbers the whole story. One of the men had given Mrs Kelly some new nails to try out. They were of a different pattern and she was using them for the first time that day. One of these had caught in the rock on her descent and she had been thrown off balance with such force that her foot had been dragged from the shoe and she had fallen headlong.

The party buried the shoe nearby and vowed to each other that they would never mention the matter so long as it could cause distress to Harry Kelly or to the friend who had given the nails.

It was strange to hear this news from Trilby when, with H M Kelly's death, I had given up all hope of hearing what happened. Trilby said the news could hurt nobody now, as the others were long since dead, and I could use the information at my discretion. It seems right to me that people should know this truth about the rare and gifted person who was our founder.

CHAPTER 5

"You could pay six shillings if you like"
1922-1923. The first journal, first Manchester Dinner, Routes in Britain and the Alps.

The Eden-Smiths were very good to Kelly in the months that followed. He often stayed with them at their house in Grange-over-Sands and this led to an incident which Len says amused them all very much; she is surprised that it happened at such an early date, but in Gabriel's diary it is the very next entry after Pat's death.

Just over a month after the tragedy, on May 28th, Gabriel took Len in the side car of her motor bike (Len lived nearby, at Cark-in-Cartmell at this time), to join a Pinnacle Club meet at Laddow Rocks. Kelly was there as well, with other Rucksack Club members. They climbed Charybdis amongst other routes and when it was time to return home Len recalls:

"Gabriel said to me, 'Now here Sprite, Kelly's coming home with me. Do you mind sitting on the back of my bike?'

"I said, 'No, not a bit.'

"We got into trouble - this is such a funny story. I had an old mackintosh and I was sitting on the back of hers, and there was Kelly - rather a big, heavy man in a way - taking up the room in the side car. She was driving the motorbike very well and we went through a place called Marple. There was an awful lot of police whistles, whistling on 'GO'. They didn't mean anything to me.

"They went on whistling and whistling and finally Kelly said, 'I think they want us.' and what happened was that my mackintosh had obscured her name-plate and we didn't stop because we didn't know anything about it. A policeman came along and said! Well, what do you think of this?' and of course I was just a young, stupid thing. I didn't think anything of it.

"'You're going to be had up for aiding and abetting this lady, hiding her name plate!'

"Of course we tried not to giggle and Kelly did his best to defend us. And the policeman said, 'And anyway, you didn't stop.' - which was true - we didn't! So about three weeks after, I was in the garden at our farmhouse. An enormous policeman walked up to the door, and I'd forgotten. I thought, 'What on earth is he coming here for?'.

"He read out that I'd got to come to court for aiding and abetting. I've got it written down, 'aiding and abetting Mrs Eden-Smith', and then he said, 'But you have the choice. You could pay six shillings if you like. You'd better think it over.'

"So then I got on to her. I don't think we had any telephone for years, but she came over and we had a good giggle about it, and Kelly too. She said, 'I don't know what you think about it, Sprite, but I'd rather pay six shillings!'

"I said, 'So should I,' but I thought, 'I'll keep this thing for ever because it's so funny.'"

The Pinnacle Club Whitsuntide Meet was again held in Wasdale in glorious weather. Wednesday, June 7th was spent on Gable, and the Wasdale party was joined by Miss Harland and Mrs Summersgill who walked over from Borrowdale, and Len, Gabriel, Ilsa Bell and Kelly from Langdale. Gabriel writes in her diary:

"Took Mrs W-Y & Miss Bell on bike to Langdale and H.M.K. rode little bike. Walked over Rossett and Esk Hause for P.C. meeting on Gable. No time for a climb. Very hot. Home 10.20 p.m."

The meeting was a committee meeting on Gable's Dress Circle. Ten pounds had been collected in memory of Pat Kelly and it was agreed to send this to Bangor Royal Infirmary with a letter expressing appreciation of the kindness and consideration of the staff.

Paddy Wells was elected Honorary Secretary in Pat Kelly's place. When the newly married Paddy came to countersign these minutes at the ensuing meeting on August 21st she signed them 'Annie Wells' by mistake and had to rub out her signature and correct it to 'Annie Hirst'.

At the June meet Biddy Wells led several of the shorter routes on Pillar, also climbs on Scafell including Jones' route from Deep Ghyll by the Arête. At least some of the other climbs were led by members of the Rucksack Club.

During the fortnight's meet in Wasdale in August it rained for twelve days running, and the reports read of long walks, farmhouse teas and games at the Vicarage, with a climb snatched here and there. Mrs Eden-Smith was present the whole time and provided transport from Seascale station to Wasdale Head. Entries in her diary include:

"August 18th. Fetched President (Mrs W-Y) from Seascale, 2.55 train. After tea did Lower Kern Knotts Crack. (Len, Dr Corbett, Mike, Biddy, Turner, Jock, Waddy, Gabriel).

"August 19th. Up at 5 a.m. to take Miss Anthony to catch 7.4 at Seascale. Fetched I.M.E. Bell from Seascale 3.34 p.m. After tea all went up to Y Boulder. Wet, mostly.

"August 20th. Steady rain all day ..."

Len says the usual place to stay on Wasdale meets was Middle Row. Once it was so crowded that she shared a bed with Lilla Michaelson and there were great jokes about the bed creaking. Len describes Mike as 'a very grand girl', not such a neat climber as her sister, but very much liked in the Pinnacle Club and in the Fell and Rock too.

Meanwhile, what of Pinnacle Club members elsewhere? During Easter 1922, Dorothy Pilley and Dorothy Thompson had been climbing in Corsica with John Pilley and I A Richards. Pilley writes of their adventures and ascent of Monte Cinto in *Climbing Days*.

Paddy married John Hirst and they spent their summer climbing and exploring in the Graian Alps, ascending several peaks from the Victor Emmanuel Hut, then moving on to the Vittorio Sella Hut from which they climbed the Grivola before being driven down by poor weather. Pilley was back in the Alps, where she and her party climbed Mont Blanc from Italy, the Blaitière, Mont Blanc de Tacul, the Requin, and the Rochefort Ridge to Mont Mallet. The previous year, after leaving the Pinnacle Club party, she had traversed the Weissmies, climbed the Zmutt ridge of the Matterhorn, the Jägerhorn, Breithorn and Klein Matterhorn before going round to Ferpècle to meet I A Richards, Mrs Daniell and R B Henderson for more climbing. Near the Bertol Hut they first met Joseph Georges and, by the end of the season, had made two new ascents with him. In 1922 he met them at Montenvers after their ascent of the Blaitière and was their guide for the rest of their holiday.

During the year the Club received the handbook of the newly formed Midland Association of Mountaineers and sent a letter of thanks, wishing them all success. The Rucksack Club Song Book music was now ready, but the Pinnacle Club had not collected sufficient money to pay for it, so they had to borrow from the Journal Fund. As regards a journal, the committee decided to defer publication and issue an enlarged handbook with meet reports; however, this decision was reversed at the annual meeting.

A lot of the committee work concerned membership. New members joined, keen climbers were promoted to full membership, and some members resigned. Poor Miss Radcliffe resigned because she was not an experienced climber and felt herself to be a nuisance. She was asked to reconsider her decision, but her resignation was accepted at the next meeting. Applications for membership were already being scrutinised with care, and two applicants had their forms returned with the explanation that their qualifications, as written, were not considered sufficient. One of half a dozen members resigning in 1923 was Miss Dutton. She was a keen member of the Fell and Rock and preferred mixed climbing. However, new members brought the numbers up to 62 and Mrs Winthrop Young, starting her third year as president asked members not to relax in their efforts to ensure the success of the Club. At the annual meeting the journal fund stood at over thirty pounds and a journal committee comprising Len, Paddy, Dr Corbett and Ilsa Bell was formed.

This sub-committee does not appear to have had everything plain sailing: its members reported back that 'it was very difficult to collect good matter for the journal. Some had been collected but the standard was not high enough.' At the annual meeting in 1924 the matter was finally put into the capable hands of Bray and Pilley, as joint editors, and the first *journal* appeared later in the year. The committee was right to attach such importance to the quality of the Club's first *journal*; as a new national club the Pinnacle Club's publications had to bear comparison with those of its peers. Our distinguished editors ensured that our journal was equally good and delightfully different. Its review in the Fell and Rock *Journal*, 1924, was not initialled, but was obviously written by an ally:

"This first number ... is more than commendable, it is excellent. From its cover, which is certainly more distinctive than that of any other journal, down to its final article, which contains a description of a crossing of the Col de Boucharou (Pyrenees) in deep snow, worthy to rank high in the pages of mountain literature, the number is one of sustained interest ..."

Committee meetings in 1923 have one or two other points of interest, the first showing a very strange reaction to standard procedure:

"The Hon. Treasurer asked that a resolution should be passed by the committee authorizing her to sign cheques on behalf of the Pinnacle Club, and pointed out that this was a request from the bank. Miss Bray expressed the opinion that this was quite unnecessary and the Hon. Sec. pointed out that for two years the Pinnacle Club had been able to carry on without any interference from the bank. After some discussion Dr Corbett put the resolution and Mrs Eden-Smith seconded. Agreed."

Bray shows sounder judgement and less prejudice in the ensuing entry:

"The Hon. Sec. asked for an expression of opinion with regard to the distinction - Full - Associate Members. She intimated that the distinction had aroused a certain amount of feeling amongst members of the Club. Mrs Eden-Smith thought it would be much better to drop the distinction. Miss Bray said that she would be very sorry to see the distinction dropped, as the Pinnacle Club was the only club with a qualification with regard to 'leading' climbs. This made the P C unique ..."

The distinction in membership is still queried from time to time, but has so far been thought a valuable and fair one, considering the aims of the club.

Meets in 1923 were in favourite areas such as Laddow, Windgather, Stanage, Alderley Edge and Buttermere. A very well attended meet in Wasdale at Whitsun saw Bray climbing Eagles Nest Direct with Mr Lamb, and Trilby climbing it a few days later with Dr and Mrs Evans. Gabriel and H M Kelly were dividing their time between the Fell and Rock and Pinnacle Club meets and did three first ascents in Hind Cove - the buttress, and Routes One and Two on the slabs. Kelly was very busy on Pillar that year as he was writing the first Pillar guide for the F & R C C.

October 13th was the Fell and Rock Dinner Meet at Coniston and is interesting because it was the day the deeds of the Memorial Hills were transferred to the National Trust. The timing of events gives food for thought, when one thinks how meetings can drag on: Committee 5.30, Annual Meeting 6.30, Dinner 7.30.

In 1923 Ella Mann had her first Alpine season. Her dozen or so expeditions included the Grépon, Dent Blanche, traverse of the Matterhorn, and the Zinalrothorn. Dorothy Thompson had an equally happy first season, climbing part of the time with Dorothy Pilley and I A Richards. This was the year in which Pilley and I A R with Joseph Georges, amongst many other Alpine traverses, climbed the Jungfrau by the North East Ridge. It was also the year in which, with Dorothy Thompson and John Hall Paxton, they had had their famous excursion 'Into Spain and Back Again' over the Port de Boucharou with François Bernard Salles, during the Easter holidays.

The year was crowned by the first Manchester Dinner at the Albion Hotel on November 10th, and a climbing meet at Stanage the next day. Len Winthrop Young remembers: "We were next door to the hotel where the Rucksack were holding their dinner, and they sent us some posies."

She also sketches a picture of Bray presiding at one of these early Manchester dinners. In her clipped, formal way she ran two sentences together and came out with the amazing statement: "Ladies and Gentlemen, you may smoke the King." Formidable as she was, she was not one to mind a joke against herself, which was just as well since she never quite lived this one down.

Early dinners were followed by entertainment in the form of singing, sketches or piano playing by members, and concluded with dancing. Bray was an excellent pianist and often played for Club sing-songs and entertainments.

CHAPTER 6

1924 - 1927. Paddy Hirst's Presidency.
Climbing abroad. First ascents. First Alpine Meet. 'Coming of Age' of Fell and Rock Climbing Club.

In 1924 the Annual General Meeting was held at the Sun Inn in Coniston. Paddy Hirst was elected president, Len Winthrop Young the first vice-president, and Biddy Wells took over from Paddy the office of honorary secretary.

During the holiday many routes were climbed on Dow Crag. The Fell and Rock had published its red guides to 'Doe Crags' and Pillar Rock during the year, and had presented the Pinnacle Club with copies. Gordon and Craig's and the Buttress Routes were as popular then as they are now. Mrs Eden-Smith was still a committee member of the Fell and Rock and was at their Easter Meet in Wasdale. She took part in two first ascents during the holiday: on April 21st she was with Kelly, Pritchard and Graham Wilson on their ascent of what has become a favourite route up Pike's Crag, Wall and Crack; the next day she watched Kelly and Pritchard, with her sons, Jock and Waddy, on the first ascent of Juniper Buttress, and joined them afterwards for a walk over the Pike and down Piers Ghyll; then she and the boys joined Kelly the following day on the first ascent of Southern Corner on Pulpit Rock. This was the last fine day, and they all went home on motor bikes in the pouring rain.

There is no record at all of the Wasdale Meet at Whitsun, but it is certain that many of our members were present among the five hundred participants in the Memorial Service on Great Gable, on Whit Sunday. In fact F & R C C archives contain a photograph of Mrs Somervell and Miss Hadfield leaving Seathwaite with the War Memorial tablet. Gabriel records it in her diary and the occasion is fully written up in the Fell and Rock *Journal* for 1924. I wonder how many of the climbers and fell walkers who go to Gable summit for the two minutes' silence at 11 a.m. on Remembrance Sunday and put their poppies by the memorial tablet realize the extent of the memorial.

A month later Gabriel and Kelly set sail for Norway, where they joined the Schaanings for a climbing holiday. They arrived in a heatwave but had very mixed weather while climbing. Extracts from Gabriel's diary vary from, 'fearful rain and wind, and an exciting crossing of a flooded glacier stream. Glad to find lighted stoves at Gjende,' to 'Raced and beat guided party, lovely day.' On July 29th they climbed Skagastölstind by the South West Arête and managed one more route before two days of heavy rain. The entry for August 2nd reads: 'Mitmaradale Pinnacle Ridge and North Peak. Very wet. Furuseth missed route off into Rungsdalen and we had to turn back at 7 p.m. retraverse the whole ridge and descend the way we had come. Hotel 11.30 p.m. A good day.'

This year Dorothy Pilley spent Easter in the Pyrenees once more and spent the summer having even more adventures, not necessarily of the climbing variety, mainly in the Italian Alps. The party included Pilley's sister, Violet. She was a Founder Member of the Pinnacle Club but was never able to come on meets; she was a doctor at the Lady Harding

Hospital in Delhi and rarely in England. She died young.

Dorothy Thompson met up with the Pilleys and their party at Arolla, and, quite by chance, had her first climb with Joseph Georges. Violet Pilley and Muriel Turner were due to climb the Petite Dent de Veisivi with him, but Muriel had done a big route on her first arrival from Paris and was too stiff the next day to view the prospect with pleasure, so Dorothy went instead. She writes:

"This, then, was my first climb with one of the most brilliant guides of his generation (although at that time known only to a few). It was under auspicious circumstances, owing to Violet's conviction that here was a grand chance to climb in rubbers ...

"That Violet and I enjoyed ourselves, dancing about that delightful rock in featherweight footgear, while someone else carried our boots for us, needs no stating."

The 1920s were the height of the 'boots' versus 'rubbers' controversy in Britain, and plimsolls were a very new idea in the Alps. Joseph was deeply interested, and made the girls experiment on sloping rock on the way down.

Dorothy Thompson did many other routes, including the Dent Blanche, with the Arolla guide, Antoine Georges.

After the Alpine holidays little climbing activity is mentioned and the New Year, 1925, began with the Manchester Dinner on January 10th. Paddy Hirst arranged a musical evening to follow. So Easter came round again, and the Annual Meeting at Capel Curig. For the first time there were no 'male attachments' to help lead the climbs. Good Friday saw rope after rope of Pinnaclers on their way up the Parson's Nose and Clogwyn y Person. Saturday and Sunday were spent around Tryfan, on Lliwedd, and walking on Siabod. Two of the new members this year were Miss Hall from the Normal College, Bangor and Miss D Arning, who lived in Manchester at that time (elected January 9th, 1926).

In 1925, Dorothy Pilley went off on a two-year tour of the world, climbing extensively in the United States and the Canadian Rockies, where she and I A Richards did a lot of exploration. The story of their climb up the North-East Ridge of Mount Baker appeared in all the papers. It was either a first or second ascent and Pilley called it a long and very beautiful expedition. She and I A Richards were married on the last day of 1926, in Honolulu.

Dorothy Pilley had left Europe in 1925 with Joseph Georges already booked for part of her Alpine season. He was left to Dorothy Thompson, 'so to speak, as a legacy' and she had what she remembered as one of the happiest seasons of her life, including a traverse of Mont Blanc; also the Grépon, Blaitière and Drus.

The *Alpine Journal* for this year contained a long article by Bray about the Kaisergebirge. She made many ascents in 1924 and 1925 with her friend Miss Marples and various guides, and she gives a very good introduction to the area. However the paragraph which interested me most was on the use of karabiners:

"The Austrian mode of climbing has frequently been censured by our English climbers, owing to their inordinate use of Mauerhaken (iron spikes or pitons with a ring at the end). There is no doubt that this is considerably overdone at present; but there is a good deal to be said for it, for though in certain places these pitons afford at times excellent hand and foot holds, their use is primarily to ensure the safety of the leader. On many of the pitches there are no belays and no firm standing places, so that should the leader fall, the whole party must be doomed. It speaks a good deal for the method that among all the accidents to the leader that occurred this year, no other member was pulled off."

Until I read this account I had no idea that any British climber in 1924 would approve of such an aid. I was intrigued to read in a later passage that the party found difficulty on a traverse because the expected peg had been removed by a previous party who thought it made the route too easy! It sounds quite a modern situation.

1926 was in the midst of the Depression and the year of the General Strike. It was a dreary time for everyone, though Pinnacle Club members, as a whole, came from the fairly well insulated world of the professions. The Easter meet was held at Torver and some members made the trip to Pillar Rock, to join in the hilarious centenary celebrations.

Paddy Hirst was elected for her third year as president and Trilby Wells and Dr Taylor were elected full members.

Mrs Isherwood had written concerning qualifications for full membership, probably pointing out that to lead a competent leader up a route was a very different matter to leading a beginner up the same route. In consequence, the wording of rule 6 was changed to the following: -

The qualification for Full Membership shall be proved ability to lead a party of Associates up an ordinary rock climb of moderate difficulty.

This rule, which stood for many years, led to innumerable jokes about the expendability of associate members.

The first official Club Alpine meet was arranged to start during the last week in July, based in Chamonix. Meanwhile, meets in England followed a familiar pattern, but exciting things were happening elsewhere. Gabriel Eden-Smith climbed many first ascents with Kelly, culminating in Moss Ghyll Grooves on July 1st, 1926. The climbers were Kelly, Gabriel and J B Kilshaw, and the ascent took one and a half hours, from 5 p.m. to 6.30 p.m.

Gabriel wrote in her diary: "A thunder shower while Harry was prospecting threatened to make ascent impossible, but the rain ceased as we descended Keswick Brothers and the warm rock soon dried ... A week of perfect weather, splendid climbing, and fulfilled ambitions (M.G.G.)"

Meanwhile Len had moved to Cambridge. Her father had made the first ascent of Store Skagastölstind in 1876, so this year was the fiftieth anniversary. As she told me:

"I was in the middle of a general strike in Cambridge and my husband was out in Geneva and I thought, 'Let's have a Fiftieth Anniversary!' I wrote to some great Norwegian mountaineers. They said, 'We're quite ready to do it. Will you come out?' 'Yes, all right.'

"And I met just on arrival, Kelly and Eden-Smith. We couldn't have done without Kelly; he was the absolute leader of the party. We did several very good climbs - mountain climbs. We had with us the future Lord Adrian, the scientist, who wasn't a lord then, - Dr Adrian - and his wife, who joined the Pinnacle Club."

Hester Adrian wrote an account of the Anniversary Climb, by Slingsby's route, for the Pinnacle Club *Journal*. This was a serious undertaking, postponed a week because of bad weather and still not easy, being covered in fresh snow. The Jubilee ascent proper, on July 21st, was by the easier Andrews Route in thick cloud and rain. The Tonsbergs and other Norwegians were together with the English party and that night there were celebrations and speeches in the hotel.

When Len went back to Norway the next time, there were lots of photos of Kelly in the hotel at Turtegro, and the Norwegians said, 'Well, he was a great man, Kelly.'

"He was," Len told me. "He did a lot out there."

Headed 'A Notable Jubilee', there was an account of the occasion in the November 1926 edition of the *Alpine Journal*.

The other notable event in 1926 was the first Alpine meet. Even before it began, Sam Hall, a lecturer at Bangor University and a relatively new member, showed her star quality by walking the 'Tour of Mont Blanc' on her own, of which she subsequently wrote a gem of an account for the *Journal*. Among my favourite passages are when she met an angel disguised as a peasant. She - " - knew he was an angel (a) Because he refrained from remarking that it was unsafe for ladies to be on mountains alone. (b) Because his directions were of superhuman lucidity, and turned out to be correct." There is also a thumbnail sketch: "Mrs Koko was very nice and kind, but she had so little spare breath that one never really made her acquaintance."

On July 25th she met the rest of the Pinnacle Meet at the Hotel Bellevue-Terrasse in Argentière: Dr Corbett the meet leader, Harriet Turner and Trilby Wells. The weather was poor and, as Dr Corbett said, the mighty peak baggers were having a poor time, but they were out to enjoy themselves, and they did. They acclimatised by having a shopping expedition to Chamonix - via the Lognon, Mer de Glace and Montenvers, and climbed the Buet the following day. The next day was spent in drying their clothes. Turner, who found herself very much affected by altitude, did no more high routes, so it was just the three of them who did the Three Cols Route the following day with their guide, Jules Vouilloz. While waiting for the weather to be right for Mont Blanc, they went up the Brévent and La Persévérance, being joined on the latter day by Paddy Hirst who had come from Arolla after doing many guideless ascents there.

At last conditions were right for Mont Blanc and Trilby, Hall and Dr Corbett set out. All went well and the weather was perfect but Dr Corbett was affected by the altitude and failed to reach the summit. She spent the night at the Grands Mulets on the way down; the others had a meal and romped down to the valley.

Miss Hall was active in the club for only a few years, after which family duties curtailed her activities, but she has always remained a member. Trilby remembered her as a wonderful walker and climber, and travelling home from Chamonix with her boots round her neck - 'She just didn't care about anything; but she was a most delightful person.'

Bray was in the Dolomites this year, and led the Funffingerspitze, and Mabel Jeffrey led a guideless party up the Haupt Turm of the Vajolet Towers. Several other members were in the Alps, and Dorothy Thompson traversed the Meije. I am not sure whether she was the first Pinnacle Club member to climb it, but Joseph Georges told her she could have led it, and members have certainly led it since. Nea Morin climbed it twice, once in 1933 with Alice Damesme and Micheline Morin, and again in 1958 with Janet Adam Smith.

1926, and Paddy Hirst's reign as president can be rounded off by quoting her own words at the beginning of the second *Journal*:

"Probably by the time the *Journal* appears I shall have joined the ranks of the 'Has-beens'. Truly some are born great and others have greatness thrust upon them. It was certainly thrust upon me with no light thrust, and just at a time when I was making the greatest change of my life - changing from one house to another. At first I felt I could not face the responsibility, but later it was borne upon me that it was a sacred duty to do what I could to carry on the work of a Club which Mrs Kelly had originated, because of our close friendship, and because of the inspiration she had always been to me. In this spirit I have striven to do my best. After five years in office - two as Secretary and three as President - I feel entitled to retire into the ranks of the ordinary member."

I met Paddy only once, at the Pinnacle Club fiftieth Anniversary Dinner. Someone said, 'That's Mrs Hirst, an Original Member,' and I, knowing nothing at all about her, saw a small, rather severe looking lady, quiet and almost colourless. Since then, I have discovered her rich humour and her tremendous exploits, and I wish I could see her again with educated eyes! Perhaps I am writing this history because, when future ignorant young things see members in their eighties, I want them to realise the rich personalities and lively minds which are to them, perhaps, masked by age.

1927 to 1929 were the years of Lilian Bray's presidency and, looking back, the first year can be seen as one of preparation for great events in 1928.

The Skye meet at Whitsun, despite bad weather, saw members exploring large sections of the ridge, and all through the year members were leading rock climbs and developing skills at home and abroad. In September 1927 Dorothy (Pilley) and Ivor Richards landed in Venice after their tour of the world and had a short Alpine season to celebrate their return to Europe. Not much was done that year but the stage was set and the characters assembled for one more great event in 1928.

September saw most people back in England, and there was a well attended meet at Castley near Almscliffe on the second weekend. Two prospective members were on the meet, Marjorie Wood and Eileen Grieg, and at the committee meeting held on the 11th they were both elected associate members. Marjorie has remained a keen member of the Club all her life, but Eileen resigned after a few years. Marjorie remembers that Eileen was a member of the Fell and Rock. She met her in Langdale and they both decided to join the Pinnacle Club. Eileen had a motor bike and side car so, as the next meet was at Almscliffe, run by the Wells sisters, Eileen came to stay with Marjorie and took her on to the meet.

In those days, the Wells were able to borrow a bungalow on the side of the Wharfe at Castley, about two and a half miles from the crags and the Wells did the catering. Marjorie writes:

"I remember my first meeting with Bray, she made us spend a whole morning abseiling off boulders - we were really put through it after I landed on my head. I remember how quiet the rocks were in those days, we could leave all our gear at the foot of the rocks and find it intact at the end of the day. The same applied to the Lakes: we could climb all day and find our things as we left them.

"Before I joined the Club I used to meet Biddy and Trilby for some climbing at Almscliffe and I bought my first pair of trousers but dared not wear them openly so wore a heavy rubber-lined mackintosh over them and went by train to Menston and walked eight miles up to Almscliffe and arrived at the rocks in a lather, dripping. I must have lost pounds! However, after one or two Pinnacle meets I became bolder.

"I think Bray and the Wells were a great asset in the first years of the Club; at a large meet they would make sure that the new members were taken on climbs by the more experienced climbers. I seemed to be taken in hand by Bray, so had a good grounding. I remember on my first Easter Meet in Wales being second on Bray's rope on Grooved Arête and was bringing Arning up when Bray called out, 'What are you doing, Wood?' I said, 'Only blowing my nose,' and was told, 'Never take your hands off the rope!' - for years after, I tended to use my sleeve.

"We seemed to have members of character in the early days. Mrs Eden-Smith was such a gentle, kindly person, and a pleasure to watch on a climb. She was such a contrast to Bray, and they never understood each other. Dr Corbett's friendship with Bray was really strange; they were so unlike. Corbett was very meek, but stood up to Bray's rudeness very well. She used to drive a huge open car at terrific speed and would often give me and Alison Adam a lift to the Lakes, driving round corners on the wrong side of the road and giving a gentle smile when we nearly hit something. Bray refused to drive with her.

"Arning was another character, but a very attractive girl in the early days; not a very neat climber, and she had a habit of holding a climbing party up while she had a bite to eat. This developed in her later years and became rather tiresome - she would insist upon having ten minutes' rest every hour to have food 'owing to my large frame' - However, she did not mind being laughed at."

On Saturday, October 8th, the Pinnacle Club's 'father and mother in one' celebrated its coming of age with a splendid Dinner and party at the Windermere Hydro. The three tier birthday cake, topped by a nightcap which on closer examination resolved itself into a model of Napes Needle, bore the legend, 'Fell and Rock Club Coming of Age: 1927.' Miss Mothersill represented the Pinnacle Club and Len Winthrop Young proposed the toast of the Kindred Clubs. This was not her first after-dinner speech; she had given one at the Fell and Rock Coniston Dinner in 1921, which she says was petrifying, and she was sick with terror all the way round Dow Crags. She went on to say, in a way which is comforting to the rest of us:

"I was always frightened. I was sick with fright because it was a very big dinner and I can't use notes because I can never read them and think I might drop them - but it went all right."

We know exactly what she said at the Coming of Age Party: "Mrs Winthrop Young, who proposed the toast of the Kindred Clubs, wittily described an imaginary assembly of relatives to greet a charming young man who had arrived at full age. First she saw the grandfatherly Alpine Club with his dome of white hair and clothes which, though old, must have come from Savile Row. There was Uncle Rucksack, such a jolly fellow with all the good and bad points Manchester produces (laughter); His pockets were fully packed with Manchester yarns. The Yorkshire Ramblers brought a present of 'pots' (laughter); uncles and aunts of the Scottish Clubs had their pockets full of Edinburgh rock; other people also showed their grit. Our elder sister, the Ladies' Alpine gave that particular polish from the metropolis and the Alps which she alone could give. And finally, the little Pinnacle comes out of the schoolroom having learnt a lot of her lessons, just in time to get her dessert or deserts at the dinner."

Other speakers included Ashley Abraham, General Bruce and Eustace Thomas, and John Hirst produced a new song for the occasion.

The Pinnacle Club's own Manchester Dinner on January 7th, led that five and three quarter year old child into her sixth year and the successes of 1928.

Easter Meet. Kiln Howe, Rosthwaite. 1928
Back Row: Dr Taylor, H.A. Turner, Mrs Isherwood, M.S. Ashton, Mrs Eastwood, H.M. Clarke, Majorie Wood.
Front Row: E.M. Hobkinson, Lilian Bray, Ella Mann, hilda Summersgill, Dr Corbett, Madge Scott.

CHAPTER 7

1928-1929. Cuillin Ridge, Dent Blanche, Women's Achievements World-wide.
Alison Adam, Brenda Ritchie, Evelyn Lowe.

Nineteen twenty eight was full of satisfying events. Pinnacle Club members made the first all-women's traverse of the Cuillin Ridge, Ella Mann led Crowberry Direct, Sam Hall climbed and explored in Iceland, Pilley and Ivor Richards ascended the North Ridge of the Dent Blanche, known then as the last great unclimbed ridge in the Alps and Nea Barnard, not yet a Pinnacle Club member, but a member of the Fell and Rock, married M. Jean Morin of the Groupe de Haute Montagne. She tells us in her book, *A Woman's Reach*, that she started climbing when she was sixteen and was for many years the youngest member of the Ladies' Alpine Club. Katharine Chorley, editor of the Fell and Rock *Journal* for 1928, says in her 'notes', "Nea Barnard gives the Club another link with the Groupe de Haute Montagne, by marrying M. Jean A Morin."

The Richards' ascent is of course mentioned in the same notes - we also learn that Kelly did many new routes on Pillar and the Napes, A B Reynolds climbed Gimmer Crack, Eustace Thomas wrote off the last of the 4,000 metre Alpines (an advanced form of munroitis), and J E B Wright, future founder of the Mountaineering Association, was misquoted in the press as saying that one-sixteenth of an inch was a good foothold for a rock-climb. However, delightful as I find these meanderings, I am being led astray.

The Pinnacle Club Easter Meet was considered the most successful so far, and the records confirm that Bray led Wood up Grooved Arête, but not that she caught her blowing her nose!

At the Annual Meeting Biddy resigned as secretary and Miss Mann was appointed.

The next big meet was on Skye at Whitsuntide. Trilby and Biddy, Bray and Corbett arrived in wet weather on the Sunday. With them were Rooke Corbett and Cook, but only Trilby, Biddy and Bray were to attempt the ridge. They stayed at Mrs Macrae's. Lilian Bray wrote in the third P C *Journal*:

"The day after our arrival (Sunday) there was a thick mist, and we spent it in making two caches as before. Monday it rained all day; Tuesday was gloriously fine and hot, and as the weather looked more settled we determined to start the following day.

"This time we prepared our breakfast the night before, making tea in a couple of thermos flasks so that we might get up at what time we liked without disturbing anyone, and we were actually off by 2.30 a.m. It was really hardly daylight, and in consequence we lost time on the way to Garsbheinn, not taking the best line across the moor.

"The day turned out hot, cloudless and absolutely airless ... We left the Pinnacle at 12.30, the heat was really terrific, and the rocks almost too hot to touch, our mouths so dry we could hardly speak ...

"We passed over the Mhadaidhs and the Bideins, we jumped the amusing little gaps between Bidein and Castail, we scrambled off Castail to the Col, and we were slowly

31

toiling up Bruach na Frithe when suddenly at 9 p.m. one of the party announced that she could not go another step. That being so, we lay down in our tracks…Our greatest tragedy occurred here. We had been hoarding one single lemon with which we hoped to moisten our lips before retiring for the night. Alas! that lemon slipped from our grasp, and we had to watch it falling faster and ever faster down the mountain side. It was perhaps fortunate that our tongues were too dry to speak.

"3.30 a.m. saw us once more on our way; we had all slept more or less; our thirst was not so acute in the cool morning, and we set off up Bruach na Frithe. At the summit we found kind friends had placed three apples for us, but strange as it sounds, my companions could not touch them, which was fortunate for me ...

"It was 9 a.m. when we finished the ridge, we had spent thirty and a half hours without water through the hottest day it had ever been my fate to climb on in the British Isles. Water seemed now of no use to us, and though we drank unlimited quantities, we never really slaked our thirst till we reached Sligachan at 11 o'clock and drank innumerable cups of tea."

This was indeed a major event. They were the first women's party to traverse the entire ridge, and they had beaten their friendly rivals, the Ladies' Scottish, by several years and on the latter's own territory. Just over fifty years later, the Pinnacle Club President, Angela Soper (Faller), was to solo the ridge in seven and a half hours. She did it on a Pinnacle Club meet, and several other members completed the ridge within the day.

This year saw the Pinnacle Club's second Alpine Meet. Trilby, Corbett and Taylor left London on July 27th and met Bray at Valsavaranche. She, lucky lady, appears to have spent the whole of each summer in the Alps, and she told them that there had been a two month drought in the region and the inhabitants were praying for rain. They stayed at the Victor Emmanuel Hut and, the day after their arrival, Bray led them up the Gran Paradiso. Trilby wrote:

"What a thrill we felt when we reached the summit - the first English women to accomplish the climb guideless. Going down, we found that the ice bridge across the bergschrund had come to grief, but taking our courage in our hands, or rather, our legs, we leapt it and soon were back again at the hut, glad enough to seek welcome shade inside."

They climbed the Ciaforon and Monciair with a guide, coming down in a storm, then climbed the Punta di Ceresole guideless. All went well until the descent of a short, difficult passage, when Taylor's abseil rope stuck and Bray threatened to cut it. Fortunately it came free.

They had other problems: Trilby had to patch her clothes every other day, and Bray's no longer fitted so neatly . . . "In a month she lost a stone. Now, supposing the President of the Pinnacle Club weighs eight stones and loses one stone per month, in how many months should we want a new President?"

Meanwhile, our Editor had already realised her dream of the past few years.

The Richards were about to start for an alpine holiday in the Dauphiné when a telegram arrived from Joseph Georges suggesting that the dry season gave a good chance of success on the Dent Blanche ridge. They immediately changed their plans and, writes Pilley, "We were still feeling irrational when we found ourselves strolling with Joseph in the shadow of the Veisivi."

The ascent began at one o'clock on July 20th, and the Richards with Joseph Georges and his brother Antoine climbed as two pairs except where the difficulties were great.

Joseph eventually found the key to the climb on the very nose of the ridge itself and they reached the summit at 5 p.m.

Having had their hearts' desire at the beginning of their holiday, the Richards found it difficult to settle to anything else; however, the glorious weather continued and they did many other routes. In Zermatt they met Geoffrey Winthrop Young, getting ready for his ascent of the Matterhorn. Later Dorothy Thompson joined them for the Grandes Jorasses, amongst other adventures.

Among the many new ascents recorded in the November edition of the *Alpine Journal* for 1928, a full page was devoted to the North Ridge of the Dent Blanche.

Pilley's notes for the third Pinnacle Club *Journal* mention her own achievement and those of other women climbers at that time:

"Turning to Alpine and general mountaineering the increasing part played by women in new and otherwise remarkable expeditions will be of interest. The first ascent of the North Arête of the Dent Blanche, the last great ridge of the Alps, by the Editor and Mr I A Richards, led by the brilliant guide, Joseph Georges; Miss Maud Cairney's variant on the N E face of the same mountain, and her first winter ascent of the Obergabelhorn from the Mountet; Miss Miriam O'Brian's first ascent of L'Aiguille de Roc du Grépon, her lead of the Mummery Chimney of the Grépon, and her exploits on the Aiguilles du Diable; Miss Sheila Macdonald's ascent of Mount Kilimanjaro, and Mrs Don Munday's explorations on the Canadian Coast Ranges (Mystery Mountain), and too many other fine performances to be chronicled here, will show that the spirit which animates the Pinnacle Club is also active ouside among feminine mountaineers.

"The advance in technical ability, enterprise and scope, to which these things testify would, we are sure, have delighted the generous heart of our Foundress. To us it shows that the inspiration from which the Club takes its being was fully justified."

Sam Hall's exploits in Iceland were also mentioned, and Sam wrote an article for the *Journal*, beginning in her usual lively style:

"I had all my life intended to go to Iceland as soon as I could afford it, and since in 1928 I realized that I should never be able to afford it, I decided to go at once . . ." Before going, she learnt enough Icelandic to be able to converse with people and stay at a farm for some days. This meant she could live very cheaply. She travelled on horseback over great stretches of desert and, as she approached the mountains, expanses of glacial plain, cut by innumerable rivers which were often deep, swift and with shifting sands. She had hoped to reach the Langjökull glacier from Hvitarvatn, but her plan broke down at the very last moment and her only shot (half successful) at that glacier was from the other side, from which she had been told it could not be done. The whole trip was witness to her bold and independent spirit and makes fascinating reading.

Several events were to take place in 1929 before the *Journal* was finally published. The Dinner Meet had been planned for the previous autumn, but took place even later than usual, in February. This spring also saw the Coming of Age celebrations of the Ladies' Scottish Climbing Club, and Biddy Wells was the Pinnacle Club's representative at their Celebration Dinner in Ballachulish. The Club's own Annual Meeting was held at Kiln How, Rosthwaite on Saturday March 30th.

For some time there had been trouble over unpaid subscriptions. The treasurer now asked for a ruling that members in arrears for three consecutive years should have their names removed from the list of membership. This was carried. Even without this rule, numbers had dropped during the year, with seven resignations and two new members; so at the meeting the numbers stood at fifty-eight.

Climbing records for the weekend show two days' climbing followed by walking over Glaramara, Saddleback and Skiddaw on the Sunday and Monday. Bray and Arning both led Arrowhead Direct on Gable on the Friday. All parties descended routes as well as ascending them, as was normal practice in those uncongested days.

The usual meets were held during the year, but one of particular interest was held at Almscliffe in September. It was led by Trilby and Biddy Wells and was Alison Adam's first meet. She had read about climbing and was very keen to try, but had nobody to climb with; then in the local Burnley paper she read something about Dr Corbett who was the School Medical Officer for the area. Corbett went to the school where Alison was teaching, to do a medical inspection, so Alison plucked up the courage to ask her about climbing and was immediately invited on a Pinnacle Club meet. She was made an associate member at the committee meeting on the Saturday evening and has been active in the Club ever since. Each year she organises a highly successful 'Yorkshire Meet', traditionally a walking meet, but some go climbing and once or twice potholing has been arranged.

At the first committee meeting in 1930, before the Manchester Dinner, two applications came before the committee, seeking full membership. The names on the forms were Brenda Ritchie and Evelyn Lowe. The committee came to the decision, however, that their application forms 'did not show them sufficiently practised in the handling and leading of novices.'

This was all very well, but Brenda Ritchie had been proposed by Pilley and seconded by the secretary, Ella Mann, in May 1929 and had been entered in that year's *Handbook* as a full member! Brenda was indeed outstanding, and the committee must have bowed to the inevitable because her name remained on the list of full members. Evelyn had been proposed and seconded by Miss Hutson and Bray, and entered in the records as a full member in December 1929; however, she had to wait till the 1931 *Handbook* before her name appeared on the list as a full member.

Brenda thinks it was Evelyn who suggested her joining the Pinnacle Club. She writes: "I remember one very enjoyable meet at the Club hut; but I don't think I went to more than one or two others - I lived much too far to go to the mountains for weekends, so that my climbing was more widely spaced, generally two or three weeks at a time, with friends or family (Evelyn and Herbert Carr, sister and brother-in-law). I started climbing with family and friends, and climbed in that way for some years, in this country and in the Alps. I also went to a good many meets with the Oxford University Women's Mountaineering Club which was formed in the early thirties - we went rock-climbing here, and had two Alpine meets - but it evaporated after a few years."

Alison Adam tells me that Brenda did many good climbs with G R Speaker and she remembers her leading many routes on the 1935 Pinnacle Club Easter Meet in Wasdale. Later Brenda led a high-powered Pinnacle Club meet in the Dolomites.

In the summer of 1929, Dorothy Thompson became the first woman to ascend the Brouillard Ridge of Mont Blanc. She had reached a peak of fitness by walking through the Vanoise with Sylvia Norman, an indefatigable walker who had written delightfully for the P C *Journal* of her chosen pastime in 'Hills versus Mountain Peaks'.

Dorothy met Joseph Georges in Courmayeur, and, with Marcel as porter they went up to the Quintino Sella Hut. They started the route at 2.05 a.m. the next morning, and completed it in almost perfect conditions, though not without an unexpected and potentially very dangerous stonefall. Dorothy wrote:

"It was not until we arrived on the summit of the Amedeo, where we paused for a meal, that Joseph really became convinced that I was not hurt. We reached it at 10 a.m." They reached Mont Blanc de Courmayeur at 2.30 p.m. and soon afterwards, as they rested for refreshment, Joseph broke the news to her that she was first woman to complete the ridge.

She went down to Montenvers the next day to find that more history had been made:

"The Montenvers, when we reached it, after a delightful walk along the whole of the climbers' terrace, was humming with activity. Members of the Groupe de Haute Montagne kept darting off to catch a train down to Chamonix. I just managed to snatch a word with Jean and Nea Morin before they, too were caught into the vortex. From my window, after ordering a bath, I saw Joe Marples below. 'Come along to the station!' she called, 'Your bath can wait! The train won't!' Hoping that no treacherous friend would purloin my hot water, I tore down and joined the general run of the traffic.

"Miriam O'Brien and Alice Damesme (the latter leading the Mummery Crack) had been putting a new angle on women's mountaineering by climbing the Grépon in a feminine party of two, dispensing with the superfluous male! With Joe herself as partner, Miss O'Brien (Mrs R Underhill) had that day led the Peigne, in another 'cordée feminine'. No wonder that excitement was bubbling and seething, with the train threatening to descend at any moment and leave them all talking!

"That evening Jean Morin, on his return to the Montenvers, played the piano to an appreciative audience, and M. (Pierre) Chevalier, curling long legs with difficulty under the instrument, sang French songs ..."

In *A Woman's Reach*, Nea tells of the great part music played in Jean Morin's life. He had studied music at the Toulon Conservatoire, where he won many awards and medals. It is yet another reminder that to know a person as a climber is to be acquainted with only one facet of their personality and life.

CHAPTER 8

"Heaven for a Bob a Day"
1930 to 1932. A Hut in Wales. More New Members.

On Saturday April 19th, 1930, the ninth Annual Meeting was held at the Crook Farm, Torver, Coniston and Miss Hilton, Custodian of the Log Book, stuck in a photograph of all the members present, posed outside the front door.

This was Alison Adam's first meeting as a member, and in her article, 'The Second Ten Years' she comments:

"The Pinnacle Club was in its tenth year, and some members must have asked themselves, 'Where does the Club go from here?' The Founder members now had family commitments, Pilley was abroad and several had given up rock-climbing. The Club needed someone with time, energy and personality to attract young members.

"To that Easter Meet came the Secretary - Ella Mann. She announced her resignation and said that Mrs Eden-Smith was willing to become the Secretary. Looking back over all these years I realise how fortunate the Club was - it got the right person at the right time . . . She was attractive to look at, with her slim boyish figure, usually in slacks (very outrageous in those days) and her hair an Eton-crop. She was a grand person to climb with, and very helpful and encouraging to new members."

Miss Bray, the retiring president, proposed Dr Corbett as her successor. This was carried unanimously. Popular as Dr Corbett was, Alison is certain that it was Gabriel Eden-Smith's personality which gave the Club its form and purpose in the 1930s.

It must have been sometime in the early summer that Susan Harper and Marjorie Heys-Jones, both to become lifelong members, first met Bray and heard of the Pinnacle Club. Marjorie writes:

"Susan Harper and I were great friends, and for some years shared a flat in Croydon. She was Scottish but had spent her life in Australia before coming to England to go to Oxford, staying on in England to teach history at Croydon High School. We met there and subsequently shared a flat for six years. She was very well read, full of ideas, produced plays at school, and persuaded me to join a fencing club to be physically fit to rock climb! Her family eventually came over to Scotland and then home was Edinburgh, and she and her sister, Chris, an artist, began walking the hills and trying a little easy climbing.

"One summer holiday, she asked me to come with her and Chris to climb in Skye. I had just had my appendix out, and it was the first time I had bog-hopped so that I was very much a third on the rope and I can remember how very frightened I was when I waited for my turns to climb on Sgurr nan Gillean!"

Chris went home and Marjorie remembers Susan leading her up a loose, long climb. "A golden eagle squawked and flew beside us, and after a very long time we arrived at the top of the mountain to find a sheep grazing.

"We got bitten with climbing, and we began to do easy climbs in Wales, learning how to climb from Winthrop Young's *Mountaineering* which we called our bible, and Abraham's book. We used to go to Snowdonia Friday evening to Sunday night. I bought a second-hand car, and we stayed at Capel Curig or elsewhere, and climbed all the easier rock. It was on Milestone we encountered Bray leading a novice who had a slight accident. We moved to help her and Bray called out: 'Why aren't you members of the Pinnacle Club?' and later introduced us to it." Marjorie became headmistress of a grammar school and Susan a lecturer at Darlington.

Meets at home followed the same pattern as in other years, though the July meet at Windgather had to be cancelled as the owner of the rocks did not wish the game to be disturbed. July saw Bray in the Bregaglia, where she climbed half a dozen peaks and traverses before joining the Pinnacle Club's second official Alpine Meet at Arolla, on August 2nd. The meet was led by Dr Corbett, the president, and the other four members of the meet had all joined the Club within the previous year. Mary Schroeder, who lived in Leeds, joined very shortly after Alison Adam. "Strange as it may seem!" writes Alison, "Bray took a fancy to her."

Mary wrote a very lively account of the Meet for the *Journal*. It is sad that we hear little more of her, for she went to live abroad and left the Club in 1935. Evelyn Lowe joined the meet by walking all the way from Lake Como - 400 kilometres in a fortnight. The last two members of the party, Heys-Jones and Harper, were both friends of hers.

In her account, Mary Schroeder writes:

"Finally from the half light emerges a figure carrying an ice axe and an umbrella, with a second figure following humbly in her wake: the President and the novice have arrived, having walked from Sion. On either side of the long table, lamp-lit, the ranks are closed and complete. We examine each other with interest... 'Fools,' says L E B 'for walking up,' but then that is her usual term for those to whom she is attached."

The party's first long route was the Petite Dent de Veisivi. Their guides were Antoine Georges, known to Dr Corbett for over twenty years, and the young Joseph Georges. After a heavy shower, the day was hot and dry, and the climb went very well.

" ... Then follows the descent over the slabs, the swing round a corner, scene of the Hopkinson accident and then after a long descent over rubble, water! We sit round the spring. Antoine's eye is arrested by my straggling socks, he pulls them up before serving the lemonade. Then with characteristic acumen Bray and her disciples head for home and tea, leaving Corbett, Lowe and myself to sleep in the sun.

"Thursday saw the departure of Bray in a skirt, under a hat with an umbrella and a walking stick - oh sight for tired eyes and most unusual! She rounded the corner, she was gone, leaving us her second best coat, her ice-axe, her water bottle, and her prunes."

After various walks and an ascent of the Dent de Salerma, they took guides again for an ascent of the Tsa from the Bertol Hut... "Merrily Antoine and Joseph hoisted us up one pitch after another. Done in that fashion, a climb naturally presents few difficulties." On the chance of another fine day, Lowe and Harper stayed up at the hut and were rewarded by the clouds lifting in time for them to climb the Bouquetins. Evelyn Lowe wrote: "The rock being iced made some of the final pitches quite difficult to negotiate, and the whole peak was most interesting throughout."

Mont Blanc de Cheilon was the last official Club climb, but Harper and Heys-Jones stayed on for another week and were able to traverse the Perroc and Grand Dent de Veisivi, Mont Collon and the North and Central peaks of the Aiguilles Rouges with

Antoine Georges. Dr Corbett went to Zermatt, where she climbed the Matterhorn with the guide Otto Taugwalder. Meanwhile, Ilsa Bell, ('Scotty') had been climbing from the Montjoie Valley, Haute Savoie, with Dorothy Thompson. While warming up for the arrival of Joseph Georges, they climbed Mont Joly and the Aiguille de la Rosalette guideless, then Joseph led them up Mont Tondu, Tête Carrée, Dome de Miage, Aiguille de Tricol and from Montenvers, the Peigne.

Some of this information is contained in the 1931 P C *Handbook*, which was the first to contain records of the previous year's meets. It was a good innovation and from this year onwards the Handbooks make extremely interesting reading, especially after an interval of a few years.

Other achievements by women mountaineers in 1930 included the traverse of the Grandes Jorasses by Geraldine Fitzgerald and Miriam O'Brien's third ascent of the N E Face of the Finsteraarhorn. G Davidson writes of a further woman climber under the heading: 'An interesting ascent of the Matterhorn.'

"Miss Ethel Whymper, only child of the late Edward Whymper, traversed the Matterhorn on August 27th, thus just about 65 years after her father's first ascent - July 14th, 1865." (*Alpine Journal*).

Ethel Whymper joined the Ladies' Alpine Club in l935, she became Mrs Blandy and was honoured guest at the Matterhorn Centenary Celebrations in 1965.

Around this time we hear a lot about the closing of the Italian frontiers and complaints about the growth of mountaineering as a competitive sport in Germany - pointers towards the troubles which were lying ahead.

That autumn the Wells sisters ran the usual climbing meet at Almscliffe, but other meets were poorly attended, and at the Manchester Dinner Meet there were more guests than members, despite offers of hospitality from those based in Manchester. This was, in fact, the last Manchester dinner as the following one was cancelled due to lack of support. Finally it was decided that dinners must be held in climbing areas and that has been the arrangement ever since. Marjorie Wood found the Manchester dinners very formal, with evening dress and dancing later, and thinks they are much better now. However, they had been a tremendous success in the early years; now it was time for a change.

The Easter Meet for 1931 was held in Buttermere. Apart from the Alpine Meet, this was Marjorie Heys-Jones' first contact with the Club. Her party had stayed the night on the way up at the house of a man at Altrincham who sold silk cloth. His name was Leech, and he was the man whom Evelyn Lowe eventually married. They arrived at Buttermere at tea time and members were eating tea round the room. Marjorie didn't understand what they were saying, as they were talking with a Yorkshire accent, though she soon came to terms with it, she says.

Marjorie Wood has clear memories of three of the members who were active in the Club at this time. Miss Hobkinson lived nearby in Leeds, and Marjorie writes: "Hobby often gave me a lift to meets and we would walk locally. She did not stay long in the Club but she was good company, very forthright; she was a factory inspector and seemed just right for the job. It was she who brought Lynn Clarke to the Club (1931) and we became great friends." E M (Lynn) Clarke was on the committee during the 1930s and remained a member till her death in 1981.

"Dora Dawson I think of with great pleasure, she was a delightful person, very quiet, with a great sense of humour. We had some happy holidays together before the war, walking in Scotland in the days when youth hostels were just starting and only remote crofts, no food provided; one collected the key from the Post Office and owned the place. Dora was small and rather plump and never seemed to feel the cold; she would turn up with a tiny rucksack for two weeks' climbing with no woolly of any kind, one thin shirt as a dry change.

We would meet in the dining car of the train at breakfast time, I joined the train at York and Dora came from London (she lived in Upper Caterham, Surrey). Always she had bought the largest cucumber she could find on her way to the station, and it formed the basis of our evening meals with a tin of salmon for most of the holiday. Dora taught German privately and we lost touch during the war; she was in the Censor's Office and I was in the army, though we wrote once a year until a few years ago."

Dora had been at university in Innsbruck, so spoke fluent German. Alison Adam had her first holiday abroad with Dora, when they went on a walking tour in Brittany.

A third member whom Marjorie remembers at this time was Nan Middleton, who must have been an experienced climber as she was elected a full member a few months after she joined. She was a live wire and not really approved of in those days as she had a lot of publicity in the papers, which the P C avoided. In May 1931 she led a meet at Wharncliffe rocks based at her 'rather primitive cottage', as Marjorie says. Gabriel and Corbett were also there, and some good, hard climbs were done. Nan did not stay in the club very long; she did not conform to the standards set by Bray and Co. and seemed an odd one out; also she married in 1932 and moved to Essex.

It must have been pleasant to climb at Wharncliffe after being drenched with rain throughout the Whitsun meet at Coniston. There was another good climbing meet at Embsay in June, but to me an interesting milestone is the first Pinnacle meet to do the Three Peaks Walk of Ingleborough, Penyghent and Whernside. The year ended with a very well attended Christmas meet at Rosthwaite, during which Taylor and Wood celebrated Christmas Day by climbing Needle Ridge on Gable.

The Easter Meet in 1932 was held at Capel Curig and the records show the first ascent on a Pinnacle Club meet of Lockwood's Chimney. The climbing party were Lowe, Heys-Jones, Lear and Harper and, as they ate their sandwiches in the rain, they noticed a cottage above the power station in Cwm Dyli which appeared to be used as a storehouse. Evelyn Lowe at once thought of its potential as a club hut and discovered that Dr Corbett, the president, and other Club members were as keen as herself. She was given the task of negotiating with the North Wales Power Company and by September had reached an agreement for the renting of the cottage on a five years' lease at an annual rate of ten pounds. For a further eight pounds the company was putting the building into habitable repair and installing electric light.

Evelyn was warmly thanked by the committee and became the first hut secretary. The hut was called the Emily Kelly Hut in memory of the Founder of the Club.

The committee met in October, following a letter from the North Wales Power Company, charging the Club with tenancy as from October 1st, 1932. It was decided that the official opening of the Club hut should take place on November 5th, 1932, at 4 p.m., and the ceremony be performed by the President, Dr Corbett. Invitation cards were printed, and sent to people who had been helpful to the club.

This was a very exciting time for Evelyn. She and her friends were busy decorating and furnishing the hut, and it was just the sort of place she loved. She had her own tiny place

The Emily Kelly Hut, Cwm Dyli

Interior downstairs

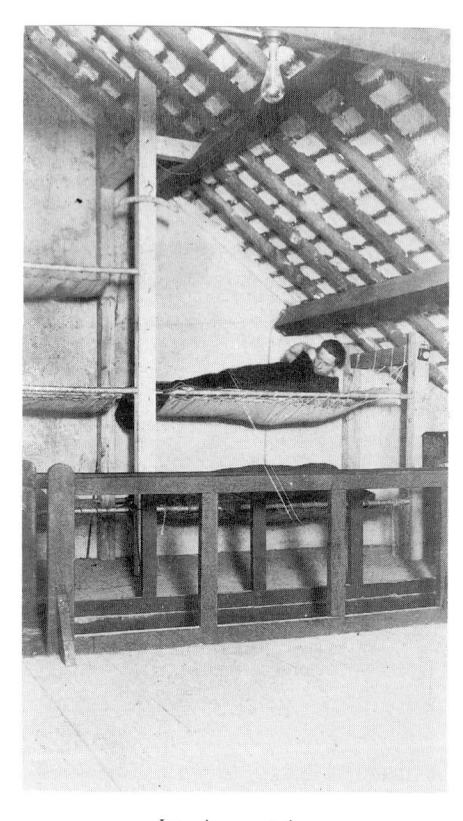

Interior upstairs

in the woods a few miles away, with just room for a bunk bed and a stove, where she could get away from the world, and she envisaged that the Club hut would perform the same service for members. The walls were whitewashed, but the shelves were left unpainted so that they shouldn't show the dirt and worry people by looking as if they needed scrubbing. On the other hand, she liked a place for everything and everything in its place, as poor sinners who mixed up the knives, forks and spoons soon found out. She wrote a 'Hut Song' for the opening ceremony, and it finished with the very true words:

> Any Pinnacler can stay
> (Heaven for a bob a day!)
> Provided that she leaves it clean and tidy!

The Pinnacle Club *Journal* contains an account of the opening of the hut; it describes the roomy dormitory with canvas bunkbeds and red blankets; the orange and blue chairs downstairs, the primus stoves, open fire and small kitchen. Dr Corbett made a simple and moving speech, then everyone trooped in for tea, cakes and a wonderfully decorated trifle in a washing basin.

The account concludes: "The feet of some of the most privileged were allowed to rest on the President's gift, a superb wool hearthrug made by herself in a pattern of ice-axes and looped rope.

"The crowd chattered and laughed, drank tea and spilt it over their very near neighbours, ate what they could reach of the good things, and gradually oozed out of the door into less congested space. The crowning glory of the Hut was switched on - electric light! And we looked hopefully for signs of envy in the eyes of members of other less fortunate clubs, whose huts have no such blessing. Outside, the sky had darkened to dusk, stars came out and frost crinkled underfoot. Most of our friends departed, and we could see the lights of their cars winding up the steep road towards Pen-y-Gwryd. A few who

Dr Corbett & her brother at the bonfire

Lowe, Lear, D Seth-Hughes, J Seth-Hughes, Wood, P Seth-Hughes.

were left with us magically produced some fireworks - was it not, after all, also Guy Fawkes' Day? - and a riotous half-hour was spent in final celebration. Supper followed, the last guests were evicted, and at length a contentedly weary band of some fifteen members were free to enjoy their first night's rest in their new Club Home. It had been a good day."

For the same *Journal*, Evelyn wrote an account of a weekend meet at the hut. We learn that people, unless they had a car, travelled by train to Betws-y-Coed, and by bus to either Capel Curig or Pen-y-Gwryd. Friday night's supper was always sausage and mash, followed by fruit and cream, and tea was made in a huge red teapot.

The opening of the hut was by far the biggest event during 1932, but it was not the only one of note. Another very interesting piece of information comes from Mrs Eden-Smith's diary: 'Nov: 27 (1932) Coniston. Walna Scar, Brown Pike, Dow Crags, Old Man and down to Parkgate, three and a half hours. Visited and had tea at new Climbers' Hut.'

This Climbers' Hut was the guest house opened by the sisters Mrs Helen Bryan and Miss Evelyn Pirie, who provided wonderful hospitality to Pinnacle Club members as they did to all climbers. They were keen walkers and moderate climbers, and both joined the Pinnacle Club at the end of the following year. Evelyn Pirie was to become secretary in 1935 and was on the committee during the 1940s; Helen Bryan became journal editor in 1949 and president in 1955, being the only president not to have been elected a full member of the Club.

Further new members had joined the Club during the summer: Harper and Heys-Jones proposed and seconded Christina Barratt, Eileen Jackson and Jean Orr Ewing, and Evelyn Lowe brought her friends Daloni and Penelope Seth Hughes. Marjorie Scott Johnson also joined at this time, followed by Sylvia Collingwood from Leeds and Ruth Hargreaves, who at the time was Ruth Heap and lived near Blackpool. Ruth was a member of parties doing first ascents in the Lake District all through the 1930s, her identity in the guidebooks slightly masked by the fact that she appears both as Ruth Heap and as R E Hargreaves. She also says that she and her friends climbed all over Gate Crag in Eskdale long before it was 'discovered' in the 1950s; it was their local practice ground.

In 1932 Jean Orr Ewing was a doctor doing research work in pathology at Oxford. She was a brilliant and charming person, having been head girl of her school and captain of the First Eleven before going up to Oxford to study medicine. Here she organised an Oxford University Women's Mountaineering Club which had successful Alpine and home meets, and in the early 1930s she organised a climbing meet in Corsica. Christina Barratt was one of this latter party. She had started climbing in 1929 and joined the Fell and Rock, where she became very friendly with Brenda Ritchie. She and her brother, Geoffrey, often climbed with Brenda's family parties. She joined the Pinnacle Club Dolomites meets in the 1950s and the Italians thought that a younger member, Anne Littlejohn, must be her daughter, which rather tickled her.

Now that the Club had a hut in Wales, it was only natural that the venue for the first Annual Dinner to be held in a climbing area was Capel Curig. Mrs Eden-Smith and one of her sons drove down on December 30th, taking five and a quarter hours from Grange. After tea at the guest house, they took Pilley and Bray down to see the hut. Gabriel was obviously providing transport for the weekend, because she met Miss Keay, the LSCC representative off the 8.32 a.m. train at Betws the next morning. She then went up Moel Siabod with Corbett, Bray, Hobkinson and Griffiths before meeting Ruth Hale, the LAC guest, off the train at 4.24. Her diary notes that the Dinner was supposed to be at 7.30, but was delayed by the late arrival of some of the guests and speakers. '35 present. A very good evening.'

Ruth Hale was to join the Club the following June, become a much loved star, and die too soon in the mountains which had cast their spell over her - the Tatras.

The President and Committee of The Pinnacle Club request the pleasure of the company of

Mr H. M. Kelly

at the Opening of

The Emily Kelly Hut

in Cwm Dyli, near Pen y Gwryd, on Saturday, November 5th, at 4 p.m.

R.S.V.P. to—
    Mrs. EDEN-SMITH (Hon. Sec.),
        Eggerslack Cottage,
            Grange-over-Sands,
                Lancashire.

H.M. Kelly's Invitation Card

CHAPTER 9

1933-35. Mabel Barker. Dorothy Pilley as President. Climbing worldwide and more new members. Climbing Days *published. Meet in High Tatras.*

In February 1933 the Pinnacle Club held its first meet at the Dow Crag Climbers' Hut, Parkgate, Coniston. Mrs Bryan and Miss Pirie had recently opened it in, as it turned out, worthy succession to the much loved Mrs Harris's Climbers' Cottage. Mrs Harris had died in 1928, lamented by several generations of climbers for her warm hospitality and kindliness.

This last weekend in February coincided with a bad snowstorm. Fortunately Bryan and Pirie were very keen skiers with a great stack of equipment, for climbing and walking were virtually impossible in the deep, soft snow. All fifteen members of the meet took to winter sports and a potentially frustrating weekend became a resounding success.

The Easter meet was in Wasdale, with a number of keen new members present. Four of them: Dr Mabel Barker, Molly Fitzgibbon, Mrs R Jennings and Annette Wilson, were elected during the weekend.

Mabel Barker had been in the parties doing first ascents on Castle Rock of Triermain and Grey Crag, Buttermere, and was getting towards the end of her climbing days, though still climbing extremely well. She was the first woman to climb Central Buttress on Scafell, (4th ascent, 1925), and the first woman, in 1926, to complete the Cuillin Ridge. She lived at Caldbeck, where she had a school, and Alison Adam remembers a hilarious Club meet which she held in her house. She was a doctor of literature and also had a science degree in geology and a diploma in geography. She assisted Sir Patrick Geddes at Edinburgh University and Montpellier University, and helped the Quakers in their work for refugees in Holland during the First World War, later holding teaching and lecturing appointments before conducting her own private school. She was a great friend of the Mallory family, and Mallory's ice axe, found on Everest, came into her possession. Interesting and gifted in so many ways, she was an inspiring person to be with and some years later was made an honorary member of the Club.

Eunice Jennings had already shown her willingness to struggle with jobs which needed doing in the hut. She was a slim, pretty person who preferred mountaineering to pure rock climbing, though she enjoyed that too. She made many friends in the Club and it was a great shock when she died suddenly after a short illness in 1937. Edith Bennett, who joined the Club later in 1933, writes that she was introduced by Eunice:

"Eunice and I met through our husbands who were both members of the Rucksack Club. We used to spend camping and climbing weekends together...once Eunice and I had a bath in the snow on the Glyders just for the hell of it! Sadly she died very young. I remember having to give the news at one very snowy Easter meet in Wasdale. After that I climbed with Annette Wilson who became a close friend."

Coniston, 1933.
Standing: L-R - Eden-Smith, Pilley, Corbett, Mrs Humphries, Hale, Ashton.
Front: L-R - Annette Wilson, Ursula Lawrie, Alison Adam.

Coniton, Easter 1934.
Back Row: L-R - Wood, B Ritchie, Arning, Pirie, Wilson, Bennett, Adam, ?
Middle Row: L-R - D.Dawson, Turner, Corbett, Pilley, Bray.
Front Row: L-R - Heys-Jones, Harper, Lowe, Eden-Smith.

Annette Wilson was a small, attractive person, quick and neat. On this occasion she had been met off the 7.09 train at Grange and brought to Wasdale by Mrs Eden-Smith in her new car. Annette was much loved Club secretary during the war years and active in the mountains till her death. When staying at the hut she slept downstairs by the fire, having been banished from the dormitory, so it is said, for grinding her teeth in her sleep! - partly true, no doubt, but it is a cosy, pleasant spot for a small person.

Dorothy Pilley Richards became President for the years 1933-36. She was back in England for the time being and agreed to be in office for a year in the first instance. Her travels had added to her prestige as a climber, if that were possible, and gave the club links with mountaineers as far afield as North America, Japan and Korea. In consequence the Pinnacle Club had requests for an exchange of journals and bulletins from the Appalachian Mountain Club, the Ski Club, the American Alpine Club and the Japanese Alpine Club.

Twelve new members had joined during the year, one being Mrs Ursula Lawrie. She and her husband had a famous alpine and polar equipment shop in London.

The climbing and walking on the Easter meet set the standard for the year, with an enormous number of routes being climbed on Gable, Scafell and Pillar. Ruth Heap, small and slight, led Tophet Bastion and Arrowhead Direct; with rock very cold and slimy, according to Gabriel's diary. Later on, during the Whitsun meet at Cwm Dyli, she and Evelyn Lowe were leading routes such as Tennis Shoe on Idwal Slabs, followed by Holly-Tree Wall, and then turned their attention to Milestone Superdirect. In fact there was a host of members leading very good routes - Wood, Harper, Pilley, Daloni Seth Hughes, Taylor, Adam, Lear, Orr Ewing and Heys-Jones stood out in particular.

Jean Orr Ewing was researching in diphtheria at Oxford. Marjorie Heys-Jones writes: "She taught me to lead and we had exciting expeditions together, one in Corsica and two in Switzerland and Haute Savoie."

There were no club Alpine meets in 1932 and 33, but those members who had the opportunity were very active in various Alpine centres and some wrote accounts for the 1932-34 Club *Journal*. I find them fresh and unassuming, though naturally filled with the delight and pride of achievement. Molly Fitzgibbon wrote of her climb of the North West Face of the Scheidegg Wetterhorn with Joseph Georges, (This ascent on August 14th, 1933, and also their traverse of Die Hörnli am Eiger were reported in the *Alpine Journal* no. 248); Susan Harper of the Dolomites; Brenda Ritchie of the Engelhörner. Biddy Deed had been in Uri and the Eastern Oberland and Bray and Corbett in the Pyrenees.

Dorothy Pilley was Editor and did not mention her own achievements, but the *Alpine Journal* no. 249 records her and Dr Richards' first ascent of Mount Conrad, Canada, on 8th September, 1933 with Conrad Kain. In 1934, Jean Orr Ewing told of her experiences in Corsica, and there is Ruth Hale's account of the High Tatras which is the prelude to the successful Pinnacle Club meet there in 1935. Susan Harper and Marjorie Heys-Jones had been to Zermatt as well as the Dolomites; a famous guide had lost his client on the Weisshorn the day before they attempted it, and they found their guide terribly flustered when they reached a certain easy slab - the scene of the disaster. On their arrival back (in the dark) at the Station Hotel, all the inmates came out to shake hands with them and congratulate them. They had certainly chosen the right day for maximum effect!

Mrs Eden-Smith's involvement with the Pinnacle Club as Secretary is mirrored in her diary. She constantly mentions giving people lifts to meets or visits to the Hut in Wales. The hut was proving itself a wonderful asset for, unlike the guest houses, all could afford to stay there. The Fell and Rock were discovering the same need and felt that they must obtain a hut or become a middle-aged club. The Ladies Alpine Club, Ladies' Scottish and ladies of the Fell and Rock were offered use of the Emily Kelly Hut and paid six pence a night more than Pinnacle Club members. (Local opinion at the time forbade any suggestion of mixed sleeping arrangements, so men stayed at cottages nearby). Fell and Rock ladies made use of the offer when A B Hargreaves instigated a most successful joint meet with the PC, F&RCC and Climbers' Club which took place in July 1934.

Between 1933 and 1934 the Pinnacle Club membership rose from 59 to 71, and the trend continued with sixteen further members elected during the year. Of these, Biddy Deed and Mary Glynne were both members of the Ladies' Alpine Club and had many routes to their credit. During 1933 Mary had traversed the Meije and the Drus. She is a relative of Owen Glynne Jones - more specifically, he was a second cousin of her mother's. Mary writes:

"My parents were excellent mountain walkers and took us to the tops of many of the mountains in North Wales but they disapproved of rock climbing after the death of Owen Glynne Jones on the Dent Blanche in the 1890s.

"The Fell and Rock was my first climbing club which I joined in 1923 and of which I am a life member. The Ladies' Alpine Club I joined in 1928 before I went to Australia and New Zealand and lastly the Pinnacle Club which I joined in 1934. I qualified by leading two sisters up climbs on Tryfan."

As it turned out, Mary had less contact with the Pinnacle Club than with the other clubs, though attending meets till the 1960s.

Other members to join during the year were Nancy Ridyard, Lucy Lambrick, J M Cobham, R Allaun, Constance Alexander, Rosalind Proctor, Nancy Forsyth, Catherine Stuart, Mary Grosvenor, Dorothy Clune, Berta Gough, Dorothy Milner-Brown and Vera Unicombe.

Nancy Ridyard was an outstanding climber and an enthusiastic member of the Club and was to be a committee member during the war years, but she resigned in 1960, and as Mrs Carpenter she has proved that her first love, the Fell and Rock, is also her last. She joined that club in 1927 and is still a member. Lucy Lambrick (Mrs Parry) served on the committee and as auditor before resigning in 1953. Berta Gough (Mrs Andrews) was very active before the war and was on the committee from 1939 till 1942; then in 1943 she met her husband, who was doing war work in Liverpool, moved to London and has never climbed since. She kept a fascinating diary of her Pinnacle Club meets, which she kindly lent me, and has always retained her interest in club affairs.

Dorothy Clune was H M Kelly's niece. Mrs Eden Smith was very fond of her and used to take her climbing. She was the subject of the article and photograph entitled 'Heyday' in *Journal* no. 4. R Allaun came from Manchester and Alison Adam thinks she was related to Frank Allaun, the Salford Socialist MP. Alison says she was a good climber, most reliable, and a splendid companion on the mountains.

Nancy Forsyth, a very fine person and one of the Club's finest climbers, was to lose her life in an accident on Ben Nevis in 1944.

Vera Unicombe is Vera Picken who still delights members with slide shows of her explorations of the Scottish Islands and the Near East. She was brought up in Abergavenny and writes:

"It was a great treat, on Bank Holidays, to be out on the hills all day. The youngest of three was in a push chair and somehow Mum and Dad carried the picnic and kettle, for we had two big bonfires to brew up tea.

"The bricks and mortar of Liverpool where I worked 1929-37 were not very enchanting and about 1930 I heard of and joined the Holiday Fellowship and went rambling almost every weekend. I can still remember the excitement of Scotland in the summer of 1932. I travelled up on the night train reaching Stirling in the early hours. The weather was perfect. At the H.F. Centre Loch Leven I met two couples who agreed to take me along the Aonach Eagach on a free day. This should have put me off for ever for the day was inauspicious from the start. However, start we did, and did the ridge in thick mist and probably some rain for we were soaked and our fingers numb with cold. No doubt it was crazy for in those days mountain walking was done in shorts. Two men refused to come with us, so there was one man and three women. We did have a rope. At that time I did not of course know it was crazy; we enjoyed it and occasionally a hole in the clouds gave a window onto the valley 3000 feet below.

"Summer 1933 I met Percy Hodladay at the H.F. Langdale Centre. He took me up Middlefell Buttress.

"There were men in the H.F. who spent weekends climbing from Idwal Cottage Youth Hostel, when they could muster transport. Back in Liverpool from Langdale I decided to organise a weekend coach party. It was successful but very harassing. Later I tried it on a bicycle - down Saturday, round the Heather Terrace and back on Sunday. Had it not been for someone called Tom (I think) I doubt if I would have got back.

"I bought a motor bike. After that it was plain sailing - almost; except for the adventures which littered the roads of North Wales. Then I could climb, but with men, and it was one of these who told me about the P.C. and encouraged me enough to apply for membership."

Conny Alexander, who also joined this year, was the person who introduced Berta Gough, now Berta Andrews, to the club.

Berta writes: "My best friend was Conny Alexander. She was warden of Idwal Youth Hostel and I spent many weekends there, where I met Alf Bridge, Maurice Linnell and Colin Kirkus who taught us both to climb. I heard of the Pinnacle Club and thought I would like to join." Another friend she met at Idwal was Annette Wilson.

Dorothy Pilley's book, Climbing Days, was due for publication in 1935 and she endured a certain amount of teasing from her friends, who wanted to know if they were mentioned in it.

In the 1934 Fell and Rock Journal she has both a review of her book and also a long and interesting article, well illustrated, entitled "More of Canada". This summer she and her husband did about 25 routes in the Dauphiné and Tarentaise, including a guideless traverse of the Meije. This route was the 'in thing' for guideless British parties just then. Brenda Ritchie was a member of a party who did it the same year, in very doubtful weather, when guided parties remained in the huts. Her account of the Dauphiné holiday is in the Fell and Rock *Journal* for 1935. Herbert Carr said that Brenda led the first rope, then Christina Barratt and Evelyn Carr followed as a ladies' rope, with Christina's brother, Geoffrey, and Herbert Carr himself bringing up the rear. He told me:

"We were greatly delayed because an overnight storm had badly iced the rocks. We reached the Doigt de Dieu as the sun set and a full moon rose over Italy - we went down the E ridge and abseiled off as soon as we could onto the glacier. Quite a day."

Molly Fitzgibbon's fine ascents in August 1934 - the traverse of the Bouquetins, and Leiterspitzen by the west arête, both with Joseph Georges - were recorded in the *Alpine Journal*.

At home, meets were well attended, with many routes climbed whenever possible. The joint meet with the CC and F&RCC which took place in July was reported as, "A pleasant innovation suggested and successfully engineered by Mr A.B. Hargreaves. Lliwedd proved the chief attraction and many good routes were done, notably the Central Chimney - Red Wall - Longland's Continuation, led by A.T. Hargreaves. This fine climb has recently been led (May 1935) by Lowe."

The Annual Dinner Meet was again in Capel Curig and made memorable by the hospitality of Mr and Mrs Hughes, the speeches and the brilliant variety show produced by Evelyn Lowe and the three Seth Hughes sisters. (Miss J. Seth Hughes took part. She became old enough to join the Club in 1937).

This was Berta Gough's second meet, and her diary gives some idea of the pretty dresses worn by members; 'I wore my flowered silk, and Conny white flowered chiffon, Smith green net. I thought Mrs Richards, the President, looked lovely in black velvet.'

Guests, as usual, were names famous in their own clubs and beyond: Miss McAndrew of the LAC; Mr Grosvenor of the CC; Mr J.H. Doughty, Rucksack Club and Mr H.E. Scott, F&RCC. 'On the following hopelessly wet day, a large company gathered at the Club Hut for tea.'

By the time of the Coniston Meet in February 1935, we had lost a Heap and gained a Hargreaves. Ruth married A.T. Hargreaves and moved to Cartmel. At the Easter Meet in Wasdale, Brenda Ritchie's leads included Botterill's Slab on Scafell.

There were no great changes at the Annual Meeting. Officers remained the same and Helen Bryan and Annette Wilson came on the committee. The Club hut had been well used, had paid off all its debts, and had a credit balance of two shillings and a penny. New members included Brenda Ritchie's sister, Mrs Herbert Carr, a good climber and very much in sympathy with the aims of the Club, but best described as a faithful though absent member. Miss Gladys Low, now Jean Punnett, had the distinction of being elected an associate member on April 20th and a full member the following day - a distinction well-merited by later events. The other member to stand the test of time is Miss Elliott, a very faithful Scottish member with considerable experience in the Highlands and on Skye.

Some of the matters which came before the committee during the year are of interest: it was decided not to support the appeal of the Lakeland Guides for the erection of first aid cabins in the hills of the Lake District (I would like to have heard the outspoken comments which must have been made about the proposal) but £5 was donated from club funds in response to the joint appeal from the Rucksack Club and Fell and Rock for the placement of first aid equipment and stretchers at the various climbing centres in England and Wales.

1935 was an exciting year for climbing, both at home and abroad. On Jubilee Day (May 6th) Menlove Edwards led M.G. Bradley, Ida Collie (LAC) and Evelyn Lowe up Longland's Route on Cloggy (Clogwyn du'r Arddu), and in August Evelyn was up there again with a party but found the rock too greasy for hard climbing and explored Far West Buttress instead. Finally, on the 9th September, Brenda Ritchie became the first woman to lead a route on this magnificent cliff. This was merely the climax to dozens of routes and fine leads by many Pinnacle Club members.

Berta Gough's diary gives us a glimpse of the August meet: "The first evening there were staying at the Hut Mrs Eden, Lowe, Clune, Forsyth and myself. Mr Kelly stayed at the Power Station House. They had supper ready for me and then we talked and went to bed at 11.15. We slept in two tier bunks like at Idwal. We got up at 8. a.m. and went and bathed in the stream in a deep pool, without our costumes. It was cold but most refreshing. Lowe cooked breakfast (all catering on meets was communal and supplied by the meet leader) and we were all ready for off by 10.0 a.m. by which time Mr Kelly had joined us. We went slowly up to Lliwedd. It was very hot work pulling up to the Llyn Llidaw. Lowe, Clune and I climbed Central Gully, Exit to East Peak, and Great Chimney, followed by Forsyth, Kelly, and Mrs Eden. It was a most enjoyable climb just within my powers ..." They were joined for the Sunday by Wilson, Procter and the Seth Hughes sisters reaching Snowdon Summit via Gambit Climb or the Parson's Nose. "Wilson and I had two cups of tea each in the new refreshment place - very posh place, all glass, Mrs Eden and Seth Hughes went down Pig Track whilst we finished off the Horseshoe, right to the end, arriving back at the hut at 7.15."

For seven Club members the highlight of the year was the August Meet in the High Tatras. Ruth Hale led and organised it, with her Polish friends, Witold Paryski and 'Taddy' Pacolaski, to guide the routes. Alison Adam, Dorothy Arning, Annette Wilson, Taylor, Bray and Dr Corbett were the other members of the party.

Their first ascent was of the Rysy, the second highest peak in the Tatra, and the night was spent in the Rysy Hut watching a thunderstorm which was to mark the beginning of bad weather for the rest of the fortnight. Despite this they did many climbs and traverses, including that of the Gierach. Alison Adam wrote the account for the *Journal* and gives an impression of beautiful scenery glimpsed between the storms, knife-edged ridges, loose rock and snow-covered icy handholds - all of which, with the good company and friendliness they met with, made everything a great adventure and unforgettable experience. Ruth's own account for the LAC *Year Book*, 1936, lists her own further routes, including two first ascents.

From the Fell and Rock *Journal* we learn of other exploits. Nancy Ridyard and Evelyn Pirie made their own route up Choire Mhic Fhearchair and 'had the thrill of route-finding among unscratched rocks'. Helen Bryan stayed at the bottom to sketch, and had a cup of tea ready for their return.

In this year, Molly Fitzgibbon was joint leader of the first Fell and Rock Alpine Meet, held at Arolla in August, and her account appears in their *Journal*. She was also the first woman to traverse the Aiguille du Plan, ascending Ryan's Route up the East Arête.

There was a meet in the Club hut for five days in November and for the first time it was described as a commemoration meet. It is now called the Anniversary Meet and always takes place during the first or second weekend of November. Part of Berta's diary for this meet reads: "...It was rather a damp day. There were 17 in the hut, very full and some of us sat round the fire and on the floor to eat our dinner...All helped with work, had breakfast in shifts...Eight went to the Ogwen Valley to climb and eight of us to Lliwedd, Mrs Richards was not well enough to climb..."

As regards the above, we find a delightful entry in the log book: "D. Pilley Richards. 4/11/35. Snowdon up PyG track, down Miners' Track, Scarlet fever convalescent. Cured."

It is worth recording that Dorothy Pilley's book, *Climbing Days*, was royally treated in the Alpine Journal for 1935 and had a three page review, initialled 'C.W.' Fifty years later, her book retains all its charm. Latterly Pilley begged us to take care of copies, as she found it increasingly expensive to replace them!

CHAPTER 10

1936 to 1939. Mrs Eden-Smith President. A headless corpse. More climbing. Ruth Hale's death. Opening of Brackenclose. Entertainments. Rockfalls. New routes.

Early in 1936, Dorothy Pilley Richards went abroad to spend a year in Canada and China, so Dr Corbett, the Vice-President, took over her presidential duties until after the annual meeting in April. Pilley had been warmly thanked at the December committee meeting for her devotion to the Club's interests during her three years' presidency. Despite her busy life and many commitments, she had attended almost all Pinnacle meets, and her prestige as a climber, writer and speaker could only add to that of the Club.

Mrs Eden-Smith was elected president, Pilley became vice-president and Evelyn Pirie was elected secretary by ballot. Other officers remained the same, but there were many new names on the committee: Ruth Hale, Susan Harper, Penelope Seth Hughes, Trilby Wells and Marjorie Wood. The only member remaining from the previous year was Alison Adam.

The cost and design of a club badge were briefly discussed, but few members were in favour of a badge at that time.

Nine new members had joined during the year. Phyl Raven, now Mrs Jackson, was young and adventurous; both she and her sister were full members, but her sister was never so active in the Club. Phyl served twice on the committee. Alicia Wilson was a member for thirteen years and made records very complicated because there were now two A. Wilsons in the Club. They often went to the same meets, and sometimes even climbed together and in 1939 when Annette became secretary Alicia was elected to the committee. Gladys Scott had been a member of the LAC for a number of years, as had Violet Cumming, Many members during the 1930s joined the Club while at college or university.

There were six resignations or deletions. It is interesting to note that Ella Mann Standring represented the Ladies' Alpine Club at the Pinnacle Club Annual Dinner at roughly the same time as she was having her name deleted from membership of the latter Club for non-payment of her subscription! She was always a close friend of members and rejoined in 1950.

As was to be expected with the enormous influx of young, keen women, climbing continued to flourish. Even the older members were doing great things:- Mabel Barker, proudly making the most of her age by saying she was in her fifty-first year, was on the first descent of Central Buttress on Scafell. She climbed with Ieuan Mendus and Jack Carswell and they all had to wait on Jeffcoat's Ledge for a party coming up. This party, led by Sid Cross, comprised Ruth and A.T. Hargreaves and one other, who was probably Mary Nelson, now Sid's wife, Jammy.

This was in June. Later in the month Evelyn Lowe, who had been ill, tested her fitness on Longland's Climb with the Seth Hughes sisters, hoping to lead the first feminine rope.

However, her arms had not regained their strength and she had to have a rope from above on the last overhang.

June also saw Susan Harper, Jean Orr Ewing and Marjorie Heys-Jones on Skye. On their way back from one climb, they stumbled across a headless corpse. Men and tracker dogs had searched the area for a whole day during May and not found it, and the girls built cairns along the route back so that the place could be identified again. Jean, being a doctor, was saddled with the task of guiding the rescue party. Wherever they went on the island after that the girls were recognised and asked the story - apparently many people had seen ghosts, especially when they heard that the head was missing! Why the corpse was headless remains a mystery.

Many parties were in the Alps during the summer, and there was yet another border incident. Nancy Forsyth and Alison Adam went to Austria. After climbing many peaks in the Stubai Alps they went up to a hut to do the Wilde Freigir. 'The hut was just on the Italian side,' writes Alison, 'and full of Italian soldiers, who were very unpleasant and marched us back over the pass at bayonet point, then stood with pistols at the ready, watching us go down the track.'

Ruth Hale spent August and September in Poland, climbing in particular with Witold Paryski and putting up three new routes: S.S.E. Face of Swinaca, the upper half of the N.W. ridge of Granarty and a point on the W. ridge of the Zabi Szczyt Nizne. Mary Glynne, who merely admitted to 'Walking in the High Tatra' in her notes for the LAC *Year Book*, joined them on this last route.

The *Year Book* records other matters of interest. The LAC had much appreciated the Pinnacle Club's suggestion of some joint meets in the British Isles, and the first took place at the Dow Crag Climbers' Hut, Coniston, 'Where not only is there a drying room, unlimited hot water for baths, and lovely food, but also climbing of every grade within easy reach.'

I think this account must have been written by Ruth Hale, who had just taken over as Hon. Secretary of the LAC on Miss McAndrew's retirement. Other Pinnacle Club members had duties to perform for the LAC in providing speeches at the Annual Dinner. Marjorie Heys-Jones with her LAC hat on, proposed the health of the guests, and Evelyn Lowe proposed the toast to the Ladies' Alpine Club.

Meanwhile, at the hut at Whitsuntide, 'Climbing and work of importance were accomplished. A masterly wall was built to support the waterpipe.' There was much climbing on Lliwedd, Idwal Slabs and Tryfan, and Milestone Buttress was 'girdled, and ascended and descended by most of its routes.'

Another good meet was held at Embsay in June, during a heatwave. It was a camping meet and the Wells sisters catered for the seventeen hungry climbers to their entire satisfaction. The year finished, or rather the New Year started, with the Dinner in Capel Curig. Guests were Ella Mann Standring, LAC; Wilson Hey, Rucksack Club; Sidney Wood, CC; and John Hirst, FRCC. Paddy Hirst was also present, so it was like old times to have the three Wells sisters there. The show was given by that other famous trio of sisters, the Seth Hughes, with the help of Lowe and Low.

Gladys-Jean Low stayed on after the meet and climbed on Glyder Fawr with Baxter:- Route V. East Wall, Lazarus, and the West Groove, - not bad for a January day.

Thus, after an arctic meet in Coniston in February, the Easter Meet came round once more. In 1937 it was held at the Strands Hotel, Wasdale from March 27th to 29th, and the signatures of members can still be seen in the old hotel records. The log book was exuberant:

A splendid meet, with the most wonderful weather conditions - positively Swiss - frost at night, crisp snow and strong sunshine by day. Long ridge and fell walks were done by most members - some tackled snow gullies and a few skied - the only rockroute done was the Arrowhead on the last and warmest day ... Two members camped ... just for pleasure. Altogether a memorable Easter Meet.

This was the year of George VI's Coronation, and Trilby Wells, jumping on the band waggon, outlined the idea of a Coronation Hut Fund, to carry out repairs to the hut and add certain amenities. It was launched with ten pounds donated from general funds.

Miss J. Seth Hughes was eighteen years old at last, and was one of twelve members to join the club in 1937. Most resigned after a few years, including Elizabeth Griffin, who was a member of the Himalayan Club and had been on two exploratory expeditions into Sikkim. Miss Littledale sent in her resignation almost immediately as a result of a climbing accident, so was given free membership for a year but in fact never came back.

The Whitsuntide holiday combined with the Coronation to give a whole week of freedom and fine weather, and many fine routes were done. Berta Gough's diary gives a glimpse of the members: "On Sunday it was very fine first thing ... We went up Lliwedd and Lowe led Longstaff and me up Paradise and Black Arête, followed by Deed, Wilson and Allaun; and B. Wells and T. Wells. When we reached the top it was very warm and we lay in the sun and met Wood, Watson and Taylor who had done the Horseshoe. The others did more climbs. Got back to the hut and had a good wash and helped get dinner ready. Went to bed at 10.15 after taking a short walk with a lovely moon."

Many people were at the hut during the summer. Evelyn Lowe spent much of August climbing in the Pass and on Cloggy, often with members of the Climbers' Club. On August 8th she attempted a lead of the Direct Route on Dinas Mot but writes that she battled in vain with the lead of the final pitches - finished by J.E. Joyce. She was with J.E. Joyce two days later on Dinas Cromlech. The entry reads, 'Columnar Cliff - Parchment Passage.' On August 12th they made the second ascent of Sunset Crack on Clogwyn du'r Arddu, and later on in the month, Evelyn was there alone, exploring and scrambling. For most people, the favourite climbs were still on Lliwedd, the Parson's Nose area, and Tryfan or Idwal.

In September came the shock of Ruth Hale's death in Poland. Her friend and climbing companion, Witold Paryski, wrote a full account of Ruth's climbing that summer, which was published in the LAC *Year Book* for 1938. Ruth had become secretary of the Ladies' Alpine Club only the year before and was as much loved by them as by the Pinnacle Club members, to whom Witold also wrote. Her obituary in the Pinnacle Club *Journal* reads:

"In September, 1937, the sad news came that Ruth Hale had been killed in the High Tatra through an accident curiously similar to that on Tryfan which took Pat Kelly from us. A moderate climb had been finished: the choice between continuing to the summit over easy ground or descending was discussed and settled by a coin which Ruth tossed. With her two Polish companions she was scrambling up from ledge to ledge over low walls when a safe-looking block which she barely touched rolled forward and flung her outwards. It was over in a second. She fell some 300 feet and was killed instantly.

"This disastrous mischance came only ten days after the ending of her greatest mountain adventure, a sixty-seven hour expedition in which her party of three had to fight through two days and nights of torrential rain and bitter cold to escape from the great cliffs of Rumanowy and Ganek on which they had been caught by a cloudburst. The leader, Witold Paryski's comment sums up what we who have also been out with her know: 'It was a very hard trial of physical and climbing experience and still more endurance and will power. One must say, without the slightest exaggeration, that Miss Hale passed the test with the highest mark. During the three days spent on the face in the most awful weather conditions she did not break down once, either physically or morally, proving as usual, the excellent companion with an enviably bright disposition.'

"It was always good to know that Ruth was coming to a Hut Meet. Her quiet efficiency and helpfulness contributed to everybody's well being. Her organisation of our High Tatra Meet put us deeply in her debt. She had made that region peculiarly her own with a number of new expeditions on highly capricious rock. It is grievous to think she will wander those ridges no more."

There were other Club members abroad in 1937; Alison Adam was in the Silvretta, where she climbed several routes; and Brenda Ritchie rounded off a rather disappointing bad weather season in the Alps with a fine guideless ascent of the Disgrazia from the Swiss Forno Hut - a long route which entailed two ascents of the Cima di Cantone, the easiest and quickest route leading directly over the summit then dropping a thousand feet the other side. Brenda said the return journey seemed endless.

Dorothy Pilley Richards and her husband were in China, then in the throes of civil war. She wrote that she had had a most interesting cross-country journey from Peking to Yunnan, whither the University had moved. As there were no students to teach, she and her husband and a friend had gone off into the Li Chiang mountains, ten days' journey from Ta Li, for some climbing. The previous summer she had climbed in the Peking Western Hills and Chang Li Coast Range, Pei Niu Ting, Eastern and Western Heaven and elsewhere.

Autumn came round again and Sunday October 3rd was the opening of the Fell and Rock Club Hut at Brackenclose, Wasdale, dedicated to the Youth of the Club by the retiring president, Professor Chorley, and officially opened by his wife, Katharine. She had furnished the living room in memory of her father and uncles, the Hopkinson brothers. Other well known names were in evidence, for A.T. Hargreaves was the first warden and H.M. Kelly the treasurer. Several Pinnacle Club members were present in their capacity as Fell and Rock members, and the reciprocal rights for Pinnacle Club members, as outlined in the *Handbook*, were later drawn up.

Pinnacle members have enjoyed many pleasant times at Brackenclose, which is such a beautifully placed centre for the Scafells, Gable and Pillar. Berta Gough, with Annette Wilson, L. Lambrick and I. Warren paid an early visit in March 1939 and wrote a vivid account for her diary:

"Annette met me at Preston Friday night at 5.30 with Warren and Lambrick. Rained all the time. Stopped for some coffee at 'Anglers Arms'. Went wrong twice on the way, once followed a road which just ended in a field. Eventually arrived at 'Brackenclose' at 12.10 a.m. The path up to the Hut was terrible, so had to leave the car at the bottom and carry stuff up. Annette and I went to farm for key and milk, lost our way going back and had to be guided by torches from W. and L. Had to hunt round for oil and trouble with primus. Had a meal and filled hotwater bottles and had hot milk in bed at 2.30 a.m. Woke up on Saturday to see it was still raining.

"I went for the milk and eggs etc. whilst Warren and Lambrick lit the fire and cooked. We spent the morning cleaning the hut as it was so wet. After lunch we went down to the farm to get 5 galls of oil, had some job carrying it back. Then Annette and I went out up Mosedale but in less then half an hour we were soaked through and came back. When we got back Sid Cross and Mary Nelson had arrived, and as they had walked over from Langdale and were also soaked, they had lit the drying room fire. At night there were 16 in, the Hargreaves, Mrs Eden, Mr Kelly, Jack Diamond, and 4 other men. We went to bed at 11.0. Mr Kelly brought us tea on Sunday morning."

This was still very much in the future when 1937 was left behind and the Annual Dinner Meet of the Pinnacle Club was held in Capel Curig on January 1st, 1938. Berta wrote:

"Wilson ... took Conny, Christine and me in her car ... I wore my blue velvet, Conny green and Wilson mauve. There were thirty-five there ... Mrs Eden-Smith was the President and looked very nice. She was very nervous over her speech but made a good one. Biddy Deed spoke for the Kindred Clubs. Mr Hirst and Mr Lawson Cook made speeches. Afterwards we had a very good entertainment by the Seth Hughes. Lowe showed a very fine lot of slides of Club activities. I have never seen her looking so nice."

On Sunday most members and some guests turned up at the Hut for tea, including a member's daughter, Joyce Hirst, and a member's son, Alastair Cooper. Daloni Seth Hughes had married Leslie Cooper in 1935 and Alastair was about eighteen months old. The famous Seth Hughes climbing partnership had come to an end, and this was the last year they were able to provide their equally famous entertainment. People's memories are a little vague after forty-five years, and nobody could tell me much except that the sketches were very funny, so I appealed to Daloni herself, who kindly wrote the following:

Easter 1938
Penelope Seth-Hughes leading Yellow Slab.

"The Annual Dinner was generally held at Bryn Tyrch, Capel Curig and it was a great occasion with a crowd of us coming, sometimes through bitter weather. Evelyn was the brains who invented and carried the burden of the entertainment after dinner, but as Penelope and I were nearly on the spot (Bangor) and she was domiciled at Deganwy, we helped her and very much enjoyed it too.

"One year Penelope and I were the front and hind legs of Pegasus, the Pinnacle Horse, and Evelyn was ringmaster with a whip who put us through our tricks.

"I never would have believed it would be so difficult to keep straight! I was fairly all right in front, peeping through small eyeholes, but poor Penelope, in complete blindness, could only do her best to follow. We zig-zagged all over the place, and several times the hind legs folded up altogether. Anyhow, our antics brought the house down, but I've never been so hot in my life before.

"Another time, P. and I were the Dolly Sisters and did an energetic dance and sang 'The Mountaineer's Anthem' specially composed by me for the occasion.

"Evelyn wrote and delivered a very amusing pot pourri of a climb, one time, and we did the 'noises off' - the rain pouring down, distracted sheep bleating, the muffled oath when a stone catapulted onto a climber's head, and the creaky flap of the Lliwedd raven overhead. It was all great fun!"

The Easter meet 1938 was based in Borrowdale, with members staying in cottages or tents. On the Saturday a large party climbed in Birkness Combe, Buttermere, and Berta Gough tells of a rockfall during the lunch break. "There was no serious damage; Wilson had her arm sprained and had to have it in a sling for the rest of the weekend and Alicia got some bruises on her back."

There is enjoyable climbing here, but this was not the last time that Pinnacle Club members were to experience rockfall on Grey Crag, fortunately without serious effects. This was the area where Cockermouth Mountain Rescue Team suffered a tragic accident due to rockfall.

The climb Berta did next day has since disappeared, also due to rockfall. "On Sunday M. Wood, Clarke, Adam, Dawson, Watson and I went to Rosthwaite Fells to climb Doves' Nests. This was very amusing as after climbing about 100 ft. up on the outside we came about 50 inside in the pitch dark. I led Alicia Wilson up the climb."

Saturday night was the Annual Meeting and the Hut Secretary's Report was especially interesting. The hut had been well used, both on meets and by private climbing parties, and many severe climbs had been done. The Coronation Hut Fund had raised seventeen pounds fourteen shillings in addition to various gifts from members and, on Trilby Wells' suggestion, a map of the district had been framed and hung in the hut in memory of Ruth Hale. Further money was available to the Club through the sale of Ruth's climbing equipment. The Power Company had been approached about renewing the lease and had not only agreed to renew it for a further five years but also to improve the drainage of the ground and to put guttering under the roof at their own expense. They were obviously happy with the Club as tenants, and the Club in its turn was extremely grateful for all the help and kindness received.

The only changes in the officers and committee for the ensuing year were due to Ruth Hale's death. Miss Allaun took her place on the committee and Biddy Deed her place on the hut committee.

Two letters were read out, offering the use of club huts: the Fell and Rock offered reciprocal rights at Brackenclose, and the Scottish Mountaineering Club offered the use of the C.I.C. Hut on Ben Nevis. Anyone surprised at the latter concession must remember the Pinnacle Club's very close association with the Ladies' Scottish Climbing Club. Mabel Jeffrey, co-founder of the LSCC and sister of Charles Inglis Clarke to whom the CIC Hut is a memorial, was to be President of the Pinnacle Club all through the war years.

The flow of new members continued: Dorothea Higgs, who lived on a farm near Dover, did well to get to as many meets as she did. She resigned after thirteen years but called in at the hut in 1973, for old times' sake. Amongst others who were members for a short time was Geraldine Sladen from Kenya, though she was working in London at this time. She had climbed Kilimanjaro and Mount Kenya, and had soon done enough leading to make her a full member. After her marriage she lived in Tanganyika and eventually resigned her membership. Cicely Wood lived in Cheshire and was a very keen member, being on the hut committee throughout the war years.

Hester White came from a climbing family, for her father had been a member of the Scottish Mountaineering Club; however, she never knew him, for he died of wounds received at Gallipoli in 1915, when she was eight months old. Hester was introduced to climbing when she went to stay with a Swiss family in 1934 and climbed from Les Haudères. She writes:

"I got well and truly bitten by mountaineering, and joined the LSCC when I returned home. Mabel Jeffrey suggested to my close friend Midge Stewart (Mrs Bullough later) that she and I should apply for membership of the Pinnacle Club. Midge joined in 1935 and I did in 1938."

Hester was at this Easter Meet, and one route she did was Tophet Bastion with the Wells sisters and Alison Adam. She found it very exciting, and not just the climbing:

"When we were half way up there was a commotion on our left, where a three-man party were climbing Lucifer. An enormous boulder broke off from Lucifer with the third man spread-eagled on it. The boulder being heavier than the man, it crashed to the ground first, and the man swung back to the rock face, where he had a pause in a state of immobility, but happily he was hauled to safety when he recovered from shock." It appears to have been a bad weekend for rockfall, Perhaps hot, dry days and cold nights put the finishing touches to the winter's erosion.

The next big Club meet was held at Whitsun in Wales. Evelyn Lowe had kept an eye on Cwm Dyli and lit the fire now and again to air it. In January she found that rats and mice had been having a feast, and there is a firm message in the Hut Book: "Please do not leave potatoes accessible to mice and Rats." An April entry reads: "Trouble with Rat again!"

On April 10th she and Brenda Ritchie, with M. Walker and N. Sims, went to Glyder Fach and led Oblique Buttress, Alpha and Beta - Alpha (VS) in particular being a delicate lead and hard to protect. On the 14th Evelyn and Brenda climbed Grey Slab on the same cliff, which they nominated a VERY good route.

Nothing so hard was done at Whitsun, when the weather was very mixed. Climbing boots had to be worn instead of rubbers and Berta, who hated climbing in nailed boots, finished Grooved Arête in stocking feet, 'which was most painful.'

Biddy Deed led Monolith Crack, one of the many times when the lie has been given to the myth that the feminine shape will invariably get stuck on this climb - though I remember a descent in the dark one November meet. It had been a near thing!

Mabel Barker was not at the Whitsun Meet; she was walking the border line between Scotland and England, which is by no means as easy as it sounds. Her account is in the Fell and Rock *Journal* for 1939.

During June, Evelyn explored above the Conway Falls for new routes, seconded by M.G. Bradley. She wrote two up in the book, but there is a pencilled note by them, 'Perhaps not new.' On 24th July she wrote up another first ascent, this time on Clogwyn y Ddisgl. She called it Long Groove. It is to the right of Rectory Chimneys, starting 'immediately below canopy roof.' It must be near Quintet Route, put up in 1935 by five Rucksack Club members and never found again (apparently). Evelyn climbed in a lot of new places, but was not one to press the fact upon guidebook writers, as her article 'The Substance and the Shadow' shows.

In July Nancy Ridyard and Nancy Forsyth led a new route on Ben Nevis almost by accident. Leading, respectively, Annette and Janet Smith of the Ladies' Scottish Climbing Club, to which they also belonged, they set out to climb Raeburn's Arête. Happily they started too far to the left, for the result is a varied and enjoyable way of reaching the First Platform on the North East Buttress at Very Difficult standard, though saddled with the name of Newbigging's Route (Far Right Variation).

The August Bank Holiday meet had very poor weather, which cleared just as most people were going home. Ruth Hargreaves had brought her friend, Jammy (Mary) Nelson to the hut, and A.T. Hargreaves and Sid Cross camped nearby. They stayed on for the rest of the week and 'most of the best climbs of the district were done under perfect conditions', but it doesn't say which ones. Jammy wonders how she escaped being a member of the Pinnacle Club, but in fact she never joined.

Many members were in the Alps during the summer, often doing guideless ascents and traverses. Pilley was in Burma, then Canada where she made two new ascents in the Bugaboo Range before returning to England. While in China she and Ivor Richards had explored the Yunnan Mountains near the Tibetan border and made the first ascent of Gyinaloko, a 20,000 foot peak. Alone and on foot she then made the three thousand mile journey from Talifu to Bhamo on the Irrawaddy (Burma) returning by another route to China (see Fell and Rock *Journal*, 1939).

The Pinnacle Club *Journal* no. 6, when it eventually came out, contained articles about many parts of the world: Alison Adam wrote of the High Tatra, Gladys Low of the Frontier Peaks round Zermatt, Brenda Ritchie of the Disgrazia and, back in Wales, of Kirkus' Slab Route on Cwm Silyn, Constance Lancaster on climbs from the Mountet Hut, Susan Harper on two Alpine holidays doing guideless ascents with other Pinnacle Club members, and Ilsa Bell on a route from Saas Fee with Cicely Hutson and Iris Blaikie. Molly Fitzgibbon wrote of the Tarentaise, Geraldine Sladen of Kilimanjaro and Mount Kenya, and Evelyn Pirie of climbing in the Atlas Mountains.

There were other articles on Scotland and Skye, poems, photos, and something of the hut's history - in fact, as good a selection as there had ever been, including a delicious strip cartoon from Marjorie Wood, entitled 'Thoughts on a first lead', and a note from Mrs Bryan about the Lake District Ski Club, formed in 1936.

Whilst the lucky ones were enjoying themselves in various parts of the world, seven members held an August Meet at Brackenclose. As Mrs Eden-Smith's report said: 'This was the first Pinnacle Club Meet to be held here but we hope not the last.'

Pilley was back in England in time for the November Meet and Halloween Party at the Club hut, and the final meet of the year was the Dinner Meet on December 31st, held this year at the Sun Hotel, Coniston, where Mr D' Aeth, a member of the Climbers' Club made them very welcome and fed them very well. Mrs Eden-Smith had had an operation immediately after the November Meet, so Mr Pigott's proposal of the President's health had special significance.

After the dinner and entertainments Bryan and Pirie welcomed a large crowd back to the Dow Crag Hut to see the New Year in with hot punch, and the celebrations lasted till the early hours. It snowed heavily during the night, so nine of them tried their skill at skiing next day. Berta, in her diary, described herself as a complete dud but enjoyed it enough to say it was one of the best dinners she had been to. It was the last one before the war.

CHAPTER 11

1939 and the early war years. Travelling to meets. Mabel Jeffrey President. Last pre-war Alpine meets. The Richards in America. Gladys Low's expeditions in the Himalayas.

1939 had arrived amid a flurry of snow, but the Pinnacle Club's ski meet at the end of February met April weather. As the report in the *Handbook* remarks: 'Our temerity in fixing a ski-ing meet twelve months ahead received its just reward in green fields and pleasant pastures.' They consoled themselves with a good, long walk, which had to suffice until the Annual Meeting at Easter.

Hester White attended the Easter Meet. She remembers the lengths she went to, to get south of the border: to get to the Lakes she had to catch a train from Edinburgh which arrived at Crewe about 2.a.m. It seemed always wet and windy and the wait for the next connection seemed endless. Wales was reached via Liverpool and a Ribble bus. That too was exhausting. Hester said: 'I like to comfort myself for my not particularly distinguished performance on the rocks by my remembrance of the state of tiredness I was in on arrival at the huts.'

This time her journey was to Wales and the Club Hut. The weather was perfect with the exception of Good Friday, which was spent by many in the recesses of Lockwood's Chimney. At the General Meeting Mrs Jeffrey was elected president and Annette Wilson became secretary. Both were wonderfully hospitable and friendly people, and evening entertainments always went with a swing when Mabel Jeffrey was there. On the Sunday night they played charades until they ached with laughter and Berta Gough said it was the best game she had ever played.

Six new members joined in 1939, but only two stayed the course. Marie Grutter was a brilliant person and a good climber who came to meets when she could, and in the 1950s brought friends and young people to the hut, accompanied by her dog, Bran. She died in 1960. Joan Cochrane has now been a member for over forty years. A good climber, she started off well by going to a very enlightened school, with: " ... marvellous trees in the garden which we were allowed to climb, in fact, they even put a plank seat up some where we could relax or finish our homework. Then I had a holiday in Sark where my sister had taken a bungalow for the summer as her in-laws lived there, and I had a great time on the cliffs. When a friend bought the three most southern Islands in the Outer Hebrides I went with her when she went to take over, and again the next year with a friend who unfortunately had no head for heights - I spent my time photographing birds on the cliffs. Then a holiday with my sister (who doesn't climb) in Skye down Glen Brittle and I was taken climbing by two young men and did Tower Ridge on Nevis unroped on the way south. Only a scramble, I know, but quite exciting.

"Next I did a milk round for two ladies - they were friends of Bryan and Pirie who were living in Surrey at that time. I was given an introduction and was invited to a meet at the Dow Crag Hut. Two marvellous days. On the first one I did Bowfell Buttress with Mrs

Jeffrey and Biddy Deed and on the second we were up and down various routes on Dow Crags in marvellous weather - wearing rubbers. Of course vibrams were unheard of in those days, it was all tricounis and I must say that although our boots were heavier I had much more confidence in them than I ever had with vibrams!" (Certainly they were not in common use, but it is interesting that the *Alpine Journal* for 1940 records that vibrams first appeared in 1935).

Joan's first meet was at the end of June. Bryan and Pirie had given up the Dow Crag Hut and were now living in Langdale. Berta records: "It was funny being at Dow Crag Hut without Mrs Bryan in charge; she, Pirie and Philippa were staying there as guests."

There had been a good meet at Whitsun, but that in August was small, for many members were in the Alps. Berta Gough records climbing Gambit and seeing Cloggy for the first time. However, the greatest excitement came at the end:

"Annette and I set out at 8.20 p.m. Just as we were leaving found we had a puncture ... Got Higgs and two friends of hers who had just arrived, and two men from the Power Station to help us change it. Could not use jack so had to lift car up onto stones. Eventually got away at 8.50 so had to rush home."

This August the Fell and Rock had an Alpine Meet in Zermatt which at least three Pinnaclers attended. Owing to the international crisis, people had to drop out at the last minute and Alison Adam found herself meet leader. Her report of climbing which made the best of rather mixed weather appears in the 1940 F&RCC *Journal*. Also writing for that kindred publication was Brenda Ritchie. Brenda climbed two routes in the Saleinaz, one of which she soloed to the top while prospecting the route for the following day! Alison Adam, Geraldine Sladen and Cicely Wood limbered up on some minor peaks before tackling the Rimpfischhorn and Dent Blanche, and Geraldine stayed on to climb the Matterhorn. Shortly after this, war was declared and Alison had a note from Geraldine saying she was returning to South Africa immediately and would Alison collect her ice axe from her aunt's house (a titled lady in the West End) and take it to the hut. Neither Geraldine nor Cicely ever came back to P.C. meets after the war.

Pilley had a serious miscarriage in 1939 and does not admit to having done any climbing. However, the Pinnacle Club News Sheet reads: "Mrs Armstrong Richards made a great recovery after her illness and managed to do some fine climbing in the Alps, including Mont Blanc, Pitz Palu (traverse), and Pitz Roseg before leaving for America with her husband, who is lecturing there."

Pilley writes: "I went off to work with my husband from 1939 to 74 in Cambridge, Massachusetts, where my husband was University Professor at Harvard. We asked Foreign Office advice and they considered it important to have English news represented by people who had been invited by America and were not just propagandists."

The Winthrop Youngs spent Christmas 1939 at the Pen-y-Pass and Len wrote a moving account for the Fell and Rock Journal. It was three months after the outbreak of war, and the Winthrop Youngs' son Jocelyn was on leave for a brief family reunion. The bitter cold of Euston Station, packed with thousands of troops on leave waiting for trains three or four hours late, is contrasted with Pen-y-Pass, where there was not even blackout on the windows. Menlove Edwards joined the family party for well-loved climbs and walks. Len's account concludes: "In a day or so we shall go to Southern England again, and one of us shortly will be on the high seas - but we cannot forget the comfort of those high hills - and our great easing of the heart."

The Pinnacle Club News Sheet came out for the first time in 1940, as a page in the *Handbook*, to keep people in touch during the war. As far as climbing went, the Alpine routes were mentioned only if they were guideless: E. Lowe, P. Seth-Hughes, V. Longstaff and G. Sladen had done some good traverses in the Engelhörner, also the traverse of the Portjengrat from Saas and (E. Lowe and V. Longstaff) the traverse of the Sudlenspitz-Nadelhorn.

By far the most enterprising climbing, however, was being done by Gladys-Jean Low, later known as Jean Punnett, who spent several years working in Bombay and Northern India. She had hoped very much to find a climbing club there but nobody appeared to be interested in climbing at all. She had very little spare cash and realised that anything she did would have to be on a small scale, and arranged by herself. Before she found employment in India, General Bruce's book *Kulu and Lahoul* had decided her to climb in the Kulu region.

The 1940 News Sheet reads: "During the holidays she did reconnaissance camping and climbing in an almost unknown and totally unclimbed range of mountains called the Ghopil Dhar. Camped at 11,000 ft with porters, and leaving the porters behind for the final peak, climbed alone to a height of 15,000 ft."

Gladys-Jean's article has pride of place in the subsequent Pinnacle Club *Journal* (no. 7), but even here her humour and flowery style mask to some extent the impact of her achievement. Furthermore, we hear no more from her; there was no public record of her one or two further expeditions and her adventurous spirit, instead of developing further in this direction, was curbed by marriage, a child, and many rather difficult years.

I think it is fair to say that up till now any woman who had climbed in the Himalayas had done so with Alpine guides and plenty of time, money and porters. Gladys-Jean, completely on her own initiative, found an unclimbed region she thought she could cope with, then selected and trained her porters.

She writes: "Chandra Ram, Channu for short, was a tough little Kuluese. He took well to boots, but was with difficulty weaned from his alpenstock in favour of an axe. He was our cook, and always officiating among the pots a few minutes after the day's march, however exacting. Chandra Singh was a gurkha and ex-soldier. From the moment an ice axe was put in his hand, he handled it as to the manner born. His policy was 'Forward'. The Kulu men were slightly nervous of the mountain gods, but Chandra Singh had the scepticism of a veteran of Marius. The only permanent non-climber was the Kuluese Atu, responsible for ata (flour) supply. He had authority to engage an assistant when necessary. Firewood was also his province. He would leap up a tree like Tarzan and fell branches to earth with his pocket battle axe, often selecting the tree under which I was snatching rest."

Gladys-Jean's first trip to the area was in 1939, and practically all her leave was spent in finding a route up the valley and forested slopes to a place marked on the map Sarangi Thach, a small alp below the snow line which was to be an idyllic base camp the following year. Of her second trip she writes:

"I was now in a better position for several reasons. Last year leave ended 1st June. This year I reached camp on 25th May, with three clear weeks ahead. At both times I had a goodly mass of tinned supplies, but this year I had in addition bags of ata for making pancakes. Last year I only had two porters, this year I had four and could divide my forces. Two for mountaineering and two to carry surplus stores by goat paths. Last year, I alone had climbing equipment. This year there were boots, goggles, ice axes, mittens, socks and

Chandra Singh on Snowfield. Ghopils in background.
Photo: Jean Punnett

scarves for three. Both years I had camera and compass.

"The sum of my evening meditations under canvas, poring over the maps 'mid fumes of kerosene was this. We would first try and climb one of the Ghopil Needles, for the fun of bagging a peak, and in order to see the other side. Was it possible to cross the col in the direction of Deo Tibba and to descend into the Malana Nala beyond? If the lie of the land were favourable, we would return to base for supplies, having marked an intermediate camp site. Then go up again and attack the traverse."

She managed to do all this. Two porters were sent to the Malana Nala with stores, and two went up the Ghopils. The final slope to the col was ice, but was coped with in an hour's step-cutting.

"The col, (16,500'), turned out to be a broad saddle and the other side was out of sight. But masses of peaks crowded into view beyond, pyramids and towers of well defined shape, dominating a landscape of glaciers. Here is the answer to the climber's dream, mountains without number, rank on rank and tier on tier, unclimbed, unnamed, unknown. Chandra Singh and I sat down on a few coils of rope apiece and made a meal of tea and chocolate. Then we set out for the top of the Grand Ghopil. The breathless precipice above Sarangi Thatch and the sheer face which takes off from the snowfield were safely below. It seemed a mere walk to the top.

"But the saddle shrank quickly to a thin ridge cornicing to the right. The home side was simple enough, but the higher the sun rose, the deeper we sank into the snow. our feet, going through the snow, now met rock, and the ice axes striking down, rang on unseen slabs. We waded slowly over slabs and drifts of snow and disapproved the more and more pronounced tilt of the rock ... At this point my inside foot went through and I had a good view of the face framed in a hole the size of my boot. We worked up towards the crest of the ridge, fancying it was safer, and my axe went through at the level of my nose. I had a view of the other side. All sky."

Eventually they reached the summit blocks and Chandra Singh belayed Gladys-Jean to the top.

"Now we could peer over into the dark corrie of the Brahma Ganga and catch a glimpse of the windings of the Parbatti." They were chased down by a storm which lasted for two days.

While waiting for the snow to consolidate, Gladys-Jean trained the porters in climbing and belaying techniques on snow and ice before setting out to cross the col, discover a descent to the snow basin beyond then find the glacier which went down to the Malana ice fall, the only break in the ridge which blocked the way to the Malana Nala. This traverse took four days and some exciting glacier work before they were once again below the snow line. Regaining the glacier below the ice fall provided some memorable moments:

"Here and there thin tongues of ice offered dubious bridges across the rimaye and over the crevasses beyond. I struck across the least rickety crest, with many a backward glance at my Tail, who were supposed to be paying out the rope. They paid it out generously and I wondered whether I was destined to glide unchecked into the rimaye. After a good deal of shouting over this rope, we all three reached the central bulge of the glacier and walked quickly down over firm ice, zig-zagging to avoid minor crevasses."

On her way back Gladys-Jean climbed the peak dominating the main Kulu Valley, the Gadi, or Shepherd of Kulu:

"Channu was my companion and we found three interesting pitches of good rock leading to the top. My object was the view. From the Shepherd, you can see the fertile Valley of the Gods in all its charm, the terraced fields of wheat and Indian corn, the orchards, the villages, each with a guardian temple, the Beas River glinting through her arch of alder trees. Beyond Kulu rise the massive ranges of Lahoul, Deo Tibba appears from another angle, and the chain of the Ghopil Dhar is seen 'from the back'. Less impressive but more climbable than from the front. A thought for next time."

Jean had two more expeditions to Lahoul. She writes:

"I visited Lahoul in 1942 and 1943, and gave myself a tremendous amount of exercise - first by walking over the Rohtang Pass and then by exploring the two valleys opposite, the Kulti Nala and the Sona Pani Nala. Both these led to vast glaciers and imposing ice falls. Further on, I saw snowfields and the line of the Great Himalayan Range, and reckoned the peaks were beyond my reach.

"Once I descended the Rohtang Pass under an umbrella, and once I came back by the light of the full moon. We decided on the latter gambit as a kind of joke to round off the trip, and never regretted it. The porters, including the faithful Channu, gained twelve hours on the return journey to their village, and I gained the most spectacular mountain view of my life.

"Need I say how tremendously interested and impressed I was, after the passage of years, by the achievements of the Expedition, P.C. *Journal* 18.

"Sheila Cormack and her party crossed the formerly remote Rohtang Pass on the post-war built road BY CAR, speeding towards their conquest of fourteen peaks in West Lahoul."

As Gladys-Jean says, these mountains do not compare with the Himalayan giants. However, it is fitting that people who nowadays find their own routes in the Kulu area and proudly get reported in national magazines should remember a girl of the 1930s who, when she couldn't find friends to climb with, had the spirit and determination to become a pioneer.

CHAPTER 12

The War Years.
War work. A German P.O.W. Camp. The Hut in wartime. 21st Birthday. Start of BMC. Deaths of Nancy Forsyth and Jean Orr Ewing. The war ends.

Back home in Britain members climbed when they could, but War Work was the order of the day. The 1940 New Sheet tells us:

P Seth-Hughes is now in the ATS (Auxiliary Territorial Service) as also is her sister Jennet. V. Longstaff is farming, and E. Worsley Lowe does WVS (Women's Voluntary Service) work, whilst G. Sladen was called home to Kenya at the outbreak of war and joined up there as a member of the FANY (First Aid Nursing Yeomanry). Cecily Wood has become a VAD (Voluntary Aid Detachment) in addition to her ordinary work.
Hester White ... now serving with WRNS (Women's Royal Naval Service).
Phyllis Raven - is a Radiographer at a Surrey Hospital.
Joan Raven - Doctor at the Royal Free Hospital.
Mrs Jeffrey - Has had a houseful of evacuees since the outbreak of war, but the last one has now returned home.
Miss L.E. Bray - Is also coping with several evacuees, so much so that she was prevented from attending the Annual General Meeting at Easter, where she was very much missed.
Mrs Eden-Smith - Driving an ambulance and doing other ARP (Air Raid Precautions) work at Grange-over-Sands.
E. and N. Wells - Have been evacuated with their charges to Nelson.
Marjorie Wood - Has been a member of the ATS for some time, and immediately on the outbreak of war was called up. She is now in camp 'Somewhere in England.'
B. Ritchie - Is doing ambulance driving at Oxford.
H. Bryan and E. Pirie - Are waiting to be called up for nursing duties as soon as the new hospital at Ulverston in completed.
T.A. Gough - Is spending half her leisure time doing clerical work for the local ARP organisation.
I.A. Warren - Was evacuated with her school to Macclesfield for some months, but has now thankfully returned home.
Alicia Wilson is doing ambulance duties in Darlington.

At some time between the 6th of August and the 2nd of September, 1939, is the first recording of Nea Morin's name in the Pinnacle Club Log Book:
"E.W. Lowe & Nea Morin: Idwal Slab: Tennis Shoe, - Lazarus - Hope - Holly Tree - Lliwedd: Central Chimney Route & Red Wall Continuation. Mallory's Slab & Great Chimney."

Seeing that every other entry is dated, it is most frustrating not to have the date for this historic entry. It must have been near the end of August for Evelyn to have returned from the Alps.

In A Woman's Reach Nea writes:

"In 1939 I brought the children to England for the summer as usual, to stay with my mother, and in August she and I went to Wales for a holiday. Miserable because finances would not run to my joining Jean in the Alps, I fortunately had an introduction to Evelyn Lowe, a very fine climber who lived in Wales. With her I did Holly Tree Wall on the Idwal Slabs and Central Chimney of Lliwedd. With other friends I led the Direct on Glyder Fach for the first time; this reminded me strongly of Chamonix climbs - in particular the final crack; I have since climbed it often, always with equal pleasure."

During September, the Log Book shows signs of romance: there are no less than five records of climbs signed C. Wood and D. Roberts. Cicely Wood was to marry David Roberts of the Climbers' Club in April 1942.

Meets for the rest of the year were cancelled, but five members, E. Lowe, P. Seth-Hughes, P. Raven, C. Wood and S. Harper, celebrated the November Anniversary at the hut.

The next official meet was the Annual General Meeting at Easter, 1940, and Berta Gough's diary gives a taste of wartime - late, crowded trains and the blackout.

In spite of the restrictions and difficulties, it was decided to hold as many meets as possible, and six were arranged for the coming year. The News Page was suggested, to keep members in touch. One item of interest in the Secretary's Report reads:

"We had been unable to hold our own Annual Dinner ... and most other clubs had cancelled theirs. As a consequence, the only dinner which had been attended by representatives of the Pinnacle Club was given by the Alpine Club in June. The President, Hon. Secretary and Editor had had the honour of attending this function, which was notable as being the first Alpine Club Dinner to which ladies had been invited."

Despite all efforts, there was only one meet held between April 1940 and April 1941, and a mere four people managed that. Two new members were accepted as associates, but their names are not recorded. I think they were Mrs Cheney, who was a member for six years, and Dorothy Gray. Dorothy immediately became very much a part of the club. Evelyn Lowe said, "... no climb or hut chore impaired her temper, nerves or appearance. A most happy person." Dorothy also was a member for six years; during her first Alpine season, in 1947, she fell and was instantly killed when running down the steep track from the Dents de Veisivi.

During the year Evelyn Lowe was married, much to the surprise of some Pinnacle Club members. As Trilby Wells said, "He was much older than she was; we thought he was courting her mother!" Be that as it may, Ben Leech was a keen sailor and respected Evelyn's dedication to her own sport. They lived in Macclesfield near his business for some years, but in 1947 he was killed in a sailing accident and she, like several members who were war widows, had to reconstruct her life.

Evelyn visited the hut fairly often during the year. Other people able to snatch a few days were Cicely Wood, Annette Wilson, Harriet Turner, Joan Cochrane and Dorothy Arning. Dorothy, from London, wrote, 'Perfect peace away from air-raids, and perfect weather. 3.9.40 - 7.9.40.'

Snatching a few days in the Lake District were Trilby Wells and Dr Corbett. Trilby tells the following tale:

"I had an experience with Dr Corbett. Our school was evacuated near to where she lived, so she was very friendly with us and with the school. I had a week's holiday due to me and Dr Corbett could get a week off, so we went to the Lake District. We stayed at the Ship Inn just outside Coniston and we had a lovely week. We went climbing, then walked over to Wasdale and spent a night at the Fell and Rock Hut. Then when it got to the last day, Dr Corbett said, 'Oh well, we'll have an easy day.' So we got a man to row us across Coniston to the other side, then we climbed up the other side and we had some coffee at a farmhouse. The man said, 'Do be careful you don't get into Grisedale Farm.' It was for German prisoners - German officers.

"'Oh, yes!' we said. 'We know the way!'

"But we didn't. And we got into Grisedale.

"We were in our climbing boots and we tramped right across the front. There was an English officer sitting writing at the open window and he never raised his head. He thought we were some of the inmates, you see, tramping along, till we got to the other end. There were two soldiers on duty and they fixed their bayonets when they saw us coming.

"When we got up to them, they said, 'How the hell did you get in here?' So we told them which way we'd come. And they said, 'You know we have orders to shoot on sight - anybody!'

"In the pocket of our rucksack we had our identity cards. You know, you always had to carry one then. We showed them those and we told them where we'd come from and where we were staying. They asked us all sorts of questions and in the end they let us go and they said: 'Tell any of your friends not to come near here.' So we said: 'Yes, we shall.'

"We went along, back to the Ship Inn. When we got there, the police had been, and they asked us more questions. And in those days if you went to stay anywhere, you had to fill up a form. If you were British, you filled up part one. When we got back police had left our forms and we had to fill up part two, which told them far more details about us.

"So Dr Corbett said, 'Now what do we do?'

"I said, 'We pack our things and first thing in the morning we go home.'

"Which we did.

"As we went - we had to go through Coniston to get to the Ship Inn, - people were standing at the gates of their houses with terribly grim faces. They had just heard that France had capitulated. So I think the date was June 1940.

"It was the nearest thing to being shot I've ever experienced."

Even at the Club hut there were some signs of war. Annette Wilson, writing the Club notes for the first *Journal* after the war, observed: "It was during the war that many of us discovered for the first time the delights of our club hut for a longer holiday than the usual weekend, and, though barbed wire and padlocked gates at the power station were a reminder of grim realities, many small parties recaptured there for a brief time the lighthearted gaiety of happier days."

In April 1940 it had been used for the first time by a school party, and members balked of their Alpine holidays were urged to remember that they had a hut adjacent to some of the finest climbing in Britain.

Easter 1941 was the Club's Annual Meeting in Cwm Dyli and in spite of restrictions and travel difficulties thirteen members turned up: Evelyn Leech (Lowe), Harper, P. Raven, Trilby Wells, Arning, Warren, Cochrane, Turner, Ratcliffe, Barratt, Grutter,

Gough, Wilson.

Mabel Jeffrey, the president, was unable to attend so Trilby Wells was elected chairman of the meeting and Annette Wilson, the secretary, had been delayed so long on her journey that the date of the meeting had changed by the time it started. As Berta Gough put it, 'We held the AGM at night.' H. Turner, the treasurer, had also been having a difficult time; during an air raid on Manchester earlier in the year the Club's entire financial records to December 1940 had gone up in smoke. Petty cash was in the safe, which she hoped would be salvaged, and the rest of the money was safely in the bank. In the circumstances her financial statement relied entirely on the bank balances.

Evelyn Leech as hut secretary and librarian, said that fewer members had used the hut so the library had been less used in consequence. 'So far the books had shown no signs of damp, but it was suggested that to prevent this, and also for the general good of the hut, some arrangement might be made for one of the men at the Power Station to light the fire once a week.'

Now she lived in Cheshire Evelyn could not do this herself.

All the Club officers were re-elected but as it seemed unlikely that two members of the retiring committee, Biddy Deed and Alicia Wilson, would be able to attend meets for some time Joan Cochrane and Susan Harper were elected in their place. Meets were arranged for Whitsun and for Easter the following year, but the war made everything so uncertain that it was proposed by Susan Harper that 'in the event of it being found impossible to hold a general meeting the officers and committee be empowered to carry on the business of the club until such time as a meeting could be held.' This was agreed.

No *Handbook* was printed this year, but an addendum of the same size and style and containing necessary information was to be issued. To the best of my knowledge, no copy has survived.

During 1941 Joan Cochrane was made a full member and five new members joined the Club including Kathleen Sykes and Freda Rylatt. Kathleen was on the committee after the war but dropped her membership when she moved to New Zealand in 1957.

Freda Rylatt was a very good climber and quickly gained her full membership. She was on the committee and had just become librarian when, tragically, she died on Dinas Cromlech on 30th October 1949.

Almost every month of 1941 there were people using the hut and August Bank Holiday was quite a big meet. It seems there was still enough petrol about for people to use their cars. The glorious weather was matched by the climbing, the bathing, and the luxury of fresh salmon for tea.

Once again Nea Morin was able to come to the hut, telling in her book how she saw a light in the window but the power station gates were bolted and barred so she climbed through barbed wire and waded the stream to reach her goal - to be told she was lucky not to have been shot by the Home Guard. Having married a Frenchman, even one who had joined the British forces and lost his life in 1943, Nea was technically an alien and later the North Wales Power Company ruled that no foreigners were to stay at the hut. So Nea was not able to join the club till after the war. On this occasion she and Joan Cochrane climbed Route II and Rectory Chimneys in very cold weather, while others found walking more attractive.

Easter 1942 was the club's 21st birthday. It was a time of strict rationing and restricted travel but Biddy and Trilby Wells were absolutely determined that there should be a cake for the occasion so as many members as possible gave small quantities of eggs, butter, sugar, fruit and so on, and the result was a cake which has become a club legend. The following is Berta Gough's final entry in her diary:

EASTER. APRIL 3/6TH 1942.

LANGDALE. I got 9.35 train from Exchange on Good Friday morning. There were not a lot travelling, the Government had asked the public not to do so. Had to change at Preston and Oxenholme.

Met Dr Corbett and two Lambricks at Oxenholme so we travelled together from there. Bus at Windermere was full so we hired a taxi. Charged us 4/- each and we arrived at the Old Dungeon Ghyll Hotel just after 2.0 p.m. Annette and Turner had arrived the day before. Also there were two Wells, Mrs Jeffrey, Gray and Higgs. It was pouring with rain so we played cards all afternoon. Game called 'Main Line', great fun. We were sharing hotel with Alpine Club. Saturday was very dull and threatening rain, so two Lambricks, Annette, Gray and I went by Stickle Tarn and Easedale Tarn to Grasmere where we had a look at Heaton Cooper Exhibition, and bought quite a lot of things we couldn't get at home. Had tea at cafe by river. Started to rain as we were walking back over Red Bank and got worse as we went on, but we did not get very wet. Very strong wind and rain at night.

The Wells had made a marvellous cake with icing and 21 candles in little roses. Mr Bulman (The Hotel Proprietor) gave us a bottle of sherry and Mrs Jeffrey presented one. We had crackers on the table with skiers on them. Mrs Jeffrey cut the cake after we had lit the candles and we all had a candle to keep. Then we had toasts and speeches. Dr Corbett spoke about early days of the Club, Biddy and Trilby told of some very funny incidents. Mrs Jeffrey outlined the history of the Club. Turner also spoke, and Mrs Eden ... Mr Bulman let us use his private sitting room all weekend ... an enjoyable meet despite bad weather. Glad I managed the 21st Meet.

As regards the speeches, the *Handbook* tells us that all original members were required to reminisce for two minutes. 'Much cake was eaten, many toasts were drunk, crackers were faithfully pulled, and a grand evening ended with Auld Lang Syne.' Much appreciated was a telegram of congratulations from the LSCC.

A *Handbook* was produced in 1942 and for the first time it contained a full report of the Annual General Meeting.

Mabel Jeffrey had now been president for the customary three years and Biddy Wells had been asked if she would take over this office; however, she refused, saying that it was fair neither to the retiring president who had had little opportunity of meeting members during her term of office owing to the war, nor to any new president, to take office whilst these conditions continue. The committee agreed and Mabel Jeffrey was re-elected with acclamation. Evelyn Leech wrote: "We felt that a club that could muster a cake with 21 candles at a time when the lights of Europe were dimmed would surely prosper for ever ... The spirit of the Club was still the spirit of its Foundress, Pat Kelly."

Several members were able to get to the hut during the summer, and in October there is a pleasant, domestic note in the log book.

"Vera Picken and daughter Gillian spent 10 days here. The weather was nearly continuously bad and climbing on the few fine days was limited to the demands of a 2 year old. We went to the top of the track on the east of the pipe line, where Gillian was introduced to Snowdon and the Horseshoe and we went down to the lake. G. will climb anything from what looks like a rock to the ruins round the hut, when I am not looking.

Perhaps she will repeat this when making her application for membership."

For the first time since the opening of the hut there was no meet in November, and for the first time in its history the Club held no Easter Meet in 1943, due both to the travel embargo on public holidays and to the difficulty many members had in obtaining time off. However, six members managed a week at the hut from April 13th to 20th, the week before Easter, and their names are enough to tell us that they tackled good routes: Evelyn, Annette, Joan Cochrane, Phyl Raven, Dorothy Gray and Freda Rylatt. H.A. Turner and a friend spent Easter weekend at the hut.

Needless to say, there was no annual meeting, and the only committee meeting during the year was a 'postal' one. Berta Gough was married in May and went to live in London. Two other members surrounded by domesticity were Vera Picken and M. Ratcliffe, both of whom had little boys.

The Easter meet in 1944 was held as planned on the weekend following Easter Sunday, at Wall End Farm, Langdale. At least fourteen members were able to attend and they climbed on all three days: Middlefell Buttress to get their hand in after so long away from the rocks, Bowfell Buttress for a full-length climb on the Sunday - 'A rather cold day,' the log book writer records ruefully, but she goes on to say: 'On Monday we spent a delightful sunny time playing about on the two routes and extras on Scout Crag.'

'It was very good after 2 years of only written communication between committee members to be again able to have a good talk - it was enjoyed by all!'

In spite of deletions of names for non-payment of subscriptions, the Club members still numbered 102. The hut had hardly been used but had been kept aired by Mrs Williams, wife of the Mr Williams who worked at the power station, and all was in good condition.

Mrs Jeffrey was elected president for a further year, or until the next general meeting. She felt it was time for others to have the opportunity of holding office, but bowed to the unanimous wish of members present.

Evelyn Leech had attended two meetings of the newly formed Standing Advisory Committee on Mountaineering, and it was agreed that the Club should be represented on this, at a cost of £3 per annum. If Evelyn couldn't go to meetings another member, probably Marjorie Heys-Jones, would go in her place. This was the start of the British Mountaineering Council, and an especially dear brain-child of Geoffrey Winthrop Young.

With everything so uncertain, no dates were fixed for meets beyond suggesting one at the Club hut in the late summer. It was decided to publish a *Handbook*.

Newly elected members were Barbara Brown, Margaret Morris and Winifred Jackson.

Barbara Brown had become keen on mountains while on a geological expedition to the Isle of Arran, then went rock-climbing in North Wales with the Oxford University Mountaineering Club in 1943. In 1946 she married and went to live in Uganda. She was a member (Mrs Dawkins) until 1968. Margaret Morris had done no rock climbing but enjoyed mountain walking; she was a member for eight years.

Wartime and the evacuation of Liverpool children to Capel Curig brought Winifred Jackson into contact with the mountains. Winifred has been committee member, treasurer and president.

The proposed meet was held in the first five days in September and those able to make the journey to the hut found the weather distinctly unkind: "Steady rain prevented us from everything we arranged to do, with the exception of Lockwood's Chimney, North Buttress of Tryfan, and Route II on Lliwedd, walks and being surprisingly happy in spite of rain, hail and storms of all kinds."

Meanwhile, Ben Nevis was the scene of a tragic accident: on the first weekend on September Nancy Forsyth and her companion Brian Kellett were killed when they fell from their climb on the crags above Allt a'Mhuilinn.

Not only the Pinnacle Club mourned Nancy's loss; she was a committee member of the Ladies' Scottish Climbing Club as well, and a keen member of the Fell and Rock.

It was hard to think of Nancy as dead. She was so calm and strong, tall, with a swinging stride and beautiful balance. She cycled from Carlisle for the Lakeland meets and had been to Rawhead only the previous weekend. Nancy Ridyard wrote in the Fell and Rock *Journal*, 1945:

"What a cosy evening we had drinking Ovaltine in the parlour with L.W. Somervell, T.R. Burnett and J.A. Kenyon. On Sunday we went to Gimmer to meet Joan Tebbutt, but the rain came down so we crossed to Pavey Ark, did the Great Gully and got down early. After tea, we parted at the top of Red Bank and Nancy cycled off to Carlisle in the pouring rain as she had so often done before."

The death of Jean Orr Ewing in the same year was another sad blow to Pinnacle Club members, though not quite so unexpected, for her life had been dogged increasingly by illness. She had been working on medical research at Oxford University and in particular had been doing valuable work in the treatment of wounds, so her death was a loss to people far beyond her own circle of friends, and to medicine as well as the mountaineering world. Jean left several books to the Club, as well as her collection of maps and journals.

We must leave 1944 on a happy note, though: Len Winthrop Young became a member of the Ladies' Alpine Club committee, and Nea Morin was elected their president.

Travel restrictions in 1945 made the Annual Meeting at Cwm Dyli a very small affair. Of interest was Evelyn Leech's description of the growth of local committees of the British Mountaineering Council. She had accepted nomination to the North Wales Committee.

Bray does not appear to have attended any meets during the war, and on this occasion she sent a proposal that subscriptions should be suspended for the duration. 'This proposal was not supported.'

Len Winthrop Young has a wartime story about Bray: "She had a fight with my Geoffrey, because I was away in the north, seeing my son whose ship had come in suddenly, and Bray was in charge of everything around Shere, where she lived. She came and told Geoffrey there might be a bomb in his garden and Geoffrey was awfully cross about this. I can see the two of them, knowing them! But it ended well. Oh, it (her manner) never altered her friendships - she was charming."

The next official meet was arranged for Easter 1946, at Coniston, but Evelyn Leech had a grand week with Phyl Raven and Eileen Pyatt in August, when they did many of their favourite routes. One or two others managed to snatch a few days' climbing as well, V.E. Day had been on May 8th and V.J. Day came on August 15th. The war had ended, but there was no November meet at the hut. The next entry in the log book comes in 1946, on March 24th, when Evelyn recorded a general airing of the hut after the winter and in preparation for a University of London Mountaineering Club Meet led by Eileen Pyatt.

People were free to travel again, but it would be some months before the threads of normal life could be picked up once more, and there were inevitable changes.

CHAPTER 13

1946-7. Evelyn Leech President. New members. National Parks. Scottish and Skye meets. Paddy Hirst on Munros.

The Easter Meet 1946 was held the weekend after Easter when the Fell and Rock kindly allowed the use of their newly acquired Langdale Hut, Rawhead. The first Warden was Sid Cross, who at that time ran the Burnmoor Inn at Boot, Eskdale; the keys to Rawhead were held by PC member, Mrs Bryan.

Twenty members celebrated the club's first Victory Meet by climbing and walking throughout the area, especially enjoying climbs on Gimmer in the hot sunshine. At the annual meeting Evelyn Leech was elected the new president and Mabel Jeffrey presided for the last time.

Another new hut had opened: the MAM hut, Glan Dena, in the Ogwen Valley, and reciprocal arrangements were approved. Pinnacle Club members have much appreciated the use of this well-planned and comfortable hut over the years.

The Ladies' Alpine Club had already celebrated peacetime by holding a dinner in November, at which the Club's representative had been Marjorie Heys-Jones.

Marjorie reported that the British Mountaineering Council had vigorous plans: the registration of professional guides in Great Britain, provision of huts in mountain centres, a first aid scheme, a war memorial to climbers, and an elementary book, *Climbing in Britain* which was shortly to be published in the Penguin series. It is interesting to see how the BMC's ideas have worked out in practice over the years.

The end of the war saw an influx of new members, five in 1945 and ten in 1946. Rosalind Hill was a friend of Christina Barratt and Brenda Ritchie. She had had one glorious season in 1937, climbing in the Jotunheim, the Tyrol and the Bernese Oberland, and she was an experienced rock climber. She is still a member.

Joyce Taylor was a great friend of Winifred Jackson; she writes: "We were sent to Capel Curig in 1941 in charge of a group of Liverpool children from Toxteth and, looking at the hills in North Wales when we arrived determined that nothing would make us climb them. However there was so little to do in Capel Curig in wartime and the children were nicely settled in with their kind hosts, so we took to walking. One of our first jaunts behind the Post Office in Capel was undertaken clutching a packet of soapflakes (Very precious in 1941 - new heights for Lux). One fine day we found ourselves near Little Tryfan. I started to go up, Winifred said I should come down - I thought I preferred to go up as I didn't like the look of down - so Winifred joined me and Hey Presto! we'd done our first ascent ...

"Looking back it is hard to imagine N. Wales at that time - it was so empty. Most of the people we met were strangers to it as we were - moved there by the accident of war. There were no groups of climbers of whom to ask advice. There was the odd man on a brief leave and of course the military from the battle school busily polishing the rock with their nails or crossing the lakes while their mates fired live ammunition at them. Apart from these we had the hills to ourselves. It must be said that I was once shot out of a chimney on Bochlwyd Buttress, where I was having slight difficulty, by the noise of firing from the lake - like a cork out of a bottle was how Winifred described it. I suppose that the emptiness of the hills and the fact that we had to rely on ourselves if we got into difficulties were all good training and may account for the fact that we still walk the hills if we climb no longer.

"A little later we had the great good fortune to make the acquaintance of Major Godfrey Bradley who had been a very good climber in pre-war days and was still climbing well. Knowing we'd done a considerable amount of walking he announced that next Sunday he'd take us climbing - North Buttress, he thought - jug-handle holds - Belle Vue Terrace for a little sit in the sun - and the climb ended on the top. We were terrified! We pleaded no equipment, etc. but Brad had a sort of Aladdin's cave of gear, so that was overcome, and in spite of our prayers Sunday dawned warm and sunny and off we went - and thoroughly enjoyed ourselves!

"After that, Brad was exceedingly kind to us. He gave us our first rope and advised us on the sort of climbs we could do on our own, and we were launched. We climbed quite extensively, disporting ourselves on the pinnacles behind the Bryn Tyrch on summer evenings and dropping borrowed CC guides when climbing on Clogwyn - we still wonder if we pioneered a new finish to that climb.

"When we went to meets after joining the Pinnacle Club I remember how overawed we were by the great names - Bray (a very formidable lady), Corbett, and nearer to us, Nea Morin and Evelyn Leech. However, hut chores proved a great leveller and everybody was so kind and helpful that we soon felt at home. There were a few unwritten rules, like never coming back to the hut empty handed - the fire gobbled up sticks and coal so we were always expected to add to the store.

"I remember the branch of evergreen that always hung over the Emily Kelly memorial board . . . The kindness of Mr and Mrs Williams (he was manager of the Power Station) and of Mr and Mrs Roberts who lived in the house next to the manager's bungalow, now all demolished).

"It was one of Mr Roberts' jobs to walk up the pipeline to Llyn Llidaw every day to check the state of the pipes and the valves at the top.

"Groceries and meat could be ordered for meets and they were left at Gwastadanas Farm and collected along with the milk.

"I took over the Hut Secretaryship (1951) from Evelyn Leech who was a tower of strength to everybody - we had planned a climbing weekend at the hut when her husband was lost. I remember Antonia, who came often to the hut as a little girl - and Evelyn's large black dog, who was not allowed to sleep in the Hut unless all present were dog lovers. I remember how shattered our little group was when Freda Rylatt was killed and how Tharby and her friend were noted for the enormous packs they carried, and how Lockwood's Chimney was almost private Pinnacle Club property."

Eileen Pyatt, who became Hon. Secretary in the 1950s, started climbing when she was about twelve, going to Harrison's Rocks with her brother Edward (author, and Editor of the *Alpine Journal*). It was he who suggested Eileen should join the Pinnacle Club, and at a BMC meeting he approached Evelyn Leech who wrote inviting Eileen to join her and Phyl Jackson at the Club hut for a week. In fact, Eileen preferred walking to climbing, so felt rather out of her depth, but they were both very kind and helpful.

Two weeks before becoming a member of the Club, Eileen led a meet at the hut, taking a party of women from the University of London Mountaineering Club for a week's holiday in weather so perfect that many climbed Snowdon to see the sunrise.

Eileen was soon to meet many Pinnacle Club members at the hut: "Of an older generation I particularly remember Lilian Bray and Katie Corbett and a more contrasting pair you could not imagine, but they seemed to hit it off. Lilian was the dominant one and was very outspoken. Katie could stand up for herself but was such a gentle soul by contrast. She was a great patience-player and always must have a game before she went to bed. Lilian was a knitter. She even knitted a carpet which we were shown when the London members were invited to tea with her. You will gather from the *Handbook* that when I became Secretary I organised walks in the country round London. They were held monthly with probably about six people attending. Winifred Jackson, Dorothy Arning and Lucy Wood were regular attenders. I knew Dorothy quite well as she and I lived fairly close together and she offered me lifts to the start of walks. (Interesting person to know but one had to be a model of patience as it took her endless time to do anything. How she got on in her practice as a doctor I do not know.) As I recollect, the walks did not continue long after I gave up active interest in the Club in 1958."

Eileen Gregory was a future bright star and president of the club. Her home was in Brighton, not an ideal centre for climbing, but in her late teens she stayed at a Holiday Fellowship centre in Langdale where they had a climbing leader on her first visit. Later, someone gave her a climbing rope that made her independent. She could always persuade someone else to come on the other end and she spent all possible holidays in Langdale. She writes: "I was taken on the Coniston meet by Phyl Raven. A man I had met on Stanage Edge insisted I joined the Pinnacle Club and put Phyl in touch with me - I had never aspired as high as to think I could join the Pinnacle Club but at Coniston the Club was very friendly and welcoming. I was seconded on my application form by Dorothy Smith whom I had met in Langdale previously and who happened to be at the meet. She left the Club and I didn't see her for twenty years, then I met her again when we moved to Cheshire. She had come from Northumberland and I had come from Kent, and we still live in the same Cheshire village - a small world -

"In Langdale I met a lad from Newcastle who belonged to the Polaris Mountaineerig Club which was supported mostly by people in the Nottingham and Derby area so I was overjoyed when I got a job in Nottingham and joined the P.M.C. and was able to climb with them most weekends. They rather limited the time I spent with the Pinnacle Club as the P.C. didn't have many meets except at Bank Holidays and these were the times when the Polaris would be going further afield and naturally I wanted to go with them.

"I occasionally met Evelyn Leech at weekends, if she came out to Derbyshire from Macclesfield, also Freda Rylatt from Sheffield. I made firm friends of a couple of lads I think she had picked up on gritstone and they joined the Polaris." In those days Eileen and Freda assessed clubs and people purely for their climbing potential!

Meets this year were held as planned. Penelope Seth Poulton, the hut secretary, went to the hut on June 5th to air and clean the place ready for Whitsun, accompanied by her seven-month-old baby Miranda. On Whit Sunday she and her sister Jennet, complete with husbands and babies, joined the meet for tea. The tolerance and even pleasure with which babies are received at the hut is a continuing tradition which has earned the love and gratitude of the writer as well as of many others.

The Scottish meet was held in the SMC Hut at Lagangarbh, jointly with the Ladies' Scottish CC, and the ten members present managed several climbs including Crowberry Ridge Direct, despite traditional Scottish weather. The report comments, 'Evenings were devoted mainly to Highland dancing, and were hilarious and exhausting.'

The largest meet was in November at Coniston, based on the Black Bull. Large parties climbed on Dow Crag every day, even though it rained, 'but the hot baths and comfort of the hotel made a soaking positively worth while, and it was a very jolly weekend.' Four new members were elected at the committee meeting held during this meet and the Hon. Secretary mentioned the several enquiries she had had from people wanting to be taught to climb, probably due to the newly published Penguin book *Climbing in Britain* or to information from the BMC, She had followed the usual procedure and invited them to come to a meet as a visitor in the first place.

A donation was sent to the Helsby Hill Purchase Fund. Members driving past this landmark on their way to Wales may reflect with satisfaction that the Club helped in a small way to preserve it for recreational use. Snowdonia itself was a proposed National Park area and the Pen-y-Gwryd entertained a royal personage for a short time when Her Majesty Queen Elizabeth visited Wales on 18th July 1946 to see its beauties at first hand.

The BMC had been busy sending out circulars and questionnaires, amongst which were postcards for all members to fill in to indicate whether they liked climbs classified by numbers or descriptions. These, (it was hoped) were filled in and returned.

Only ten members managed the Easter meet in 1947. However, among the guests at the club hut were Nea Morin and her daughter Denise. Nea finally became a member in November. Saturday was very wet, an excellent day on which to hold the annual meeting, though not so good for four hotel dwellers who had to walk down to the hut through torrents and puddles. Their return was made rosier by good measures of the President's port. However, people climbed on Good Friday, Sunday and Monday, with nine people going up Amphitheatre Buttress on this last day. Evelyn led a prospective member, Nea led Denise, and Joan Cochrane and Freda Rylatt led the last two ropes. When the weather wasn't raining it was cold and very windy, and members left on the Tuesday morning in a blizzard.

One matter to come before the annual meeting was the choice of a design for a bookplate. Miss J. Tebbutt had submitted several designs, which were narrowed down to two by the committee, then the final choice was left to the members present. The design chosen shows a young woman climber standing relaxed against a rock, absorbed in reading a book.

Also considered were hut fees, which were increased to two shillings for members and an extra sixpence for guests. It was decided to make the *Handbook* a little less confusing by including maiden names in brackets after the names of members who had married since joining the Club.

There were seven new members in all, during the year. Nea has been mentioned; Stella Magri was amongst a group who came from the London area and was very active for a few years; Dora King was much loved - a good climber who held office or was on the committee all through the 1950s and early 1960s. She also joined the Ladies' Alpine Club. It was with sadness that members heard of her death in 1982.

The second meet of the year was Whit week at Glen Brittle, and with Evelyn Leech and Nea Morin there, great things were done. Also present were Freda Rylatt, Dr Corbett and the Wells sisters, and from the MAM, Mrs E. Burton. The meet record reads:

This meet owed much of its success to the kindness of Cyril Machin, who invited us to join in all the excursions which he arranged for the MAM party. With them we traversed the Dubhs, and we went by bus to Dunvegan Castle. Other excursions and climbs included the Window Buttress and Inaccessible Pinnacle, the White Slab route on the Ghrunnda face of Sron na Ciche, the Alasdair to Dearg ridge, Eastern Buttress Direct of Sgumain, Cioch slab and upper wall, both routes, the Direct and West climbs to the Cioch, and Mallory's Slab and Groove on Sron na Ciche.

The two hostellers spent three days in getting to Glen Brittle, through missing a connection at Stirling. They filled in the weekend by ascending Ben More from Crianlarich, the Tower Ridge from Glen Nevis, and then when they felt they were all set for Skye at last, they found themselves on the wrong boat, bound for a 36-hour trip round the outer isles, not touching Skye at all. The sun-drenched Cuillins looked tantalising; however, with four other hostellers who had made the same mistake, they transferred to the mail boat for Rhum, and from there a lobster boat brought them across to Loch Brittle in the evening.

Paddy Hirst was also in Scotland this year. She was rarely able to attend Pinnacle Club meets, but that was by no means an indication that she had given up mountaineering - far from it. By degrees, she and her husband had been caught up in the passion known as munroitis; not an all-consuming passion, because they also went to the Alps when they could, and climbed in other areas, nevertheless it was a steady love affair. Munro's 'Tables giving all the Scottish mountains exceeding 3,000 feet in height' had first appeared in print in 1891 in the *Scottish Mountaineering Club Journal,* but were not published as a general guide till 1921, so it was in the 1920s that 'Munro bagging' first became popular.

Paddy Hirst wrote in the Pinnacle Club *Journal* (no.7): "In May, 1925, my husband presented me with a car for my birthday and a fortnight later the two of us started off for a tour in Scotland with the intention of climbing some of its mountains en route. It was MY holiday, so I planned the routes, chose the places we should visit and the peaks we should climb... We had such a marvellous time that we decided to make a Scottish holiday an annual affair. A year or two later, when staying at Loch Laggan Hotel, we met a well-known member of the SMC who was just finishing the Munros. He suggested we might begin to collect them, and as we had by this time climbed quite a number of the Scottish hills, the suggestion took root and in future we planned our trips with that end in view. Henceforward we always took with us a tent and provisions so that we were quite independent if there was any difficulty in getting suitable accommodation.

"We became so interested in munroing that besides our annual fortnight in May or early June, we began to spend Easter, New Year and other weekends trying to reduce the 543 Tops. (We religiously did the tops as well as the separate mountains.) We had decided from the first that Ben More on Mull was to be our last Munro, and this we accomplished in June, 1947; and in August 1947, we did the last top, Cairn Dearg, S.W., of Ben Nevis. But for the World War, we should have finished the task much earlier; we did not visit Scotland from 1939 till 1943. By that time our longing for Scotland was so intense that we could stay away no longer, so we bought bicycles, took them by train and for some years used them to reach the distant hills.

"Looking back I realise what a tremendous amount of enjoyment I have had out of munroing; many happy hours have I spent, deciding which peaks to do next and planning the routes. Frequently, when we started off, my husband had no idea what was in store for him and he jokingly used to say to me he was 'just the chauffeur'."

In the late 1950s Eric Maxwell compiled a list of 'Munro baggers' and a short history of the sport entitled *Quod Erat Faciendum* and sent copies to John and Paddy 'With the compiler's compliments'. They were the eighth and ninth people to complete the Munros and the fifth and sixth to complete the tops as well. Paddy was the first woman to complete them and was to remain the only one for many years. Despite the principle of 'ladies first', John Hirst is firmly on the list as eighth and Paddy the ninth; the differences between principles and practice are very strange!

Several members were able to go to the Alps this year. Dorothy Pilley Richards and her husband climbed twenty-three routes, all guideless and one, Piz Miez by the west ridge, a new ascent. They had also been out in 1946 and done almost as much.

Kathleen Sykes worked for the United Nations Relief and Rehabilitation Administration in 1946 and had been hoping to be posted to a mountain centre but wrote from Ausbach - her hopes were not realised, but she was doing interesting work with displaced persons - Baltics, Poles and Ukrainians. She spoke of their energy in training and establishing themselves and of the lack of privacy which was one of their greatest hardships - families partitioned from others only by blankets. Her work lay in arranging jobs or training for displaced persons within the local community. The account in the 1946 *Handbook* is a small piece of history and a reminder of the aftermath of war.

For Dora King, 1947 was her first season abroad and she climbed the Wetterhorn and Schreckhorn; Marjorie Heys-Jones had a good season in the Bernina and Bregaglia and Alison Adam climbed the Dent du Midi.

Nea joined the GHM International Meet based at Les Praz, Chamonix and climbed with her friends and family. Her entry in the LAC *Year Book* reads: "Traverse of the Moine up SW ridge down ordinary route, Dent du Géant, Dent du Requin, by the Chapeau à Cornes arête (all *cordée feminine*. Leading). Traverse of Mont Blanc du Tacul by the Aiguilles du Diable, without the ascent of the Isolée (guideless). Mont Tondu (with Denise Morin). Aiguille de l'M (with Denise and Ian Morin)."

Poor Dorothy Gray fell to her death coming down from the Dent de Veisivi this year, during her first Swiss season. It was a bad year for accidents; John Barford, friend of many members and BMC Hon. Secretary and author of *Climbing in Britain* was killed by rockfall in the Dauphiné.

At the hut, Evelyn Leech led a pleasant meet for the stay-at-homes and was there several times before the November meet, climbing alone or with various friends. For a weekend in September she was joined by Joan Cochrane:

"September 10th: Cracks Route on Dinas Mot (wet).

" 11th: Central Chimney Route, Lliwedd (wet)", says the Log.

The October meet in Yorkshire had perfect weather, but the picture for the final meet of the year was of wet clothes steaming by the fire, and members working off excess energy in gymnastic trials of strength on the beams.

CHAPTER 14

1948-1949. 1st post war dinner. Meets and members. A post card from Chamonix. A reluctant president. Gwen Moffat. Alpine meet. Freda Rylatt's accident. E.H Daniell.

The new year of 1948 began in fine style for the Pinnacle Club. The first post-war Dinner Meet was held from January 3rd to 5th at Coniston, and hospitality was returned to the many clubs who had been less tardy in this respect. The weather was traditional: "while torrential rain was falling outside, we were diverted by the witty speeches of Dr T. Howard Somervell, Miss I Blaikie of the LSCC, J Cochrane, and the President. Dr Somervell's speech caused some of us to look in our Bibles to find Isaiah's reference to the Pinnacle Club." (The reference is not recorded. Surely it wasn't XIII v.4, 'The noise of a multitude in the mountains'!) "Stella Magri entertained us with a delightful little ballet, with climbing as its theme.

"Large parties walked up to Dow Crag, and on the first two days rain held off until after the climbs were started, though we were invariably pretty wet by the end of the day ..."

The next meet was the Annual General Meeting and a cold but sunny Easter saw 22 members at the Club hut. The report reminds us that rationing was not yet over: "The arrival of the party was heralded by a deluge of about 40 parcels at the Power Station. More tins came out of these parcels than had ever been seen before, and some magnificent stews were cooked in a bucket. The primuses and fire stood up well to the strain of cooking for 19 persons, and the electric kettle worked overtime providing incessant mugs of tea. During the weekend there were several walking parties who spent considerably more strenuous days than the climbers....

"The annual meeting passed off successfully and members not staying at the hut were fortified for their return journeys to the Pen-y-Gwryd and various farms, by glasses of port, shandy, or ginger beer."

Of the six new members joining in 1948, two are of special interest: Peggy Wild and Winifred Marples.

Peggy and Winifred were living in London, but had little else in common except their love of climbing. Winifred (Jo) Marples had been a member of the Ladies' Alpine Club since 1922 and had accompanied Bray and other Pinnacle Club members on many Alpine routes. She led a rope on the first guideless ascent of the Aiguille du Roc au Grépon. She had always enjoyed rock climbing and it is surprising that she had not joined the Club earlier. She came into the Club as a full member.

Peggy Wild joined as a girl who enjoyed walking and camping and was renowned for the enormous rucksack she carried. She developed into a very sound climber and was outstanding in introducing to the hills teenagers, with whom she had much sympathy and endless patience. When I first knew her she was working at the Plas Gwynant Adventure School and Club members were delighted and proud when she was appointed Chief Instructor. This meant she was busy at weekends, but she usually called in at some time during a Welsh meet. Now she has retired, perhaps she will have more spare time.

The Easter meet went on all week for some people, ending with three wet days of which the final one was spent by Nea Morin and Evelyn Leech in spring-cleaning the hut, after everyone else had gone home.

The Whitsun meet was a joint one with the Ladies' Scottish at their hut in Glencoe, Black Rock Cottage. Evelyn wrote: "The late running of the Whitsun trains shortened our weekend by a fine Saturday morning, and two of us who had sworn to break our fast at Black Rock broke it on Stirling station with a sausage and bitterness of spirit. However, when we arrived at noon to find Riona Barclay at the bus stop to meet us, kettles on the boil at the hut, and all our heavy packages of food and sleeping bags portered across from Kingshouse by our hostesses, bitterness evaporated in the sunshine which enveloped Rannoch Moor. This high standard of hospitality was kept up throughout our visit, and we can only hope that plague, pestilence, or murrain may someday drive the LSCC southwards, when we may have the opportunity of giving them our best bunks while we sleep on the ground!"

The weather remained perfect, and climbs included the Crowberry Ridge and routes on the Rannoch Wall, Church Door and the Chasm. On the Monday, "by a great effort of will the entire hut party rose and caught the early bus down the glen; M. Johns and A. Adam went off to the Aonach Eagach Ridge from the Devil's Staircase to Clachaig, with M. Wood, who turned back from Am Bodach in order to finish her sketches of the day before; when we saw the finished pictures that evening we thought she had spent her time wisely, and felt a little envious of the gift that allows the Buchaille in morning and evening light to be carried home when the holiday is over. C. McNair and S. Magri, E.W. Leech and P. Raven, went up Bidean nam Bian by way of the Hidden Valley and Stob Corrie nam Beith. C. McNair and S. Magri descended to Clachaig, and E.W. Leech and P. Raven to Glen Etive, where they found tea with home-baked scones and home-churned butter and wandered home to Black Rock very happily beside a river which offered gorgeous bathing pools round every bend."

Mabel Jeffrey and Hester White were also on this meet, joining the climbing parties at the weekend.

The August Bank Holiday meet at the Club hut was not blessed with such good weather, when some of the party did Route II in a thunderstorm, augmented by a plane crash on the Cwm-y-Llan side of the mountain.

The Alpine weather was equally unsettled and few people managed many routes. Eileen Gregory was one who climbed eight routes, including the Requin and Grépon, several of them with Freda Rylatt. We are very lucky to have a postcard which Freda sent Winifred Jackson from Chamonix. Winifred writes: "She was famous for the amount she could get on a few square inches." It reads:

CHAMONIX - MONT BLANC
Aug 18 (1948)
Dear K.,
Hope you've been having better weather for your holiday than I have. One and a half weeks of rain and snow with one or two good days & only one ascent in pleasant conditions. Did you go to Glen Brittle I wonder. Perhaps I will see you at the P.C. November meet. Eileen Gregory whom you may remember from the Coniston November

meet, is here and keeps cheerful under the wettest and most trying conditions. We are camping and going to huts. Surprisingly enough I am the only one left camping; everyone else has retreated to the CAF Refuge because of spraying tents. We really have had some deluges. When I was buying a new rope at Brigham's I was awfully tempted to buy a beautiful lightweight tent & paid far too much for it. But it has been well worth while because in spite of being so fragile it has withstood torrents of rain, & I've thoroughly enjoyed using it. When the weather is bad, camping is some solace for no mountaineering. We've been to 4 huts so far, & done 3 ascents in wet & cold - on some days I've been absolutely miserable. The one ascent in sunshine was a delight. We've had a guide all the time. I for one have been thankful because of the bad weather, & now feel more confident about finding my own way about. We might do without in our third week. Eileen and I feel we shall stay on till the end in hopes of good weather. We arrived here in pouring rain, & conducted to the camp site my spirits sank to zero level. All we could do was dump our rucksacks in the rain. Then the registered luggage had not arrived. This was almost too much to bear, because my suitcase contained my tent & all my clothes. However we found that we could spend that night at the CAF Refuge close by. This was indeed a blessing - it rained all night, and next day was fine for pitching tents. We have only done minor ascents so far due to bad weather conditions. Am enjoying it though - on the whole. - Eileen by the way has a non- leaking tent but has her brother with her, so they are at the CAF Refuge.

Yours F.

This was Gwen Moffat's first Alpine season, of which she was to write so entertainingly in the Club *Journal*. She joined the Club the following year. Pilley as usual had been very active. She and her husband had spent the winter snowshoeing in the White Mountains of New Hampshire, USA, but came back to the Alps for the summer and appear to have done as much as ever, though perhaps more passes than peaks are mentioned - the only indication that the Richards were deterred in any way by the weather.

Pilley and Eileen Gregory were both at the Yorkshire meet in October, along with Alison Adam, Bray, Corbett, E.M. Clarke, H.A. Turner, Biddy, Trilby and Marjorie Wood. The meet was based at Grassington.

"On Saturday, in delightful weather, the party walked to Malham Cove and returned via Gordale Scar, a distance of about 20 miles up hill and down dale. Sunday ... up the river to Kettlewell and on the Arncliffe Fell."

I cannot help contrasting this peaceful autumnal scene with Pilley's snowshoeing expeditions or her toils up the Aletsch Glacier in doubtful weather, yet each was a valid experience to a mountaineer and enjoyable in its own way.

The final meet of the year was a rather small Aniversary Meet at the Club hut - Eileen Gregory, Mabel Jeffrey, Dora King, Evelyn Leech, Freda Rylatt, Annette Wilson, Lucy Wood and three visitors had good days on Lliwedd and Tryfan.

Once again the New Year, 1949, was to commence with a big dinner meet at Coniston. Nancy Carpenter, née Ridyard, and Ruth Hargreaves came to this meet, their first for some time. Bray and Corbett were there, Bryan and Pirie, Gabriel, Mabel Jeffrey, H. Turner, E. Leech, M. Wood, A. Wilson, F. Rylatt, and newer members F. Denny, P. Wild, H. Winter plus many friends and relations. It must have been the first dinner meet that the Wells sisters could not attend.

"After justice had been done to the excellent dinner provided by Mrs Robinson, our President and Vice-President amused the company with a programme of slides showing the emergence of women climbers from the skirt to the trouser stage, and the perils of climbing in the garments worn, perforce, by the pioneers of our sex. These were followed by slides of Wales and Skye taken by Mrs Jeffrey. We have to thank Mr Appleyard and the F.& R.C.C. for the operation of and loan, of the excellent lantern."

Mabel Jeffrey and Evelyn Leech had each presented photographic slides to the club, which were to remain in Evelyn's care for the time being. Sadly, many of the things which Evelyn sought to keep safe for the Club were lost when she died. I do not know what happened to the slides.

This was the end of Evelyn Leech's third year as president and the committee agreed that she should approach Biddy or Trilby Wells to see whether they would accept this office. Bray wrote nominating Trilby, so she was asked first, but both refused to stand. After some discussion it was decided to ask Miss Bray to try and persuade Trilby Wells to accept nomination, and two other names were suggested as alternatives. Who can tell whether Bray ordered or persuaded Trilby? At any rate she agreed to be president.

Thus everything was prepared for the 1949 Easter Meet and Annual General Meeting.

Easter saw the Club hut full to overflowing and six members staying at the Pen-y-Gwryd. Evelyn Leech chaired the meeting until Trilby's election as president.

Under the three year rule, all officers were due for re-election but as there had been a change of president it was decided to elect a new secretary the following year and a treasurer the year after that. As it was, there were four new committee members.

Marjorie Heys-Jones gave the BMC report, which concluded: "The Council was taking an active part in opposing any schemes which would result in spoliation of the countryside, notably the proposed electrification scheme for the Snowdon area, and in this she was sure it would have our full support."

The last sentence is well worded. The electrification scheme in question included a new reservoir in Cwm Dyli, and a new and bigger power station below it. The *Alpine Journal* for May 1949 drew a vivid picture of huge spoil heaps,, dams and the desolation of the old lake shores in dry weather, concluding: "It is to be hoped that the powers which have just given us a Bill for 'preserving and enhancing natural beauty.' will not let these schemes materialise, at any rate in this unique bit of Welsh country." Fortunately they didn't. I can find no mention in Club records of this scheme to bury the hut in an artificial lake, but it must have been in the forefront of everybody's mind.

Two guests who became members during the meet were Ada Kindleysides (now Ada Shaw) and Gwen Moffat. Gwen describes her first meet in *Space Below my Feet* and the reaction when, halfway up Lliwedd, she said she couldn't come on the Alpine meet that summer because she was expecting a baby in July. Ada writes: "I well remember Gwen Moffat - no-one realised she was pregnant straight away. Of course in those days we climbed a lot on Lliwedd and invariably approached it via the pipeline - Gwen will tell you that the worst part of the day for her was the daily plod up the pipeline. Once on the rock (minus boots), she floated, curling her toes round the holds, and was a delight to watch."

Ada came climbing because she liked mountain walking and enjoyed the ridges and scrambling best. "What really spurred me on was reading Dorothy Pilley's *Climbing Days* - then I bought Barford's Penguin, *Climbing in Britain* which listed clubs and the names of their respective secretaries. Pilley had written about the formation of the Pinnacle Club and Barford included the Club in his list so I wrote to the secretary at the time, (Annette Wilson), and she wrote a very friendly letter back saying 'Come to a Meet!' So that was the beginning and that first meet was a marvellous experience.

"The people I climbed with on my first meet, apart from Evelyn, were Joan Cochrane and Phyl Raven, both of whom were very good climbers and great fun to be with. Joan still has the same twinkle in her eyes as she had back in 1949!"

On the Sunday Ada was one of the party which climbed Evelyn Leech's own climb on Crib-y-Ddisgyl, the Long Furrow, which, as the *Handbook* reports, 'They pronounced to be a fine climb.'

During the year eleven new members joined the Club. These, apart from Ada and Gwen, were P. Whinnarah, M. Garner, C.B.R. Cooper, J.M. Coates, P. McCall, D.B. Kidd, M.E. Oliver, D.N. Morin and E. Teague.

Miss Teague lived in Cambridge and was a member for only two years, and Miss McCall from Liverpool for four. Pat Whinnerah was a member for a little longer, but by 1952 she had married John Duerden and gone to live in Tanganyika. They were on an expedition to Kilimanjaro in 1951, and they discovered large deposits of sulphur as well as climbing the mountain. Diana Kidd lived in South London and was on the first Alpine meet after the war. She was a member for eight years. Madge Garner became Mrs Gillespie two years after joining the Club and rarely came to meets but obviously valued her connection with the Club and remained a member for 32 years. Joyce Coates was a member for 14 years and Maud Oliver for 19. Denise Morin (now Lady Evans) is Nea's daughter; she had already climbed many routes at home and in the Alps and was now old enough to join the Club, of which she is still very much a member. Catherine Cooper was at the Pen-y-Gwryd Hotel when she joined, and had climbed the popular routes on Idwal Slabs, Tryfan and Lliwedd. She soon moved to Anglesey, but spent many years in Glasgow before returning to Wales.

The highlight of the year was the Alpine meet, led by Evelyn Leech. Five members approached the meet via the High Level Route from Verbiers to Zermatt, and Evelyn noted the difference in the Pas de Chèvres since she first went over it on her way to Arolla: "Like so many other things, the Pas de Chèvres is not what it was in my young days: then one practised a neat trick with an axe on the holdless bit of the face; now one climbs up iron ladders, changing ladders half way, as it might be trains at Clapham Junction.

"The Hotel de la Poste was still there and had changed for the better since my first Pinnacle Meet in 1930, led by Dr. Corbett. I remembered it very well and I recognised the landmarks; I remember feeling suitably shy and hanging back from leading the Dent de Satarma; but what I remembered best, was Dr. Corbett's firmly benevolent leadership and her kindness to a bunch of greenhorns; and if my own party noticed an added gentleness - but perhaps they noticed none!

"Our three nights in the huts might have been thirty from the way that every touch of civilisation in Arolla charmed us: none of the High Level party had carried more than the legs of its pyjamas over the Rosa Blanche, and some not even these, but the legs were faithfully laid out on the beautiful beds by the bonne at the Poste and we were spared knowing how long she hunted, or what she thought!"

Members on all or part of the meet were Marie Grutter, Winifred Jackson, Diana Kidd, Dora King, Evelyn Leech, Jo Marples, Phyl Raven, Freda Rylatt, Horatia Winter, and

Annette Wilson. The *Handbook* account tells us: "No accommodation being available in Zermatt, the second week was spent largely between the Schönbiel Hut and the Fluhalp Hotel, and for the third week we had a most excellent flat in Zermatt. Climbs done included Rosa Blanche, Petite Dent de Veisivi, Pointe de Zinal, Matterhorn (Zmutt Ridge by some, Hörnli by others), Rimpfischhorn, traverse of Adler and Allalin Passes and Wellenkuppe."

On this very happy meet, guides were engaged for those who wanted them; Otto Taugwalder and Carl Biener on the second week, and Alexander and Otto Taugwalder for the third week. They guided the less experienced members and also led Dora King, Phyl Raven and Freda Rylatt on the Zmuttgrat on the third week while Evelyn, Horatia, Diana and Marie traversed the Hörnli and Italian ridges and spent a day in Italy. The parties reunited for the Rothorn, which was to be the climax of the meet, but morning brought new snow and a bitter wind:

"The only chance was to try for the Wellenkuppe if the weather cleared later, 'and that will be rather nasty,' said Otto placidly. Thus warned, a very select party prepared to follow Otto, Freda willing and Marie somewhat press-ganged. Later still a tic-tac message was brought in: 'Otto says it is not as cold on the glacier as he expected (what had he expected? we wondered, when we got there). Would Evelyn form another party and follow? I formed a party by the simple expedient of selecting Horatia from the shuddering remainder, and she, in spite of having left her winter pants in the valley, nobly followed me.

"On the glacier we re-roped, Freda and I together ... Every now and again the wind blew us to a standstill, at the same time picking up handfuls of hailstones and throwing them in our faces; however, the glacier was in an interesting condition ... The best things come to an end and so did the glacier, but when we rounded the last snowy corner we were suddenly out of the bitter wind and climbing on fine warm rock. Marie ... had a severely cut finger and I lost my way and found it again: altogether a good day. That night the meet broke up with an excellent party, wine and women in plenty and the guides who had climbed with us."

Freda and Horatia had another week in Zermatt, guided, and climbed Monte Rosa, Lyskamm and Castor, then returned to climb the Rothorngrat. Evelyn and Dora went over to Saas Fee for their last three days, 'and enormously enjoyed the Nordgrat of the Weissmies with an old friend, Heinrich Supersaxo, who remembered and asked after every Pinnacler he had previously met. It was sad hearing to him that so many had embraced husbands or domesticity or both ... 'and she was so good...'

"By traversing the Weissmies by the Zwischbergen Pass and sleeping at Almagel, Dora and I were able to spend our last day on the long traverse of the Portjengrat from Portje; and it seemed a fitting end to this 1949 Meet that we should follow in the footsteps of those other Pinnaclers in the Alps, the first to hold an Alpine Meet."

In September Phyl Raven was back in Wales with Joan Cochrane. The weather was rather wet, so they did traditional routes such as Amphitheatre Buttress; however, they finished by climbing the Cracks on Dinas Mot. Joan wrote in the Log Book: "Boots and/ or socks. Greasy. Jointly led." To the last remark Phyl added, "Nothing of the sort!" The following weekend was the Yorkshire meet, and autumn had come round again.

The Anniversary Meet was at the end of October this year. Many members who had been on the Alpine meet were there: Evelyn, Freda, Winifred, Diana, Dora. Also there were Joyce Coates, Catherine Cooper, Nea, Patricia McCall, Harriet Turner, Lucy Wood and Maude Oliver. The Saturday was spent on ever-favourite Lliwedd, half in the cloud, but Sunday dawned bright and sunny. Some went to Lliwedd again, Evelyn took a party of novices up the rocks to Lockwood's Chimney, and four people: Nea, Tony Moulam, Catherine Cooper and Freda Rylatt went to Dinas Cromlech to climb Flying Buttress. This lovely, easy climb with its sound rock and splendid situations was to be the scene of a totally inexplicable tragedy. Freda was leading, climbing easily as always, when she fell and was killed. The whole Club must have been in a state of complete shock. Ada Shaw writes: "I remember for some reason I couldn't get to that meet and what a shock it was to read of the accident in Monday's newspaper, particularly as about a fortnight earlier I'd had a weekend with her in Derbyshire (she lived in Hathersage). We climbed on Stanage both Saturday and Sunday and achieved lots of routes. I recall that on Sunday (to try and convince her friends and neighbours she was off to church) she met me at the appointed place dressed in a skirt and coat, and dodged behind a wall later to change into climbing clothes! I also climbed with Freda at the Whitsun Meet, 1949. I remember this well because I'd travelled by train overnight and had met up with Freda at Betws around 6 o'clock on the Saturday morning. I don't think I had a very clear idea how I was going to get from Betws to the hut but Freda was in no doubt - she intended to walk! I was a bit taken aback by this and managed to thumb a lift in a milk lorry for us, I think as far as Capel. However we got to the hut, had some breakfast and set off for Y Garn. Actually until I looked into this I hadn't realised that I only knew Freda for such a short time."

It is obvious that Freda went straight to people's hearts. In the *Journal* Annette Wilson wrote: "Freda's love of the hills, and her joy in climbing on them, was deep and real; it did to a quite unusual degree dominate her life, and she deliberately sacrificed her career to it by refusing, except for a very short time, to take up any post away from the north country ... Her strength and endurance were a legend in the Club and because she enjoyed this advantage she would always seek in some unobtrusive way to lighten the burden for weaker members of the party ... She was essentially unassuming, never boasting of her feats on rock or in any other field; ... We have lost a fine climber, a grand companion, and a true friend."

Evelyn Leech wrote a poem where words and metre combine to give the sense both of desolation and of triumph:

> The kind heart is still,
> The strong stride is done;
> The joy in the hill
> In the rain, in the sun
> But kindness and strength
> Her brief race run,
> Live on here the length
> Of our days in the sun.
> In our minds still engendering
> More joy, more befriending,
> So life without ending,
> Eternity won.

A subscription fund was started for a memorial to Freda, and her parents gave Freda's climbing equipment to the Club. In her own village of Hathersage they gave a memorial window to the Parish Church of St. Michael. It was dedicated on Sunday, May 25th, 1952, by the Lord Bishop of Derby, and the inscription reads:

"A.M.D.G. The gift of her parents in memory of a beloved daughter, Freda Isabel Rylatt, B.A., F.L.A., who lost her life on Dinas Cromlech October 30th, 1949."

A death more easy to accept was that of Mrs Daniell, an original member of the Club and better known as the novelist E.H. Young. She died on August 8th, 1949, and her executor, R.B. Henderson, was most anxious that the Pinnacle Club should have some fitting memorial. He visited the hut some time in the autumn, and wrote afterwards to Annette, as secretary: "I should indeed have been surprised if I had found anyone at the hut when I called. It was a lovely climbing day and of course everybody was out on the mountains.

"I am giving instructions to our local bookseller to send you all E.H. Young's books now in print. This is only 5 of her 12 - the others will follow as they become available.

"Mrs Daniell was a wonderful climber. I never saw anyone like her - unless it was Winthrop Young before he lost his leg..." "You may like to have this sonnet written by M.S. Gotch (Headmaster of the Bentley School Calne) who also climbed often with Mrs Daniell.

"As a novelist she reigns supreme".

The sonnet is entitled Quiet Now, and is a moving tribute. It is strange that two members about whom people were moved to write poetry should die within three months of each other.

There was much discussion at committee meetings as to what form a gift should take. A wireless was suggested but received strong opposition. In the end the memorial gift was comfortable mattresses for the bunks in the hut, and there is an inscription in the dormitory to this effect. Her books are still in the library, to be enjoyed by members.

Mrs Daniell had a great interest in education, which was the reason for her close association with the Bentley Grammar School, where she set up prizes for Greek history, philosophy and drama. R.B. Henderson deserves a mention. Born in 1880, and a former headmaster and Oxford don, he had been giving weekly talks to Bentley sixth-formers and was interviewed by them for the school magazine:

"Under cross-examination we found that Mr Henderson must have been very active in his youth ... He rowed both at school and at Oxford and got an oar for being head of the river. He liked riding, getting a taste for it when he had his own horse in World War I. He also mountaineered in Switzerland and was carried away once by an avalanche, ...

"He considers Salisbury Cathedral is the most beautiful piece of architecture he has ever seen. The greatest man and woman whom he has met are Vaughan Thomas and E.H. Young and the greatest cricketer very definitely W.G. Grace.

"... His remaining ambition now is to get on into the next world as early as possible.

"We take this opportunity of offering our warmest congratulations and best wishes for his new post of lecturer in charge of the teaching of Religious Knowledge in the University College of North Staffordshire."

Not everyone takes up a new challenge at the age of seventy.

CHAPTER 15

1950 - 1951

Menu cards - Marjorie Wood starts a tradition. Hut maintenance. Club badge. Climbs and meets. Sid and Jammy at ODG. Alpine routes. Pat Whinnerah on Kilimanjaro.

The Annual Dinner Meet at the Black Bull, Coniston, ushered out the old year and welcomed the New Year of 1950. Marjorie Wood was asked to provide the menu cards for the dinner and for the first time the Club had cards with beautiful, original paintings on each one. Ever since then, the Club's menu cards for each annual dinner have been its special pride and joy, and other artists have joined with Marjorie to supply the necessary pictures.

Biddy and Trilby Wells arranged the fun and games for New Year's Eve, and the days were spent climbing on Dow Crag. After the usual bite of lunch in the cave, small parties would detach themselves and disappear into the mist, to be seen no more until they arrived back at the hotel, though they heard of only one party embarking on the wrong climb. By lunch time on Sunday the mist had deteriorated into heavy rain and all parties arrived back very wet and dripped happily on the lounge carpet whilst they had tea before their journey home.

The Easter meet this year was based at Middle Row, Wasdale, where twelve members were staying, and was memorable mainly for the weather and the contrasting comforts of Mrs Naylor's cooking and good fires. Nea Morin, camping by Angle Tarn with her children, Ian and Denise, and accompanied by Evelyn Leech, tells a graphic tale of gales, storms and demolished tents, in *A Woman's Reach*. By the end of the weekend the tops were deep in snow. Peggy Wild was camping up Mosedale and appeared at intervals to thaw out by the fire. Those indefatigable walkers, the Wells sisters, Bray and Corbett, made a circuit of Scafell via Mickledore, Eskdale and Burnmoor on the Friday, and on Monday a party reached the top of Scafell Pike while the Morins battled back to Langdale through gales, hailstorms and deep snow.

By contrast, the annual meeting was a very calm affair. Trilby Wells took the Chair as President and Annette, concluding her secretary's report, thanked all who had helped her during her years of office and forgave all who had not. She was retiring after eleven years in the post and the handwriting in the minute book, which had remained the same for so long, changed to that of Marjorie Wood. The vote of thanks to Annette was accompanied by a book token in recognition of the key position she had held through so many difficult years.

Much of the meeting's business concerned huts. The Climbers' Club had written, offering the use of their Cornish hut, the Count House at Bosigran, to Pinnacle Club members. The offer was gratefully accepted and details were published in the *handbook*.

Meanwhile Evelyn Leech was trying hard to improve the facilities in the Club's own hut.

In the Hut Secretary's report, Evelyn described the arrangements she had made with the Power Station for the erection of a drying room annexe at the end of the hut, this cost being met by a donation of £5 each from Mrs Jeffrey and the hut secretary herself, as retiring president. Trilby Wells then said she would like to donate the same amount. Unfortunately the agreement of our landlords to this scheme and its implementation were two quite different matters. By the following year the meeting was talking of getting estimates, and the year after that it was decided that the expense was prohibitive. Contractors were unwilling to take on a job where all materials had to be manhandled across a primitive bridge and a few hundred feet up the fellside. This has been a problem ever since. Eventually a new coke stove was put in, to the left of the door, and was surrounded by drying racks.

The question of a Club badge was raised again this year and received a much more favourable response than it had in 1936. Enquiries were made as to cost and choice of materials, and designs were asked for. The one chosen was by Marjorie Wood.

Miss Jocelyn Moore was elected an associate member at this meet. She was at Lady Margaret Hall, Oxford, and wrote a letter to the committee, which was discussed at the May meeting, suggesting that the Oxford Women's Mountaineering Club be allowed to co-opt itself to the Pinnacle Club, as the men's section was debarring women from its meets except on very minor occasions. The committee had quite a lot of discussion about this: it would be good to have extra people using the hut, but on the other hand there would be no room for them at the larger Pinnacle Club meets. "It was thought that as their members would only be at Oxford for three years, they would want to keep their individual club and have their own meets, some of the Pinnacle members to attend when possible to give assistance... They would pay visitors' fees at the hut." Records do not indicate that they took advantage of this offer, and Jo Moore's relationship with the Club had hardly a chance to blossom; she was killed when the bivouac at the Col Eccles was destroyed by a rockfall in 1952. Eileen Healey wrote for the *Handbook*: "The club has lost one of its most brilliant young members with the death of Jo Moore ... That season she had already made a guideless ascent of the Brenva ridge and appeared to be all set for a first-rate season's climbing. Her climbs included the Drus, Grépon East Face and S.W. ridge of the Fou ... Her toughness and good nature made her the best of mountain companions."

Another member joining this year was Jean McCann, now Jean Brazier. She had been in the services during the war and writes: "At the age of 24 I was released from the Wrens and started being a student; to complete my liberation I started walking and hostelling in the Lake District. After some time I wanted to climb so joined a Mountaineering Association course in Langdale. One of the members was Maud Oliver, who was already a Pinnacle Club member. She put me in touch with Annette Wilson and in due course I was invited to a meet at Cwm Dyli. I vividly remember arriving there to find a blazing fire and a welcoming Annette."

Almost immediately after joining the club Jean moved to Bristol, to work for the BBC, "which made things difficult: not only was I far away but also I worked weekends and public holidays as nearly all programmes were 'live' in those days.

"The next summer I joined Cyril Machin's climbing party in the Cuillins and did some classic routes. Halfway up the Inaccessible Pinnacle a young man stopped to watch and (yes, you've guessed!) the following year we were married and settled in Bristol.

"Between 1953 when I took the twins (prenatally) up Galdhopiggen and 1972 when *they* took *me* up Romsdalshorn nothing at all happened except for a few lovely weekends when Joan Cochrane picked up a Bristol P.C. group (Annette Wilson, Dr Corbett, Sue Gibson and me) and took us up to meets in her Landrover."

Jean thinks she would win the booby prize for Pinnacle Club attendance, but more evident to me is her tenacity of purpose, only to be expected of Pinnacle Club mums. Now she is back in the hills though walking, not climbing, and went to the Dolomites a week after writing to me.

The first meet after the 1950 annual meeting was at the Club hut at Whitsun. Nea Morin and Denise were able to go down a week early and had six days' very pleasant climbing before the main meet arrived. Denise led Tryfan North Buttress and Milestone Direct and Nea led harder climbs; Tony Moulam joined them on one day to lead Scars Climb on the Terrace Wall. This Very Severe climb had been put up by Wilfred Noyce and Menlove Edwards, and as Tony Moulam wrote in the guidebook published six years later: "It has strong character of its own and is challenging in layout."

The 26th May saw the arrival of Evelyn Leech, who led M. Innes of the LSCC up The Cracks on Dinas Mot, but on the next day, when everyone else arrived, it poured with rain. This was a joint meet with the Ladies Scottish, who were met at Capel and taken to Ogwen by car, after which most of them walked over to the hut via Heather Terrace and the cairned track, getting soaked to the skin of the way. A few stalwarts climbed Milestone Direct. There were several camping parties and the hut was more than crowded, so Saturday evening was hilarious, with Scottish reels and dancing, sketches, songs and charades. Fortunately the weather improved on Sunday so several people did the Horseshoe while other parties climbed on Lliwedd, Tryfan and Crib Goch Buttress.

Just over a week later Nea was back to do two V.S. climbs on the East Buttress of Clogwyn Du'r Arddu; the entry in the log book reads: "Chimney Route & Sunset Crack, Cloggy. with A.J.J. Moulam leading."

A month later Nea and her family were in the Dauphiné, where she took them up the Pic Nord des Cavales, then she and Denise climbed the Barre des Ecrins, Denise's first 4,000 metre peak, and traversed the Cinéastes. Eileen Gregory was also in the Alps, in Chamonix, from where she climbed the Eveque-Nonne Traverse, the East Ridge of the Droites, the East Face of the Grépon, traversed the Drus and climbed the Moine arête of the Cardinal Verte.

I think other, more secretive people must have been in the Alps, for the August meet at the hut was a very small affair: Maude Oliver and a guest, Annette Wilson and Peggy Wild who had brought her friend, Doreen Tharby. "P. Wild had a strenuous time as usual, arriving at the Hut Thursday evening, doing the Horseshoe on Friday, up at 6 a.m. Saturday to cycle to Bangor to meet a friend and walking over from Ogwen via Tryfan N. ridge and the Bristly Ridge to the hut."

Joyce Taylor, who had taken over as the hut secretary, had a wet stay at the hut at the end of August and just missed seeing Evelyn Leech who had brought her baby girl, Antonia, for her first sample of hut life. Evelyn just wrote, "Evelyn Worsley Leech and Antonia, Sept. 4th-6th." It meant a lot to her, and at tea time on the Sunday of the November Meet she brought Antonia for her introduction to the Pinnacle Club.

The final meet of the year saw the New Year in on the Sunday night. Thick, wet snow fell and John Hirst, who was to have been one of the speakers, and Paddy were unable to get through. Fortunately Molly Fitzgibbon, the LAC representative, came to the rescue and gave an excellent speech. Lawson Cook and H.M. Kelly were the guests of honour, and Mabel Jeffrey showed colour slides of Scotland. Finally, everyone enjoyed the party games organised by the Wells sisters.

In February Eileen Gregory led a very wet meet in Edale. It was almost a non-event because the only two people to turn up were non-members: J. Parry and P. Bennell. Undaunted by the rain, Pat Bennell became a member and remained one till 1970. Eight years later the Club met her again under most delightful circumstances. She was now Mrs Patricia Holt and had a farm guest house near Slaidburn, where for two years running she tempted the Pinnacle Club Yorkshire meet away from Yorkshire into Lancashire - and never have we been more royally treated! Not only that, but she and her husband found time to come and join the members for the last few miles of a walk.

By contrast with the February meet, the Easter meet caught some members without their ice-axes - it poured with rain in the valleys and snowed on the tops as Ada Kindleysides, Eileen Pyatt, Peggy Wild and Doreen Tharby walked over from Llanberis on the Friday, and everyone was horrified when Peggy and Doreen insisted on pitching their tent in the deluge. Saturday was bright and sunny and Nea Morin led a party on the Crib Goch ridge; snow conditions made the descent from the col to Llydaw as interesting as any part of the route. Next day parties found blizzard conditions on the tops and on Monday, "even the campers came in at last."

The Annual General Meeting was held on the Saturday night. The membership of the Club was 111, of whom 48 were full members and the secretary pointed out that an important aim of the Club was to encourage members to lead climbs but that no associate members had qualified for full membership since 1946. This meant there was often a shortage of leaders on meets, and she stressed the importance of new, young members becoming leaders. During the librarian's report she suggested that the Club should stock up with all the new climbing guides.

The BMC report contained two matters of historical interest: it was the year of the Festival of Britain and climbers were asked to provide hospitality to visiting climbers if required and, secondly, concern was felt over the proposed railway up the Matterhorn (fortunately still in the future)!

The seventh Pinnacle Club *Journal* had been published in 1950, edited by Mrs Bryan. Reviews were good, and Evelyn Leech's "Snowdonia - my Measuring Stick" was particularly liked. Copies of the *Journal* were sent to the parents of those mentioned in obituaries: D. Gray, N. Forsyth and F. Rylatt.

The Karabiner Club had acquired a hut near Coniston village and wrote suggesting a reciprocal arrangement. "It was decided to agree to this arrangement but to admit women members only to our hut," read the minutes.

This year Denise Morin was elected a full member of the Club. One of the members joining during the year was Annis Donnison, who married and became Annis Flew a few years later. A good climber, she soon became a full member and an efficient hut secretary who has had many family holidays at the hut. I called in at Cwm Dyli with my family one summer in the 1970s and my boys, who were about the same age, were quite overawed by her high-powered, intellectual and charming ménage. Annis said mildly that girls developed faster than boys at that age.

Joyce Taylor and Winifred stayed on after the meet and were joined by two friends, Chris Woods and Moggy Dew. Each was to join the Club within the next few years, but on this occasion they had a very snowy time and no climbing at all. I think it was Joyce who came for a day in the middle of April and climbed on Teryn Bluffs with Tony Moulam. "Second ascent" is written by one entry, but there is no signature. Joyce came for a few more days at the end of May, and another visitor was the London University Mountaineering Club.

In June the committee had agreed that the hut could be used by a group of Rangers from the Girl Guides Association. They came from all parts of England and were between the ages of 16 and 21. The correspondence had been with Miss J.M. Cobham, Chairman of the Devon Training Company of Girl Guides, and she herself was a rock climber and former member of the Club (1934-6). Their first exploit was a night ascent of Snowdon, starting at 1 a.m., presumably on the eve of their arrival, so they fully justified their title of "English Land Ranger Adventure Camp". This set the tone for a good fortnight's activities.

Following closely on their heels came Dorothy Pilley Richards and her husband on one of their all too brief visits from the U.S.A. Pilley wrote, "Arrived from Shropshire.

"July 12: Horseshoe of Snowdon.

13: To Beddgelert - ten mile walk in the rain.

14: Glyders and down to Ogwen.

15: Yr Aran down to Beddgelert.

16: Milestone Ordinary, North Arête Tryfan.

17: Away over Siabod."

- All good, energetic stuff by the future author (*Fell and Rock Journal* 1953) of "Middle Alps for Middle Years."

Meanwhile Sid and Jammy Cross had taken over the Old Dungeon Ghyll Hotel in Langdale, and the Pinnacle Club Whitsuntide meet was held there. Blessed with good weather and the famous hospitality, it was the foretaste of a long and happy relationship.

Whitsun may have been sunny, but August Bank Holiday was wet, and in the hut were a typical, happy-go-lucky group: "An attempt was made to find Lockwood's Chimney during a lull in the afternoon, but after a few false starts this was abandoned in favour of dinner."

Luckier people were in the Alps, in fact Eileen Gregory was in the happy position of going to the Alps twice a year at this time: once for skiing and once for climbing. In August she climbed the Aiguille de Roc, the Pélerins, the Fou, and the Mont Blanc traverse. Dora King climbed several good routes in the Zermatt area, I think with guides, and Nea Morin visited three different centres, the first of them with her family, Denise and Ian. Denise had had her appendix out less than three weeks previously, so was not expecting to climb, but she managed two routes on the Engelhörner, followed by the Monch and Jungfrau.

From here Nea went on to the Chamonix valley with Tony Moulam, where they climbed the Aiguilles Dorées and the Grépon. They had it to themselves, but Nea said the Aiguille de Roc looked like a Samivel illustration, festooned with climbers - perhaps one of them was Eileen Gregory!

Nea's final centre was Briançon, whence she climbed four routes with friends in the Alpine Club. Throughout her season she led or shared the lead; she was sad to have no cordées feminines but relished, "the unusual pleasure of a light rucksack and a far lighter burden of responsibility on the climbs."

Gwen Moffat was also in the Alps, with Vicki Russenberge, having left Sheena with her parents. Gwen writes: "I did the Marinelli Couloir then with him but nothing else in the Valais except being benighted on the Rothorn and bullied up only the top third of the E. face of the Strahlhorn (first ascent and not worth it. No wonder it had been left by everyone else).

But we did go to the Civetta in the same season and did numbered ascents of the Via Andrich on the Torre Venezia, the Via Tissi on the Torre Trieste, and the only route (at least then) on the Campanile di Brabante. All first feminine ascents - and all, highly dramatised, in *Space*."

Another member's exploits were being highly dramatised in the *News Chronicle*, whose reporter truly gave of his best: "It lives in legends of Africa and Abyssinia, in the lands of the Wanagoli and Wasambari - the treasure of Kilimanjaro.

"Kilimanjaro . . . towering 19,000 feet, the highest mountain in Africa, an extinct volcano whose glaciers send down a thousand rills which combine to form the Pangani river."

After further build-up we learn that five Sheffield University graduates climbed Kilimanjaro and found enormous deposits of sulphur. Among their number was P.C. member Patricia Whinnerah, who had married John Duerden of the Climbers' Club and gone out to Kongwa, in Tanganyika, where he worked as an entomologist. For their vacation they joined the group climbing and exploring Kilimanjaro, making two journeys to the top because their porters refused to carry equipment up the last 4,000 feet, and doing three-hour surveys. The ridge of sulphur was formed on the middle crater, "about 200 ft down inside the mountain." It must have been exciting, taking part in this expedition. Sadly members never heard of it first hand, for Mrs Duerden lost touch with the Club and resigned her membership a few years later.

Back in England, September gave perfect weather for the Yorkshire meet, held at Austwick, but the November meet at Cwm Dyli was not so lucky - especially disappointing as Pilley had made a special effort to attend before returning to the United States.

The Annual Dinner was held in Wales for the first time since the war. Marjorie Wood led it and wrote: "Two of our guests responded nobly to our last minute requests for speakers, Miss Welchman of the Ladies' Alpine Club and Mrs Walker of the M.A.M., making excellent speeches in spite of a few hours' notice, while Mrs Leech helped the Club out of a difficulty after G. Moffat wired to say she could not attend to propose the health of the guests and kindred clubs. For the first time at a dinner all the speeches were made by women."

I think it was the first and fortunately the only time that every single speaker bar the president, had to be replaced at short notice, though there are good tales to come of speakers falling by the wayside in subsequent years.

CHAPTER 16

1952. Gwen Moffat and Morins at the hut. Nea Morin President. An influx of new members. Alpine Climbing Group. Girl Guide Association. London Section. Alpine routes.

As spring came, in 1952, Gwen Moffat became homesick for the mountains. She and Sheena had wintered in Brighton with her parents and she had been working at the theatre there. During the winter, she had also given her first radio broadcast. Now, as she writes in *Space Below my Feet*:

"I packed our bags and with Sheena, my radio, a cot and mountains of luggage, we left Brighton one glorious morning and headed north ... We moved into the Pinnacle Club hut just before Easter. I had very little money and no food, but once there was a roof over Sheena's head, the minor anxiety of what was to happen to us evaporated."

The Club's official Easter meet this year was in the Lake District, but just before Easter Gwen was joined by the Morin family: Nea, Denise and Ian. The log book makes fascinating reading:

"April 11th, 52. N.E. Morin. Chasm and Needle's Eye on Glyder Fach. D.N. Morin & G. Sutton: Central Route on Cyrn Las.

"April 12th. N.E. Morin Grooved Arête, Belle Vue Bastion, Gashed Crag on Tryfan. D.N. Morin and G. Sutton: Munich Climb and Long Chimney on Tryfan.

"April 13th. N.E. Morin, Crib Goch Buttress and Gambit on Crib y Ddysgyl. D.N. Morin with Ian McNaught-Davis - Main Wall on Cyrn Las. With Dick Viney attempt Fallen Block Crack on Crib y Ddysgyl. Very wet and we come down after many gyrations.

"April 14th. With Geoff Sutton attempted Curving Crack on Cloggy. Wet. Rescue of I McNaught-Davis."

I don't know whether Ian is aware that our log book records the errors of his youth!

The next day Patrick Thompson looked after Sheena while Gwen and Denise soloed Milestone Direct and did Wall Climb, and on the 16th Gwen climbed with Charles Marriott, Denise's Godfather, on Lliwedd. On Good Friday evening Pat baby-sat for Gwen once more while she went up to the Pen-y-Gwryd for a drink, and she met Johnnie Lees, whom she subsequently married and divorced. She described her first impression of him as "a tall and talkative man with legs like a kangaroo." Years later I first met him when I went on a course in mountain rescue and self-rescue techniques. He was in charge of the course and I wondered whether to mention Gwen or not, but he talked quite a lot about her when he knew I was from the Pinnacle Club.

Johnnie saw Gwen back to the hut before walking back to his tent in upper Cwm Glas and the following day he collected her to go climbing in the Pass.

Meanwhile Denise had been climbing with Charles Marriott, and had also done the Direct Route on Dinas Mot and Nea on the Grochan with Johnnie Lees. An April 23rd Gwen had an interesting ascent of Lockwood's Chimney with Pat Thompson and wrote: "Because of bathing the baby etc. and trying to get the water to run, we did not leave the

Gwen Moffat on Milestone Superdirect.
Photo: S.R.G. Bray.

hut until 8.10 p.m. It was Pat's first climb. I reckoned we only needed light as far as the chimney which is always dark anyway. We managed as far as the crack below the chimney - which was wet and slimy and Pat didn't like it, so abseiled and found a variation on the right which is a lot wetter and slimier. It was dark by now. We did the chimney by torchlight, spending an hour on it - a very interesting experience. Came out on top feeling very like speleologists." Apparently it didn't put him off climbing, for Margaret Darvall met Pat Thompson later on an M.A. course.

It looks as though Denise left the hut after April 23rd, and Gwen hitched with Sheena to various local climbing areas. On April 27th she climbed Trilon on Carreg Wastad with Geoff Roberts and Bill Trench. This VS climb had been put up four years earlier and became very popular. At the beginning of May Gwen mentions several climbs, some with Johnnie, and soon after that she became warden of a youth hostel, so her climbs are not recorded in the log book.

Meanwhile the Pinnacle Club had held a very successful Easter meet at Gateside, Coniston, where Bryan and Pirie had a new guest house. Nea Morin was elected president and some of the items discussed at the meeting were the raising of the annual subscription to fifteen shillings, further drying facilities at the hut (a sectional hut was suggested for a drying room), and new bunk canvases. These latter were being supplied free by the Climbers' Club and it was hoped they would be fixed by Whitsuntide.

On the Sunday the new committee met for the first time and a memorial to Freda Rylatt was discussed. Mattresses had been bought to supplement those given in memory of Mrs Daniell, but something special to remember Freda was needed. This matter was finally settled in 1955 and Mr Kirby of Duffryn, who had already made a bookcase, completed the memorial by making a seat which bears her name.

Nineteen new members joined the Pinnacle Club during the year. This was an enormous influx, but many were members for less than ten years. Ruth Ruck joined for nine years, for three of which she was hut secretary, as she lived close by near Beddgelert. She and her family had come from a suburban environment to take on a Welsh farm, and she wrote a delightful book about it, *Place of Stones*. She donated a copy to the club library. Mrs Beryl Work also lived in Beddgelert; she was assistant hut secretary to Ruth Ruck, but left the Club in 1960. Jessie Byrom lived in Cheshire and had been climbing and walking for many years before she joined the Club. She remained a member till her death in 1982. Dr Sheila Allison is now Dr Hennebry. She moved from the north east to Middlesex on her marriage and was rarely able to attend meets, but has kept an interest in the Club.

Margaret Thomas, now Maggie Turner, climbed with the Bangor Club and also was one of the group who eventually founded the Chester Mountaineering Club. She writes: "I cannot remember how I first came in contact with the Pinnacle Club. I do remember why. The male section of the Bangor Club was becoming somewhat chauvinistic and I felt the need to first bring more women into that club and begin leading myself, then I felt the need to join a club with a high reputation which did not depend on men!"

She remembers her first meet, "It was very wet. Jack Longland appeared and persuaded a group to do Lockwood's Chimney."

Peggy Wild's friend, Doreen Tharby, had already become part of Club history with her camping and walking exploits and she continued to take a full part in Club activities for many years, mainly because of her friendship with Peggy.

Maria Rinetta Leggett - Rie to her friends - was a Dutch girl who came to England during the war and had been married to a member of the British forces. She only took up climbing when she found herself alone in London and needing to make new friends and a life for herself. She had a very good job at the Dutch Embassy, translating, as she was fluent in English.

Denise Wilson (née Shortall), who gave me this information, says Rie helped her parents financially as they were retired and dependent on her to quite an extent - "Which is why we never got to New Zealand (She and I were going to emigrate, but her parents needed her contribution). She climbed mainly with a group from London."

Rie proposed herself modestly as an associate member then proceeded to enumerate such routes as the Grépon and Requin in the Alps and leads such as Avalanche, Red Wall and Tennis Shoe in Wales. Certainly she was only on the threshold of her climbing career: she was to lead great Alpine routes, marry a climber and have two children. Fortunately there was no foreknowledge of her tragic illness and death to mar the fruitful, happy years ahead of her. When she joined the Club she was sharing a flat with Joyce Hughes, who became a member at the same time with almost an identical application form. Joyce has written the following account:

"My interest in climbing developed as a result of my move from Derbyshire to London in 1950, when I was introduced to a group of people calling itself the BRMC. Their training ground was the sandstone outcrops, Harrison's Rocks, High Rocks and the rest, in Sussex; it was a time when new climbs were being done, and it was there that I met Nea and Denise Morin, and learned from them about the Pinnacle Club.

"In the early fifties petrol was still rationed and few people had transport of any kind, although motor cycles were beginning to be used. Trips to Wales and the mountains were therefore not easily come by. Looking at diaries I realise that my period of intense interest in climbing lasted a comparatively short time, over the years 1950 to 1955, when I married and developed other interests. During this time I had two holidays in Skye and four trips to the Alps, two, privately organised, to Chamonix, where we attempted some of the then popular routes, the traverse of the Grépon and the Meyer-Dibona route on the Requin among them (1952).

"In 1951 I met Rie Leggett, as she then was, at Harrison's Rocks. Camping was not restricted in those days, and in summer it was usual to sleep out or camp in the bracken on top of the rocks (we used to complain about being kept awake by the nightingales). There was a favourite picnic spot under the overhang at the foot of Moonlight Arête, and I remember being regaled there with strawberries and yoghurt by John Hammond, who was later to die on Mount Cook. As always happens in retrospect, summers at Harrison's were always fine and warm.

"It was Rie who was the motivator of the two of us as an all female rope. We later shared a flat and planned together a number of weekends and holidays in which we ticked off our fairly modest ambitions in the way of Welsh climbs. We also had a memorable holiday in Skye, where we insisted that a male acquaintance who joined us should occupy middle position on the rope. Since the rope was a ninety-foot over-weight nylon, (itself a rarity in those days) this presented some problems, and we had a fairly epic descent of the Inaccessible Pinnacle, where the shortness of the rope was quite a handicap.

"I think it was either Nea or one of her brothers who first suggested that we should join the Pinnacle Club, as a natural consequence of our interest in all-female climbing.

"I rather dropped out of Club activities after 1955 but Rie remained active, pairing up with Denise Wilson and becoming a member of the Alpine Climbing Group, one of its first women members."

I have left Suzanne Long until last because she has been intimately connected with the Club ever since she joined and is a tremendous source of information and anecdote. She has served four periods as a committee member, has been secretary, dinner organiser, and, for the last ten years, auditor of the accounts. She is no less active on meets at home and abroad, though whatever the situation she always looks neat and elegant. She merited the following paragraph in Evelyn Leech's amusing article for the 1958 Journal, 'Such Stuff'.

> Suzanne turned up the other night ... literally turned up, for she was hanging upside down with her foot wedged, addressing a young man in that gentlest of voices, and in a sentence rich in the letter R. Her foot being wedged, meant that her hands were virtually free for other work, so she was tucking in loose strands of hair and using a lipstick, which, when it dropped at my feet, I noticed was one of those two-tone jobs, one being labelled "Mountain Magic" and the other "Discretion", and I remember thinking 'grooming may be important, but surely not when one's upside down.'

Sue writes the following account: "It was in 1947, on a walking holiday in North Wales, a difficult time for me (Sue's husband had been killed in action a year after their marriage), that I discovered the mountains and climbing. At that time life had little meaning to someone struggling to pick up the threads as a civilian and a widow; trying to find an aim for a lost future.

"The end of our walking brought us to Idwal Cottage, passing Tryfan in the evening light with the sun red over Adam and Eve. The cottage was full of the climbing fraternity. My reaction was immediate - I wanted to climb.

"But how!

"Next year my friend and I based ourselves at Idwal and were taken climbing on Rowan Tree and Ivy Chimney on Tryfan, fortunately by some lads with good climbing technique. During this holiday we discovered P-y-G and returned there the following year. Meanwhile I had discovered Dorothy Pilley's *Climbing Days* and Barford's *Climbing in Britain*. There I read of the Pinnacle Club, the then secretary's address being in Bath. Right on my doorstep, but I had nothing to offer.

"It so happened that P-y-G had mislaid our booking and we were bedded out next door with the Lockwoods. How fortunate for me. There I heard all about the formation of the Club, Mrs Lockwood being one of the early members. Mr Lockwood, who incidentally was the architect of the Power Station, discovered Lockwood's Chimney and was full of anecdotes of wide hips getting stuck at the chock stone. He spoke of his failure to have Sally Lockwood accepted as a member, despite her having successfully scaled the chimney - not surprising really, as Sally was a dog.

"From this source I was directed to the hut in Cwm Dyli and on investigation met Nea, who was leading a Girl Guide group. By this time Annette, the secretary, had moved to Bristol and with Nea's encouragement I contacted her. Thus commenced a very happy association. We both worked in the city, I had transport and we would slough off our workaday blues on the first leg of our journey to Wales or the Lakes.

"On these journeys I was regaled with much information as to the exploits and characters of the older members and can still remember the feeling of awe when meeting Dorothy Pilley for the first time at a November meet; also amusement at a discussion overheard between her and Dorothy Arning over petrol expenses, when Pilley said, "I'll give you a cheque." and Arning replied: "Oh, no, I'll have cash if you please!"

"I never knew Annette in her leading days, but she was an extremely neat climber, a tireless walker, and the fastest person I know downhill - she bounced down like a rubber ball.

"In those days we always came to dinner meets in Joan Cochrane's Landrover. We would collect Dr Corbett, who always sat in front with Joan and Annette, while every so often the back would be filled with myself, Jean Brazier, my friend Peggy, and quite likely others picked up on route: Esmé Speakman from Gloucester and Evelyn Leech if she had been visiting in Hereford. Dr Corbett was the most imperturbable passenger - unlike the rest of us it was never necessary to stop for her for any reason, and on one never to be forgotten occasion when she gave Joan the O.K. at a crossroads and a bus missed us by a tissue paper distance, while we wilted she murmured gently: "What a naughty bus!" - shades of her heyday as a demon driver!

"Another deathless memory I have of her at the 'Sun' in Coniston, at dinner sharing her meal, one forkful for her and one for 'Lady', a golden retriever.

"During the 1950s we were not faced with the problem of queueing to climb and the Milestone Buttress on Tryfan was a popular start, to continue onto the East Face climbs. Sometimes we would walk from the hut, up the miner's track to the East Face routes and Idwal. Craig yr Ysfa and Lliwedd were also very popular, in fact my first official climb with the club was on Ridge Route on Lliwedd when Dora King led Annette and me. As we relaxed on top Dora turned to me and said, "My name's Dora." I felt at that moment that I had passed muster and was acceptable.

"To a lesser degree we did the odd climb in the Llanberis Pass, where even then you might have to wait for a climb, and the Parson's Nose was popular as an alternative way up Snowdon."

The hut was well used during the year, with a large party of Rangers and Guiders coming again in June, with Nea Morin and Beryl Jennings helping to lead the climbs. This was followed by a large Pinnacle Club meet at the beginning of August at which Sue Long was one of seven new members elected. At the same meet Ada Kindleysides, "who had led two novices up two climbs during the weekend," was elected a full member.

Eileen Pyatt was keen to form a London Section of the Club and asked committee approval for a small amount of money from Club funds to cover postage. This was readily agreed to by the committee members present, who were Dora King, Ada Kindleysides, Eileen Pyatt and Annette Wilson. The next committee meeting was held at the Yorkshire meet in September, when the committee members present were Trilby and Biddy Wells, Dr Corbett and Marjorie Wood. They were worried at the thought of a London section, in case it tended to split the Club; they also considered that Club funds should not be used in this connection and that this was a matter to be brought up at the annual general meeting. All ended amicably however and the 1953 *handbook* contained the following announcement:

"London members.

"An active group had recently been formed in London to organise walks and visits to local sandstone outcrops. Any member of the Club who wishes to receive the circulars, which also give details of lectures, etc., in London, may be obtained from the organiser (Miss E. Pyatt)."

This section flourished during Eileen's active years with the Club but was not continued afterwards.

This year considerable difficulty was experienced in finding a venue for the annual dinner. Even London was seriously considered, though few people wanted to hold the dinner away from the mountains. In the end it was postponed until February, 1953 and held in the Old Dungeon Ghyll with a record number attending. The November meet of 1952 was also a record in the number attending, with 24 squashed into the hut in rather cold, wet weather. Pilley, Arning and Marie Grutter were there and it was Shirley Bull's first meet. The hut had been well used during the autumn by both climbers and family parties; A.C. Wood, now Mrs Roberts, came with her husband and two young children. One of their expeditions was up Snowdon, and, "On the return D. Roberts felt he had emulated Atlas," a feeling not unknown to other parents of tired families.

After the November meet, however, the hut remained empty until the following March.

There are few records of Alpine activities in 1952. Denise Morin had done a number of climbs with French friends, including a traverse of the Meije; Pilley produced a fine crop of peaks, passes and traverses; and Eileen Gregory's peaks included the Chardonnet, Grépon and Mummery-Ravanel.

CHAPTER 17

1953. Bunny Bull meets the Great Ones. Morin family climbs. Alpine Climbing Group. Gwen Moffat first woman guide. Everest climbed.

Although the Pinnacle Club had to wait till February for its 1953 New Year celebrations, the comfort and hospitality provided at the Old Dungeon Ghyll made the delay worthwhile, and the occasion was made memorable by John Hirst and Harry Spilsbury's varied repertoire of humorous songs. They sang a few to enliven the dinner speeches and were persuaded to continue afterwards – the highlight of the meet. The weather was fine and warm enough for members to enjoy climbs on Pavey Ark and Bowfell Buttress.

By contrast, the conditions at Easter were Alpine and misty and the log book reports that: "N.E. Morin, S. Long, S. Kelly thought they did Bristly Ridge (in descent) and meant to keep the precipices on their left but were led astray by A.B. Hargreaves who bounced before them like a parched pea down a bottomless gully."

When tackled about this thirty years later, A.B. remembered the occasion well. He said it was a perfectly good route in summer but the snow had made the bottom section dangerous so they had to climb all the way up again. Here his conscience smote him because of the extra energy they had used up, and he fed them all with chocolate to keep them going. Alas, the ungrateful Pinnacle Club recorded the gully but not the chocolate! At the annual meeting the subscription was raised to 15/– to help pay for the *Journal* and the treasurer proposed that the ten remaining original members should be honoured by being elected Honorary Members of the Club. This was carried unanimously.

There was news of Harrison's Rocks in the BMC report: the possibility of leasing the area had been explored but the practical difficulties of access had not been settled and a proposal to start pig–rearing below the Rocks was being resisted vigorously.

There were many applications for membership and a limit of 150 Club members was considered but the decision deferred. However, it was agreed that all applicants must attend at least two meets before their nomination could be considered.

It was high time there was some ruling on this; earlier in the year two applicants, having been told they could not become members without attending a meet, had come to the hut for a night and left after breakfast. They had been informed that they would not be elected till they had climbed with the Club, and in fact they never joined. Perhaps all they wanted was cheap accommodation in Wales.

The new conditions of membership meant that only one person qualified during the ensuing year – and even she should have joined the Club in 1952. Shirley Bull had been brought to the November meet 1952 by Sheila Allison, and writes: "When it was torrenting with rain on the Sunday, my proposer and I went off to do the Glyders only to find on our return that the committee had met early and gone home so my application had to wait 'til '53!"

Shirley Bull, 'Bunny' to members, writes that she will never forget her first meet: "Dr

Arning was giving a lift to Sheila Allison and me and she drove us up on Friday – an experience in itself. The drive was punctuated with little incidents like, 'Oh my god – it's a dual carriageway,' as she shot up the wrong side, slammed into reverse and backed down the fast lane to take the other side. There was also the traffic light where she got out and jumped about in the road saying she had cramp. However the most abiding memory is that she drove with the sunshine roof open. Sitting in the back, by the time we were snaking up the A5 into Wales in the dark and the drizzle, I was numbed in brain and body. At the hut the fire was already crackling in the grate and as I thawed out Sheila informed me of the names of people in the photographs round the fireplace. Shortly we went upstairs where some old ladies (probably younger than I am now!) were settling to their various comforts, hotties, bed socks and a bottle of rum (surprises!). "Hallo Arning."

"Hallo Evelyn, Hallo Dorothy."

"I looked at the portly figure owning the latter name and rushed downstairs to look at the photo by the fire. The resemblance was nil but somehow I knew – that back upstairs I was is the presence of the great Dorothy Pilley whose exploits had already become known to me and whose book I was still trying to obtain. A further trip downstairs confirmed that the other was another familiar name to me – Evelyn Lowe (by then Leech). They were friendly to the aspirant, but at 22 in those days one felt a mere youngster and I unpacked my kit in awed silence.

"Shortly afterwards there was another arrival with greetings and kisses (more surprises) all round. Further trips to the photos confirmed that Nea Morin was now in our midst. That night I hardly slept with excitement and the incredible snoring duet which emanated from the two Dorothys with a volume which filled the hut and seemed to vibrate my very bunk.

"It could have been on this first Anniversary Meet that a group of us did the Milestone Direct. Nea led up first; she danced prettily up the first pitch. 'It must be dead easy,' thought I, 'After all she has a daughter who is also a student, so she must be old enough to be my mother; even though she was a brilliant climber in her day, that day must have long since passed. When it came to my turn my tricounis slithered all over the polished rock, breathless pantings and struggling followed. When eventually I stood beside Nea I had a totally different view. Nea climbing was an aesthetic experience in itself.

"I think it was on this meet that I first met Sue Gibson (Long) with her intelligent dachshund Otto. It was certainly pouring with rain but then it was always raining on meets, it seemed to me! Before bed he had to go outside. The tip of his pointed nose went out; he returned. "Out," said Sue. Otto reversed putting the necessary portion only outside the porch he lifted his leg and returned. Club members, unable to copy, were jealous.

"I couldn't go on any other meets that year as I was training for the European Rowing Championships but the following November I got my Associate membership.

"On the Anniversary Meets one usually met Annette Wilson. As an early riser I always got up first and made tea which enabled one to start the whole hut moving. Annette slept downstairs and as soon as she had her tea she used to tease the fire into life and so rekindle that special atmosphere one always feels at Cwm Dyli. I remember on one occasion when it had rained continuously that it was quite a feat to get to Annette sleeping under the window because the water rising through the stone floor created a lake between us. Annette too, like Evelyn, was a good liaison with the natives. To me the hut seems strangely isolated now when it has lost the two inhabited houses and the constant throb of activity, human as well as engine, from the power station."

Bunny says she did not come from a climbing background and she terrified her mother by climbing rocks at the seaside. As a teenager she read any mountain literature she could lay hands on, and as soon as she reached university she joined the mountaineering club. Here she learnt more about the Pinnacle Club, which she had first heard of in Colin Kirkus' *Lets Go Climbing*, and Sheila Allison took her along. Getting to meets for weekends was almost impossible without a car or extra time off. She writes: "I got my first car in 1955 and it revolutionised things for me – though the drive from the south was 250 miles and it took me 6–7 hours of hard driving. I think 1955 was also the year of my first vibrams – not that they were much help as it was always wet. Heather still has as one of her earliest memories the sight of the sparks which flew from my tricounis as we descended in the dark. I remember this experience from earlier as we returned along the deserted A5 in the dark – the thoughts of a deserted A5 now!

Heather Monie joined the club in 1959. Bunny met her when she was just going skiing and they made a pact that Bunny would take her climbing and Heather would take Bunny skiing.

Even when Bunny found it hard to attend weekend meets, she was able to join the walks arranged for London members. She writes: "It was here that I first met Bray who must have been nearing 80, yet she and her unlikely poodle dog nearly walked the boots off the rest of us. Heather remembers driving through Shere very early one January morning with snow deep on the ground – and Bray's bedroom window was flung wide open. It was about this time that Heather and I were driving down to the Hut in sloshing rain when we met Bray in a skirt, plastic mac and what looked like lacrosse boots. Unforgettable was the righteous indignation with which she rejected our offer of a lift, 'I'm going for a walk!'

"Corbett was of a gentler mould. She stayed in hotels at the end of her life when she came up with the Bristol contingent in Joan Cochrane's landrover. They found her always cheerful, always grateful, always looking on the best side of things. Once on a Yorkshire meet I was objecting to a large dog which pestered me at breakfast but Corbett called out, 'Here boy, come and worry me.' She then fed alternate mouthfuls – on the same fork – one to the dog then one to herself." (Obviously her usual procedure, and strange in a doctor!)

Bunny herself is known for her fast cars, her fine photography, and her recently published guide to the Black Cuillin Ridge. She writes: "I do not think there is much to tell about the *Black Cuillin Ridge – Scrambler's Guide*. When Heather and I first went there we found a lack of information about the ridge apart from the pure rock climbing. Bit by bit we explored what could be done and built up a note book. It is much wider and also more idiosyncratic than that which was sent for publication but we felt there was a need for a guide which would serve as an introduction to the non–rock–climber. I do not accept the criticism in *Climber* that it was not very adventurous as it dealt only with the usual routes. If you know that, you don't need it. Seeing the explosion which is occurring in the use of mountain areas, I was in two minds whether to do it in case I caused further ravages, but it was pointed out to me that this would happen anyway. Hence I went ahead with the *Scrambler's Guide* and was very 'chuffed' to have it published by the S.M.C. – and written by a woman! – when one thinks of that chauvinistic male preserve."

Going back to the Easter meet 1953, April 10th has an entry to pinpoint the attitude of those who had suffered a week of the weather conditions: "Caernarvon. The Majestic.

'My Wife's Lodger', 'Submarine Base'. Warm and dry for 1/9!"

This was the one rest day Nea and Denise Morin allowed themselves in a fortnight's climbing which included hard routes despite the weather. On their final day they led through on Longland's route on Cloggy, finishing in a snowstorm. N. Lawton was in a second party which had to abseil off.

The mother–daughter team of the Morins had reached full strength. Nea had translated Maurice Herzog's *Annapurna* in collaboration with Janet Adam Smith thus earning the money for an Alpine season in 1953 and, in her book, she has written a full account of their very successful season. Their routes included the traverse of the Vajolet Towers, Kleine Zinne Nordwand, First Sella Tower; Jägigrat, Weissmies ascending by the North Ridge and descending the West Face, Matterhorn with Nea's 17–year–old son Ian, who also joined her for the Rothorngrat and a trip to Arolla by the Col d'Herens. In celebration of *Annapurna*, Nea and Janet Adam Smith hired a guide, Bernard Perren, and climbed the Schalligrat to the summit of the Weisshorn, descending by the East Ridge.

Other Pinnacle Club members in the Alps were Dora King doing the High Level Route from Fionnay to Zinal and climbing peaks on the way, Dorothy Pilley Richards with her usual crop of routes including the Zumsteinspitze–Dufourspitz of Monte Rosa, Eileen Gregory who traversed the Meije before going to the Chamonix area for routes including the Requin, the East Ridge of the Plan and West Face of Pointe Albert.

Although she was a founder member of the recently formed Alpine Climbing Group, Gwen Moffat was unable to go to the Alps this year. Members of the ACG had to be under 40, climb routes T.D. and above in the Alps, and were therefore a very select group. Other women members also of the Pinnacle Club were Eileen Healey, Denise Morin and Nancy Smith. Nancy later left the Group; she was to become a Pinnacle Club member in 1960. This year Gwen was awarded the British Mountaineering Council Guides Certificates, both Grade 2 for mountaineering and Grade 1 for rock climbing of a higher standard, and became the first woman Guide.

The hut at Cwm Dyli was well used during the year. Maud Godward was there at the beginning of June and wrote: "June 2nd, 2.30 a.m. received news, Everest climbed Friday, May 30th." The weather was cold and wet, so she and her companion celebrated by climbing Lockwood's Chimney and Spiral Stairs.

Nea Morin, Evelyn and Antonia Leech arrived early for the November Anniversary Meet, "for a grand tidy up. – bought new American cloth for the table and for upstairs – new washing bowl and a splendid doormat and hammer." The weather for the meet proved the accuracy of Bunny Bull's generalisation by being 'terribly wet'.

Of interest is the Oxford University Women's Mountaineering Club meet on December 5th–9th. The members of the party were J. Newby, A. Percival, B. Coates and Denise Morin who wrote, "N.B. this is a resuscitation of the O.U.W.M.C. which seemed to fizzle out after J. Moore's presidency." Also of note is the fact that they found the causeway across Llyn Llydaw six inches under water and had to paddle through. The causeway has been high and dry in recent years.

The Morins spent Christmas week at the hut. They found the wreck of an aeroplane in Cwm Silyn, but the entry about Hound's Pinnacle on the Tremadog cliffs is the most intriguing: "Much shoulder bunting (spoonerism) and abseiling on hibernating vipers." After this crazy, happy family party the hut waited quietly until February 27th and the Annual Dinner Meet at the P–y–G.

CHAPTER 18

1954. More new members. Maud Godward and the M.A. Manchester University W.M.C. Kay Boucher's experiences. Nea's Pinnacle Club Alpine Meet.

Easter was fairly late in 1954, with Easter Sunday on 18th April. The meet was based at Gateside, Coniston, and seventeen members plus a guest, Chris Woods, enjoyed the homely hospitality and wonderful weather.

Christine Woods was an outstanding person, and a great friend of Winifred Jackson, whom she had first met at university in 1932. She was slow to come to the mountains and even slower to join the Pinnacle Club, but once she became a member she gave herself wholeheartedly to forwarding its happiness and success. Her illness and death in 1973 were a great blow. As part of her obituary, Winifred Jackson wrote: "She found peace and relaxation in the mountains and few would have guessed, meeting her there, how extravagantly she used her superb vitality in coping with the demands of a busy and very successful professional life. She was the first woman member of the Yorkshire Veterinary Society and became its first woman president as well as being president of the Association of Women Veterinary Surgeons."

Maud Godward and Isobel Wake, now Isobel Lawton, are still active members of the Club, and can speak for themselves.

Maud says: "Since youth I had been a keen mountain walker with my younger brother but when he got married this came to an end. I saw in a daily paper, looking over someone else's shoulder in the London Underground, a row of girls and boys joined by a rope, on a rockface. I saw the headlines which proclaimed the newly formed Mountaineering Association under the old guide Jerry Wright. I bought my own copy of the paper, found the address and joined forthwith. In my time, a tremendous lot of young people owed all their climbing life to Jerry Wright. I had no climbing contacts and my parents were positively anti-climbing. When I took it up, I had to leave (as one could in those days!) all my gear in the left luggage at Euston and I am afraid I had to deceive my family as to where I was going for the weekend or who with!"

Maud found out about the Pinnacle Club from John Barford's book, so wrote off and became an aspirant member. She continues: "Another useful contact I made outside the Club was Elizabeth Coxhead, author of the attractive climbing novel, *One Green Bottle*. I probably met her through the Mountaineering Association as she was a great one for encouraging young climbers although very unclubbable.

"I learnt to climb from George Dwyer, Jack Henson and Jim Cameron in the Lakes; also Gwen Moffat occasionally. They all acted as tutors to the M.A. and I soon realised they were privately available, so I was climbing every weekend with one or other of them, and met other clients of theirs with whom I also climbed independently. George was a splendid person, a lowland Scot of immense personal integrity and a very reassuring tutor, although he had gruff words for those who dithered. Jack Henson lost much of his ability after his hand was crushed in the Himalaya, although he did his best to go on. Jim Cameron was highly competent and still guiding after the M.A. broke up.

"In Switzerland I learnt from Gottlieb Perren and his younger brother Bernhard when they were employed by the Mountaineering Association. From them I learnt ice and snow methods. Bernhard was 18, his elder brother 23 or so.

"My recollection of Gwen as a tutor is of delicate movements performed on a severe climb in Wales, wearing tricounis. I already had vibram-soled boots and I remember thinking that in tricounis I could probably not have followed.

"On my beginners' Alpine course my companions were Penny Storey and Joan Busby. Once seen, the Alps had to be a 'must' every year, and I can look back on ten glorious Alpine seasons, climbing with the Perrens and other Swiss, and a number of French guides, mainly from Zermatt and Chamonix but also other centres, and including some of the most celebrated routes; during this time Penny and I, and Joan and I, did some very modest guideless climbing.

"I found the Pinnacle Club, to my surprise, with only a few outstanding members, and on being made a full member I was able to rescue a meet, (Whit. 1956) which was on the point of being cancelled by Blanche Eden-Smith, no longer able to carry on. I invited some of those women I had contacted in the M.A. and Margaret Darvall and Penny Storey came.

"Thanks to my previous climbing expeditions to Skye with Elizabeth Coxhead I had learnt my way about there, and had two charming companions there on the first meet I led for the Club.

"In those early days for me, it was of course Nea Morin who held the Club together and inspired everyone, and worked so hard giving us practice at Harrison's Rocks. Our spirit was tremendous. I remember seeing Nea descend a grade 5 route facing outwards, which others had difficulty ascending facing inwards.

"I became a tutor for the Mountaineering Association after I had passed their Beginners' and Intermediate grades. At that standard I was appointed a Beginners' Tutor and among my trainees was, I believe, Janet Cox whom I proposed for the Pinnacle Club at age 16. She was not allowed to join at that age, although even then one could see that although pretending to be following a leader she was obviously a natural climber whereas I had had to be shown what sort of holds could be used and how to use them. I was always a careful climber" (Maud puts an exclamation mark and others can testify to her carefulness!), "and I like to think no-one who came on my beginners' courses left without knowing how not to fall off and how to be prepared for the fall of others. I also made a point of abseiling with just the rope round the body – a method I was very glad to have been taught myself to carry out with complete control, either slow or fast, – and without falling out of the rope. It always seemed to me that one might have a rope handy but not necessarily all the slings belts, carabiners and what-not in an emergency.

"My favourite courses for beginners, in Wales for example, were on the Milestone and the Slabs, and the Gribin, with a few others – on Tryfan and in the Pass, thrown in if we had very promising people. I am sure I never put anyone off and usually heard from my ex-pupils that they had gone on and were now in the Alps or, that they would always remember the experience of their lives although they were not going on climbing! I also led courses in the Lakes, of a similar nature. I enjoyed these courses very much indeed and felt I was giving back to climbing what it had given to me, in however small measure."

While the Pinnacle Club were having their Easter Meet in the Lakes, Sylvia Greenwood was leading a Manchester University Women's Mountaineering Club meet at the hut in Wales. They were so energetic that they exhausted themselves and confessed to praying for rain near the end of the week. Amongst other excitements they rescued two male climbers from S. Gully on Tryfan and led a French novice, a lady aged 61, up Parson's Nose followed by the Clogwyn-y-Person arête – "Madame wished to do something more exciting than PyG Track. We fed and bedded her and took her back on motor bike. Madame now satisfied."

Their next entry reads: "Lliwedd – Ridge route – Long cavalcade of 3 ropes – much knitting – crochet pattern may be obtained on application."

It is good to savour the fun and vitality of this group.

Whitsun saw the Club meet at Cwm Dyli and Kay Boucher trying to find the hut in the early hours after travelling up on the coach from London. Finding the door bolted and barred she slept under a boulder till woken by friendly cows. Stiff and cold, she wandered down to the Power Station, and her diary gives an eye-witness account of the routine in 1954: "This time I met a man with a kettle, and he invited me in. He showed me round and gave me a very interesting talk about the station, which is supplied with water from the pipeline from Llyn Llydaw. At 6.45 a.m. he directed the pipewater through one of the generators to warm it up, and at 7 a.m. sharp another man arrived and got it going for the day. Being a Saturday, the Llanberis Slate Quarries were closed, and only one of the three generators was working. Two produced 10 KW each, and the third and latest produced 32 KW. This at the time was being overhauled. When the kettle boiled, we settled down to a cup of tea."

Kay needed a cup of tea, for her critical mind, razor keen for new impressions, was in for a shock:

"About 8 a.m. I said goodbye and made my way to the Pinnacle Club Hut. The door was unlatched, and on knocking and entering, I saw unspeakable chaos. The downstairs was unequally partitioned off by the stairs from the back of the hut – it was possible to walk all the way round them. On the left were clothes hanging and lying everywhere, boots and a coal shovel scattered, odd parcels and food near the stairs, and a mop. Immediately opposite the door was a green and brown contour map of Snowdon and district to the memory of a member killed, and to the right was more chaos. Two beds were in this part, an elderly woman (Annette) was still in one, and the other was trailing clothes on the floor. Somebody was trying to lay the table, and clearing gear away, another was washing up, and a fourth (Evelyn) was cooking breakfast on a primus, dressed only in her underwear, for a small child named Antonia. A dead fire spilled tin cans, ashes, bacon rinds and egg shells into a basin underneath, and the whole scene was utterly depressing ... I was directed upstairs to the dormitory, where a couple of girls about my age woke up and asked the time. I chose the only bunk on the third storey, and then went with one of the girls for a wash in the stream. After that we had breakfast of scrambled eggs and sausages, flakes and tea, and then I did the washing up. Fortunately the Hut has electric light, and water could be rapidly heated in an electric kettle, after having been brought from the stream in buckets.

"There was no attempt made to sweep or tidy the Hut, and about 10.15 a.m. or so, we set out in cars for the Idwal Slabs... When we eventually got back to Cwm Dyli, we found that others had arrived, and lit the fires so we were soon dry. Dinner was of mushroom soup, ham, eggs, lettuce, tomatoes, radishes, onions, beetroot, Christmas pudding and Ideal milk and coffee. It was very good indeed and most welcome. Whilst some of the others did the washing up, I sharpened knives and then helped Sue, Sheila (a school teacher) and Sylvia (studying maths and physics at Manchester University) to cut up meat for tomorrow's supper ...

"Sunday, 6th June 1954. I woke up at about 6.30 a.m., saw the rain pouring down and went to sleep again for another hour. Two girls brought round mugs of tea whilst we lazed around. Peggy and Beryl left early to go round the Horseshoe..."

It poured with rain, so they spent the morning reading, "from a very good selection of books in the hut," then had a scratch lunch, "chicken broth of doubtful age and origin," and went for a walk, fetched milk and water, and came back for a good meal of soup, stew, rhubarb and rice, coffee and biscuits. Breakfast cost 2/-, the evening meal 3/- and everything else such as tea, sandwiches and cakes, was included.

After the meal, Isobel asked Kay if she would like to go up to the Pen-y-Gwryd. A group of them drove up in the car – "and we spent a pleasant hour there, talking.

"The old shoe locker at PYG has now been converted to a climbers room, complete with pinewood walls and old logs for seats. Most of the Everest team have signed their names on the ceiling there, as well."

The following day it was still raining, but they climbed Lockwood's Chimney then went for a walk over the Glyders. At 8.10 that evening, Kay's coach picked her up outside the Pen-y-Gwryd, and someone shared his supper with her.

"It was very good, and we slept soundly until we reached Birmingham at midnight – in pouring rain. A traffic diversion, due to an accident, awoke us temporarily, but I, at any rate, slept more or less continuously until we reached the Blue Boar at 2 a.m. for coffee. At soon after 4 a.m. we made a diversion to drop Ted Warr at his front door at Elstree (the MA meet leader), complete with four tents and personal kit, and then lost several other people before we all piled out at Euston at 5 a.m., – and still raining hard." Kay made for the ladies waiting room and, using her rope as a pillow, slept on the floor till the Underground trains started running and she could go home.

"So ended another mountain weekend. The weather had not been kind to us, and I was profoundly thankful that I had not spent it under canvas. The visit to Cwm Dyli had been interesting though the standards were not quite what I expected. One day I saw a tin of pilchards – part of the emergency rations; the date on the tin said May 1949! It was just that sort of place. I only climbed with younger members, but I felt that on Tennis Shoe, at any rate, I was climbing as well as any of them. Lockwood's Chimney was just unfortunate and to be repeated at the earliest opportunity. (N.B. I never did!) No one seemed very keen on going out in the rain – quite understandable, but not a very good policy for a few precious days' holiday. Possibly I have the Mid Surrey Ramblers to thank for my attitude, of come sun, come snow, out we go! Nevertheless, it was a good weekend and I enjoyed it."

Kay bravely sent her diary, as she puts it, "in all its embarrassing entirety", but in fact the intolerance of youth adds spice to this detailed and well observed account – all true, but interpreted in different ways by different eyes.

The main event for the Pinnacle Club was the Alpine Meet, held from July 25th to August 7th. Nea had promised to lead an Alpine meet in her final year as president and she wrote the report: "On July 25 and 26 twelve of us assembled at the Union National des

1954

From S.I. Gibson

Sue Gibson on Pointe des Ecrins.

From E. Pyatt

Le Bez, 1954. 'We all fitted into the taxi !'
L-R: D. Tharby, P. Wild, A. Wilson, S. Long, N. Morin, R. Leggett, E. Pyatt.

A. Flew, S.I. Gibson, N. Morin, R. Leggett.

Aiguille de Sialouse.

Centres de Montagne chalet at Le Bez near Briançon in the Dauphiné – Annis Flew, Beryl Jennings, Joyce Hughes, Phyl Jackson, Rie Leggett, Suzanne Long, Peggy Parkinson (prospective member), Eileen Pyatt, Doreen Tharby, Peggy Wild, Annette Wilson and myself. We had one guide, Louis Perramon – "Pépé" – and one moniteur, Pierre Imberty, attached to our group. Only Peggy Wild was feeling tough enough to take advantage of an offer to take two of our party round by car, starting in the early hours of Monday morning, to the Val Venion to climb the Aiguille Dibona by the Boell route."

The party went up to the Glacier Blanc hut from where various groups climbed the Pic Louise, Pic de Neige Cordier by the E Ridge, the Ecrins by the S Face and the Montagne des Angeaux before crossing the col du Monetier back to Le Bez.

"August 1 was a well-earned rest-day. August 2 we bussed up to Pont de l'Alp and walked through the meadows to the Pics de la Bruyère which we traversed. On August 3 Annis, Rie and Joyce climbed the Roche des Corneilles with Pépé and Pierre. August 4 round to Ailefroide again and up to the Lemercier Hut, 2,704m. August 5 six of us traversed the Aiguille de Sialouse, 3,576m., the local Grépon, Pépé with Annis and Joyce, myself and Rie, Pierre with Phyl and Suzanne. We had hoped to climb the Pic Sans Nom as well, but were too slow. August 5 Annis, Eileen, Peggy W., Peggy P. and Rie traversed the Pelvoux, 3,948m, descending by the Glacier des Violettes. The rest of us tidied up the hut and took all the spare gear down. On August 7 the party broke up after 14 days of fine weather during which we accomplished eight expeditions.

"The meet was voted a great success; this was mainly due to the efficiency of Georges Lambert, in charge of the U.N.C.M. at Le Bez, to the enthusiasm, patience and good temper of Pépé and Pierre, and to our luck with the weather. N.E.M."

It must of course be added that the success was due also to Nea's contacts, planning and expertise, and, not least, her loving care for all the party.

Other members had been profiting by the good weather in the Alps. Eileen Gregory had to her credit the Piz Palu traverse, Piz Roseg-Eselgrat, Piz Benina-Biancograt, Casnile-East Ridge, Punta Rasica traverse, Domes de Miage and Aiguille de Moine S.W. Ridge. Maud Godward's many routes included the Dent Blanche by the Viereiselgrat, and the Kanzelgrat on the Zinalrothorn. Gwen Moffat was in Chamonix with John Lees, but had mixed weather; they queued along the Forbes Arête of the Chardonnet and climbed the NNE ridge of the M in the rain, then climbed the Moine and Eveque from the Couvercle Hut.

Dorothy Pilley Richards' activities ranged from USA to the Alps to the Kolahoi Glacier in Kashmir; she wrote her account from "Golden Gleam House Boat, Srinagar". Lucky Dorothy!

With so many members in the Alps, the August Bank Holiday meet at the hut was a small affair. Slightly larger was the Yorkshire meet, held at Wharfedale during September, and the November meet became a real reunion. Peggy Wild wrote this report:

"At this meet we had the unique pleasure on entertaining at the hut two French guides whom we had met in the Dauphiné. They were spending a 'holiday' potato lifting at a camp near Shrewsbury so D. Tharby and P. Wild picked them up in the early hours of Saturday morning and drove them up to the hut. After a lengthy breakfast we at last managed to get round to Tryfan where most people, including the guides, did the Direct. The weather was reasonably good – a gentle rain with no wind, but the rock was cold. Later while on our way up the North Ridge, the clouds parted momentarily and we saw to our delight that there was snow on the tops. Soon we were on the summit of Tryfan where we found it several inches deep. We descended by the South Ridge and Heather Terrace from where we pointed out to Pépé and Jules the start of the well-known climbs of which only the first few feet were now visible. In the evening the guides were introduced to the Pen-y-Gwryd...

"Sunday was a beautiful day but we found Lliwedd very greasy... Jules and Pépé were quite impressed with Welsh climbing. Annis Flew qualified for full membership with a very fine lead of Avalanche. As we came out into the sunshine at the summit on that warm, still evening, it was hard to believe that it was November. P.V.W."

This year, for the first time, members were asked to send lists of climbs done during the year, for inclusion in the *Handbook*. Only seven people responded and unfortunately the idea never caught on. The climbs of the highest standards were rarely done on meets – perhaps mainly because of the weather! – but also because of a strong tradition that leaders should hold themselves available to help those less brave or skillful than they, so many of them are not recorded. Eileen Healey regularly led VS, and mentioned Trilon and Pharaoh's Wall in the Pass and Great Slab on Cloggy. Rie Leggett had a long list of Severes including Rienetta at Tremadoc, which bordered VS (it has since suffered rockfall).

Maud Godward qualified as a full member of the Club, with an impressive list of climbs in many areas and the old campaigner, Mabel Jeffrey had skied and ski-toured in Scotland and Switzerland, and spent June in Norway. Dora King listed climbs and ski runs, and Brenda Ritchie's list of climbs and solo scrambles showed that she was still very active, though climbing was no longer her main interest.

The Oxford University Women's Mountaineering Club had two meets at the hut during the year; one in June and one in December, and Beryl Jennings led a Cave and Crag Club meet there in November.

Annis Flew, her husband and a friend were there just before Christmas and walked and climbed their way over to Ogwen and tea – only to find that the refreshment hut was shut. There is no record as to how they got home again. Finally Maud Godward brought her friend Margaret Darvall to the hut to see the Old Year out:

"Woke to rain and slept again. Breakfast 12 noon. Flake Traverse on Dinas Bach just complete by dark. Large tea at Pen-y-Pass followed almost immediately by large dinner a Pen-y-Gwryd.

"30/12/54. Summit of Crib Goch & back in mist, & gale at times."

It sounds to me like just enough activity to make the self-indulgence really pleasurable. Thus Margaret Darvall is introduced to the Club.

CHAPTER 19

1955. Mrs Bryan President. Hard climbs. Margaret Darvall. Denise Shortall. Welsh 3,000s. Alpine routes. Hut in disrepair. LSCC Himalayan Expedition 1955.

Almost without a murmur the Annual Dinner Meet became established in February rather than at the New Year. In 1955 it was held at the Pen-y-Gwryd where, in spite of a hotel proprietor's nightmare of snow, a fluctuating number of guests, burst pipes and a flooded bedroom, Chris Briggs made the Pinnacle Club welcome and comfortable. During the day members ridge-walked and skied and at night after the meal and speeches they feasted their eyes on Dennis Kemp's slides of Corsica.

The Easter meet in Coniston had poor weather, but afterwards it improved enough for hard climbing. Nea and Denise climbed Overhanging Bastion on Castle Rock of Triermain; while Ann Clarke and Muriel Baldwin, who were guests at the meet, stayed in the area to climb four good routes with friends: Asterisk and Gimmer Crack in Langdale and Mickledore Grooves and Central Buttress on Scafell. Ann Clarke married Geoffrey Sutton and joined the Pinnacle Club in 1957 as Ann Sutton.

The Annual General Meeting was held on the Saturday, April 9th and of particular interest was the hut secretary's report. Expensive repairs were necessary, but the hut was still on a yearly lease from the Electricity Board. The full impact of the situation was to be borne on the committee later in the year, but meanwhile the hut secretary put the matter forward in a businesslike manner: "Decorating materials had been purchased and left at the hut and a notice put up suggesting to members that they could get to work on wet days. A sinking fund had been proposed to draw on for repairs, there being a clause in the agreement with the N Wales Electricity Board requiring the Club to keep the hut in good condition."

Mrs Bryan was elected as the new President; she has been the only associate member to hold this office. Evelyn Leech became Editor and Suzanne Long was designated the next Hon. Secretary, to come up for election in 1956. "She had revealed her talents by acting as secretary at the November committee meeting."

Lilian Bray proposed the vote of thanks to the retiring President, Nea Morin, saying that very few presidents had done so much to attract new members and praising the way in which the Alpine meet was organised.

The Pinnacle Club was making strenuous efforts to find a hut in the Lake District at this point, so far without success. The hut sub-committee reported the possibility of a barn at How Farm in Coniston, but nothing ever came of it. Still thinking of accommodation, the Club made reciprocal arrangements with the Cairngorm Club, which gave us the freedom of Derry Lodge (at the commencement of the Lairig Ghru), and Muir of Inverey, for 4/- a night.

Five new members were elected during 1955, two of them future presidents: Margaret Darvall and Denise Shortall. The others were K. Boucher, J. Griffiths and A. Horsford.

Jean Griffiths was a small, friendly and very active climber who came on many meets. When she joined the Club she had seconded many routes and led through on routes up to about Very Difficult standard with another girl, Pat Martin. She was a friend of Pat Daley and Eileen Healey, through whom she heard of the Club. She became a very good climber and was also a great walker, having done the Marsden-Edale Colne Rawsley and the Welsh 3,000s, the latter as a circuit. She was killed in the Berwyns with her friend Vin Desmond, when they fell through the cornice from the only really steep part of the ridge in poor visibility. It was on a Polaris meet, so was an especially great shock to that club.

Anne Horsford had attended the three grades of M.A. courses before applying for membership and, although never very active in the Club, retained her membership for over twenty years.

Despite being so critical on her first visit to the hut, Kay Boucher – Kay Hewins since 1957 – has always been proud of her Pinnacle Club membership, though injury put paid to climbing almost as soon as she was elected. Her first taste of the mountains came when she stayed at the Pen-y-Gwryd with her father. This inspired her to go on a climbing weekend at White Hall, Derbyshire, run by the newly-formed Central Council for Physical Recreation and organised by Cyril Machin.

She writes: "There I met two young men from the south London area where I lived who told me of a local rambling club, and through them, I met my husband, whom I married in 1957. In the meantime, and through this rambling club, I became part of the Travelling Climbers Grapevine. In the early fifties the law did not permit that private coaches could advertise that they were going to such a place at such a time, because that would be competing with public transport; they could only be booked by a private organisation who could not advertise the fact. So the grapevine operated and magically, climbers appeared from all over the place at a given meeting point on a Friday night, swathed in ropes and rucksacks, and drove off along the A5 all through the night, arriving at the farm below Tryfan between 4 and 5 a.m., pitching tents, catching up on some sleep, breakfast, climbing or walking all weekend, back along the A5 (had to be over the border before closing time!) and to sleep in the waiting room at Euston Station by say 4 a.m., waiting for the first underground trains. Then home, bath, and off to another week's work and study.

"Looking back, I don't know how I had the stamina, but it was a wonderful time. I can remember meeting the coach outside the Park Lane Hotel (to the fury of the commissionaire!), and on the way back from Wales one icy night a packet of butter freezing in the doors just before closing time, so everyone had to leap out through the emergency doors to be in time for a drink." Kay remembers, as the writer does, using Williams' barn, in the Ogwen Valley, as an Alpine hut in bad weather.

Kay had climbed in Austria and also done the Haute Route from Chamonix before joining the Pinnacle Club in 1955 and that spring she and five friends went on a more enterprising expedition – the Kunigsleden through Swedish Lapland, then branching over the mountains to Narvik. They carried heavy loads, reckoning that they needed to be self-sufficient for ten days, and had bad weather for the entire trip. They met antagonism from the Swedes and Lapps and were frightened, ten years after the end of the war, to find evidence of German occupation. This was in addition to the natural hazards of mosquitos, bogs and glacier-fed rivers. The Norwegian side produced the worst bogs yet encountered and by now they were quite out of food, so it was a ragged, exhausted and hungry group who were seen by some Norwegians, fêted and fed and given a free taxi-ride into Narvik.

Unfortunately Kay developed back trouble which went from bad to worse and concluded her rock-climbing career.

Margaret Darvall's achievements as a mountaineer are quite extraordinary when one considers that she started climbing at an age when many people have already given up. She writes: "I was born in Berkshire and spent all my early holidays in Dorset. I never saw a mountain until I was over thirty, though I had plenty of exercise walking with a brother of 6ft. 5, and scrambling on Dorset limestone. The first mountains I saw were on the Welsh border. I was fascinated by the spiky shapes and spent hours hunting down their silhouettes on the skyline. None of my friends shared my tastes.

"On my first visit to the Lakes I did Striding Edge in sandals and a wide cotton skirt which kept snagging on the rocks. My first ascent of Snowdon was by the Llechog track (I still think it makes the best walk up), again in sandals and a skirt. I wasted a lot of energy skidding inside the sandals, – it was a fine day but with mud about. The first climbers I met ran a guest house in North Wales. On their advice I did Tryfan by the North Ridge on my own, in borrowed slacks and crepe soled shoes. Then they took me (again in borrowed slacks and shoes) and some others up Crib Goch and I was hooked. I bought a pair of boots, and went to Buttermere. It was spring and London was balmy but there was still plenty of snow on the mountains. I knew nothing about equipment and walked with my map (cloth backed in those days) wrapped round me to keep out the wind. I remember going up a gully on Harrison Stickle facing out, which for some odd reason seemed easier than facing in. And I followed someone's tracks in the snow along the High Level Route on Pillar, hoping I could cope with where they led me – no axe of course.

"About this time I chanced on Frank Smythe's books in the library and devoured them. He doesn't write well but his enthusiasm comes through. I still thought climbers were a different sort of animal, born, not made. Then I saw the advertisement of a mountaineering lecture. I couldn't get in as it was packed to the doors, but there were stalls outside with leaflets about Mountaineering Association courses and I grabbed one and booked a course for Easter. I was lucky to have Scotty Dwyer as a tutor.

"That was the year many people were killed on Snowdon. All the tops were plastered with snow and ice. It was quite a time before I discovered that it was possible to climb on warm rock without blowing on one's fingers before moving. I was over 40 by then and there was rarely anyone less than twenty years younger than me on the courses. It was a race to get enough skill before old age caught up with me. I might have managed if I hadn't started skiing at over 50 and wrecked a knee.

"I wanted to join a club but the Fell and Rock and the MAM would have nothing to do with me unless I was introduced by a member. I didn't dare try the Pinnacle Club as I took it for granted that they were all tigers and would turn up their noses at me. Then I met Mary Glynne and Nancy Smith at Scotty's. Mary suggested I should try the Fell and Rock, I expect because they had a London Section, and with her introduction I was welcomed there. The first climbing friend I made through the London walks was Betty Emery, a delightful person and a good climber. Sadly she was killed on Ben Nevis not long afterwards. It was through her that I met Maud Godward at an LAC meeting and she introduced me to the Pinnacle Club. I was lucky to come in at a time when Nea was still active and with endless time and patience to give to new members. Eileen Healey did the same.

"There was a pleasant footnote to my mountaineering this year, 1985, when I was invited to Mary Glynne's 90th birthday party as a token mountaineer – I think the only climber there apart from family. I felt it gave me a respectable ancestry in the climbing world, as Mary was Owen Glynne Jones' niece and a member of Geoffrey Winthrop Young's climbing parties at Pen-y-Pass.

"Probably the best holiday I ever had was in Turkey. In 3 weeks in the mountains we once saw some Austrian climbers, otherwise nobody but nomads and our donkey men. There were no useful maps, only verbal information from Sidney Nowill, an AC member in Istanbul. More of an empty wilderness than the Himalayas are now and some good climbing. Probably the hardest lead I ever did was on Erciyas. It added piquancy to the Turkish trip that I first heard about the mountains there from Whymper's grand-daughter, Nigella Blandy. East Greenland was beautiful and even emptier, but our climbing there was hampered by too heavy loads and rotten rock."

Denise Shortall, now Denise Wilson, first heard of the Pinnacle Club from Rie Leggett. She writes: "I met her the weekend of my eighteenth birthday in June 1954, when I was in Wales with someone who knew the group Rie was with. It was a beautiful sunny day and we were both dying to climb whilst everyone else just gossiped, so as we were in the Pass under Dinas Mot, Rie and I introduced ourselves and sloped off and climbed The Cracks. I remember she was amazed when I produced gritstone pebbles to make runners in the twin cracks and she amazed me in return by telling me there was a club for women climbers, and inviting me to a meet.

"I started climbing on local gritstone. When I was sixteen I went to work at ICI Blackley, Manchester, and met someone who went out to Chew Valley on a Sunday. Prior to that I was a real 'towny' and didn't know hills existed! but I did like all games and thought this sounded interesting. At Chew Valley, Laddow etc. I met the Cromlech Club of Manchester and through them the Rock and Ice so progressed from local gritstone to weekends further afield and eventually the Lakes and Wales. By the time I met Rie I was climbing every weekend – rock gymnastics only, though – and always as a second. I went to the Alps for the first time that summer with the Rock and Ice and climbed with Ronnie Moseley. He and Joe Brown and Don Whillans were there for the whole summer doing things like the West Face of the Dru.

"I went along to the Pinnacle Club Meet mext Whit – completely unprepared and unheralded! I was dropped at the P-y-G – it was dark and late and I had no clear idea where I was going and Rie wasn't due till the early hours. I remember paddling the river – I didn't know there was a bridge – and then climbing in through the bedroom window as the door was always securely locked in those days. A voice said, 'Who is that?' and I caused consternation by replying 'Denise', because it was Nea whom I had clambered over and she certainly wasn't expecting her daughter! However I was made welcome and given a bed and the next day I really met all these tough women – frightened me no end. We stormed off over the Glyders – all those fragile-looking white haired ladies – I had never walked so far in my life before – carrying ropes too as we were going to climb on Glyder Fach."

The Whitsun meet at the hut was a very successful one, blessed with perfect weather. There was a strong party of Pinnacle Club members (Rie, Sue, Nea, Ada, Eileen Pyatt, Doreen, Peggy and Annette), and included among the nine guests were Margaret Darvall, Janet Roberts, Denise Shortall whose arrival she has already described, and Penny Storey.

They all walked over to Tryfan on the Saturday and climbed various routes before walking back over the tops or via the miners' track. On the Sunday Rie, Denise, Nea and Janet Roberts went to climb the Direct on Glyder Fach and Nea tells in her book how they linked up with Annis Flew and her husband Tony, who were having trouble with the top pitch. She writes: "I became impatient and made myself rather unpopular by insisting that someone else should be given a chance and suggesting that this should be our young prospective member. Denise Shortall led it easily without a moment's hesitation, and with such airy technique that she reminded me of a butterfly."

Denise's account of this is a little different. She writes: "We did the Direct Route and I had to demonstrate my inserted gritstone pebble runner again and also hand jamming, which was a Rock and Ice/gritstone acquired technique. I felt a bit chirpy after that but was quickly reduced to size when they all rushed down to Llyn Bochlwyd and plunged in starkers whilst I cowered behind a rock all prim and trying to pretend I wasn't with them. What an introduction! In spite of which, I went on more meets and joined the following year. When I broke up with Ronnie it was marvellous to know I still had climbing companions, as I was really hooked on the game by then."

In later years, when Denise was married with a young family and came out about once a year, many of us were impressed and a little envious of the way in which she would lead VS climbs with perfect ease! She does so still.

August Bank Holiday weekend saw Dr Arning, Gwen Moffat and three guests at the hut, and Doreen Tharby camping with Peggy Wild at Llidaw. The party climbed on Lliwedd while Arning walked over Lliwedd and Snowdon. There is mention of loose rock on the routes and Gwen wrote in the hut book: "Cloudy but very hot. No rain now for 29 days here; Lliwedd as dry as a bone." After that they climbed in the Pass and the next visitors to the hut were Rie Leggett with her parents and brother. There is a nice 'thank you' note in Dutch.

Doreen Tharby and Peggy Wild spent the night of August 6th at the hut, to clean up after their week's camping and also to record Peggy Wild's achievement as the first member of the Pinnacle Club (as far as I know) to do the Welsh 'Three Thousanders' within a day: "On Friday (5th) P. Wild did the walk over the fourteen 'Three Thousanders' ably supported by D. Tharby who met her with welcome cups of tea and much needed food on the Llanberis Pass and at the foot of Tryfan then waited at Aber with the car. The weather was scorchingly hot."

Meanwhile other members were in the Alps. Annis Flew was in the Dauphiné, in good form after climbing to VS standard in Wales, and her routes included the Aiguille Dibona by the Boell route and the traverse of the Meije. Dora King climbed in the Engelhörner and did several routes from Saas Fee as well as visiting other areas. Nea and Denise Morin engaged a guide, George Lambert, for an ascent of the Ecrins by the Pilier Sud, then climbed other routes guideless. Ian Morin joined them for the Pic du Glacier Blanc, South Ridge Direct, then in the Mont Blanc area they climbed the Dent du Géant and the Mer de Glace Face of the Grépon. Denise Shortall had been to Chamonix in July and climbed the West Face of the Pointe Albert and the North Ridge of the Peigne.

As well as more traditional routes, Eileen Gregory visited Central Switzerland for the Salbitschensudgrat, Huhnerstock-traverse and Oberaarhorn. Dorothy Pilley Richards' list is worth having for the sound of exotic places: "Kolahoi Glacier and hills around Srinagar Kashmir. Adam's Peak, Ceylon. Mt. Harmon, Lebanon. Uludag, Turkey.

Olympus, Parnassus, Kylene, Greece. Albris, Pitz Padella, Pitz Ot, Pitz Vadret, Tschierva, Schwarzhorn, Sarsura, Grialetch, Vorab, Passo Cassandra, Piz Tremoggia, Piz Scalino, Breithorn, Kl. Matterhorn, Alphubel by Rotengrat."

During the summer Gwen Moffat seconded John Turner on Spectre, Clogwyn-y-Grochan, but sounded (in *Space Below My Feet*) so cross about the way she climbed it that one hardly dares mention it. The guide book of the time reads, "Exceptionally severe. Exposed, strenuous and delicate also. Probably the most difficult climb in the valley."

After a walking meet in October, the final meet of the year was the November Anniversary Meet at the Club hut. There was no shortage of leaders on this occasion and two notable guests were Dorothea Gravina and Anne Littlejohn. In the hut book is a postscript to the meet: "If anyone finds a 5,000 lb carabiner (Stubai, screw, large, moffats for the use of) and hemp waist line will they kindly hang it on the ham hook over the table. Please do not use the hemp for towing cars. G.M."

The Club hut had been causing a great deal of concern during the year. In April the committee had agreed that the window frames should be renewed without waiting for a fabric report and on 28th May the surveyor's report was studied, also a covering letter by the architect who had prepared it, , Lt. Col. Goodchild, A.I.A.A., (who gave his services free). It concerned a great deal more than the windows and was a damning and chilling document exposing evidence of missing tiles, wet rot, woodworm, decayed rendering and defective plaster; adding in addition that the cottage was not a worthwhile structure on which to sink a lot of money.

The committee viewed this report with considerable consternation, especially as the agreement with the Electricity Authority stated that the hut was held on a yearly tenancy, that six months notice to quit was all that was necessary on either side, and that repairs must be executed within six months of receiving the notice. They agreed to investigate the possibility of buying the hut, as they would then feel more justified in spending money on it, and asked Ruth Ruck to approach the Electricity Board through her friend, Mr Goodchild. As to where the money was to come from, it was decided to leave this over until they knew whether it would be needed, but in due course several members said they were willing to loan money to the Club, should it be required at short notice.

Little did poor, helpful Mr Goodchild realise the indignation of Pinnacle Club members at his comment that our beloved hut was not a fine old specimen of a Welsh cottage! The remark still lives in the memories of older Pinnacle Club members.

Unfortunately a letter read at the next committee meeting stated that the Electricity Authority was not prepared to sell. There was a long discussion and it was firmly established that not only were members very keen to keep the hut but that also there was little possibility of finding a hut elsewhere. This being so, committee members decided to ask for a longer lease, approach the Power Station 'in a guarded manner' to find out which builder worked for them and whether he would estimate for the repairs, and get essential work put in hand as soon as possible. There was fear that the Electricity Authority might not agree to a longer lease if it was felt the Club was going to do the repairs notwithstanding, hence the low-key aproach.

During this year the Pinnacle Club agreed to reciprocal rights with the Chester Mountaineering Club, who had a hut at Llanberis and a very small one at Capel Curig. It was considered unlikely that Club members would wish to use each others' huts, but it was a friendly gesture. Another club with whom we arranged reciprocal rights (in

January 1956) was the Mountain Club of Stafford, whose hut was near Dinas Mawddwy.

Six members attended a committee meeting held in London on 25th January, when a number of hut matters were dealt with. After requests for use of the hut by a party of schoolboys and a Liverpool Venture Group had been agreed to, subject to hut repairs having been completed, the committee went on to discuss the main reason for the meeting. This was a letter from the North West Electricity Board offering a lease of three years and on a yearly basis thereafter. They also asked to know what repairs, etc, the Club intended to carry out. The offer was accepted and Ruth Ruck, the hut secretary, agreed to get a builder's estimate for all items on the architect's report and inform the N.W.E.B.

Thoughts at the Annual Dinner Meet, held at the Old Dungeon Ghyll in February 1956, were far from domestic worries and builders' estimates. After the meal a talk and slide show were given by Mrs Monica Jackson of her expedition to the Himalaya with two other members of the Ladies' Scottish Climbing Club. The trip took them into the heart of the Jugal Himal in the spring of 1955. The other expedition members were Betty Stark and Evelyn Camrass, and Betty and Monica were joint authors of the book about the expedition, *Tents in the Clouds*, published in 1956 and so successful that it was reprinted the following year. As the expedition was planned in the British Isles and obtained publicity and sponsorship, unlike Gladys Low's quietly planned trips from Bombay in the 1940s, it dawned on people that this was something special. It was hailed as the first women's Himalayan expedition, and Monica Jackson wrote:

"Of course, when we realised that we would be pioneering in more senses than one, we were quite pleased, since it seemed to us that this might improve our chances of obtaining financial backing. On the other hand, we thought it would mean that we would have to contend with a good deal of prejudice at first. Both these surmises proved correct."

The book makes very good reading, especially as the party surmounted many difficulties to succeed in doing all that they had hoped to do – to find a way to the heart of the Jugal Himal, explore the last large unexplored area of the Nepal Himalaya, climb an unmapped mountain and give it a name. Would the Pinnacle Club ever do anything like this?

CHAPTER 20

1956-1957. Dinners. The hut. New members. Dorothea Gravina. Eileen Gregory's first Himalayan trip. Deo Tibba. Greenland. Norway. Rie and Denise in the Alps.

Easter fell fairly early in 1956 but the weather was fine and warm. The meet was based at the Club hut and led by Nea Morin in the absence of the President, Mrs Bryan.

There were climbing and walking parties every day, although the Club made a tactical error on the Saturday in aiming for Amphitheatre Buttress on Craig yr Ysfa.

There were so many parties climbing it, or waiting to start, that members turned their attention to Amphitheatre Rib, which was also crammed. Nea, with her brother, O. Bernard, and Megan Rowlands, climbed the route, but two other parties traversed off and scrambled to the top. There were three guests at this meet: M. Kellett, M. Rowlands and N. Smith. This was Nancy Smith's first meet, but she appears not to have climbed with Club members, except perhaps on the Friday. On the Monday she climbed Main Wall on Cyrn Las with Geoff Roberts, Jack Longland and Alan Hargreaves. On the same day Nea Morin was at the tail end of a party including Chris Bonington, Ian Morin, Richard Brook and Denise Morin, who climbed Great Slab on Clogwyn du'r Arddu and stretched from top to bottom of the cliff!

The meet report concludes: "A profit of £1/5/0 was made on the catering for the meet and this will be spent on a new primus stove which Beryl Jennings is obtaining for us at cost price."

The Annual Meeting on the Saturday was held at the Club hut and Eileen Pyatt gave her final Secretary's Report before handing over her duties to Sue Long. She recorded, but did not draw attention to, an alarming trend towards the eating of dinners! "The meets were not, in general, so well attended as last year with the exception of the Annual Dinner, at which there were 55 members and guests. We have been represented at Dinners of other Clubs as follows – by Mrs Leech at the Rucksack Club Ladies' Night, by Mrs Morin at the Climbers' Club Summer Dinner, by Miss E Gregory at the Fell and Rock Climbing Club, by Miss R Leggett at the Oread Mountaineering Club, by Mrs A Flew at the Mountain Club, by Mrs D King at the Ladies' Alpine Club, and by Mrs J Brazier at the Bristol University Mountaineering Club. We received an invitation to send two representatives to the Chester Mountaineering Club Dinner but were unable to find anyone to attend."

The hut was of course the main concern and Nea Morin, as Chairman, outlined the situation: the promised three-year lease, and the major repairs that must be attended to. It was agreed to postpone publication of the *Journal* for a year as all spare money would be needed. Ruth Ruck, who had done valuable work obtaining an architect's report and builder's estimate, wished to resign and Annis Flew agreed to take her place if it could be done efficiently by somebody who did not live locally. As an incentive, it was agreed that the hut secretary could use the hut free of charge and also that her husband be permitted to stay there. Annis was Hut Secretary for the following nine years, seeing the repairs successfully completed and further improvements installed. This showed especial dedication, as each of her visits to the hut involved a considerable journey.

As regards insuring the contents of the hut, Dr Arning had made inquiries, but when it was found that Sue Long worked for the Prudential Assurance Company, the matter was placed in her hands.

During 1956 Penny Storey, Susannah MacRae, Isabella Taylor, Megan Rowlands, Dorothea Gravina and Anne Littlejohn were elected members.

Megan Rowlands was an experienced Alpinist and mountain walker who had recently become interested in rock climbing and led to a fairly modest standard. It is interesting to note that she was elected a full member immediately (as were Anne and Dorothea), whereas Denise Shortall, who had shown such formidable powers as a rock climber but was young and unknown, was made an associate member in the first instance. Megan married and ceased her membership within a few years. Susannah MacRae had done some climbing with her brother, who was very keen, so Esme Speakman recommended the Pinnacle Club to her and Margaret Darvall introduced her to members. She came pretty regularly to meets until she was married and busy with a family, and had a cottage ner the Post Office in Glen Brittle, Isle of Skye, where Pinnacle Club members could stay.

Penny Storey joined through meeting Nea Morin at the Ladies' Alpine Club, and writes: "I have always been interested in mountain walking and scrambling but came to more serious climbing late in life. I was in my forties when I joined the P.C., and I found myself at the November Meet being led up Horned Crag by Maud Godward, who was qualifying for full membership.

"I am (was) more of an alpinist than a dedicated rock climber and did a number of Alpine routes including the Weisshorn Nordgrat, Zinalrothorn Nordgrat and Rothorngrat, Matterhorn and Dent Blanche.

"My main climbing companions (apart from my sister who gave up and did not join any clubs) were Maud Godward and Margaret Darvall. We did a bit of guideless climbing in the Alps of which the best was the Couronne de Breonna, sharing leads with Maud. My last alpine style climb was Mount Olympus in Greece in 1967. My climbing career was severely hampered later on by family responsibilities."

Sadly these commitments prevented Penny from accepting the office of secretary or even standing as a committee member and when at last her position eased she was turned down as not well enough known.

Since she stopped climbing Penny has travelled extensively: wild life safaris in East Africa, trekking and flower hunting in Kashmir, the Seychelles, Senegal, Mediterranean Islands, and nearer home in France and the Scottish Islands. She had a distinguished career in the Foreign and Commonwealth Office, and the Club was proud when she was awarded the MBE for her work.

Isabel Taylor has spent her holidays in Shetland for the last twenty years, since her husband, Bertie, became bothered by arthritis and took up fishing, but they come to a dinner meet now and again to meet old friends. She writes: "I did a little climbing as a student and then about 1952-53 did two Mountaineering Association courses in North Wales. Having married a Wayfarer, he decided that I must join the Fell and Rock. Then we met Maud Godward whom he already knew and she invited us both to a P.C. Dinner at Dungeon Ghyll. Then I went to another meet (Wasdale Head) and Maud and Margaret

Darvall proposed and seconded me for membership. This was a much simpler process than counting Lakeland summits for the Fell and Rock. Janet (Cox) did her first lead with me as second on Pinnacle Rib. Bertie was there too, keeping an eye on proceedings, He felt very responsible, as Janet's father was also a Wayfarer and she was still at school at that time.

"My first visit to Cwm Dyli was for a dinner meet. I arrived late on Friday evening and crept up to bed. Next morning, being uncertain as to the 'form' I opened one eye very cautiously and beheld a rear view in tan meridian bloomers. This proved to be Pilley, so I felt that I was really one of the girls then."

Anne Littlejohn was already a keen member of the Ladies' Scottish and was elected a full member. Margaret Darvall says that she climbed for years without telling her mother, and covered her tracks by writing postcards in advance and having them posted from the seaside. At one time she used to be at the hut about one weekend in three and Margaret often went with her.

Margaret writes: "She was writing a climbing guide to Rhum and I went there with her two of three times. She was a very tough and energetic and sometimes eccentric climber. She worked at the Veterinary Research Station at Weybridge and retired early, commuting her pension, to buy a half derelict farm in the Scottish Lowlands and stock it with Dorset Sheep, the breed she had got accustomed to in the south – I believe they have the rare gift of producing two lots of lambs a year. Unhappily the farm didn't prosper and I doubt whether she now had either the time or the money for climbing, though she is still a Ladies' Scottish member." Anne resigned from the Pinnacle Club in 1977.

Dorothea Gravina also joined the Club as a full member. She comes of a family with the good old Yorkshire name of Briggs. Their estate had been at Rawdon, but they were living in Bradford when Dorothea was born. Dorothea grew up during the Great War, with brothers at the Front. After the war her brothers took advantage of a resettlement scheme to go to South Africa and grow oranges. They called their estate Rawdon after the old family estate back home. During the years that followed, Dorothea felt at home in many parts of the world, and some of her adventures are recorded in 'Moments', which she wrote for the Pinnacle Club *Journal*, but we have since prevailed upon her to tell us a little more of her life.

Dorothea grew up as a keen Girl Guide, joining in 1918 and absorbing all the sense of adventure, self-reliance and friendship that it provides. She became a Sea Ranger, and has stories to tell of life on the old ship, *Implacable*, in Portsmouth harbour: being woken in the morning by traditional cries of, "Show a leg, show a leg, the sun's burning your eyes out!" walking the yard arm, manning her own boat, *The Dauntless*, which name incidentally describes Dorothea very well, and rowing the Admiral, known, I regret to say, as "Ginger Pop", all round the harbour.

When the International Chalet at Adelboden, Switzerland, was built for the Guide Movement in 1932, Dorothea was working there before it opened and stayed on as a member of the staff, leading parties up the surrounding mountains, until her marriage two years later. A great-grandson of Liszt, her husband was a fine musician who had developed into an outstanding conductor, in demand to conduct many famous orchestras. They built a house in Merano, in the South Tyrol, and life held many riches, with music and friendship, skiing in winter and climbing and walking the mountains in summer. They had two little boys by the time the outbreak of war came to ruin their happy life.

It was evident that the Germans would overrun the South Tyrol, and Count Gravina insisted that Dorothea and the two boys should move to Switzerland, where Dorothea's mother was living at the time. Dorothea says that this was very sensible as she would most certainly have quarrelled with the Germans and been shot. Dorothea and the boys, Michael and Christopher, lived in the Baby Chalet, which had been built for the personal use of the American lady who had provided the money for the International Chalet at Adelboden. The latter was now closed for the duration of the war. There was no call for orchestras and conductors in wartime Italy, and Dorothea's husband joined the Italian army, in which he had served with distinction during the Great War. When he had leave she would slip across the frontier to join him for a few precious days in Venice.

Finally they decided that Dorothea and the boys must go to America while there was still a chance. With her third son, Tim, well on the way, they had an exciting journey, creeping along the South of France to Spain, then taking a flying boat to Bermuda. She was safely in America when Tim was born.

When the war was over, they came to England where for many years their home was a gypsy caravan near Maidstone in Kent. An uncle paid for the boys' education and when they were all safely at Marlborough or beyond, Dorothea turned her thoughts to more adventures: she booked for an M.A. climbing course in Skye. The leader of the course was Gwen Moffat, who was extremely impressed by such an outstanding 'beginner'. Gwen wrote in a letter to Nea, 'She is 53 and I first met her in a Beginners' Course in Skye when she had more energy and enthusiasm then anyone else and, among other things, stopped a clumsy student falling off the ridge when I was too far away to do anything. . . I think she will make a splendid addition to the Club.'

Margaret Darvall met her first on the November Meet in 1955, and the second time they met, in London, Dorothea said: "Lets go to the Himalayas." Thus started the British side of the women's expedition to Cho Oyu.

Isabel Taylor has mentioned the next meet, which was at Whitsun in Wasdale. It was the last meet till September as the August meet was attended by Gwen Moffat alone. She climbed with a novice, and with John Lees who wrote up a new route on Dolmen Buttress in the Hut Book. She was the only hut resident all summer, apart from two women's university clubs and an Outward Bound girls' course from Plas-y-Brenin run by Nea and Denise Morin with Philip Cunningham and Charles Evans.

Meanwhile members had been fairly busy in the Alps and elsewhere. Eileen Gregory had her first trip to the Himalayas. She spent a few days exploring alone in Kulu before being joined by Frances Delany and having a mini-expedition while waiting for Joyce Dunsheath and Hilda Reid to arrive. Eileen reached a 17,000 ft summit with one of the porters. When the party was complete, they crossed to Lahoul and set up an advanced base at Concordia, from where they ascended several peaks. In Eileen's account for the Pinnacle Club Journal she writes:

"Following the curve of the glacier and camping at the foot of Gunther's Peak (climbed by Mr Gunther in '53), Frances and I and two Sherpas arrived at the summit, the highest point reached by the expedition (about 21,000 ft.). The view was rewarding of course, but was particularly interesting as Mr Gunther had had bad weather, and we were able to solve some of the mysteries which he had left. We found that his Lion Glacier did not exist. Frances, an experienced surveyor, was able to fill in a section of the map ...

"Joyce was very keen that the four members of the party should climb a peak together, and, before Joyce and Hilda descended to Shigri, I suggested that we should all try the convex summit above Concordia. This did not turn out to be a good idea as I had the last thousand feet to ascend solo, and then had to make my way along a thrilling ridge to the highest point. I resolved not to go out again without some of our porters." With two Sherpas and a Ladakhi, Eileen later climbed the Chapter House and Cathedral, and finally, when the others had gone home, she found two Ladakhi climbing companions and made her way towards Deo Tibba.

"We started over a col from Nagar to the Malana Nullah, expecting to make the best of doubtful weather and cross south to the Parbatti valley. As the weather improved we were able to continue up the Malana Nullah, and eventually pitched camp on the watershed ridge at the head of the Jagatsukh Nullah, which Frances and I had visited in May. From this camp I employed the last fine day before the monsoon in climbing Deo Tibba by the watershed ridge. All went well on the ascent, although the snow was soft and deep on the slope leading to the final dome. It was a large summit, different from the sharp points of the Barashigri peaks. There was a sea of cloud below us as we started down. By the time we had reached the top of the watershed ridge the snow was very soft and it was necessary to cut steps in the underlying ice. Cutting for the descent worked very well, the men would do the cutting while I stayed at the top of each pitch to safeguard the party. I had little confidence in my pick stuck in the ice, and I knew I should have to stop a slip before it developed into a fall, but I was not put to the test and we reached the bottom safely... "

Eileen makes everything sound so normal and thoroughly under control, but the underlying message is that she possessed a cool head and exceptional stamina and climbing skills. Joyce Dunsheath, in her more detailed article for the Ladies' Alpine Club, says that Eileen, "On hearing details of the proposals, . . decided to give up her job as a bio-chemist and join us as equipment and climbing leader." Eileen travelled out by sea with the bulk of the equipment, while Hilda and Joyce journeyed by car and Frances went by air from Nairobi. They were lent surveying equipment by the Royal Geographical Society and received a substantial grant from the Mount Everest Foundation.

Denise Morin was another Club member exploring new territories and she records: "First ascents of Mount Atter and of eight other peaks in the Sukkertoppen region on Hamburgland, West Greenland." She wrote an article entitled "Taterat and Tupilak" for the Pinnacle Club *Journal* and her achievement was also recorded in the LAC *Year Book* as follows: "Among new members we are particularly glad to welcome Denise Morin. No doubt she has had more opportunities than most to become a good climber, but she is now a mountaineer in her own right. Her lecture to the Club in January on an expedition and new climbs in Greenland which she undertook last summer with her brother and three young friends (average age of the party was 24) is a fine example of enterprise and skill."

Beryl Aston (Jennings) and Peggy Parkinson were members of a party which spent a fortnight of bad weather in Norway but nevertheless managed to climb several peaks. Peggy was in a group which climbed Vinnufjell from Grasdal in really foul weather conditions, taking 14 and a half hours, and was told that it was the first ascent of Vinnufjell by a woman climber.

Several Pinnacle members were in the Alps. Penny Storey's ascents included the Midi-Plan traverse, the Forbes Arête of the Chardonnet, and the Zinalrothorn by the Rothorngrat. Margaret Darvall joined her for the last climb, then they tried their hand at guideless climbing and led through on the Riffelhorn skyline. Maud Godward's guided ascents included the Courtes, Midi-Plan traverse, Grépon, Petits Charmoz, and Breithorn by the Young-grat. Dorothea Gravina had a guide for the Strahlhorn and Rothorngrat, but climbed the Wellenkuppe, Trifthorn, Matterhorn, Dom, Täschhorn, Alphubel and Monte Rosa guideless. As usual, Pilley recorded climbs in the USA and Europe, but this year's queens of Zermatt were undoubtedly Denise Shortall and Rie Leggett. They had intended going out as a party of four, but two had dropped out and Denise and Rie had bad moments deciding whether they ought to have a guideless expedition to the Alps as a party of two, but the results justified their decision. They started off with the Rotengrat ridge of the Alphubel, followed by the Kanzelgrat of the Zinalrothorn.

Denise wrote: "Pouring rain cheated us of another peak the next day and we returned to Zermatt, where we danced, ate and slept our way through two days. By Saturday we were bored with the gay life, and in spite of the still doubtful weather we set off for the Matterhorn Hut. As usual, Rie and I walked up to the hut in shorts, and it was still warm even though it snowed on us that day.

"There were no English-speaking people in the hut, and our arrival without a guide, and wearing shorts at an altitude of 11,000 ft., caused great mirth. The tables were turned, however, when the guardian came in. He immediately guessed who we were and told the others a long tale of the climbs we had done. From then on we were treated with great respect, and one or two even came to shake us by the hand."

Rie in 1956.

After the Matterhorn, they went back to the Rothorn Hut and climbed the delightful rock ridge of the Trifthorn followed next day by the grand finale of the Wellenkuppe-Obergabelhorn traverse, returning to Zermatt down the Arbengrat ridge.

Denise wrote an article for the ICI magazine, which was reprinted in the Pinnacle Club *Journal*, entitled "Les Dames Anglaises".

Nearer home, Gwen Moffat married John Lees in June and they spent a fortnight climbing in the rain on Skye, redeemed by Slav route on the Ben and Clachaig Gully in Glencoe. Denise Shortall, who was climbing in the same area, mentions a new route to the right of Ossian's Cave.

September brought a new departure for the Club in a meet at Avon Gorge, led by Annette Wilson. She said a considerable number of hard routes were led, and commented, "Our members enjoyed the unique experience of climbing with ship's sirens echoing from the rocks around them. The sound of car horns from the Portway was perhaps less enjoyable but it all combined to make this meet a little different from the rest."

Annette was also leader for the Anniversary Meet at the Club hut in November which was exceptionally well attended. Dorothea Gravina is listed as a 'friend' but was elected a member during the meet. She brought two of her sons, Michael and Christopher, to take part in the climbing. When she left at the end of the weekend she forgot her handbag. Shirley Bull writes: "Annette opened it in front of all to ascertain its owner.

"'Countess Gravina,' she moaned, 'and with sons – and to think I wrote to her as 'Miss'!'"

Annis Flew, the Hut Secretary, was unable to attend the meet, but she and her husband came to climb for a day during October, and the log book entry shows that they left things ready: "Delivered Elsanol & soap powder & primus prickers, also screw tin opener. Mr Fawcett will deliver 2 sacks of coal (2cwt) next week for November Meet."

Denise Shortall was at the hut that weekend and climbed Babel on the Grochan (VS) – "Very hard, conditions bad." There were few further visits before Annis came once more in February 1957 to check that all was in readiness for the Annual Dinner Meet.

CHAPTER 21

1957. A winter ascent of Snowdon. Mur y Niwl. Eileen Healey President. 3,000s in 9 hours. Alpine Club Centenary. Dolomites meet.

The Dinner Meet was on February 23rd, 1957, and we have no less than three accounts of one particular outing. The *Handbook* notes: "The weather was not altogether kind to us, Saturday being a day of unrelenting rain, and snow at higher levels. Despite the inclement weather parties ploughed their way through soft snow on Lliwedd while one party, led by Dr Charles Evans, whom we were very honoured to welcome as our guest from the Climbers' Club, climbed a perilous snow gully on Snowdon. Another party following behind decided to put prudence before valour and retreated."

Nea Morin's account can be read in *A Woman's Reach*. She calls it 'poor man's Eigerwand' and says of Charles, who had become engaged to Denise, "I began to think a less intrepid son-in-law would suit me better."

One of the party was a young prospective member, Judith Hall – prospective because she was not yet eighteen. She was so keen on climbing that she worked all her holidays at the Pen-y-Gwryd and went out with any climbing partner that she, or Chris Briggs, could find for her in her spare time. She kept detailed climbing records in a diary, beautifully illustrated, with little sketches of hard moves. The following is Climb no. 26, and is entitled,

FIRST SNOW CLIMB.

"Date – Saturday, February 23rd 1957.

Companions – Charles Evans, John Clegg, Nea Morin, Denise Morin, Jim Simpson, Eileen Gregory. Place – Snowdon.

Climb – A gully, slightly right of Great Gully, nameless. Footgear – Boots (Tricounis).

"It was half term, and having arrived at P.Y.G. at 7.10 am, walked down to the hut, unpacked, had breakfast and returned, I waited for everyone to go out. Charles asked if I should like to go with him, John Clegg, Denise and Nea Morin, Jim Simpson and Eileen Gregory, on a Snowdon gully. I accepted with delight, as I had been very keen to do a Snowdon snow climb, especially since reading *On Climbing*.

"We left at about 10.30 am, and walked up to Pen y Pass, and thence up the Miners' Track. Either sleet, snow, rain or hail was falling, at any rate slightly, all the time. We climbed up the track, in gradually deepening snow, passing a small camp, with occupants still inside. We then left the track, and started climbing a steep snow slope. It was really enjoyable, plodding up, through snow over two feet deep. We reached a level part, and then climbed again. By this time we were in mist, and this was our undoing, for we missed Great Gully, which we had intended to climb, and found ourselves in a steep place, to the right of Great Gully. We roped up – in the order in which we had been climbing – Charles, myself, John Clegg, and Eileen, on the first rope, Nea, Jim and Denise on the second. The climb was really quite hard – at any rate in parts, where icy rocks were on the surface. After we had been climbing for a short while, we heard another party behind, but they realising that we must be on something quite hard, as they had caught us up from a long way behind, turned back, for it was too cold to wait around. At one point, just as I was about to start climbing, I felt a jerk on the rope – John had been pulled forward, by Eileen's slipping, however, both stopped." (Nea writes that all except Charles, Judy and herself, were wearing vibrams and felt very insecure). "In several places, steps had to be cut, or ice chipped away. Owing to the continual fall of sleet, etc. we were soon wet through, and got very cold waiting. In one place I had a very awkward stance onto which to bring up John.

"We finally reached the top of the most steep part, and moved together to the summit of the mountain. In parts, the slope was icy, with a very thin covering of snow. This, those wearing vibrams found difficult. In other places, the snow was much thicker. We reached the summit, in a blizzard, and tried, without success, to find shelter by the cairn, while waiting for the second rope. We then walked to the start of the P.Y.G. track and descended into shelter from the wind, to wait for the others. Then we all slid and plodded down the snow slope. At one stage John, who was below, and moving faster than I was, pulled me off a rather more delicate part and I had a short slide, stopped by the rope from above. We unroped and floundered down. John and Eileen went on ahead. The cloud had cleared a bit and the colours were beautiful. With stops to admire the view and to eat, we continued down the P.Y.G. track, in my case continually going through the snow to the streams underneath. It was dark before we got down and we paddled through every possible stream. On reaching the Pen y Pass, we went in for a drink and then made best possible time to P.Y.G., arriving at 6.40 p.m. Every garment was sodden. After changing, I had my dinner in the office, owing to lack of space and joined the others for coffee and speeches. Afterwards Charles treated me to a sherry and we then went into the Billiard Room for a talk, with slides, on four women's expedition to the Himalaya. Afterwards, dressed in an odd mixture of wet, dry, tidy and untidy clothes, we walked back to the hut, after a cold but enjoyable day, and the fulfillment of one of the smaller of my ambitions."

The "Four women's expedition" is described more gracefully in the *Handbook*: "After dinner we had the pleasure of seeing Miss E. Gregory's slides and hearing about her Himalayan expedition. It was a great thrill to listen to such exploits from one of our own members. We are very grateful to Commander Showell Styles for loaning and operating his projector."

Judith had her eighteenth birthday during the year, so joined the Club later in 1957. She had first seen the mountains when she stayed at the Pen-y-Gwryd with her family in 1952. They started their holiday with a walk round the Snowdon Horseshoe and on subsequent days climbed several other 3,000 footers. She writes: "During the beautiful summer of 1955 I spent the summer holidays working at PyG. On my days off I was introduced to rock climbing by Christopher Brasher. I climbed with many different people, including Charles Evans, when he was having photographs taken for his book *On Climbing* (see plate 6). I worked at PyG every subsequent school holiday and climbed in all conditions. At 18 I became a member of the Pinnacle Club – introduced by Margaret Darvall.

"In August 1957 I went on a French mountaineering course to Contamines. After that, training and working as a nurse restricted my climbing activities considerably. Free weekends were unheard of then! However, I did part of my midwifery training in Bangor in order to be near the mountains and also I spent 3 months working as 'nanny' to Charles and Denise Evans' eldest son in Bangor, between jobs." (Denise had 'au pairs' so that she would be free to climb. However, they were usually keen climbers so she had pity on them and invited them out, then had to find a baby-sitter to baby-sit for the baby-sitter!)

"I worked in South Africa from June 1964 – June 1965 and had 3 weekends in the Drakensberg mountains – which are spectacular. The highlight was a long walk, with a rocky scramble at the top, up Cathedral Peak – 9,800 feet, led by a Zulu guide who could yodel!"

Judith is now Judith Huskins, with three teenage boys, but meanwhile her diaries take us right back to the 1950s and early 1960s with a freshness and a singleness of purpose which concentrates much more on the climbs than on the people she climbed with. She did nothing of extraordinary difficulty, sometimes because she was too modest about her skills – she was afraid of being a nuisance. Often, however, Judith chose an easy route because she was introducing a beginner to climbing. Even when seconding, she was kindly towards young men less able than herself:

"On the second section there was one quite hard pitch, where Jeremy had some difficulty, and then came off. He then got up, and I followed with little difficulty, being third person (always easier)!" This was on Amphitheatre Buttress in midwinter and she proceeded to take over the lead. (Jan. 2nd 1957).

There is no entry in her diary for Easter 1957, but the Pinnacle Club met once again in Wales.

Margaret Darvall and Dorothea Gravina with her sons went up two days early and camped, as there was still a Manchester University WMC meet at the hut. In pouring rain they did the Snowdon Horseshoe 'in reverse' and next day, in better weather went up the Glyders and Bristly Ridge. That evening everyone else arrived.

This meet was well-attended and very active, with at least two groups climbing to VS standard. Many popular routes had to be avoided as they were packed with the Easter crowds. Winifred Jackson and Chris Woods went to Amphitheatre Buttress but changed their plans when they found eight parties ahead of them. Two days later Dora King was to avoid Bristly Ridge because it contained a long crocodile of ramblers singing Negro spirituals.

The youngest guest was Antonia Leech, aged seven, who climbed Lockwood's Chimney and the Ordinary Route on Idwal Slabs as well as walking up Snowdon.

Several members stayed on after the end of the meet and Sylvia Greenwood started from the hut at 4 a.m. on April 24th to complete the 3,000ers by 9 p.m. On the same day Denise and Nea Morin and Eileen Gregory were in a party which climbed Mur y Niwl. Nea writes about the expedition in *A Woman's Reach*:

"Mur y Niwl on Craig yr Ysfa was a brilliant discovery of Tony Moulam. He made the first ascent in 1952 and it had the distinction of being called the finest expedition in North Wales ... I wanted to do this climb and in fact had hoped to do it with Denise. However John Disley, chief instructor of the Climbing Centre at Plas y Brenin, Capel Curig, invited Denise to climb it with him. He did not want to take more than one person and I was feeling rather disgruntled when I ran into Peter Biven, whom we had met in Cornwall, and Trevor Peck ...

"Peter said yes, he would like to do Mur y Niwl, and no, he didn't mind how many people came ... Somehow this straggling and slightly hilarious party did not seem quite in keeping with the seriousness of the expedition, indeed almost an insult to this great Mur y Niwl, the Wall of Mists. But although we were all undoubtedly rather rock-happy, we were tremendously impressed with the cliff and with the beauty and originality of the route."

At the end, Eileen Gregory said it was a route she would never lead – but she led it a fortnight later.

Philip Gordon, a great nephew of Geoffrey Winthrop Young, was in Wales this April, and on 26th he led Denise, Nea and Eileen up Spectre on Clogwyn y Grochan. The following day he climbed Brant Direct with Denise and on 28th Nea joined them for Munich Climb on Tryfan.

The Annual General Meeting took place as usual during the main Pinnacle Club meet. There had been quite a lot of discussion at committee meetings during the year, about replacement of officers, because Rie Leggett, who had offered to take over as treasurer had then decided to emigrate to Australia. Ada Moss (née Kindleysides) was approached to see whether she would do the job, then Rie decided not to emigrate after all. Mrs Bryan had been president for only two years but had been able to attend very few meets or committee meetings and Nea, as vice president had virtually been doing the job for her. Mrs Bryan wrote a letter of resignation, hoping that a young, active member would be able to take over, and Eileen Gregory was eventually persuaded to accept the position. Finally, Evelyn Leech, who was editor, had had no journal to edit and now had other things to do. Nea Morin agreed to take on the work. New committee members were Ada Moss and Margaret Darvall.

Repairs on the hut had been completed, money had come in well, and Winifred Jackson, retiring as treasurer, hoped the Club would feel justified in publishing a journal as soon as possible. She also proposed that calor gas should replace the primuses for cooking. Everything ahead looked rosy, especially when Eileen Gregory said she was willing to lead a Dolomite meet if there was sufficient demand.

Members joining during the year were Ann Sutton, Margaret Dew, Patricia Parsons, Jill Robinson, Jean Punnett, Pat Daley and Judith Hall.

Jean Punnett was Jean Low, now married, whose membership had lapsed for six years. Ann Sutton has already been mentioned as Ann Clark, a medical student and brilliant climber who married Geoff Sutton. Her leads included Gimmer Crack, Mickledore Grooves, Moss Ghyll Grooves, Unicorn, Birthday Crack and Brant Direct, so her entry form was most impressive and she was elected a full member. She kept her membership till 1973.

Mog Dew is best known to Club members for her beautiful pictures of Alpine flowers for the Dinner menus. She thinks there is nothing of interest about her climbing experiences, but I suspect that many a member will have sympathetic fellow feelings as they read her account! She writes:

"I started to walk in the mountains when I first met my husband. He stayed at P-y-G and I stayed with the Lockwoods to make it quite proper! He tried me out on the fishing bank first, on a very windy day and in an extra big gust I was blown in, much to Lockwood's delight. Next I was tried out on the hills. I wept bitterly, in despair and terror, on the track leading from the Glyders to Tryfan and again crossing all the swollen streams. His method was always to walk well ahead and I had to get on with it.

"Eventually I progressed from Wales to Skye. There we met Winifred Jackson, Chris Woods and Joyce Taylor (now Beard), the start of our friendship and many holidays together, in Wales, Skye, Kintail, Glen Coe, Ireland and Austria. They were scrambling rather than climbing holidays, with the occasional climb, but never severe.

Winifred and Chris took me as their guest to several P.C. meets and to stay at the hut, and eventually I joined the Club in 1957.

"In 1961 to celebrate being 40 I went on a climbing course at Plas-y-Brenin with Sally Westmacott. After that she went from strength to strength and I went into a decline, as my husband wouldn't trust me to lead and I didn't trust him any more!"

Pat Daley started her climbing career by joining the Polaris M.C. (Nottingham) in 1953 after reading an article about the club in the local newspaper. She writes: "I was looking for something a bit adventurous and it fitted the bill! Eileen Healey and my friend Jean Griffiths took me to the Pinnacle Dinner in 1954. It was a very snowy weekend and there were two or three Pinnacle parties on Bristly Ridge. We were all so muffled up we didn't know each other again at the Dinner.

"I became a member in 1957 but was not very active with the Club until about the middle sixties when I started to go on some of the meets." Pat had her first son, Alastair, the year after she joined the Club and her second son, Tim, in 1961. She was rather quiet and unobtrusive about her climbing skills and it was not until 1966, when she led routes on a damp, cold meet at Stanage Edge, that she was considered for full membership.

Pat writes: "In the 60s and early 70s my main interest was in rock climbing in Wales and the Lakes. I tried to improve my standard and to do some leading, and I think the best I managed to lead throughout was Eagles Nest Direct on Great Gable, Curving Crack on Cloggy and Mickledore Grooves on the E. Buttress of Scafell. The latter was inspired by reading an article in the Pinnacle Club *Journal* by Ann Sutton called '3 slabs on Scafell' in which she described the climbing as 'serious and beautiful but never desperate'. I needed a shoulder and a push to get me up the first overhanging pitch, but thereafter it was okay. Chocs and wedges were a bit of a novelty then, and I was quite proud of getting them in, but my second said, 'actually Pat you are supposed to put the *metal* against the rock, not the rope!'" She seconded a number of routes on Castle Rock of Triermain; and Deer Bield Crack, near Grasmere, which she calls a real collector's piece – and so it is.

Pat's services to the Club include three years as a calm, efficient and friendly Hon. Secretary at a time when she was the third secretary in three years and the Club badly needed some stability (1970-72).

The hut was well used in the summer by families and climbing parties. Anne Littlejohn came for two weekends with Beryl Coates, a non-member, for an attempt on the Three Thousanders. On May 11th they both completed them in just under twelve hours; on June 22nd Anne Littlejohn, accompanied by Beryl for half the route, completed them in 9 hours 6 minutes. Both walks started from the hut – no conservation of energy by starting from Pen-y-Pass or camping out on Snowdon and starting from the highest point! On the first occasion they returned over Carnedd Llewelyn and Craig yr Ysfa to the A5 north of Capel Curig. For Anne's second walk there are the following details on the log book:

"Dep P C hut 7.20. Crib Goch 9.15. Snowdon 10.0. Elidir Fawr 12.15. Y Garn 12.55. Glyder Fawr 1.40. Glyder Fach 2.0. Tryfan 2.38. Penyole-wen 4.17. Carnedd Dafydd 4.39. Carnedd Llewelyn 5.18. Yr Elen 5.27. Foel Grach 5.59. Foel Fras 6.21. Time 9hr. 6 min. Weather: dense mist from Elidir Fawr to Glyder Fawr, with rain and cold wind; otherwise clear and cool. Descended to road about 1 ml beyond Rowlyn 8.30.

Far from needing a rest after this effort, the next day they both walked the Snowdon

Horseshoe.

Many members were abroad in 1957, some perhaps in Zermatt for the Alpine Club Centenary celebrations. I can find no record of Pinnacle Club members there, but Denise Morin was asked to take part in a film made to celebrate the Jubilee Year and conducted herself creditably on Suicide Wall at Idwal, at the end of May. This was the year of her marriage to Charles Evans, and they spent their honeymoon in the Himalayas.

A small, but very competent group of Pinnacle members joined Eileen Gregory on her Dolomites meet: Brenda Ritchie, Christine Barratt, Anne Littlejohn, Sylvia Greenwood, and a guest, Iris Lemar. Brenda, with her knowledge of the area was able to organise the climbing throughout the meet and also secured the services of Johann Demetz as a guide on some of the routes. They climbed many routes from the Sella Pass, then walked over to the Vajolet Hut and did several routes including the traverse of the Towers. Anne Littlejohn wrote an account for the *Journal*.

On Nea Morin's recommendation, Judy Hall went on a climbing course for young people organised by the Union Nationale des Centres de Montagne. She was the only English person on a course based at Contamines and she wrote a lively account for the *Journal*. They had good training and climbed several routes, culminating in a traverse of the Courtes from the Couvercle Hut. Judith did not have to be too modest in her private diary, and confides: "I was very pleased to be the first girl to reach the hut, – about 20th altogether out of 85... Some of us in our group, only some of the boys and myself, climbed a chimney about 30ft high and very strenuous ... The guide then asked me if I should like to climb a pitch to the right of the chimney. This, he said, was a compliment. Some compliment!" She was in the top group, but was disgusted to find that they were to climb technically more difficult peaks while the second group achieved her ambition of climbing Mont Blanc!

Apart from Eileen, the only person to list her climbs for the *Handbook* was Pilley, who spent the winter snowshoeing in the White Mountains of New Hampshire and came to the Alps in the summer to climb such routes as the traverse of the Wildstrubel, the Grand Combin (on which they were turned back by a storm) and the Velan.

Autumn was ushered in with a meet in the Avon Gorge, where only Eileen Gregory and Anne Littlejohn braved the wet and slimy rocks. By contrast the Yorkshire meet was held at the evocatively named Laburnum Farm, Appletreewick and Sunday at least was graced by a glorious autumn day which lived up to this cosy and peaceful-sounding venue. Miss Bray was present, and stayed till the Monday.

This was the last meet of the year, for the November meet had to be cancelled due to foot and mouth disease. The committee were able to climb at Stone Farm and Harrisons, for they held a meeting in Nea's house at Tunbridge Wells, and the year had not quite ended for the climbing fraternity, though the occasion was somewhat different: on December 9th Eileen Gregory, together with Suzanne Long, represented the Pinnacle Club at a reception, graced by the presence of H M the Queen and H R H the Prince Philip, which was held at the Great Hall, Lincoln's Inn Fields to celebrate the Centenary Year of the Alpine Club.

CHAPTER 22

1958. A new treasurer. Janet Cox. LSCC Jubilee. A festive Christmas. Eileen married. Collapse of a barn wall. Mollie Taplin. Dorothy Lee. In mother's footsteps.

For Marie Grutter, her friend and a dog, 1958 started at Cwm Dyli with walks and climbs in the snow, and there was still a lot of snow and ice about at Easter, though it did not prevent people from rock-climbing. The Annual Meeting was held on the Saturday and amidst more happy accounts of the year's activities, the treasurer reported that no less than 34 members were in arrears with their subscriptions. On the other hand, the response to the hut fund had been generous and had relieved to some extent the drain on Club funds for the repairs carried out at the hut.

Unfortunately some cheques had had to be returned to the senders as they had not been presented for payment within six months of drawing. Keen and willing as the new treasurer was, she seemed not to realize that cheques were of no value to the club until they were banked! In fact she was a very busy professional person and was eventually persuaded that it would be less worrying for her if Ada Moss took over the club finances. Ada (now Ada Shaw) had found herself an occupation for the following twenty-four years and would have gone on for longer but Club members started to worry about what would happen if someone had to take over as treasurer without the benefit of her expertise!

In Nea Morin's capable hands, the first *Journal* to be produced in eight years was well on its way. She expected it to cost something in the region of two hundred pounds for 200 copies. In view of the cost of the *Journal*, subscriptions were raised to £1 a year for members over 23 years of age. Due to the expensive new calor gas cooker (an opinion was expressed that a 4-burner table model would have met the club's needs), members felt justified in raising the hut fees to 2/6d for members and 3/- for guests, plus 6d for use of the oven. Mrs Leech raised the question of members' husbands sleeping in the hut, from the point of view of inconvenience to any other members who might be staying there. "There was a very full discussion on this," read the minutes! but it was decided that members' husbands could stay at the hut if there were no other bookings. Any member arriving without booking would have to put up with the inconvenience.

Members joining during the year were Virginia Debenham, Jo Scarr, Sheelagh Dack, Janet Cox, Bertha Rostron and Freda Wilkinson.

Bertha was a sound climber of considerable experience, and a member of the Lancashire Caving and Climbing Club. During her years in the Pinnacle Club she certainly pulled her weight, and she led very enjoyable meets based on the hut in Torver, Tranearth.

Josephine Scarr had been climbing for three years, and led such routes as Longlands on Clogwyn D'ur Arddu and The Direct Route on Glyder Fach. She resigned from the Club in 1972, a few years after going to live in Australia, but members follow her career with interest for she is a very gifted and attractive person whose first book, *Four Miles*

High, is an account of the start of her own climbing career, her leading of even harder routes, and her two successive expeditions to the Himalayas, the second of which was the Pinnacle Club's Jagdula Expedition.

Janet Cox, (now Davies), was old enough to join the Club at last, and did so at the November Meet. She says she started walking with her father in the early fifties and liked being in the hills but as she was always so far behind him she never really felt that walking was 'it'. When Maud Godward invited her to her first P.C. Dinner in 1956 she felt very overawed, at 15, to meet all those – to her – ancient climbers, but she must have got something out of it, as she persevered. She was getting keen on rock climbing but as no-one as her school was interested she relied on her father and the P.C. The following year she went on a Mountaineering Association course on Skye, led by Hamish MacInnes. She writes: "This really fired my enthusiasm – I loved Skye and was much impressed by Hamish's life-style! In 1958 I went to university, joining the Climbing Club which was pretty anti-women but I gradually was accepted." For such an outstanding climber, it took Janet a surprisingly long time to realise her potential, which became apparent during the 1960s. She writes, of more recent years: "During the 1970s I became bogged down in children, making the odd foray out with Helen Jones or Niki Clough. Niki and I were planning another Himalayan trip when she died last Easter (1982). This last year I have been getting out much more regularly, climbing mainly with Ginger Cain, who also lives in Plockton. This year we broke back into Scottish VSs, having struggled up numerous desperate Severes. So hopefully this is a middle-aged revival, which I gather is happening with a lot of women in their 40s or so."

Cwm Dyli was well used in 1958, with two parties from Oxford University WMC; a family party of Joyce Tombs, her husband and friends, including the new arrival, John Richard Tombs; and many visits by members and guests for climbing:

"May 3rd-4th. D.N. Evans, C. Evans, J. Hall – Kirkus' Route on Craig Lloer."

"5.7.58. Oxo, Craig y Wenallt: J.R. Lees, V. Bray, G. Moffat." John had put up this route in 1953.

In August, Annis Flew and her husband mixed climbing days with hard work at the hut: replacing windows and panes, fixing bookshelves and a new shelf for the saucepans, struggling with the water supply till Annis "no great lover of water", fell into the stream, and doing a hundred and one other jobs. On a climbing day they triumphed over The Direct Route on Glyder Fach, which had caused them trouble before.

At the Whitsun Meet the Pinnacle Club had joined with the Ladies Scottish Climbing Club on Ben Nevis to help them celebrate their Jubilee Year. Strong winds and bottomless snow made the Douglas Boulder an epic and long climbs out of the question, so the party went for long walks instead. As they filled the C.I.C. Hut and Steall Hut, they had the mountain almost entirely to themselves. After the meet, Nea Morin went on to Skye with Brenda Ritchie, Monica Jackson and Dorothea Gravina and they climbed many favourite routes such as Cioch Direct, Crack of Doom and Window Buttress.

Nea was able to go to the Alps this summer; the previous year, she says, she had spent all spare money on Denise's wedding. With Denise and Micheline, she chased fine weather till they reached the Dolomites, where nevertheless their routes were accompanied by thick mist or thunderstorms. Being very keen to climb the Spigolo del Velo on the Cima della Madonna and wary of doing it guideless in such doubtful weather, Nea and Denise hired the guide, Giacomo Scalet for a carefree, happy ascent. When Denise went home, Nea joined Janet Roberts in the Dauphiné for a guideless traverse of the Meije, not knowing that it was to be her last major Alpine route. She writes:

"I am glad now that my last big climb in the Alps was guideless; in retrospect I enjoy every minute of it, although I didn't at the time. Had Janet and I been with a guide on the Meije he would have found us exasperatingly slow. All pleasure would have vanished had we been hurried and harried, and made to feel that we were not doing as well as we should. As it was, and with the luck of the weather, we were able to go our own pace and to appreciate our freedom to do so."

Other P.C. members abroad this summer were Pilley, wandering freely through Switzerland with ascents and traverses of medium-sized peaks; Maud Godward and Penny Storey led through on several routes and hired a guide for the Weisshorn Traverse.

Dorothea Gravina and Margaret Darvall made guideless ascents of the Aiguille de Toule, Tour Ronde and Dent du Géant as well as guided ascents of harder routes. Dorothea had a guide for the Rochefort Ridge and Mt Mallet and the Midi-Plan traverse, but saw herself up Mont Blanc, the Dent Blanche and many good routes in the Dolomites, such as the traverse of the Vajolet Towers. Annis Flew also was in the Dolomites climbing classic routes, guided, in the Sella Pass area.

Norway was popular as well. Marjorie Wood and Alison Adam were on a walking tour through the Jotunheimer, climbing mountains en route, and Eileen Healey's list reads:

"Norway – Horrungane: Söre Dyrhangsringen (S. face), Store Skagastölstind (Heftes Renne) Midtmaradel (E. face). Romsdal: Romsdalhorn (S face and N face), Kuannsdalstind (up W ridge down N ridge) Venjatind (up W ridge), Trolltindene, Bispen (S face) and Kongen. Sunmöre: Smorrshedtind (S W face), traverse of Armstrong-Vigdal gorge on Slogjen." She also lists her British rock climbs: routes such as Longlands on Cloggy and Overhanging Bastion on Castle Rock.

Autumn came round again and Chris Woods led a Yorkshire Meet at Grassington – in fine enough weather for climbing as well as walking. All other accounts of September and October mention wind and rain, though Denise Shortall with Denise and Charles Evans climbed a 'slimy' Belle Vue Bastion in October. Quite good routes were climbed at the November Meet as well, in spite of 'rain blowing in hard gusts'. "E. Healey and S. Macrae disappeared towards Cwm Silyn and had started the Ordinary Route before the other members could find the foot of the cliff. After various problems with cows, three ropes followed Eileen. They consisted of Charles Evans, B. Keatinge and D. Evans; A. Flew and P. Wood, N. Morin and Ian Morin. At the top of the cliff the wind was strong enough to lean on."

This was the last meet of the year, but the hut continued to be well used: by Gwen Moffat, the Magog Club (including Joan Beattie and Jo Scarr), and a Morin-Evans family party of seven who cooked their Christmas turkey in the oven and stayed a week. "Very successful. Hut looked most festive with Xmas tree and decorations (by Denise) – all complete with wine, crackers, liqueurs, cigars, etc. etc.

"26th. Gashed Crag. Terribly slimy and wet but not cold. Came back to a wonderful Boxing Day dinner at P.Y.G."

Sue MacRae brought a party to the hut to celebrate the New Year, closely followed by the Manchester University W M C meet. Meanwhile Annis Flew and helpers had called in to do some hut maintenance and admire the decorations.

The festive season was closed officially with a very proper entry in the hut book, dated

January 6th: "Visited Hut and removed decorations. P. Storey, M. Godward."

It must be unheard of for the president of a men's club to change his name in the middle of his term of office, but this is what happened in the Pinnacle Club when Eileen Gregory married Tim Healey in the summer of 1958. The Club was perhaps a little slow to organise a proper response to this event, but they made up for it at the Annual Dinner Meet held at the Pen-y-Gwryd in February 1959 when Nea presented Eileen with a wedding gift. After the meal, Mrs Eve Sims gave a talk and showed a film of the Women's Overland Himalayan Expedition. It was a good thing the occasion was a festive one, for the weather was awful.

The Easter Meet and Annual General Meeting was a much smaller affair, with equally bad weather and a great deal more excitement. Easter was the last weekend in March and the meet was held at Wasdale Head in the Wastwater Hotel and Barn. During the Saturday night the wall of the barn collapsed and the inmates emerged, fortunately unhurt but considerably surprised, to be comforted with coffee and a bed on the hotel floor. Janet Cox was there too but slept so soundly that she never heard a thing and woke in the morning to wonder where everyone had gone. Maud Godward was the meet leader and seems to have felt personally responsible for the barn wall, apologising profoundly for the unexpected occurrence.

"Sunday, in almost continuous heavy rain," reads the report, "nearly everybody went over Black Sail and Scarth Gap to Gatesgarth for tea, glorious scones . . . Clothes were dried and the barn party slept in the lounge."

The following day saw the intrepid party on Slingsby's Chimney, Scafell. Janet led one of the ropes, climbing with Mollie Taplin, whom she met for the first time on this meet. While at Birmingham University she climbed mostly with men, as there were no keen girls, but Mollie lived in Birmingham as well so henceforth they climbed a lot together. Janet's comment on Arrowhead and Slingsby's is: "Rain, fog and icy wind according to my records – wouldn't do it now!"

Dorothea and Margaret, arriving last at Slingsby's, were advised not to follow; so they went up Scafell via Lords Rake and thence to Scafell Pike where they helped rescue a walker with a broken leg. Dorothea helped carry the stretcher and Margaret took charge of the family. Dr Arning whose walk had also been interrupted by the rescue, saw the party down to Hollow Stones then pressed on over Mickledore and Esk Hause before returning to the hotel.

For once the *Handbook* records a "Bray" story: "The indefatigable Lilian again went up to Styhead and subsequently caught the night train home, pausing at the door of the hotel to comment, 'I never saw such a dirty anorak' to Eileen, just back from Scafell." Another famous one, hitherto unrecorded, concerns a time when Mabel Jeffrey's climbing partner went home early and Mabel asked whether she could join Bray's party. Bray replied, "You can come up this climb if you like, but you can't use our rope." One of her remarks was: "Wood'll carry the ropes; she's as strong as a horse." Bray cast a critical eye over everyone on the rocks and held post-mortems on each route – an irritating and high-handed person, remembered with affection. Will present members engender such fond memories?

The Annual General Meeting had been held on the Saturday night and Bryan, Pirie and Bertha Rostron came over for it. Amidst news of the Club, the secretary wished every success to members visiting the Himalayas in 1969, – to Nea Morin on Ama Dablam, and our president Eileen Healey, Dorothea Gravina and Margaret Darvall on Cho Oyu.

Dorothea Gravina was elected Hon. Secretary, to take up office when she returned from the expedition and Ada Moss was treasurer. BMC news recorded the purchase of Harrison's Rocks, and the appearance of jumars: "These are light metal devices which facilitate ascending fixed ropes".

One item under Any Other Business was the investment of Club funds. National Savings Certificates were purchased and the Club decided to have a flutter with five Premium Bonds, purchased in the Treasurer's name. Fortunately for Ada's feelings, she was never required to hand over the jackpot.

Among members joining during the year were M. Taplin , D. Lee and P. Wood.

Mollie Taplin, who became Molly Porter on her marriage, did one of her first climbs with Margaret Darvall, who remembers her as very keen but nervous. Mollie says this was due not to the climbing but to her being in awe of the distinguished company, which included Dorothea Gravina, Nea Morin and Eileen Gregory! She was impressed also by their kindness and generosity to a novice.

She had been captivated by mountains since her first visit to the Highlands and read every mountaineering book she could lay hands on. After reading *Mountaineering in Scotland* by Bill Murray she wrote to him, with the result that he introduced her to rock-climbing.

She joined the Pinnacle Club when she went to teacher training college in London, and when she qualified and moved to Birmingham she spent every weekend in Wales or the Lake District. In 1960 she joined a major expedition to Spitzbergen. Another member of the expedition was John Porter, whom she married, and they opted out of city life, moving to the Cairngorms where they both became winter climbing instructors at Glenmore Lodge.

She has made many mountaineering trips to the U.S.A. and writes: "We've been all over the mountain States in most seasons for many years, and mountain deserts and canyon lands too. I also was a member of the first British Women's Expedition to Peru, in 1971 – Barbara Spark came too. We did some first ascents in the Andes then. I also went to Kenya, Canada and Arctic Norway."

Mollie followed Gwen Moffat in obtaining her Guide's Certificate and she became increasingly involved in the local mountain rescue team. She became a team member in 1963 and helped shape the very professional service needed to cope with increasing accidents in the Cairngorm area. Of her eighteen years with the team she spent more than ten as Team Leader and Secretary. She was Vice-Chairman of the Mountain rescue Committee for Scotland for about three years. She also trained a search dog with the Search and Rescue Dogs Association.

Mollie's life was so full that she lost touch with the Pinnacle Club, resigning her membership in 1971, but members follow her distinguished career with interest.

Dorothy Lee had been a member of the Ladies' Alpine Club for several years and had a number of Alpine peaks to her credit, which must have led her to an enjoyment of rock climbing for its own sake. She was a keen hockey player as well as loving the mountains, and she was a splendid person to have in a club. She had become treasurer of the Ladies' Alpine Club a year after joining, and in 1965 she became secretary of the Pinnacle Club – always welcoming and often in charge of meets. Early in the 1960s she developed an arthritic hip, which put a stop to climbing and made going downhill rather painful but even when her outdoor activities were curtailed and she was unable to come to Pinnacle Club meets we heard of her organising events for the Alpine Club and she sent neat and charming little paintings for the menu cards at Pinnacle Club dinners. She died in 1983, having more or less refused to admit that she was ill.

Pat Wood, now Pat Henry, was a strong leader and very self-reliant, who was elected a full member. She is a dentist, and is described as tolerant, unselfish and imperturbable in Jo Scarr's book about the Jagdula Expedition, which was probably as good a testing ground as any – but this is looking into the future.

April 1959 saw the start of the second volume of the log book. The hut was well used and records suggest a wet spring and glorious summer. The Whitsun meet was in the middle of a heatwave and there were thirty people sleeping in and around the hut. Vera Picken came with her two daughters, who had an escort of five PC members on their first climb. Later in the year Gwen Moffat brought her daughter Sheena to the hut and they climbed Horned Crag. The step across was difficult for a 9 year old, but achieved without assistance.

CHAPTER 23

1959-60. Ama Dablam. Cho Oyu. Good routes – hut parties – hut troubles. More new members. Jo Scarr on Kaisergebirge Wall. Dauphiné meet. 1st ascents on Rhum. Midland Spitzbergen Expedition.

Meanwhile the action moves to the Himalayas, for on March 29th Nea had left Katmandu with the Ama Dablam Expedition, and had started the long walk to Base Camp. The expedition leader was Emlyn Jones, and another member, George Fraser, was brother of a Pinnacle Club member, Mollie Agnew. George, with Mike Harris, was last seen on the ice pyramid about a thousand feet below the summit of Ama Dablam on May 21st. Nea wrote: "They were both going splendidly, it was a brilliantly fine day, and it seemed that all was set for final victory.

"To get a better view I climbed up Ambu Gyabjen (about 19,000 ft) but I started late and by the time I reached the top clouds had obscured the upper slopes of Ama Dablam and Mike and George were never seen again." The next day was warm; there was the rumble of avalanches on all sides and the weather was bad for the next four days. Nea herself had walked in while recovering from a knee damaged at Harrison's Rocks, and her hip gave her considerable trouble also. When walking out, she could feel that permanent damage was being done, but even so she could appreciate the thrill of being on a Himalayan expedition. One camp was on the same site beside a torrent coming from the Dudh Kund, a high lake, where Denise and Charles had camped on their honeymoon. Earlier, Dawa Tensing, the Sirdar, had pointed out to her 'his' peak, which they had all climbed together. Summing up, Nea wrote:

"During the expedition I learned how the body can adapt itself to conditions that one would normally consider crippling, and yet still be capable of great physical effort, an experience which in itself is tremendously worth while. And even had I been able to forsee that it would end my climbing days, I still think I would have taken the opportunity to go. It was of course a bitter disappointment to me not to be able to play a fuller and more useful part in what was almost certainly my last serious mountain endeavour. Yet just to have been a member of a Himalayan expedition, to have known some of the splendid people who live among them, were experiences I had never dreamed would come my way and for which I shall ever be grateful."

The Women's International Expedition was later in the year. The leader was Claude Kogan, and the objective Cho Oyu, 26,750ft., lying about 20 miles north west of Everest. Claude had already reached within 2,000 feet of the summit and had high hopes that an all-woman party could reach the top. Pinnacle Club members were Dorothea Gravina, Margaret Darvall and Eileen Healey (Gregory). Margaret, as Principal of her secretarial college, took on all the secretarial work at the British end and Dorothea, who wrote an account for the Pinnacle Club *Journal*, comments that her secretarial pupils must have had a surprising grounding in expedition work. "Margaret and I." she continues, "set off by boat from Marseilles at the beginning of July, 1959, seen off by our leader Claude

Kogan, and Micheline Rambaud, another French member in charge of photography. We got used to saying goodbye to Claude about six times on the gangway for the benefit of the press."

After many adventures, including hornets and leeches, the whole expedition arrived at Namche Bazar, and seven of them visited Thyangboche Monastery while waiting for the weather to clear. Dorothea continues the account:

"We left Namche on September 10th having taken on more of the local toughs as porters. The way now grew more and more barren and ever more beautiful, icy peaks rising up in all directions. This was yak country and we passed many groups of these always melancholy animals, with their long black hair and their tiny feet, looking like animated hearthrugs. Both ends look alike. One can never by sure till it moves if one is looking at the north or south end of a yak. We bought one in Namche and it walked sadly with us to Base Camp where it was most basely slain behind a rock and put in the freezer."

Once Base Camp was reached, all went according to plan until Claude and Claudine were poised at Camp 4, 24,000 feet, hoping to make a successful summit bid. The weather deteriorated, heavy snow fell and the temperature became much higher. Soon avalanches were falling on all sides and two Sherpas were caught as they descended. One managed to free himself after two hours but the other was too deeply buried. After a few days, Dorothea and Jeanne, with Phu Dorje, were able to reach the site of Camp 4, but saw nothing but spent avalanches, not a sign that any human being had ever been there. "It was a perfect day, deep blue sky, the shining summit just above us and magnificent peaks in all directions. At last the weather had settled."

Dorothea, as deputy leader, brought everyone off the mountain. When the shock and grief had subsided a little she determined that there must be another women's expedition as soon as possible; there must be success and happiness to counteract people's reactions to the heartbreaking tragedy.

Back in the Alps nearer home, members were having their own smaller adventures. Freda Wilkinson and Janette Curtis had a climbing holiday in Austria and crowned it with an ascent of the Matterhorn from Zermatt, all guideless. Gwen Moffat went to the Dauphiné where she climbed the Aiguille Dibona by the Boell Route and the Stoffer variant, the West Peak, the Soreiller by the South Ridge, Les Bans voie normale, Pic du Says East Ridge and descent of central couloir. Maud Godward climbed the Besso, Obergabelhorn, and Pic Nord des Cavales, and Dorothy Lee joined the Ladies' Alpine Club meet for two or three routes.

The 28th July saw Jo Scarr and Muriel Baldwin driving to the Alps in a Ford van. They were heading for the Dolomites but stopped off at Chamonix en route to climb the Forbes Arête, where they had a perfect day and sunbathed for an hour on the summit; and to do the first guideless feminine ascent of the Aiguilles Dorées. On this latter route (the E-W traverse) which is very long, they encountered difficult snow conditions and had to bivouac. Nea Morin thinks they may well have been the first feminine party to traverse the Forbes ridge. Back home, Bertha Rostron did the Colne Rowsley walk; with her husband and a friend she did the circuit of the Welsh 3,000s, in 23 hours, starting and finishing at Cwm Dyli. Climbing lists show that Cwm Silyn and Tremadoc were becoming popular.

The traditional Yorkshire meet in September saw a good many Yorkshire lasses present: Marjorie Wood, Chris Woods, Trilby and Biddy Wells. Isobel Lawton, Alison

Adam and Evelyn Clarke nipped over from Lancashire and Bray came up from Surrey for a long weekend. They stayed at the Hill Inn, Chapel-le-Dale in glorious weather and went for enormous walks.

As usual, the Anniversary Meet was a big one. Denise introduced her small son, John M C Evans to the club and Nea showed her Ama Dablam slides; then Jo Scarr showed slides of the Forbes Arête, the Dorées and, in the Dolomites, the Sella Group, traverse of the Vajolet Towers, and San Martino. The weekend was wet and misty, so climbs were traditional – Milestone, Monolith, Gribin Facet, Lockwood's and Flying Buttress.

Once or twice during the winter Jo Scarr used the hut for parties from Plas-y-Brenin, where she worked:

"November 25th. Very, very wet, cold day, so I brought a party of Outward Bound girls here for a brew-up before doing Lockwood's Chimney. They (fourteen year olds) were fascinated by the hut, never having been inside a Welsh cottage before . . .

"February 15th 1960. Brought a party of twelve boys from Ipswich here for the night – I hope this does not come under the title of "mixed party". Snowdonia really snowbound – it took us two hours from Plas-y-Brenin to Pen-y-Gwryd in a Land Rover, digging out various other vehicles en route. Then plodded down here in deep snow & a really biting wind. Comfort of the hut much appreciated by the group."

"A week of horrors follows," reads the log book. "Rentokil men come in, as arranged, to cope with woodworm. While spraying hut they receive several electric shocks. CEA inspect and turn off electricity.

"April 2nd. A. Flew, P. Wood, AGN Flew arrive in rain. A. Littlejohn here already, spring cleaning.

"AF to Beddgelert looking for electricians ...

"Main worries: how to restore electricity supply – pay Rentokil bills – and keep foreigners out of our Elsan. Camper caught in flagrante delicto: padlocks the answer..."

Things were straight just in time for an Oxford University Women's Mountaineering Club meet, followed immediately by the Pinnacle Club Easter Meet.

Dorothy Arning was present, and perhaps this was an occasion when she travelled up with Nea. Nea had a story of taking over the driving and of suddenly seeing a foot appear in the wing mirror. Arning had cramp in her leg, and had stuck it out of the back window. When sleeping in the hut, Arning snored very loudly; if people complained, she offered them sleeping pills.

This year there were thirty present at the meet and, although some were camping or sleeping in plastic bags, they were almost all having meals in the hut, which was very crowded indeed. One day of rain and snow and three days of splendid sunshine saw the climbing of many fine routes. "A Flew led Belle Vue Bastion (with D Evans and M Agnew) and M Baldwin and P Wood did Erosion Groove and Lion on Carreg Wasted ..."

The Annual General Meeting on the Saturday evening was held in a somewhat dim light, as the hut was still waiting to be rewired for electricity after the alarming experiences of the Rentokil men. The Hon Secretary's report is stamped with Dorothea's personality and style. She remarked on the strong entry of keen young climbers and hoped this tendency would continue, to maintain a vigorous core of good climbing.

"A very cheerful Whitsun Meet was held at the hut in glorious weather; 11 members and 5 guests (3 of whom had since seen the light and joined the Club) succeeded in resisting nearly all temptations to sunbathe and a lot of climbing and walking took place in all directions . . ."

"Members would be glad to have news of Mrs Armstrong Richards, still struggling to recover from injuries received in a motor accident. She wrote from Florida, mentioning three swims a day and a lot of bird watching, but her hip was no better and she could not walk. (It was agreed to send a cheering message from the meeting)." Dorothea outlined the Himalayan and Alpine expeditions, and continued: "It is nice to report that this expedition business is becoming a confirmed habit in the Club, M. Taplin having joined a party going to Spitzbergen in July, and M. Baldwin and P. Wood hoping to join an enterprising expedition to Afghanistan and the Hindu Kush this summer. It is hoped that this growing volume of expedition experience in the Club will stimulate members to further enterprise in this line..."

Expenses were high in 1959, read the treasurer's report, due to the cost of the *Journal*. The cost of 200 journals had been £227, but it covered eight years and was three times as thick as the ones that followed. Everyone felt happy and relaxed with the finances in Ada's capable hands, and Annette Wilson, the auditor, was warmly appreciative when she proposed the adoption of the accounts. This was Eileen Healey's last meet as president and she earned a very special vote of thanks. Winifred Jackson was unanimously elected in her place.

Enthusiastic climbers joining the Club during 1960 included five who were made full members straight away: Nancy Smith, Bridget Keatinge, Muriel Baldwin, Millicent Bishop and Mollie Agnew. Eveleigh Leith, Frances Blackhurst, Anne Sutcliffe and Hester Willink became associate members.

Muriel Baldwin was an experienced VS leader with many routes to her credit, at home and abroad, but she resigned the year after her election, as did Millicent Bishop, who had much the same qualifications. Hester Willink was a member of both the LAC and Pinnacle Club for about three years, but her interests must have changed. Bridget Keatinge became Mrs Andrews; she resigned in 1968. Frances Blackhurst became Mrs Dewey on her marriage and resigned in 1972.

Anne Sutcliffe, now Anne Wood, joined partly because her aunt, Marjorie Wood had been encouraging her to do so for many years. She loved mountain walking and hoped to be able to go up mountains in a more interesting way, but a couple of wet climbs cured her of this! She decided to stick to walking and scrambling, which she is still very fond of, at home and abroad. Anne was a member of the party sleeping in the Wasdale Head barn at Easter 1959, when the wall collapsed, and her most impressive memory is of Dorothea Gravina's cool-headedness in an emergency: she was up on her feet and out to see what could be done before the rest of them had gathered what was happening. 1960 was Anne's first Easter hut meet and she says it was very memorable for the people who were there and the marvellous atmosphere: Nea, Denise, Margaret Darvall, Dorothea, Eileen, Suzanne – people who had been and who were about to go on expeditions.

The Hon. Eveleigh Leith had joined the Ladies' Alpine Club in 1951 and was their journal editor when she joined the Pinnacle Club. A lover of outdoor adventure rather than a hard rock climber, she nevertheless had a good and delicate technique with a fine balance. She often climbed Severes with Nancy Smith, had been skiing since 1935, including glacier skiing and had ascended many Alpine peaks, both guided and guideless. Her brother had an estate in Scotland and she went up every year for the beating in the grouse season, which she much enjoyed. She had never tasted fish and chips till two

Pinnacle Club members with a more plebeian upbringing introduced her to this delight. To talk to her was to hear of a different and fascinating world, and to those who knew her well were disclosed a variety of skills and enthusiasms. She adored the ballet, especially Sadlers Wells, and for over twenty years she ran the Sadlers Wells Ballet Benevolent Fund and had a gift for finding money to help injured ballet dancers and those who fell by the wayside. She was a member until her death in 1984.

Mollie Agnew lived in Scotland, but had climbed all over the British Isles as far south as the Avon and Cheddar Gorges, leading to severe standard and seconding much harder routes. She was an enterprising member for a few years and retained her membership till her rather early death in 1983.

Nancy Smith calls 1960, when she joined the Pinnacle Club, "a sort of second flowering." She had done very little for a while, after her husband's death, and being more than fully occupied in a single-handed doctor's practice in Lancashire. She was born Nancy Heron, and a born climber – her mother has a photo of her, aged two-and-a-half, high up an apple tree, two yards beyond the reach of an anxious-faced aunt who stood with outstretched arms. As a child, Nancy climbed all the local gritstone: Ilkley Moor, Almscliffe, and Otley Chevin. She writes:

Nancy, aged 18, on Murray's Route, Simian Exit.

"I visited the Rockies in 1939 and then started proper rock-climbing with the Leeds University Climbing Club in December '39 and was leading the lads on my first meet –

Dow Crag in snow and ice." She has a photo of herself belaying a beginner on Murray's Route, Simian Exit.

When they went to Wales, she stayed at the YHA hostel at Idwal - or if it was full she bivvied in the Chapel porch. Inside the hostel was a big photo of her future husband's great uncle, Owen Glynne Jones, and the motto "It matters not how long we live, but How". (His ice axe came into Mary Glynne's possession and she gave it to the P-y-G).

"One day," Nancy continued, "I met an old member of the Pinnacle Club, Phyllis Thompson, and I led her up Holly Tree Wall, hauling our sacs after us – on to Continuation Wall and up to the summit of Glyder Fawr and down the other side, down to a little surprise she had for us – there were four of us, the other two had walked up, not climbing – to the Pinnacle Club Hut – my first visit. There was a heat wave, but the hut was cool and damp and mouldy. It seemed unused. We stayed three days. It was too hot to climb so we got up and did the Horseshoe by night, arriving on the summit of Snowdon as dawn came with mists filling the valley. I had no idea then that there was a road round or a P.Y.G. and Pen-y-Pass – I thought that across the mountainside was the only way to this wonderful little hut! Miles from anywhere – in another world."

This was in 1942, and Nancy wanted to join the Club then, but Phil dropped out of things and Nancy didn't know anyone else.

Nancy spent Whitsun that year on Pillar Rock, camping at Black Sail with no tent and only bread and water because the hostel was full. She took a beginner up all the old Abraham routes (she never climbed again!) and then hitch-hiked back. Nancy was picked up by an old buffer of a driver, who looked like a retired Army Colonel but surprisingly he was really interested in Nancy's enthusiastic descriptions of all the climbs she had done. When he could get a word in edgeways he introduced himself; he was Ashley Abraham! He told her she must join the Fell and Rock Climbing Club, and that he would propose her. This he did, and Nancy felt highly honoured, also at his continued interest in her climbing. Several of her friends joined the Fell and Rock as well and later on, when she met Cym, he was in the Climbers' Club so she camped outside the huts when they were in Wales (as women were not allowed in the hut) but when they were in the Lakes the Fell and Rock was hospitable to them both.

While working as a psychiatrist at the Southern General Hospital in Glasgow, Nancy became an honorary member of the Lomond Club. She couldn't join because it was a men's club, but she did many good routes with them and in particular with Tommy McGuinness, with whom she had her first Alpine season in 1947. They climbed the Breithorn and the Matterhorn and also did the Untergabelhorn Ridge – because they liked the look of it. She says they had no guide except the 1896 Swiss Baedeker. The ridge was very long, loose and dangerous and, so far as they could see, untrod by human feet. Dogged by bad weather when they went to Chamonix, they came to Grindlewald and attempted the North Face of the Mönch, thinking the Eiger too hard and the Jungfrau a cheat because it had a train up it. But they were wounded by fanatical German climbers ahead who were hacking out great ice steps and dropping the chunks down on them. They had to retreat – badly bruised.

In 1945 Nancy became a house surgeon in Leeds Maternity Ward. She went to Ben Nevis at the New Year with Molly Till and John Cook, whom she had known since his days as a schoolboy at Bradford Grammar. In fact, John introduced Nancy to Cym, who followed John as President of Cambridge University Mountaineering Club. This New

Year they stayed at the Nevis Hut and went up the N.E. Buttress in a very strong wind and poor visibility to find arctic conditions on the summit. Someone was there, however, and they found Tommy McGuinness and his friends snug in a tent and welcoming them with a cup of tea.

In June 1951 Nancy and Cym went off to the Alps on a motorbike with all their gear, only to find that the weather was unsettled and there was too much unstable snow about so early in the season. They decided to go to the Dolomites via Central Switzerland and reached the Susten Pass to find the road blocked. They had not believed the signs as there seemed to be quite a bit of traffic heading in that direction, but when they came to a 40ft wall of snow they realised that the traffic comprised workmen clearing the road. As they were turning away in frustration and despair, some workmen pointed out the gang working at the other side of the snowdrift. The road was clear to the hairpin bend below their own blockage, so they got out their climbing rope and tied it to the motorbike, which they belayed down the snow slope until it was safely on the clear road ahead.

Nancy and Cym had to drive to the Brenta Dolomites before finding rock in condition for climbing. With Italian guidebooks and an imperfect knowledge of the language they had differences of opinion up the Campanile Basso and a few other hard routes, almost certainly putting up their own variations on the Bimbo di Manaco (V), the Cime Ceda (IV) and the Cima Tosa (V). Nancy writes in the *Fell and Rock Journal* for 1952 of their first ascent of the North Ridge of the Badile that season, of their descent from the Falso Passo di Bondo in a storm, their bivouac outside the Badile Hut, which had not yet opened for the season and was barred against all comers, and their return to the Sciora Hut the following day.

With Cym Nancy climbed such routes as the Mer de Glace face of the Grépon and, what she considers her best route of all, the Aiguilles du Diable in 1950. This was the first British guideless traverse of the whole route, including the Isolée, from the Torino Hut. A party which included Gaston Rebuffat's brother was also on the climb, but missed out the final peak. However, they waited for Cym and Nancy to complete the climb then all went on to the top of Mont Blanc de Tacul and the Italian summit but dared not go on in thick cloud to the French summit as they would never have found the hut. Cym and Nancy had to lend the other party a rope, also Cym led the way down in the thick mist, all of which was a great boost to their morale.

On reaching the glacier, the men raced off to catch the last téléferique. It was a long way across the Géant Glacier, and uphill, and they were still roped together. Nancy was tired and plodding ... she could have plodded on into infinity at her own pace but they all had longer legs and were super-fit men. She kept going as long as she humanly could and then collapsed, totally breathless, sitting in the snow and sobbing because they'd miss the last funicular and she had let them down!

Instantly the men were all contrition and consternation. They stopped for rest and refreshment, made their way to the Torino Hut and had a celebration meal – a much finer ending to such a superb day, thinks Nancy, than a dash for the téléferique, even had she been capable of it.

Soon Nancy's whole life was to change. While coming back from work in a snowstorm one night, Cym ran his motor cycle into the back of a lorry which had been parked without lights, and was killed.

During the bad time that followed, Nancy answered an advertisement for a doctor to be in charge of a women's gynaecological unit at Sulaimaniya in Iraq. This was not a job under British sponsorship but was working directly for the Iraqui government and she had no idea till she arrived what it would be like working as an employee of a Muslim country. The site of the women's hospital was a shed full of dung and she was apparently supposed to construct a fine new building with her bare hands. The crisis came when the wife of a government official required surgery to remove an ovarian cyst from her abdomen. With difficulty, Nancy obtained facilities in the men's hospital, where, in the ceiling of the operating theatre swallows were flying to and fro, building their nests. As well as the danger of nesting material and bird dirt dropping into the open wound, Nancy had doubts as to the proper sterilising of the instruments. When she finally removed a very large cyst and handed it to an assistant, the assistant immediately rushed out to the anxious husband who was waiting outside and threw it into his arms, causing pandemonium – it was as big as a football. Nancy says she ran away.

She set out to climb a local mountain, but in this attempt she was thwarted by the desert heat. When her tongue stuck to the roof of her mouth she realised that she was suffering dehydration so had to descend before reaching the summit. Nancy writes: "Nea was instrumental in bringing me to the Pinnacle Club. I found her with her two brothers doing very hard things on Harrison's Rocks where I escaped sometimes from being a house surgeon at the Kent and Sussex Hospital, Tunbridge Wells." By the time Nancy joined, however, she was in general practice in Lancashire.

During the week after the Easter Meet Anne Littlejohn and Denise Evans came to the hut for some climbing; firstly a day on Tryfan: "Terrace Wall Variant. Down N. Buttress Route to Terrace Wall again. Cheek, leading through. Cheek again, leading through in opposite order. Honour now being satisfied, descended N B traverse for third time and called it a day.

"April 24th. Western Gully on Black Ladders (we hope)"

Evelyn and Antonia Leech were there at the same time, climbing and walking for five days before leaving to camp in the Lledr Valley. Two days later, Gwen Moffat came with Sheena. There had been a drought for a fortnight and, in spite of all the work on the dam and the water supply, the water had sunk below the level of the pipe. So the hut was now without power and water.

All through the summer Annis and Tony Flew came with various companions and climbed a good many routes – Soap Gut, Pinnacle Wall, Sabre Cut, The Direct Route on Dinas Mot and others. Meanwhile Tony planned a dam to rival the Kariba. By the beginning of June the electricity worked, sand and cement had been assembled at the dam and Tony Flew and J. Whittaker slaved to complete the structure; but the first Saturday in June was to be notable mainly for the action on Kaisergebirge Wall.

The incident makes a sensational start to Jo Scarr's book, *Four Miles High*. She was leading Kaisergebirge, seconded by Muriel Baldwin, and was twenty feet above her last runner when she knew she was coming off. The peg held, and acted as a perfect pulley: as Jo came down Muriel had been pulled up and was now some way off the ground, with someone hanging on to her legs. After a rest Jo led it without any hesitation, followed by Pat Wood and Muriel. The log book reads: "Saturday 4th. After a thorough and sensational testing of the vital runner JMS made a second and successful attempt on Kaisergebirge Wall, followed by APW and EMB."

The guide book description of the time reads: "Extremely severe. Very exposed ... A good deal harder, technically, than anything else on the cliff."

On the Sunday, everyone managed prestigious climbs on the Pass before steady rain drove them to the hut for an official opening of the dam.

A fortnight later Denise Evans with Mollie Agnew and Ray College with Annis Flew, climbed Curving Crack and Longland's on Cloggy. The crack was wet and greasy in parts, Longland's in good condition and Denise on form with a vengeance after the birth of her firstborn. The following day a party left for the Direct on Glyder Fach and Annis' entry records ruefully, "Led to top pitch and failed as usual!" The hut was busy all summer with people doing the Three Thousanders in training for the Alps – "We hope we recover in time!" – climbing, and family holidays.

The LAC and Pinnacle Club joined for a meet in the Dauphiné during the last two weeks in July. As the report says, "This was a most memorable Meet ... as all the participants happened to be P.C. members, cooperation was excellent." Those taking part were Janet Cox, Margaret Darvall, Maud Godward, Dorothea Gravina, Ada Moss, Nancy Smith, Penny Storey, Isabel Taylor and Frances Tanner, a prospective member. They congregated at La Grave to meet their guide, Gilles Josserand who, with his humour and enthusiasm, added considerably to the joys of the meet.

As training they climbed the Pic de la Grave and the ridge route on the Rateau. Before dawn the following day they were off to the Refuge de l'Aigle, "perched dramatically above the Glacier de l'Homme, with fantastic views to distant Mont Blanc and the Valais peaks. Even more dramatic were the large stones which came bouncing down at us on the glacier. The next day a party climbed the Pic Orientale de la Meije, followed the day after by a long traverse of the Meije ridge, over the Doigt de Dieu to the Zigmondy Tooth, all in crampons owing to icy conditions; but for lack of one more long rope to ensure a safe return up from the gap, we could not attempt the final Grand Pic ..." Other climbs were the Bruyére Arête; and the slim peak of the Dibona simultaneously by the voie ordinaire and the Boell South Face route. The top was a little crowded when they met. This was the last complete route, for attempts on the Ecrins and the grand Pic de la Meije were foiled by bad weather.

This was part of a very good climbing year for Janet Cox; she was seconding much harder climbs and climbing a lot of gritstone. She led Molly Taplin up Skylon and Unicorn in the Pass and Great Slab on Cloggy.

Dorothea had a good year as well. Anne Littlejohn wrote an account for the *Journal* of the Whitsun Meet, joint with the LSCC, at Lagangarbh, Glencoe. It concludes: "By Monday only PC members remained. In perfect weather M Agnew and D Gravina climbed Agag's Groove, descended by Curved Ridge and hurried on to traverse Aonach Eagach ... In the evening, on hearing the glowing accounts of the splendid views enjoyed by the Aonach Eagach party, A Littlejohn, on an impulse, proposed a midnight ascent of Ben Nevis in order to view Lochaber by moonlight and watch the sunrise from the summit ... M Darvall and D Gravina received the suggestion with enthusiasm ... There cannot be many who, like Gravina, have climbed Agag's Groove, traversed the Aonach Eagach and ascended Ben Nevis all within the space of some sixteen hours."

Anne Littlejohn was engaged in writing a guide to the Isle of Rhum at the beginning of the 1960s and she and Margaret Darvall led through on two first ascents on Allival Slab. Later in the summer Margaret went to Switzerland and, with Maud Godward, traversed from Grindlewald to Grimsel via the Strahlegghorn. In the Bernina Alps she climbed Piz

Tschierva and Piz Corvatsch with Joan Busby.

Eileen Healey was in the Dauphiné for part of her Alpine holiday, and her routes included the S Ridge Direct of the Pointe des Cineastes and the W Ridge of the Pic Nord des Cavales. Bridget Keatinge climbed and ski-toured in the Silvretta and led Pic Coolidge in the Dauphiné.

It is good to know that Pilley had recovered enough from the road accident to reach the Geltenhutte and climb the Arpelistock.

The major event of the summer was Mollie Taplin's trip with the Midland Spitzbergen Expedition. The members of the party included Jim Kershaw from Cardiff, Tony Daffern, Harold Manison and Mollie from Birmingham, John Porter from Leicester and Gill Howarth from Sale. Their objects were to attempt unclimbed peaks and to survey and sledge in almost unknown country. They arrived in Magdalene Bay in the afternoon of July 5th and spent seven weeks on the island. They used the Franklin Glacier as their highway to the interior and spent a week climbing, sketching, surveying and skiing before negotiating the Waggonway Glacier and moving on to their next camp.

Mollie wrote for the *Journal*: "In spite of poor weather, at our next camp we climbed a further five peaks, one requiring a two-day effort, as well as providing an ice-wall of technical interest... Soon we were on our way again sledging farther inland to establish our third camp at the foot of Cafe Top, an impressive hog-back peak of about 4,000 ft."

This journey proved difficult and dangerous with poor conditions and bad visibility. Three of the party lost much equipment and spent five hours climbing out of a crevasse into which a collapsed snow bridge had deposited them, before staggering the last few miles to the new camp.

After days of bad weather, they climbed a fine peak several miles across the snow-field, then moved camp once more to the highest mountains yet, and spent the following days climbing intensively before being compelled to start the return trip to Magdalen Bay, and the little ship 'Lyngen' on which they were to return home. Mollie's full account is in *Journal* number 9.

There was a pleasant meet at Austwick in September, but most of the returning wanderers waited until the November meet before exchanging stories of their summer exploits. Dr Katie Corbett had died in June, aged 82, after a short illness, and had asked that her ashes should be scattered over Snowdon, so it was decided to do this at the Anniversary Meet. On the Sunday ten members (A Wilson, D King V Picken, S Long, S Bull, A Moss, H Monie, M Darvall, M Godward, led by Lilian Bray) ascended the Miners' Track to a point above Llyn Llydaw and there scattered the ashes of Dr Catherine Corbett, past President and Original Member of the Club. The ceremony did not go without a slight hitch for nobody had thought the jar would require an implement to unscrew the stopper. Fortunately the well-groomed Sue had her nail-file handy. Lilian performed the ceremony for her friend, pronouncing the words "In memory of Katie".

After the November Meet the hut was deserted till Annis and Tony Flew called in for a pre-Christmas visit. They fitted new Dunlopillo cushions to the seats, fetched kindling for the fire and left Warfarin down for the 'voracious mice' – a thoughtful Christmas present which the latter appear to have ignored.

CHAPTER 24

1961-2. Winifred Jackson President. An accident. Hut matters. Preparing for the Jagdula Expedition. Alpine routes. *Space* published. 'Women's Kulu Expedition'. Meets and membership.

There had been a lot of discussion on whether to hold the Dinner Meet at the New Year as had been done in the past, rather than in February. In the end it was decided to hold a New Year Dinner as well, comfort lovers staying at the Pen-y-Gwryd and hardier souls at the hut. Bunny Bull and Heather Monie stayed at the hut and were provided with sausages in case they got hungry. These sausages were superfluous, to say the least, as the log book records:

"S. Bull and H. Monie joined the P.y.G comfort-lovers in wet and disappearing snow for:- Crib Goch and Snowdon, Tryfan by North Ridge, Church and Cnicht; all punctuated with frequent wining and dining and SAUSAGES. N.B. The mice have been fed twice daily."

The Club's new President, Winifred Jackson, was at the head of the table on New Year's Eve, when seventeen members and relatives sat down to a really outstanding meal. The New Year was welcomed in in the bar to the accompaniment of rattling spoons and song. During the evening they saw Nea's colour slides of Ama Dablam and Chris Briggs' of Spain, Chris thus showing his versatility in providing not only the meal, but the entertainment as well.

Any occasion was notable with Winifred presiding. A teacher, soon to be appointed headmistress, she was a serenely good president, kindly and dignified, with an imposing figure. When anoraks with kangaroo pockets arrived, Bunny Bull chatted happily to Winifred about their usefulness: "I keep my camera in mine; what do you keep in yours?"

Winifred eying her with kindly tolerance looked remarkably like an oil painting of some benevolent College Founder. "Me," she replied simply.

Winifred presided next at the Annual Dinner. 1961 was the 40th anniversary of the Club's foundation, and efforts were made to mark the whole year as one of special celebration.

The Annual Dinner Meet, held from February 17th to 19th, packed out the Pen-y-Gwryd Hotel, and by turning the billiard room into a dining room Chris Briggs managed to accommodate 55 for the meal. Original members able to attend were Bray and Mrs Hirst, Biddy and Trilby Wells, and there were Club members from every decade – forty in all, which was a singularly appropriate number. At least ten were staying at the hut, among them Judy Hall, whose diary records three climbs with Anne Littlejohn. Judith wanted to lead Flying Buttress but there was such a queue for it that Anne led two other routes first. At last Judith did her lead, which was to qualify her for full membership but for this she must be seen by someone in authority and be seconded by an associate member; she records this event in her entry for the following day:

"Companions Julia Papworth and Frances Blackhurst. Footgear – boots. After waiting some time for various members of the Club to decide what they planned to do, and then get started, and also for the Committee to adjourn, we left P.Y.G. at about 10.45 a.m. and drove to the Llanberis Pass.

"Evelyn Leech accompanied us to the foot of the climb in order to observe my leading, as I wished to qualify for Full Membership of the Pinnacle Club. At the foot of the climb was a large party of beginners from the Mountaineering Association, who had only just begun. Had we got here earlier we would have missed them!"

Her frustration is obvious, but the Pass was sheltered and the waiting quite pleasant as they did scrambles in the sunshine. The climb went even better than the day before, so Judith attained her ambition and returned happily to London.

The main event of the weekend was of course the Dinner, and the official guests included Mrs Don Munday of the Canadian Alpine Club. Ken Tarbuck of the Wayfarer's Club was the chief guest and main speaker. Ken was the big authority on nylon rope; he had lectured up and down the country, written books and evolved the Tarbuck Knot, the learning of which was a major achievement in everybody's Beginners' Course in rock-climbing. He was introduced by Denise Evans, who proposed the toast to the guests in a most entertaining speech, ending up in a burst of song in praise of Mr Tarbuck. The evening concluded with slide shows.

Marjorie Wood had been unable to illustrate the menu cards this year, so for the first time an appeal had been broadcast to all members; a great stock of talent was disclosed, and the cards were unique and charming as ever.

A glance at the log book shows that Margaret Darvall and Denise Evans had snatched a chance to climb Central Trinity Gully in January and that several members had climbed up to VS standard in the Pass on the Sunday of the Dinner Meet. The committee meeting that Judith Hall mentions on the Sunday morning was a short one to elect Barbara Spark and Frances Tanner to membership. The following weekend Barbara brought a group of students to the hut, something she has done since on many occasions. Many young people, when meeting members of the Pinnacle Club ask: "Do you know Barbara Spark?" and go on to enthuse about the hut, its primitive delights, and its beauties as a centre for field studies.

This first party certainly left the hut in excellent order, with the fire laid, tea towels all newly washed, coal brought up to the hut and stacks of firewood.

Barbara was still at the beginning of her climbing career, a vivacious girl with red-gold hair. She and Jo Scarr were already planning their small expedition to the Himalaya, for which they received Pinnacle Club recognition, so Barbara's membership was a matter of some urgency! She is now Mrs Don Roscoe.

Frances Tanner started climbing when Nancy Smith went to Kirkby Lonsdale as a trainee assistant to try general practice after Cym's death and her experiences in Iraq. Frances realised that climbing meant a lot to Nancy and was determined to try it – not having a clue what it was all about, though she had always been a keen walker. She became a very steady second, though she rarely had the courage to lead. Soon after she moved to Lancaster in 1965, her mother went blind, so Frances was rarely able to come on meets. Once when my children were young she came over for the day and I bravely led her up Moss Ghyll Grooves. The climb was new to me, and her ideas on where the route went were very reassuring. I wondered how she would find the step across in boots, but she had no trouble at all. When she reached the top, she said "What shall we climb now?" being used to Nancy and her abundant supply of adrenalin. Mine, however, was all used up!

The 1961 Easter Meet and Annual Meeting were held in Wasdale during the first three days of April, and Saturday saw twelve members walking the Mosedale Horseshoe in the rain. Sunday was fine enough for Great Gable and favourite routes on the Napes, but the climbing was overshadowed by a serious accident to a walker, who was hit by a falling stone. Arning and Nancy Smith provided the first medical attention, whilst others set off for the stretcher at Sty Head, but unfortunately the walker, a Mrs D Clay, died. All well-known places were very crowded this weekend, so the Club went to Yewbarrow on the Monday, in search of open space. Some climbed on Overbeck and also did a route called Mossy Face, (they called it "Messy Rib") – the latter for sentimental reasons since Brenda Ritchie had led the first ascent. It is hard to think of any other reason for climbing something with such a name.

The Annual Meeting was held at the Wastwater Hotel. The secretary's report recorded with sadness the deaths of two founder members, Dr Corbett as already mentioned, and Dr Taylor at the age of 89. Two younger members were even harder to lose: Jean Griffiths, killed near Cader Idris; and Marie Grutter, the brilliant scholar, tutor and linguist, through illness. The last named had climbed Red Wall and Longland's with Maud at the Whitsun meet two years before, and three weeks later she, with her dog, Bran, had brought three members of Elford Youth Club to sample hut life. Writing of Marie, Evelyn Leech listed her achievements in the world of education and talked of her love of people, recalling with quiet wit her real affection for the hut, "sometimes bringing some student who longed to climb, or some teenager in need of elevation." Her expertise in languages had made her a tactful and fluent liaison officer during the Club's first Alpine meet after the war.

The hut secretary's report mentioned a generous gift from Biddy and Trilby Wells to help with major repair bills, the largest of which had been for woodworm treatment. During the woodworm spraying, when the hut had suddenly become alive, walls and all, with electricity, the complete rewire demanded by the Electricity Board had been done very quickly by Mr Worswick of Llanllechid at a cost of £18.

Questions had been asked at the February committee meeting as to why the new heating-stove required repair; it appeared that people had been standing on the open door of the stove in order to reach the drying rack and that the door had broken off in consequence.

At this time the *Journal* was being published every two years so it seemed sensible to economise on the *Handbook* by making reports briefer, and the rather unrepresentative climbing lists were omitted altogether.

Matters of interest in the BMC report showed that the Council had been hard at work in the area. Merioneth Planning Authority had refused the Mountain Club of Stafford permission to build a climbing hut in Cwm Cowarch, and the BMC helped the club win the appeal. Pinnacle Club members enjoy using this very pleasant hut today.

A new threat to the environment was the proposed nuclear power station at Wylfa Bay for which pumped storage accumulator installations would be needed; and surveyors had been seen in the area round Llyn Idwal and Llyn Boclwyd. The BMC was one of many groups which had lodged passionate objections.

A North Wales Committee had been formed to deal with local matters and Denise Evans was the first Pinnacle Club representative.

The BMC was compiling a hut list for the use of member clubs. It was with some reservations that members agreed for Cwm Dyli to be included. They could foresee all sorts of problems arising if the whereabouts of the key was known to all and sundry (it was kept in a special place in the power station and was easily available). It was a well-known ambition of certain members of the Climbers' Club to gain admission to the hut – but the thought of unknown members of other clubs made this threat pale to insignificance!

Three outside parties used the hut between Easter and the Pinnacle Club meet at Whitsun, for which one group drove up from London overnight. Dorothy Lee, Hester Willink and Dorothea Gravina arrived in the early hours and were out on the Carneddau when Annis came to make sure the hut was in good order.

The following day was spent on short routes nearby, for the Jagdula Expedition had a date with the photographer from the *Manchester Guardian*. As Dorothea put it: "Jo Scarr, Denise Evans, Pat Wood, Barbara Spark, Dorothea Gravina, all members of the Jagdula Expedition, draped themselves in suitable dramatic poses round various Himalayan boulders."

This was a very exciting meet for everyone, with all the fun and anticipation of preparing for an expedition. Vera Picken had brought her young daughter Mairet on the meet, so she must have had a wonderful introduction to the Club. She was one of a large party who climbed the Teryn arête the next day then continued round the Snowdon Horseshoe and back down Crib Goch. Dorothea wrote that the weather was wonderful, hot sun and a cloudless sky which called for lots of halts to look at the view and lie stretched out in the sun. Jo Scarr and Denise Evans did Curving Crack on Clogwyn du'r Arddu.

Dorothea wrote another note for June 30th – July 1st:

"JAGDULA EXPEDITION
The whole team succeeded in getting together in one place for the first time, but our activities were decidedly complicated by the arrival of an eight man team from Associated Television, undeterred by thick mist and drizzling rain. Crackstone Rib however was clear and the remainder of Saturday was spent in dramatic attitudes against skylines and disentangling ourselves from trees. Our greatest anxiety was for the safety of the TV team, but they showed great courage and determination in scaling the heights of Carreg Wastad. Sunday breakfast round the camp fire lasted most of the morning, followed by the Racks where Denise met a terrifying daddy longlegs. By this time the weather had turned gloriously hot and sunny and a philosophical calm descended on the whole party. Much work on expedition matters was done in the intervals, tents put up and down, lists gone over. Our next meeting will be in Delhi next March. Frances Tanner and Nancy Smith did Lockwood's Chimney. Expedition members present, D Evans, J Scarr, B Spark, P Wood, N Smith, D Gravina."

Two prospective members on the Whitsun meet were Mary Kershaw and Mabel Oldham. They had lived in Betws-y-Coed for fifteen years and ran a guest house. Keen walkers and leaders of the easier rock routes, they had introduced many young people to safe hill-walking and rock-climbing and were discovered by Gwen Moffat, who introduced them to the Club. They were elected members at a committee meeting held at the Guide Club

Greetings from members of the
Jagdula Expedition 1962
(Pinnacle Club)

L-R - *Barbara Spark, Nancy Smith, Jo Scarr, Denise Evans, Pat Wood, Dorothea Gravina.*

in Belgrave Square on July 5th and were almost immediately called upon to render service, for Annis was going to the United States for four months from September to December and Mabel and Mary were well placed to keep an eye on the hut while she was away. Mabel and Mary were two charming middle aged ladies and their enterprise and stamina were not immediately apparent, but they went off in their own quiet way and did walks such as the Welsh Three-Thousanders and kept an eye on the hut at the same time as working very hard to make their guest house a successful and happy place.

With the President and Secretary both living in the south of England and Dorothea a keen member of the Guide movement, several committee meetings were held in Belgrave Square during her term of office. At this particular meeting there was much discussion on the process of electing new members, especially that it was not up to a prospective member to apply for either full or associate membership, but merely for membership. Rule 6 in the *Handbook* should be changed also, for there was no mention of attendance at two meets being a necessary qualification. Nea Morin was asked to draw up a resolution to go before the General Meeting.

Nea had other matters on her mind as well; she had been looking at the bleak surroundings of the hut and thinking that the addition of a few small trees would be very attractive. On June 9th, with the help of her friends, she planted four "pre-memorial" rowans. She came again at the end of August with her son, Ian and her sister-in-law, Micheline, to attend to the Morin Rowan Grove, which seemed to have taken root sturdily. Sadly the sheep must have discovered a good meal, for there is no rowan grove now.

The Coopers and Poultons had had a grand family party in the hut during early August, and when Nea's party came along, in torrential rain, they were glad to find another family group, Sue Long and her friend Peggy Reece with her small son, before a blazing fire – and with their feet tucked up because the hut spring was working overtime. It would have been miserable to arrive all wet and find the hut cold, deserted and flooded, but this was a different matter. The whole party helped lay the linoleum, well scrubbed by Peggy, and the following day was fine so they had all the books in the library out in the sun for an airing and to be checked for mould.

Near the end of the Morin's stay, Annis turned up with her new baby, Harriet, aged seven weeks. Nea's report reads, "Much baby worship."

Bertha Rostron and Denise Wilson also had baby girls in 1961. Like Denise Evans they came back to climbing again as soon as they could. Ada Moss married Derek Shaw.

Dorothea was obviously training for the Himalayas this summer. She did several peaks and traverses in the Engadine with Margaret Darvall, and they progressed to the Bregaglia, joining Fay Kerr of the LAC and Eveleigh Leith for such routes as the Monte Rosso Traverse. Knowledge of this latter route encouraged Margaret and Eveleigh to climb Monte Rosso guideless later on, while Dorothea and Fay had a guide for the Badile Traverse, ascending the North Ridge and descending the South. Finally Dorothea joined her son, Tim, for a guideless ascent of the Haslerippe route on the Aletschhorn.

Janet Cox was in the Alps with Nigel Rogers, of the Climbers' Club and Alpine Club, whom she married the following year. They were driven from the rains of Chamonix to the Bregaglia, where they made a guideless ascent of the North Ridge of the Badile.

Margaret Darvall and Maud Godward linked up for some routes from Saas Fee, and Eileen Healey was having a final year before starting her family; she and Tim went to the Atlas Mountains in Morocco and when she wrote about her adventures for the Club Journal she said their holiday still seemed to have had almost more than they hoped for. They went in April, and Anne Littlejohn was able to go as well. They concentrated on the Toubkal area and climbed about fifteen routes. During the summer, Eileen was in Zermatt for the Matterhorn traverse via the Hörnli and Italian ridges, the Triftjigrat on the Breithorn and the traverse of the Zinalrothorn via the Rothorngrat and North Ridge.

During the year, Gwen Moffat published her first book, *Space Below my Feet*, to the accompaniment of very good reviews. In fact that in *Mountain Craft*, the magazine of the Mountaineering Association, could almost be called a rave review:

GWEN MOFFAT WRITES A LITERARY CLASSIC.
The author of this book is the only woman professional guide in Britain; she is one of our most competent and experienced rock climbing leaders, and an alpinist. She was chosen as the leader of a women's Himalayan expedition but something went wrong and she has not yet achieved her ultimate mountaineering ambition.
She has been an army driver, a deckhand, a chambermaid, a hostel warden, a script-writer and a tutor of the Mountaineering Association. The book she has written is an important contribution to mountain literature. [Then follow one and a half columns of enthusiasm, concluding:] Every reader in search of splendid authorship and every mountaineer looking for deeper understanding of climbers and their sport will find both in this remarkable work.

The review in the LAC *Journal* had more spice and less sugar: Whether or not one admires her style unreservedly, nobody can deny that she can write most mountaineering authors under the table ... A large number of the characters in the book are fellow-climbers, some of whom are well known, and this, combined with the fact that vistas of the author's private life are revealed to us, enables the reader to revel in all the sensations of a really pleasurable gossip . . . An unusual book by a courageous woman.

Thirty years later we know that the reviewers were speaking the truth. Only the other day someone said to me, "You know, I still think *Space* is the best climbing book I have ever read."

At the time there were jokes going round that all the men Gwen had ever climbed with bought copies in frenzied haste to find out what she had said of them. As to the allusion to the women's Himalayan expedition, Gwen was perhaps tempted to lead one, but as a professional guide she had everything to lose if anything went wrong.

On 23rd July the Women's Kulu Expedition, sponsored by the Mount Everest Foundation and Royal Geographical Society – in other words, Jo Scarr and Barbara Spark – set off from Plas y Brenin after a wonderful party and send-off with wine, folk music, presents and a farewell cake decorated with marzipan mountains, a baby Land Rover and a signpost marked – "Himalayas 8,000 miles."

At home the November meet at the Club hut was described as memorably bleak with plenty of snow already on the ridges, but there was plenty of rock climbing shared with very active guests: Sylvia Yates on her second visit and Jo Fuller for the first time. Janet Cox and Jo Fuller were whisked off to Tremadog to climb hard routes, presumably with Nigel Rogers and Brian Fuller, and seconded one of Joe Brown's new routes, the Grasper, and Jack Longland's Helsinki Wall respectively. Everyone else climbed in the Pass, where several guests were leading routes, sometimes climbing together. This led to the following entry in the committee minutes of a meeting held in December:

"It was also emphasised that prospective members at Meets are not allowed to lead rock climbs and that responsibility in this matter rests with the Meet Leader."

Oh dear!

Vera Picken was elected Secretary at this meeting and, despite her sin of leading routes before election, Sylvia Yates became an associate member.

Jo Fuller became an associate member on the last day of 1961 and celebrated on the first day of 1962 by climbing North Buttress on Tryfan with Dorothea and Tim Gravina in glorious weather, deep powder snow and Alpine conditions. Nancy Smith had brought her skis and had a marvellous time. After seeing the New Year in at P.Y.G. she "Skied down to the hut in the dark – fast and exciting."

This was Dorothea and Pat's last meet before the Jagdula Expedition. They were all set to drive out to Delhi in their Hillman Husky where they planned to meet up with Jo and Barbara in time to welcome Denise and Nancy, who were travelling out by air.

By early 1962 Winifred Jackson had heard from Jo Scarr and Barbara Spark of the success of their Kulu expedition. Their adventures on the way out included an ascent of Mount Olympus in Greece and a rock climb with a lonely and amorous young Greek; however, they arrived safely at the roadhead of Manali on September 12th and set off three days later for the Bara Shigri Glacier with three Ladaki porters, three ponies and three donkeys, obtained with the aid of Major Banon of Sunshine Orchards. Their porters, Wangyal, Jigmet and Atchuk had already been on two expeditions that summer and were experienced and trustworthy. The trek to base camp took seven days, and there was a serious set-back when Jo developed an abscess and had a fifty-mile round trip to reach a doctor. Meanwhile Barbara, with Wangyal and Jigmet had done two carries up the glacier. "The glacier is horrible," Barbara said gleefully, "Huge wobbly boulders with ice in between."

Jo, in her account for the PC Journal, continues: "How right she was ... After a day's load-carrying up this slag heap, I decided my abscess had been a blessing in disguise."

During the following five days three camps were set up, with the top one at 18,000 feet from which they were in a position to attempt their objectives, Lion and Central Peak.

They climbed both peaks, then moved camp up another branch of the glacier:

"Above the ice fall the only camp site free from danger of avalanches was a small table of level snow surrounded on three sides by wide crevasses. On the fourth side was a narrow crevasse, which we just hoped would not suddenly open up and leave us stranded.

"Next morning we set off first to look at the low col lying to the north of our camp, and after an easy scramble up scree reached its top only to find a very long ice slope down the other side, far too steep to be a practicable pass down into the next glacier basin. It seemed that after all we would be forced to return to the Bara Shigri by the same route, but we still had one day left before we must go down. Studying the surrounding peaks, only one looked even faintly possible, the un-named twenty-thousander directly above our camp site. From bearings and photographs we have since identified this as 20,495 ft., marked on the Survey of India map, but at the time we were not at all sure which peak it was, since the topography of this area did not agree with Lynam's provisional map at all.

One of the ridges from 20,495 ft, ran down to the col on which we were standing, so we set off to try and find a route up it. The rock was steep but sound and we had some excellent rock-climbing, but after five hours we were still less than a third of the way up the mountain, so had to abandon the route as impracticable. On the descent we discovered a much better route, however, zig-zagging on ledges straight up the east face, so decided to try for the summit by this route the next day. There was no time to put a camp half-way up, we would have to do it in a day from our camp at 19,000 ft., or not at all.

"Leaving at 6.30 a.m. we made rapid progress up the section we had come down the previous day, but farther up the angle steepened, and we came to a huge vertical rock wall, holdless and unclimbable. It seemed to be hopeless, but Wangyal, a wizard at route-finding, found a snow couloir round the side, and on we went. At 2.30 p.m. we reached the heavily corniced snow ridge leading to the summit. Keeping well down from the edge we battled along, a strong wind driving snow into our faces, and mist blowing eerily around, obscuring any view. At 3.30 p.m. we reached what we thought was the summit, only to see about fifty yards away and fifty feet above us another pinnacle, the true summit. It was clearly climbable, but would have taken us at least an hour in those conditions, so we eventually decided that with only another three hours of daylight left for descent, those last fifty feet were not worth a night in the open and possibly frostbite, and after all, what were fifty feet in twenty thousand?

"As fast as possible we climbed, scrambled, and slid down, and at dusk reached the vertical wall where we resorted to abseiling. For once I had no compunction about abandoning pitons and karabiners. The abseils brought us onto easier ground but now it was completely dark, and still a thousand feet of rock and snow lay between us and our tents. A bivouac seemed inevitable, but we determined to keep moving down as long as possible. Teeth chattering in the biting wind, we gingerly felt our way down the scree-covered ledges, very conscious of the thousand foot drop to the glacier below. Progress was very slow, and several times we came to an impossible section and had to retrace our steps, but after four hours we glimpsed level snow ahead, the glacier! It took another hour to find the one and only snow bridge across the enormous bergschrund, and then we were down. The walk across the snow basin to our camp was not without its hazards, Jigmet fell into a crevasse on route, but we were all still roped and hauled him out again. At 10.30 p.m. we reached the tents, exactly sixteen hours after leaving them. This ascent (and descent!) had been definitely the most interesting and memorable of our three peaks, and we celebrated into the early hours, on tea, soup, and a baby bottle of brandy."

They hurried down next morning and reached base camp the following day with supplies reduced to a quarter pound of margarine and one spoonful of jam – their ration scale had been accurate!

Their return to Manali took five days, and the ponies had to struggle over the Rhotang Pass after a heavy fall of snow, the end of the good weather the expedition had enjoyed almost continually for the past five weeks. Jo and Barbara wintered in Delhi, teaching in a school while waiting for spring and their next expedition.

All this was very good news to the Club when members met for the Dinner Meet at the Old Dungeon Ghyll Hotel in Langdale and there was much celebration.

Shirley (Bunny) Bull led the next meet, the Easter Meet, at the Club hut in late April. Due as she said to the Himalayas and babies, this was a very small affair with sixteen members present at the annual meeting and twenty-two apologies for absence.

Arising from the minutes of the previous year was the amendment to rule six, concerning qualifications for membership. Nea had prepared the revision, which was fully discussed and resulted in the wording more or less the same as at the present time:

Qualifications for full membersip included ability to lead climbs of a certain standard (Difficult standard was stipulated, but this was very much a minimum requirement) and competence to take charge of parties on these routes, also readiness to take a share in the activities of the Club. Any candidate for membership must take an active part on two official meets, and associate members would be promoted to full membership on the initiative of the committee.

Vera Picken had taken over from Dorothea Gravina as Hon. Secretary, and her report started on a sad note, for Penelope Poulton, one of the famous Seth Hughes sisters, had died. The membership stood now at 124, and members who had joined since the previous Easter were Mary Kershaw, Mabel Oldham, Sylvia Yates, Jo Fuller, Sally Westmacott, Marjorie Tanner and Sheila Crispin.

Something has already been said of Mabel and Mary, who were sincerely thanked for their help given to the Hut Secretary. Their idea of a warm welcome for visitors included special journeys to light the fire in readiness for their arrival – an impressive act of kindness.

The two members who joined right at the end of 1961, Sylvia Yates and Jo Fuller, were already experienced climbers, though Sylvia's application form was low-key: "Rock climbing in Ireland leading to V. Diff standard. Climbs in Wales include Longland's, Great Slab, The Cracks, Nea. One season in Zermatt – Breithorn, Rimpfischhorn, Trifthorn & Dom by Festigrat." Nancy Smith says she never knew Sylvia to be daunted by a climb. After a few years, Sylvia moved to Switzerland and she lives now in Ireland where she met Ingrid Masterson and introduced her to the Club.

Jo was married to Brian Fuller and had seconded many hard routes in England, Scotland and Wales: such things as Kipling Groove, May Day, Swastika on the Etive Slabs, and Cenotaph Corner. She had also been involved in many new gritstone routes. At the time she joined, she led to about V Diff standard but soon developed into a very sound VS leader.

In her four years' climbing Sally Westmacott had tackled middle-grade routes in several areas and up to VS in Derbyshire. Abroad, she had traversed the Zinalrothorn, Nadelhorn and Rimpfischhorn, Tour Ronde and Tsantaleina amongst other climbs. She had joined the Ladies' Alpine Club in 1959 but usually climbed with her husband, Michael. She joined the Pinnacle Club because she was not eligible for the Climbers' Club, but when they opened their ranks to women she became a member and resigned from the PC in 1976. She and Mike were in America for some years, and she is a very sound and experienced climber, having always remained keen, and does a lot of work with young people, judging by her constant pleas for cast-off rock boots.

Marjorie Tanner was a maths teacher at a grammar school in Essex, so had a punishing journey whenever she came to Wales for the weekend. She had been a keen walker for a number of years before she started climbing, and was a most delightful person to talk to. Unfortunately her Head did not entirely approve of the head of the maths department going off on climbing weekends; especially when Marjorie had quite a bad fall while leading Flying Buttress one damp day. Before this, she had been prepared to take over as Hon. Secretary. Sadly, she resigned from the club in 1971.

Sheila Crispin lived in Coniston and when she showed an interest in climbing her parents insisted that she should have proper instruction, so she learnt with Jim Cameron. After the first once or twice he had her leading, and after that she climbed with him as a friend and saved her money for other things. She joined the Pinnacle Club shortly after her eighteenth birthday and already led climbs to Severe standard as well as enjoying skiing and mountain walking. After leaving school she qualified as a vet. and now works at the University of Bristol. She has always been a safe, strong person in the mountains, and was medical officer on the Pinnacle Club Lahaul Expedition in 1980.

The final meet before the summer was held in the Club hut at Whitsun. Most people arrived very late, some in the early hours of Saturday morning, so they were late starting out and the whole party, – Margaret Darvall, Suzanne Long, Annette Wilson, Vera and Mairet Picken, Doreen Tharby, Maud Godward, Penny Storey, Marjorie Tanner and Peggy Wild – went to Teryn Slabs. The whole party, that is, except for Dr Arning. They may have been slow, but Arning was slower, and she was left behind, locked in the hut.

As it was padlocked on the outside by Annette, who stressed that the whole thing was an accident, Arning had to squeeze her not inconsiderable bulk through the top of the ground floor window (according to one account, and the upstairs window according to another), thus attaining a first descent (of one or the other). Nobody records what Arning did after that.

That evening Ruth Ruck called in at the hut and invited all present to Ty Mawr for coffee the following morning. Her book about the farm, entitled *Place of Stones*, had recently been published and several members had already read it, so they were very keen to see round Ruth's domain. Afterwards the whole party went on to Cwm Silyn but they hadn't thought to bring a guide book so after a bit of scrambling about they went up via a gully and returned to the hut for a cup of tea. Some climbed Flake Traverse in the Pass after this, amongst them June Hunt, Sir John Hunt's daughter, who had arrived late the previous evening for her first experience of the Club. The whole weekend sounds a happy sort of doddle, but something must have impressed her, for she came again!

CHAPTER 25

1962. Jagdula Expedition. Other trips. Anne and Sylvia at the Hut. Froggatt Meet. Reunions and climbs in Wales. An accident and a news bulletin. Tin trays.

Jagdula Expedition Christmas Card. The arrow points to Dorothea.

The most comprehensive account of the 1961 and 1962 Himalayan Expeditions is Jo Scarr's book, *Four Miles High*, but at least two shorter accounts were published: Nancy Smith's "Himalayan Holiday" in the P.C. *Journal* and Denise Evans' "The Jagdula Expedition 1962" in the LAC *Journal*.

Dorothea and Pat had an adventurous drive out in their Hillman Husky and finally, driving day and night to make up for lost time, arrived in Delhi on 12th March to be greeted by Jo and Barbara.

The following week was an exhausting round of clearing stores through customs, completing formalities, re-sorting eqyipment and visiting friends, so it was a sleepy quartet who stood on the tarmac in the pre-dawn greyness to welcome Nancy and Denise at Delhi airport. During the succeeding days they saw a few of the sights of India, were photographed for television and had an interview with Nehru before driving to Nepalganj and the kindly welcome of Miss Anna Tomasak at the American Mission Nursery.

That evening they met their Sherpas. The sirdar, Dawa Tensing, had been with Denise and Charles Evans when they climbed in East Nepal on their honeymoon, and had been Charles' sirdar on Kanchenjunga. He was an old friend to Denise, and the others liked him at once. He told them he had come out of retirement for one last expedition when he heard that Evans Memsahib was coming.

The Jagdula River flowed through one of the wildest areas in the world still unexplored, about eighty miles north west of Dhaulagiri, and entailed a two hundred mile walk-in from Nepalganj. John Tyson had taken an expedition to this part of Nepal in 1961 and at the time the Pinnacle Club had been afraid that he would climb Kanjiroba's highest peak, a beautiful snow pyramid, which they thought they could climb if the approach was not too difficult. In fact, Tyson concentrated on a different group of mountains but was able to give them a great deal of advice about the approach.

Nancy wrote of the three-week approach march: "Snowy peaks of the high Himalaya over a hundred miles away came into view each time we crossed a range of hills. At Sitalpati our expedition dog joined us and came the whole way. At Jarjakot we changed from thirty-eight ponies and thirty-eight pony men to sixty-eight coolies, because the going was too rough for horses, and shortly after we dismissed our armed escort. Over the high hills, through the rhododendron forests and along the hot sultry Bheri River valley we walked, avoiding its many deep gorges by high detours. We usually set off about 4.0 am after a cup of tea and a Ryvita biscuit, and walked until 10.0 am. Then a large breakfast and maybe a bathe in river or waterfall. Then off again at noon in the heat of the sun and on until evening and camp. In nineteen days we had covered the two hundred miles to Kaigaon, the last village, at a height of about 9,000 feet."

They sorted equipment here, then followed the river to the north-east to make camp just above the junction of the Jagdula and the Garpung Khola. Denise and Nancy, with three Sherpas, explored up the Jagdula Valley to try and approach their peak from the west, but found the route difficult and dangerous with thorn bushes and loose rock. They turned back with reluctance for they had no idea whether the prospects would be any better on the unexplored east side of the range. This, however, proved much easier. Jo and Barbara set off first, round the southern end of the Kanjiroba Himal, following the Garpung Khola in a north-easterly direction along a well worn yak track. In two days they reached a high, wide valley and established a Base Camp at twelve thousand feet, later moving this to a higher position.

Nancy wrote: "We found another camp site on the sloping valley side, and a spring coming out of the rocks. There we dumped our loads and the Sherpas set to and dug out stones and levelled places for all our tents, and built a dry-wall shelter for the kitchen tarpaulin, for this was to be our home for the next two or three weeks.

"Meanwhile the five of us, light as air with no loads, set off up the ridge above after Dawa. We were in high spirits and going to have a look, approaching Our Peak and exploring the unknown... We had no rope, no crampons, no overboots ... Dawa was forging ahead in deep snow going in up to his middle. We all followed behind feeling oddly like a bunch of kids on a Sunday School outing... There were one or two rocky pitches where Dawa waited for us ready to hold a hand if we needed help and even if we didn't. This dear old veteran of so many expeditions was egging us on, perhaps wondering in his wise old head if this bunch of hilarious girls were really mountaineers at all."

The summit of Dawa's peak was 17,500ft, and for Pat and Nancy it was their first Himalayan top.

The party spent the last few days of April, during which it snowed frequently, in climbing minor peaks and measuring out a baseline and building cairns for Jo's survey. On April 19th Dorothea and Nancy set out with Dawa to find a site for Camp I in their attempt on Kanjiroba, taking with them tents and food. The weather was bad and on the descent Nancy lost the route and was avalanched down a gully. Fortunately she was not badly hurt and writes: "The others tried to put me to bed then but I was so full of joie de vivre, and so thankful to be still alive, that we had an uproarious evening in the tent that night. We ate tinned pears for supper and a vague memory of a bit of verse came to mind: "With possible extinction adding flavour to stewed pears." Michael Roberts. Dorothea capped it all by saying 'Somewhere up there in the snow we've hidden the stuff for Camp One. Now there's a little puzzle for Denise and Jo to go up tomorrow and see if they can find it!' It snowed all day and we had visions of our dump being buried deep in the snow and lost for ever. They were rather cross that we hadn't even put a tent up."

During the following days Camp One was set up, Camp Two established above the ice fall and Camp Three at about 20,000ft, high up on the final ridge. Jo, Nancy and Denise spent an uncomfortable night there and were away to a late start the following morning.

Denise writes: "The ridge continued airy and exposed, though not technically difficult. Most of the time we were on the very crest or, because of cornices, a little to one side. The snow was still very soft and we were scarcely ever able to get a satisfactory axe belay. By mid-day we had gone about two-thirds of the way to the summit and were still hoping to reach it when we came to the foot of an ice pinnacle that had been prominent from afar. We knew that we must contour it on the left, that is, north side of the mountain, for here the top of a small glacier abuts against the ridge. But now the weather, so fine to start with, was deteriorating rapidly and we were soon enveloped in cloud... Twenty minutes later it was snowing more thickly than ever and we turned back. Visibility was so poor that we could only see a yard or two ahead and had we not been following a ridge we would have had great difficulty in finding the way ... We came to a place where the ridge appeared to divide: which way had we come? The mist lifted for a moment and we just had time to make out our two little tents beneath us. When we reached them we tumbled in thankfully. The blizzard grew fiercer as night came on until we thought we must soon become airborne. But the tents stood up to it. Next morning we had barely emerged to see how much new snow had fallen when Dawa appeared, followed by four Sherpas with empty pack-frames.

"'Niche!' he said, grinning, pointing downwards, and we all went down to Base Camp."

Not until May 10th was the weather fit for another attempt, and by that time Dorothea was in bed with a sore throat and high temperature. The others went up to Camp Two and arranged for Jo and Barbara to have first attempt at the summit, to be followed by the others next day. They reached the summit at 9.30 on May 14th. The others were ready at Camp Three but by now Denise was ill with flu and had to miss her chance. She went down to Camp Two with Jo and Barbara and saw Pat and Nancy reach the summit at about nine'o clock the following morning.

Jo and Barbara decided to spend a week surveying on the west side of Kanjiroba, taking a Sherpa and going over the col above Camp One into unknown country, now that the mountain had been climbed. Meanwhile the others moved down to the lower base in the Garpung Khola. Kagmara I, the highest peak to the east, had attracted Denise from the first, and she and Dorothea determined to climb it. Denise writes:

"Pat and Nancy had joined us by now and we spent the next day carrying a camp up to the glacier below the north face. The seracs growled and grumbled all afternoon and evening and snow fell thickly. The next morning however the weather seemed to be clearing and Dorothea and I set off with Mingma and Pemba Norbu, while Nancy and Pat followed with Ang Pema. The climbing was steep and invigorating, with here and there an icy bulge where hand and footholds had to be cut. From below it had looked as though the lower part was the steepest and that the angle eased off higher up, but in fact the slope was concave and steepened considerably towards the summit ridge. We reached the top at midday and started slowly down, taking great care with the top slope which, covered with fresh snow, felt as though it might avalanche. We were just negotiating an awkward corner where the snow tended to come away in slabs from the ice beneath when Pemba Norbu, who was bringing up the rear, shot past us with a dismal shriek. Dorothea, next on the rope, brought him to a stop.

"We reached camp to find Jo, Barbara and Ang Temba, all looking much thinner after a successful week of exploration on the west side of Kanjiroba.

"It was by now May 23rd and we only had a few days left before starting on our homeward journey. We put a camp on the col between Kagmara I and II, and from it were able to climb Kagmara II and III and a small peak south of the Kagmara Lekh overlooking the Tibrikot valley."

We take up the story from Nancy's account: "The snow was getting very soft and wet, avalanches more frequent and it was the end of our allotted time in the High Himalaya. So reluctantly we packed up and sloshed down to Base Camp.

"There was a Tibetan tent pitched below us in the valley, with hand-woven sacks for trade and a herd of seventy-four yaks. We counted them. This was a stroke of luck for us as we hired sixteen of them to carry the remains of our stuff back to Kaigaon.

While four of us went back with the yaks, Dorothea and Jo travelling light with three Sherpas, went over the Tibetan Col. Jo took more bearings on the peaks for her map and they had a wonderful time exploring unknown valleys and up to the Phoksumdo Lake. Finally they met us, coming down another valley and joining us over a week later at the Indian check-point, at Dunai on the Thuli-Beri river to the east.

"There is neither time nor place for the real story of our walkout. It was completely fascinating, and had all the excitement of a new route, with the issue in doubt until the last few days. This was due to the wild habits of yaks, the problem of yak transport and the difficulty of hiring coolies or beasts in the wild desert region to the north. We still followed the Bheri river almost up to its source high on Dhaulagiri. The Barbung Khola is the same river, and the geography here had everything. I doubt if anywhere in the world could be found a walk to equal this in contrasts of climate and land formation. Over the Balangra Pass with wild rhubarb growing, and far more Alpine flowers peeping through as the snow melted. Down to Tibricot, with its wild dogs, paddy fields and a hot dusty river valley with afternoon dust storms. Up the Barbung Khola we went, getting into ever wilder and more desert country to the north of the High Himalaya, where the rainfall is nil. There were great gorges and chasms and pinnacles and the odd architecture of erosion, like the Grand Canyon in Arizona. Then over three high passes where we all suffered from altitude sickness at 18,000 feet, even our dog and the Sherpas, and on to the edge of the high plateau of Tibet. We came round the north of Dhaulagiri and down to the more prosperous and irrigated valley of the Kali Gandaki River. There were horsemen and their horses decked out in embroidered cloths like the film of the battle of Agincourt. Coming up the valley were decorated mules carrying supplies for the Tibetan military encampments we had passed near the frontier. With the irrigation were apricot trees and barley growing, Tibetan villages and refugees. Then down to the paddy fields again and maize on terraces and thick impenetrable steamy forests with rich green undergrowth, masses of ferns and dahlias and exotic lilies and orchids. We were plagued by leeches and soaked in monsoon as we splashed on over rushing torrents by precarious bridges, up and down thousands of marble steps on the hills over to Pokhara with Annapurna to the north.

"From the airfield at Pokhara we flew to Katmandu; a cocktail party at Boris' a welcome from Charles Wylie, then flying out to Patna, Benares, Allahabad, Lucknow and train back to Nepalganj. Then home in a Boeing 707 and London next day was simply absurd. This was how Denise and I landed back; the others have a different tale."

The others had a two month overland journey ahead of them, but first they were shown round Kathmandu by the Sherpas. Jo wrote: "Our faded tartan shirts, jeans and delapidated baseball boots were more suitable for this wandering round squares and bazaars and drinking with the Sherpas in their favourite chang houses than for attending the official functions given for us. We felt most self-conscious in this garb but everyone else seemed delighted to see mountaineers in their ordinary expedition clothes.

"At last we could delay our departure no longer. The Sherpas were leaving on their three-week walk back to their homes in Sola Khumbu, and Dorothea, Pat, Barbara and I were returning to Nepalganj and then Delhi. Ahead lay the 8,000-mile drive back to England, behind three enchanting months in West Nepal, surely one of the most delightful countries in the world."

For members with shorter holidays nearer home there were still exciting placs to visit. Sally Westmacott went to North Africa and climbed a number of peaks in the High Atlas, and several members and prospective members joined the Ladies' Scottish Alpine Meet based at Saas Fee, or made up their own parties elsewhere in the Alps. At home the hut was well used, in particular by Anne Littlejohn and Sylvia Yates who snatched four separate breaks during August and September:

"Made acquaintance of Main Wall today: went with piton in pocket and PAs in rucksack, but needed neither. Situations splendid but technically just a teeny bit disappointing ...

"1 Sept 62. Entirely deceived by plausible announcer who had distinctly promised sunny intervals ...

"9 Sept 62. Rain not heavy but horizontal. Arranged library books and journals, cleaned windows, allowing better view of rain.

"22 Sept 62. Anne Littlejohn and Sylvia Yates. Ever since having been taken up the Nose Direct (by a perfect stranger, one February afternoon – need one add that the descent was made in total darkness?) one of us had had an ambition to lead it, when conditions should be a little warmer, drier and lighter. We had to dispense with the warmth but at least the rock was dry and sufficiently illuminated when Sylvia floated up it this morning. The final crack was an unseen lead because, as we discovered later, the perfect stranger had finished by the last pitch of Diagonal Route."

Nea on the Boulder

Nancy on the Boulder.

On Brown's Eliminate.

Froggatt Meet 1962. Photos: Frances Tanner.

Marjorie Tanner and June Hunt arrived that evening, having climbed North Buttress, and presented a brown woollen rug to the hut. When Annis and Tony came the following weekend they were much impressed by the gifts, cleaning and climbs. They climbed on the Saturday but on the following day of rain the hard-working Hut Secretary wrote with venom in the Log:

"The Hut Sec. has long regarded the Hut Lavatory (let alone its emptying) with distaste verging on loathing. Setting out through the rain with a bucket of Snowcem, I soon found our 'dry' walling was not the properly prepared surface the makers recommend..."

At the beginning of October the Pinnacle Club had its first gritstone meet for many years, staying in the R O Downes Hut at Froggatt. This is the Climbers' Club Hut in memory of Bob Downes, who died on a Himalayan expedition. The meet was led by Janet Rogers (Cox), and was a tremendous success, well photographed by Frances Tanner. Also present were Denise and Nancy back from the Himalayas and a good mix of established members and guests.

Froggatt Edge is a great place for party pieces – Janet's was Sunset Slab and Nancy's Three Pebble Slab. Members led the ever-popular Green Gut, top-roped Brown's Eliminate and enjoyed other choice delights all along the Edge, but the most spectacular photos are of Nea and Nancy surmounting the overhang on the Boulder. Sunday saw similar performances at Stanage.

Nancy and Frances went straight to the hut after the Froggatt meet and Nea stayed with Denise in Bangor. On October 11th they climbed Sabre Cut on Dinas Cromlech, followed by Nancy doing Cenotaph Corner on a top rope held by Denise and Nea. This shameful deed did not go unnoticed, for when they went down they found Jo Scarr and Barbara Spark at the bottom, and all went off to the Pen-y-Gwryd for a celebration dinner. Two days later Nea, Denise and Charles Evans were able to join Jo, Barbara, Nancy and Frances for yet another celebration dinner at PyG. In spite of all the feasting, they appeared to be in good form, and a number of other friends came up at the weekend to keep the climbing standard high – Anne Littlejohn, Alwine Walford, Sylvia Yates and Sybil Washington. Sylvia and Anne climbed Unicorn before the weather broke and October departed midst rain, hail and biting wind.

These hail showers continued during the November Meet but there were several climbing parties. Mabel Oldham was with a group climbing on Tryfan, and towards the end of the Saturday afternoon she was leading her sister Mary on Second Pinnacle Rib when she fell while making a traverse right at the top of the final pitch. Her rope jammed in a crack, which saved her to some extent. She and Mary were helped down by members of the Keele University Climbing Club, and met near Heather Terrace by the Ogwen Cottage rescuers. Mabel had arm and shoulder injuries and was taken to Bangor Hospital, refusing morphia and stretchers! (Thus reads the account in the Log Book).

Apparently Mabel fell about fifty feet and ended in a very awkward position so it was fortunate that Keele members were climbing nearby. They were warmly thanked in a letter from Winifred Jackson, and in reply they said: "We are particularly pleased to have been of assistance to the Pinnacle Club. We have often enjoyed the help and advice and very pleasant company of Annis Flew (on Lliwedd of course) and are happy to have repaid this debt of gratitude, at least in part. Please send our best wishes to Mrs Oldham. I am told that despite her injuries, her spirit that night was quite remarkable."

They could hardly have written a more tactful letter.

On the Sunday morning Annis and Vera visited Bangor Infirmary and found Mabel extremely groggy and awaiting an operation. She had a broken rib, arm and collar bone, but eventually made a good recovery. However, this was not quite the end of the matter for on the Saturday evening the following news item had been broadcast:

"In Wales, an RAF Mountain Rescue Team has been battling its way through heavy rain tonight to rescue a woman reported lying unconscious on Tryfan Peak in Snowdonia. Police said the woman had apparently fallen during a storm in the afternoon. No more details have been given."

By 8 a.m. the following morning the news bulletin was substantially correct, but that was too late to prevent a night of worry for the families who heard the announcement.

June Hunt, who had been with Annis and Vera on Tryan and helped with the rescue, wrote to Vera:

"I did feel most dreadfully tired after all the events of Saturday and the drive home seemed endless ...

"The most astonishing thing about the whole incident was the speed with which the BBC got hold of the news. Luckily my family missed the announcements but apparently it got on the air – even the Club was mentioned – before we got back to the hut! It seems there must be some mean person in Ogwen somewhere who phones everything straight through. I've noticed that few falls are ever reported from Coniston area, and yet Jim Cameron told me his team is often called out ..."

Vera wrote to the BBC for the relevant extracts from the news bulletins and, after thanking them for their cooperation, continued:

"I suppose if we have an accident we must expect some publicity and the extract read at 8 am on 4.11.62 is more or less correct, but I feel that the reference at 9.30 pm 3.11.62 was made rather prematurely. Not only was it incorrect but since there were about 24 women climbing in Snowdonia that weekend (Pinnacle Club alone) relatives and friends who heard the announcement would have been caused unnecessary anxiety. I, for instance, had left four children at home, aged 14-22 ..."

The BBC, in the person of a lady with the charming name of Betty Kitkat, replied that they were well aware of the anxiety that could be caused; and continued: "We well understand your feelings about our first report ... but the work of the RAF Mountain Rescue Team in the circumstances was news of general interest, and we did not feel justified in withholding it. We gave our authority (the police), and it could be expected that relatives of climbers known to be in the area would telephone for details as they became available."

So the matter rested.

The hut continued to be well used throughout November; Sylvia Yates and Anne were determined to climb Babel, which Sylvia led on the 11th in a biting wind, "nonchalantly, followed shiveringly and with respectful slowness by AL and Denise Evans, who had come along the Pass just at the right time."

The New Year meet, held on the last weekend in December, was especially joyous, for all the members of the Jagdula Expedition were safely home and able to attend. Winifred Jackson wrote: "It was a very happy informal Dinner occasion. there was plenty of snow ... Skiers and skaters and tin tray experts did well."

It is pleasing to think of Pinnaclers seeing out this happy, successful and eventful year, tobogganing down the hillside on tin trays.

CHAPTER 26

1963-1965. Dorothea Gravina's presidency. Floods in the hut. Members. Meets.
Helen Goodburn finds friends in Nea and Denise.

People at the Dinner Meet in 1963 remembered it for the glorious weather with frozen waterfalls, snow and ice sparkling in the sunshine, fitting weather for the showing of Denise Evans' film of the Jagdula Expedition on the Saturday evening. Dorothea Gravina, who was camping as usual, had pitched her tent near the Pen-y-Gwryd so as to be handy for the dinner but called in at Cwm Dyli for Sunday breakfast, cheerful and indefatigable. At Easter she became president for the next three years, and this meet had memorable weather as well – wind, hail and torrential rain. On the worst day Dorothea led a 'swim' up Glyder Fawr and back via the restorative Pen-y-Gwryd while the Sensible People endeavoured to have a lazy day amid the springs of water in the hut. Sheila Crispin, signing herself 'Cherub' – a nickname she earned at school because she was not one – drew an inspired illustration in the log book.

"Well girls, we must learn to live with it"

On the following day, in continuing rain, everyone grabbed an implement and dug drainage trenches in all directions. "This fevered activity was watched with astonished interest by the Power House men and kept us happy all day," reads the meet report. There is a picture of this, too.

At the Annual Meeting, Evelyn Leech was made an honorary member in recognition of her many years' service to the Club. Vera Picken said a young, active person should arrange the climbing venues, so Jo Fuller was appointed meets secretary and nine meets were arranged instead of the usual six. A sad note was the death of Mrs Eden-Smith. She had been in a nursing home since July 1962 after having a leg amputated; nevertheless it was sad to say goodbye to an original member whose personality and enthusiasm had done so much to shape the Club. Harriet Turner, who had served the Club so well as treasurer and auditor, had also died. She left the Club a small legacy.

Two new members had been elected in November 1962: June Hunt and Fiona Lewis. Mrs Lewis was a member for about twelve years.

June is daughter of Sir John Hunt, of Everest fame, but regrets that her enthusiasm was far greater than her ability. She came to climbing through a love of mountain walking, and went on a Mountaineering Association course in Wales taught by Fred Taylor. One day, she says, he waved his hand at Cwm Dyli and made a complimentary remark about the Pinnacle Club, whose hut it was. It came as a shock to find later that the imposing building she had seen housed not the Club but the power station!

After that she had many climbing holidays with Jim Cameron, the Lake District guide and finally became a Pinnacle Club member in a most unlikely way. She met Joan Cochrane at a testing session for 'Mensa' applicants. Mensa, despite being composed of the brightest people in the land, had stupidly given a large number of them the wrong room and, when they finally found them, refused to let them take the test that day. Joan and June went off to tea at Fullers to console themselves, talking mountains, and Joan proposed

June for the Club.

Joan's farm prevented her coming on meets, but June found herself made very welcome, especially by Marjorie Tanner, who used to pick her up from Stratford on her way to climbing weekends at the hut. She always led the climbs and was a great companion. June is now June Ginger; she married a Californian in 1963 and they have lived in an avocado grove ever since, except when using June's hobby of bird watching as an excuse to travel the world.

At this time Anne Littlejohn was working at the Veterinary Laboratory near Weybridge in Surrey and Sylvia Yates was based in London, but all through the year Anne wrote long essays in the log book of the climbs they had done, joined on occasion by Jo Fuller and Denise Wilson. In June, Jo Fuller led Sylvia up Merlin at Tremadoc, her first of many VS leads. By the end of the year Sylvia had well over twenty VS leads to her credit and Anne had gleefully recorded remarks she had overheard from male climbers: "Disgusting confidence" on Longland's; "S.Y. strolled up Scratch, layback and all, somewhat to the chagrin of a male party who jammed and slinged their way up it, inch by anxious inch, at a very respectful distance behind us."

During the summer they were involved in two rescues of fallen leaders. In each case the seconds were without gloves and had badly burnt hands. The traditional waist belay, with this inherent danger to seconds, remained in use until the advent of the Sticht Plate in the mid seventies.

Six Pinnacle Club members planned to go to Chamonix in the summer – Jo, Sylvia, Anne, Denise Wilson, Nancy Smith and Pat Wood. They met briefly in Wales in July, climbed Soapgut, and made plans till all hours. Nancy and Denise travelled to Chamonix together and dashed straight out for a training climb – The Petits Charmoz, the M and the Pointe Albert – three peaks on the first day! When the others arrived they did the same training climb and Nancy and Denise fulfilled one of Nancy's great ambitions – the N W Ridge of the Blaitiére – strenuous, serious and long – descending by the Arête Bregeault and arriving back at their tent after a 17 hour day. While they had a well-earned rest day the others climbed the NNE Ridge of the M, then all went up to the Couvercle Hut. The others were indignant when Jo's husband claimed her as a climbing partner, altering all her plans, so only five of them climbed the SW ridge of the Moine and traversed the Courtes. After that the weather broke, so Denise and Nancy climbed the NNE Ridge of the M with Frenchmen pinching their calves on the crux and made a getaway for Switzerland and the E Ridge of the Weisshorn. Sylvia, Pat and Anne climbed the Plaques Route on the Requin and the Forbes Arête on the Chardonnet and almost succeeded on the Midi in poor conditions before going home. It had been a joyous and successful holiday, and the routes on the Blaitiére and Weisshorn were both first feminine ascents.

Meanwhile Dorothea Gravina dashed across Europe on a moped to lead the Pinnacle Club and Ladies' Alpine Club joint meet at Zinal, where members found great enjoyment on the rock ridges all around. Pinnacle Club members were Doreen Tharby, Peggy Wild, Eveleigh Leith and Sue Long; Mary Fulford and Livia Gollancz, who were LAC members on the meet, joined the Club in the autumn.

Margaret Darvall, Marjorie Heys-Jones and Dorothy Lee with two imminent Pinnacle Club members, Alwine Walford and Katharine Gebbie, were climbing in Turkey, making a number of guideless ascents, and Sally Westmacott climbed in the High Lebanon before returning to the Alps for routes around Arolla and Zinal.

1963-65

Janet Rogers was climbing in the Alps with her husband, Nigel. They started with two good rock routes on the Cima Picolissima, then went to the Bregaglia for the NE Face of the Badile, still a very serious climb, of which all the early ascents had taken two days. They rounded off their holiday with a visit to the Mont Blanc area for the N Ridge of the Peigne.

Mary Glynne was on a trip round the world; when she reached Japan, she climbed Fujiyama.

At home the hut was much in use for clubs and family parties – the Flew family and the Coopers and Poultons.

September saw the returned wanderers meeting at Froggatt, Yorkshire and the hut. Anne Littlejohn and Sylvia Yates resumed their ticking off of VS climbs, and on September 28th had the fun of going to Cloggy to watch the first televised climb done live by Joe Brown, Don Whillans, Ian McNaught-Davis and a Frenchman.

The following weekend was the Anniversary Meet, with good climbing but the first sign of trouble in the Nantlle Valley. Three people trying to climb the crags round Nantlle found themselves turned off each in turn by angry farmers. The farmers had a legitimate grievance, with sheep-worrying, litter and damage to fencing, but their protective measures with dogs and guns were somewhat extreme.

Three new members were elected during the meet: Cynthia Agnew, Mary Fulford and Livia Gollancz.

Cynthia lived in Maryport, Cumbria, and had been on the Buttermere meet run by Margaret Darvall a few weeks before. She had loved fell walking since childhood and had been rock-climbing since she was seventeen. Now she led climbs of all standards, including such taxing routes as Eagle Front in Buttermere and snow and ice climbs on Ben Nevis. She was on the committee during the late 1960s, but moved to Scotland shortly afterwards and lost touch while her family were growing up. She came back, with her daughter, for the 50th Anniversary celebrations of the opening of the Club hut.

Mary Fulford grew up in a hillwalking family, so selected Bangor as a suitable place for her further education, as it combined mountains and the sea. She knew she would not have a chance to graduate, for her parents could only afford two years at college for her, but in those pre-war days she was thrilled to have two years rather than disappointed not to have longer. At Bangor, in 1935, she was introduced to rock-climbing by a boyfriend, a daredevil who had been expelled from school but became a reformed character when introduced to rock-climbing. Mary was invited for what she thought was a picnic, but found herself being roped and led up the Idwal Slabs. Her main feeling was embarrassment because her blue and white spotted frock kept blowing over her head. During the following week she acquired not only a pair of second-hand slacks but another boyfriend who climbed. He took her up Milestone Buttress and she was hooked – riveted! She says:

"Between the two of them (I know I was very false, never telling one about the other) I received some very good training.

"One evening when I was having a tutorial with my biology tutor I saw on her table D. Pilley's *Climbing Days*, which I borrowed."

Before Mary left for work in London she was introduced to Connie Alexander and invited to join the Pinnacle Club but, alas, she had no money to afford the sub or train fare to meets. However, her aunt gave her £3 for her 21st birthday and she bought her first pair of climbing boots, nailed with tricouni no 2 hobs and muggers on the back. Mary writes:

"I have them still. During most of the war years they remained unused, carefully Mars-oiled by my supportive Dad." Mary and boyfriend no.1 each married a non-climber, so when the two of them, being out of training, took a long time over a celebration climb in 1945, their respective spouses became worried, angry and suspicious! Mary decided a women's club was the answer and joined the Ladies' Alpine Club. Anne Littlejohn met her in Switzerland and finally linked her with the Pinnacle Club, giving her lifts to Wales. Mary writes: "Her work was research into what caused sheep to abort their young. I can tell you that the back of her car was not for the faint spirited! Anne believed in a very toughening regime. No little luxuries in the diet. Bread and fried black pudding were the chief ingredients of the evening meal, with copious draughts of strong tea and an orange for pud. - If she did not judge her own rucksack to be heavy enough, she would add a few miscellaneous stones to it." Mary remembers Anne's generosity in letting her lead an all-day Alpine climb, and looks back on two special highlights in her own career: the women's expedition to East Greenland in 1968, where they were exploring where no-one else had trodden – a marvellous sensation; and a trip to Peru in 1972, where three of them climbed in the Velcanota region.

Livia Gollancz says that her route to the Pinnacle Club was devious. During the 1940s she worked in Glasgow as a musician and made friends, independently, with two different members of the Ladies' Scottish Climbing Club. However, she never had free time at weekends, so it was not until she gave up music to become involved in the publishing firm founded by her very famous father, and moved to London, that she was able to join and go on Scottish meets. She is now Chairman and Joint Managing Director of Victor Gollancz Ltd. In Scotland she met Esme Speakman, who introduced her to the Ladies' Alpine Club, and through the LAC she met Nancy Smith and Dorothea Gravina, who eventually talked her into becoming an associate member of the Pinnacle Club. She says: "I was a very clumsy rock-climber, and knew I would never become a full member, but I frequently went to Wales on weekends with a small party led by Anne Littlejohn, staying at Cwm Dyli. I attended one or two Pinnacle dinner meets, and a few weekend meets; but in recent years have been too busy with my other activities (singing and gardening) to be very active in the hills – indeed, the Dolomites meet where we last met must have been my most recent appearance with the Club."

The Dolomites meet was in 1972. I shared a room with Livia and she, eternal student, studied Italian while I read a Mills and Boon novel. I had never met one before, and it seemed a most inopportune time to be caught red-handed! She told me she was also taking singing lessons. These must have been of an advanced variety, for when we were returning home on the train from Bolzano and Livia discovered that Meena and I had been unable to book couchettes she told us that she had the perfect method of giving us an empty carriage with plenty of room to lie down. She closed the door, drew down the blinds, and proceeded to entertain us with operatic arias for the next hour or so. The train filled up; night approached, but nobody ventured to enter our carriage! "There," she said, "You should be all right now." and she left us to sleep in comfort.

Nancy Smith tells me that Livia, who is much in demand as a soloist, loves to try out her voice where the acoustics are good. She finds part of the London Underground particularly suitable and Nancy has waited, in a semi-detached way, while Livia tried out an aria at the top of the escalator.

Even after the November meet the hut was well used till the close of the year, and indeed throughout the winter, by a number of parties. Anne and Sylvia climbed Yellow Groove and Lion, "and another unseen VS bit the dust." That night they did not sleep well, being kept awake by a rat dragging stones across the floor. They wrote, "We spent an agreeable half hour nailing a couple of flattened tins across the hole."

All through January and February 1964, Sylvia and Anne continued to explore Welsh crags and try new routes; on 29th February they climbed their first HVS lead, Erosion Grooves, and the following day, the log book says, Sylvia rather meanly deserted her party for a chance to climb Brant Direct and Karwendel Wall, both in the Extremely Severe grade.

Easter was at the end of March and Dorothea presided at her first Annual Meeting. Club membership stood at 126, meets had been well supported, and Pat Wood had been invited to join a scientific and climbing expedition to the Peruvian Andes in 1965. The secretary went on to report the scandalous behaviour of some male climbers 'Apparently not of very high repute', who had parked their cars at the Power Station, claiming to be married to Pinnacle Club members. Moreover, some had asked for the hut key – not husbands but intruders! Members were asked to help men at the Power Station by always going for the key themselves.

This was the time when the Nature Conservancy was worried about the numbers climbing at Tremadog and allowed only those who had been issued permits. The Hon. Secretary had a supply of these. Miss Turner's legacy was discussed and members decided to spend it on cheerful curtains for the windows, later deciding to buy these anyway and to spend the money on a table. The bulk of the meeting was spent in revision of the Rules of Membership.

It had become obvious through the years that a number of very good climbers had been welcomed as full members because of their climbing skills but had made no real contribution to the Club. Many had resigned after a year or two. Members thought that full members should have proved themselves not only good climbers but good Club members as well. The new rules, which included circulating the names of prospective members on the twice yearly Club bulletins, did much to ensure this. New members who had joined the Club since November 1963 were Kathryn Walton, Annabelle Harrison, Sally Belfield, Judith Pillar and Katharine Gebbie.

Kathryn was an experienced climber who led to VS standard. In 1964 she was injured in an accident which killed a member of the Cockermouth Mountain Rescue Team during one of their practice sessions and shocked the British climbing world. She was going out with this member at the time, so it was a terrible experience for her. She was a Club member for eight years.

Annabelle Harrison (now Barker) lived in Betws-y-Coed and was at college in Aberystwyth when she first came to Club meets. She often led routes with Sally Belfield, who was a college mate. She had been mountain walking since she was sixteen and climbing for about two years, leading to Severe and seconding harder routes. Within a year or two she married Bill Barker and climbed to a much lower standard while their children were growing up, but now has a wide experience of climbing, mountaineering and skiing, and regularly organises her own mini expeditions to the Himalayas, exploring remote territory.

Katharine Gebbie was a member of the Ladies' Alpine Club, enterprising, and very experienced on snow and ice. She enjoyed rock routes on big cliffs and was friends with

Margaret Darvall and Alwine Walford. Her work has kept her in the United States for a number of years and she has climbed in many parts of the world; she and her husband came on the Pinnacle Club trip to Kashmir organised by Alwine Walford in 1979 and climbed several routes.

During the spring and early summer of 1963 Sylvia Yates was having a final burst of activity before going to live and work in Switzerland. She and Anne Littlejohn spent two days in the Pass and notched up nearly two thousand feet of Severe climbing, walked from the hut to Cloggy, where Sylvia led Curving Crack on sight, and Great Slab, and they also spent a day on the Wenallt, sampling Shake and Bovril – steep climbs requiring arm strength and confidence. Annabelle Harrison was climbing hard routes with friends and a new visitor to the hut was Kate Hall, who partnered Sally Belfield. Denise and Charles Evans had a family party at the hut with their two baby boys, Chuck and Robin; "Lovely weather for nappies. Barbara Spark took Denise Evans up Crackstone Rib on Tuesday afternoon."

It was a good summer for family parties: Tony and Annis Flew introduced Joanna (15 weeks old) to the hut and brought a number of parties of European visitors: "Lockwood's – Anglo-German ascent with precious little common language!"

Later came the Beard family, then a large family party of Coopers, Poultons and Campbells. The entry written by a family visiting from the Netherlands brings poignant thoughts: they were Rie Herbert's family (Rie Leggett, who had done the Alpine routes with Denise Wilson) and she had died of cancer the year before, leaving a husband and two little children. Her parents had written their first entry nine years earlier when Rie brought them to Wales to show them the hut.

By summer Sylvia Yates was in Switzerland and she joined the LAC meet led by Dorothea Gravina, teaming with Dorothea when the others climbed with guides. She also joined Nancy Smith and Pat Wood at Courmayeur for the Tour Ronde, the Géant and the Mayer-Dibona route on the Réquin. They encountered two thunderstorms on the last-named route and had to bivouac.

This year Barbara Spark was involved in a bad climbing accident on Pillar Rock in Ennerdale. It was after this accident that Cockermouth Mountain Rescue Team placed the rescue box at the foot of the rock, asking that the three clubs involved in the accident should give donations towards it – which the Pinnacle Club was

Dalmazzi Hut. Nancy, Ian, ?, Joe Brown, Pat, Sylvia, Mary Stewart, Tom Patey, Chris Bonington. Photo: Frances Tanner.

happy to do. When the time came to go to the Alps, Barbara still had both legs in plaster, so her partner, Pat Wood, joined Nancy Smith's party. Frances Tanner says that when they went up to the Dalmazzi Hut they were surprised to find it full of tough British climbers: Joe Brown, Tom Patey, Mary Stewart, Ian Clough and Chris Bonington, who were having their meal before going up to the cirque to reconnoitre their route for the following day. The Pinnacle Club were going up to decide on a route for Nancy and Sylvia when a chap festooned with slings and a crash helmet, also British, came running down. His partner, with whom he had never climbed before, had come to grief when they unroped to glissade, and was lying helpless on the glacier. Nancy says that Tom Patey, who as a doctor knew exactly what to do, probably saved the man's life by lying underneath him on the glacier to keep him warm until the stretcher arrived. The stretcher was of the heavy, old fashioned type and was very difficult to manage in spite of eight people carrying – it was getting dark too. Just as they reached the hut, a storm broke.

Pat Wood, Sylvia Yates, Nancy Smith. Photo: Frances Tanner.

The following morning, going over the ground, looking for a lost torch, they saw how close they had all been to injury and possible annihilation. Huge boulders had rolled down the scree, obliterating the track that they had been on. Certainly, if such a strong party had not been at the hut the injured man would have died.

Also in the Alps this summer was Margaret Darvall; she climbed from Courmayeur and traversed Monte Rosa before going on to other areas for guided climbing. Janet and Nigel Rogers had started their summer holiday in the Dolomites with routes culminating in the Torre Venezia before moving to the Mont Blanc area for the Peigne and Mont Blanc de Tacul. Janet wrote an account of the Aiguilles du Diable for the LAC *Journal*.

Amongst other routes this year, Eveleigh Leith and Livia Gollancz climbed the Gran Paradiso and Livia climbed the Matterhorn.

Sally Westmacott was now living in America and had been one of a party doing a number of first ascents in the White Mountains and in Alaska. The best rock climb was the first complete ascent of Sam's Swansong on Cannon Mountain, over 1000 feet on granite and graded Hard VS, with her husband Michael, Alan Wedgwood and Phil Nelson.

Nea Morin's name has been conspicuous by its absence. She had had an operation earlier in the year and celebrated her recovery by going to the Moelwyns in May where Nancy Smith led her up Kirkus' Direct. This summer she was camping at Courmayeur above Palud, which campsite became something of a meeting place for Pinnacle Club members.

Back in England there were four meets during the autumn, culminating in the Anniversary Meet at the Club hut during the first weekend in November. Twenty-eight members and guests were present at sometime or another and both days were fine enough for climbing. Saturday night was booked for the usual committee meeting, which raged on until the small hours. News had come that the houses by the Power Station would be demolished and this made members wonder whether the tenancy of the Club would be affected. All in all, the committee had a lot on its mind.

Under the new ruling, names on applications for membership had to be circulated to members, so the four people approved at the meeting became members in 1965. These were Peggy Foster, Gael Hutton, Christine Sheard and Alwine Walford.

Peggy was married with a family and had been mountaineering and climbing for a number of years. A sound Severe leader, she was a tall, strong girl with a lot of stamina and was an active Club member for about ten years, leading several Lake District meets.

Christine Sheard had walked and climbed extensively in Scotland and the Lake District before becoming a member of the Pinnacle Club; she had been to the Dolomites and had been on a rock and ice course in the Stubai Alps. A very keen member and great fun to be with, various reasons have prevented her coming on meets in recent years. With her husband a member of the Gritstone Club, she led one or two highly successful meets based at their hut near Ribblehead.

Alwine Walford was born in the North West Frontier Province but when she was six her father, Dr Vosper, became doctor at the Mission Hospital in Srinagar, Kashmir. He was a keen mountaineer and Alwine was much influenced by him, so at nine years old she was off with him, climbing Himalayan mountains. Soon after this she was sent to boarding school in England and says she spent the next few years waiting and longing to go back to Kashmir. This she achieved in 1939 when she was eighteen and, to her great joy, the war prevented her returning to England to complete her education. She stayed to teach at a school in Srinagar, and she says:

"I was lucky enough to get summits over the next few years, of no great technical skill but just hard plod and scramble, such as Mahadeo, Haramukh, Zabur Ridge and a string of peaks above Gulmarg." Alwine's father was very friendly with a high-ranking officer in the RAF, who stayed with the family and realised that Kashmir was a perfect place for airmen to rest and recuperate during service in the Far East. Many of these young men wanted to go out with Alwine, who tolerated the dances for their sakes and was delighted to have them as climbing partners even though some of them had their work cut out keeping up with her. There were one or two outstanding climbers and, acting partly on Dr Vosper's suggestion, young officers such as Wilfred Noyce organised climbing parties in the Sind Valley.

When Alwine was 21 she married Hugo Walford, who was much more interested in sailing than in climbing – a relaxed person who never tried to impress her with his mountaineering ability; a lesson, perhaps. In 1944, a few months after the birth of their first child, Alwine joined an RAF party who were camping at Sonamerg to attempt Tajwas

Peak at the head of the valley. Alwine had not recovered her full strength and the long walk up the Sind Valley from Srinagar to Sonamerg left her drained of the energy required to reach the summit. However, she met John Jackson, who was later on the staff of Plas y Brenin, and he made her realise that she must get some 'proper' rock-climbing in Britain. She took this very seriously, climbing mountains in Austria for a fortnight to get fit and finishing with a flourish with an ascent of the Wildspitze before joining Maurice Guinness for a two-week climbing holiday at the Pen-y-Gwryd. This was in 1951, and she proceeded to the Scafell Hotel in Borrowdale for further climbing with Maurice Guinness and Rusty Westmorland. She was in good hands, for Rusty was very keen to give women confidence in leading climbs. When he was seconding Alwine his encouragement and knowledge of the route gave her a considerable advantage over less experienced parties. She says that when parties ahead were having trouble on a route he would quietly point out to her where the good holds were, enabling her to dumbfound them with her speed and finesse.

Alwine's introduction to climbing with other women came in 1956, when she joined her friend, Monica Jackson, of the Ladies' Scottish Climbing Club, for what she describes as her first epic taste of Skye – two weeks of fine weather! As a result of this she joined the LSCC and found that on many occasions she was coming to North Wales and staying at Cwm Dyli as a guest. She made many friends in the Pinnacle Club and finally joined in 1965.

Alwine has had four holidays in Austria and the Alps, been three times to the Dolomites and has climbed in Turkey, the Rocky Mountains, Long's Peak and the Grand Canyon, Cyprus and Crete. During her presidency of the Club she organised a Pinnacle Club trip to Kashmir, whose members climbed and explored in four different mountain areas.

Alwine and Margaret stayed on after the November Meet to climb Lockwood's Chimney before driving home, and the hut's only visitor before the new year was Evelyn, to light fires and air the place while cataloguing sixty-five books given to the club by Bryan and Pirie.

The 1964 Annual Dinner and General Meeting were held in February rather that at Easter, by popular request. The whole weekend was tremendous fun, with guest speakers Tom Patey and Dennis Gray and home speeches from Dorothea Gravina and Kate Hall, who proposed the toast to the guests in verse. It was Helen Goodburn's first meet and she writes: "What an introduction! the Rock and Ice had joined in the occasion and after dinner Tom Patey livened things up with his accordion. I loved meeting all the old ladies with the wonderful stories of climbing long ago. I had an appalling cold and had lost my voice. Denise Evans plied me with rum and blackcurrant all evening – heady stuff for a poverty stricken student. I remember committing a terrible faux pas. Two of us were offered a lift back to the hut and invited the driver, Dennis Gray, in for coffee to find Annette installed for the night on her accustomed bench in front of the fire. Would I ever recover from this black mark? The whole weekend, including the initial drive down the track in the dark on the back of Sheila Crispin's motor bike, Annette on her bench, Evelyn's black dog, stories round the fire in the hotel is all imprinted on my mind. I went to lots of meets after that. In the hut Kate and I were often the only young ones and I seem to remember being much in demand as a leader. I remember Dorothea leaping naked into the river to bathe in the morning and much smoke from the fire. I remember when Dorothea brought Dawa Tensing to stay at the hut and was very impressed when he called me 'memsahib'. We heard him praying in his tent. I remember seeing Lilian Bray, striding out from the Gwryd in her skirt and boots. There was a climbing elite that appeared on a few meets – Janet Rogers, Jo Fuller, Denise Wilson and others. I aspired to join them."

Helen had always longed to climb mountains but had been told by her mother that "Snowdon was for experts", so she had to wait until she was at university in Bangor before becoming better acquainted with them. She joined the mountaineering club and writes: "On the freshers' meet the buses disgorged us at Ogwen Cottage and I was very disappointed to be told that I had to just walk round the lake since I had no boots. However the walk round the lake turned out to be a trip up Bristly Ridge, over the Glyders, back by the Devil's Kitchen and 12 miles back to Bangor. Not a bad day out in Clark's shoes. I was hooked.

"Two days later I had bought a pair of boots and was taken round to the Pass to do Flying Buttress. I had no grant and no money for clothes or equipment. It was the winter of 62/63 and a heavy fall of snow came in October. I learnt to dress in many layers, pyjamas, tracksuit, shirts, sweater. I couldn't afford even a decent anorak. It was very cold that winter and I learned to walk fast uphill and downhill in whiteouts or on still, clear days. I couldn't use map or compass so must keep up with the boys for my survival. All the rest of the girls had long since been 'burnt off', part of a deliberate policy. I had warning enough of the dangers on my first day out in the snow. The rescue team brought four bodies down to Ogwen Cottage, stuffed them in the Landrover and then climbed in themselves.

"Girls were not welcomed in the mountaineering club. Not only was no allowance made for their lack of speed but they were also expected to endure the foullest crudities of songs, speech and behaviour. The technique of obtaining climbing partners, apart from boyfriends, was difficult. One had to wait till the monsters were weakened mentally by alcohol, get them to agree to climb with you in front of witnesses, and hold them to it.

"No amount of such unsubtle persuasion could make them allow me to join them in the Alps. One day one of the older students, who knew his way around a bit, announced that I should join the Pinnacle Club. I had never heard of it. He bundled me into his van and dragged me off to the Evans' house. He dropped me off at the gate, and told me to go and knock on the door and to ask Denise Evans if she could help me to join. I was terrified and frankly overawed by the whole idea. As I walked up the path Denise and Nea were sitting in the garden. I was immediately welcomed, put at my ease and given lots of useful advice. Nea insisted I should go and climb in the Dauphiné with a French organisation called the UNCM. Some of the French kids were about as welcoming as my colleagues in the mountaineering club until one day on a mountain top we met an old guide who called out, "Which of you is Nea's friend?" Immediately I was deemed to be an O.K. person. Yet another reason to bless the day I met Denise and Nea came when I was introduced to the P.C."

CHAPTER 27

1965, 1966. Dawa Tensing in Britain. S. Angell's first meet. Matterhorn Centenary.
New members.

*June 1965. P.C. group with Dawa Tensing at Cwm Dyli.
L-R: Helen Jones, Annette Wilson, Margaret Darvall, Dorothea Gavina, Dorothy Lee, Seated: Shirley Angell with Timothy. Photo: I. Angell*

April 1965 records a very special visitor to the hut, with a very special signature, quite unreadable to most but with a translation by the side. Dawa Tensing was on a three months' visit to this country, not his first, for he had been up Lockwood's Chimney in 1955 with George Lowe and John Hunt, and recognised his surroundings immediately on this occasion. This time he was brought by Charles, Denise and Chuck Evans, walked round the hut and visited the Power Station. Denise wrote his achievements in the hut book:

"Everest 1924, 1935, 1951, 1953 (S.Col), 1956 (S.Col twice), Cho Oyu 1952, Makalu 1954 with NZ Expedition, Kangchenjunga 1955 (Sirdar), Annapurna IV 1957 (Sirdar), & II 1960. Dhaulagiri 1958 (Sirdar) and Ama Dablam 1959. Pinnacle Club Jagdula Expedition 1962 (Sirdar)."

A few days later Frances Tanner, Pat Wood and Nancy Smith came up for the weekend and had a celebration supper with Dawa on the Saturday, then Barbara Spark was able to join them for a walk over the Carneddau – in arctic conditions but a wonderful day.

There were more visitors before the Whitsun meet, notably three teenage girls who were given a wonderful introduction to the mountains by Peggy Wild. One of them, Linda, had her fourteenth birthday and they celebrated the great occasion by climbing Snowdon by the Pig Track.

The Whitsuntide Meet was the first one I ever came to. Ian and I drove up from Leicestershire with our son, Timothy, who had his second birthday that very day, and were welcomed by Dorothea, who strode down the hill from the hut and helped us with all our camping gear. Dawa was Dorothea's guest, and several people took photos of Dawa and the two-year-old Timothy, who seemed to get on well together. I was thrilled with the whole weekend, climbing at Cwm Silyn with Marjorie Tanner then on the Wenallt with Kate Hall and Helen Goodburn, and having a day out on Cnicht while Ian gave Timothy a good camping holiday, fetching wood and having adventures by the stream.

I had grown up loving mountains, for my parents loved walking and my sister, Coral, and I were encouraged to do gymnastics and climb trees and rocks. My father was a vicar and when I was eighteen we moved to Whitstable in Kent, where we had a lovely garden and orchard. On the day of our arrival he received an agitated phone call from a parishioner who had glimpsed Coral and myself at the top of adjacent poplar trees in the vicarage garden. He said, truthfully, that he thought this perfectly natural, and our reputation spread like wildfire.

Unfortunately my father had a very serious illness when I was a child and his legs went numb if he walked for long. Our walks were punctuated by long waits while he lay down with his legs in the air, waiting for the feeling to come back. In the end, my parents stayed in the valleys while Coral and I ran up and down the nearest summits. When we finally went on organised hill-walking holidays we found we could beat most people hollow.

In 1956 Coral gave me *Rock for Climbing* by Douglas Milner for my birthday and wrote in it, "Let's go climbing!" so we went on an MA Beginner's Course in Borrowdale with 'David' Davies. It rained all the time, but he made it enjoyable. The following year she gave me the CC Guide to the Llanberis Pass and we went there on an Intermediate Course with someone called Stan. Stan took advantage of Coral at the top of every pitch. Fortunately I was less attractive, so went second on the rope until Coral and I were deemed capable of leading each other.

One of the young men on the course was Alwyn Spires, a founder member of the Rugby Mountaineering Club, who was so impressed with our act that he invited us to the second meet. Thus began long but happy coach journeys up the A5 for camping and climbing weekends in the Pass or at Ogwen. One evening we were relaxing outside the Vaynol Arms when my attention was drawn to a young man, high in a tree, with his foot tied to a branch by his bootlaces. He was called Angell, which we thought at first was a nickname. Later he danced a polka with me, up and down the road. It was love at first sight!

Before I got married I was determined to become competent in the Alps, also I passionately wanted to climb the Matterhorn. Since a school trip to the Belvedere (when my red suede shoes left pink marks in the snow) I had been two or three times to the same place, only to be rained off. I went on a course in Austria, led by Peter Gentil and we climbed one or two peaks every day, but after ten days I received a press cutting from my mother which read "Mad Dog Ian Climbs It Solo!" Ian had climbed the Matterhorn without me! I told Peter Gentil I'd have to go straight to Zermatt. He said, fine. Why not try the Zmutt ridge? but I thought the Hörnli would do: all I wanted was to get to the top. In Zermatt, Bernard Biner fitted me into the laundry room at the Bahnhof and it rained for three days! Ian was in Chamonix, I met no friends and I no longer had money for a guide. I sent Ian a telegram "Please come to Bahnhof, Zermatt" which reached him just as he was setting off for a route, but he hitched round by the following morning. We asked a guide in the village whether the Matterhorn would 'go' and he said, yes if we took two guides, so we bought some food and went up to the hut that afternoon. I cried most of the way – I was so sure it would rain again. Next day I led all the way up and the top felt marvellous, especially as a passing guide said I climbed well. Ian said I was all right on rock but had a lot to learn about snow and ice – I still have. From Zermatt we went to Chamonix where I had booked for a MA Alpine Intermediate Course and Ian left me camping in Snell's Field.

The leader of this next course was Doug Scott, earning money while at university. I was the only woman and the rest of the party must have found me unbelievably sickening. I was fit, acclimatised, and could keep up with Doug's chosen pace (the shape of his calves is imprinted on my memory) and I was the only one who had climbed to VS standard. From the Couvercle Hut I led the second rope on one or two routes, then Doug led me on the Mummery-Ravanel. In perfect weather we all climbed the Forbes Arête on the Chardonnet then went to traverse Mont Blanc, aiming to spend the night at the Vallot Hut before going over and descending by Mont Maudit.

It was still early when we reached the Vallot from the Tête Rousse Hut and I met a French boy who wanted to climb Mont Blanc but his father was unwell and he had nobody else to climb with, so I told Doug I'd just nip up to the summit and back with this lad. Of course Doug had to come too, feeling responsible, and on the top we met Chris Bonington and Don Whillans, the first pair on the summit after their ascent of the Frêney Pillar. Doug knew them and Chris said to him, looking at the French lad, "You didn't hire a guide, did you?" A photographer arrived by helicopter and photographed the four of us on the summit, because the press thought the Frêney Pillar was being ascended by French climbers (who were also on the route) and that they would have photos of a first ascent achieved by France. – So I got into the papers that year, as well as Ian!

We never did do the traverse. The others in our party had a leisurely trip to the summit while we fed the four conquerors of the Frêney on a stew made up of all our spare food. Doug says it was this course which convinced him he could never stand being a guide.

When Ian and I started a family we soon found that a baby makes it harder to climb together, and especially hard for me to go to the Alps, so I wrote to the Ladies' Alpine Club to ask if I would be acceptable on a meet. Lindsay Urquhart replied, recommending the Pinnacle Club. Dorothy Lee wrote a welcoming reply to my enquiry, and on our way up to the Whitsun meet we gave a hitch to an old friend, Bud Metcalfe, who knew Kate Hall (Webb) and said she had just joined the Pinnacle Club, so I went in eager anticipation which was not disappointed.

Kate Hall's application was approved at this meet and she was finally elected in September.

1965 was the centenary of Whymper's first ascent of the Matterhorn and many people were in Zermatt for the celebrations. Ian and I left Timothy with my parents for one week and dashed out for a few routes but there was so much new snow that we managed only the Wellenkuppe and Trifthorn. I was a little apprehensive as I was expecting another baby. Our vicar from Markfield, in Leicestershire, was Chaplain at the English Church for the celebrations and we had promised to give out service sheets and ring the bell for the service at which Sir John Hunt (as he was then) placed a wreath on the altar in memory of Charles Hudson. Our Vicar, Frank Food (nicknamed Heavenly Food), conducted the service and the Bishop of Leicester gave the address. Others have done justice to the many events of that festive week; for me the fun lay in meeting friends such as Margaret Darvall and Dorothea Gravina, and in playing a small part of our own.

Wanderers were back in Britain by September. Jo Fuller started the month by traversing the Welsh 3,000s solo in 7 hours 48 minutes, and called in at the hut next day: "Aching knees! Many cups of tea and coffee were consumed before I could face the journey back to Ynys Ettws."

The following day (3rd) Nancy Smith writes: "Rain. Reading, Writing – no Rithmetic."

Cynthia Agnew led a meet based at Dale Bottom Hut near Keswick, which belonged to Yorkshire Mountaineering Club at the time. Alison Adam ran the Yorkshire Meet in Wensleydale and Christine Sheard the Froggatt meet. There were 29 people at the Anniversary Meet, some not arriving until the Saturday morning because of the fog on Friday evening, made worse by bonfires and fireworks, it being Guy Fawkes night. Margaret Darvall picked me up from Shrewsbury Station in her Morris Traveller, already well filled by Alwine, Grizel Paterson and all their gear, but the weekend was worth the complicated travel arrangements.

Throughout the winter months the hut was well used by groups from Bangor Grammar School or the University, led by Barbara Spark and often including Helen Goodburn and Sheila Crispin. Good use was made of the dry ski slopes at Plas y Brenin on wet days. Helen says she and Sheila did quite a lot of walking with a hugely pregnant Denise Evans this winter. The two of them acted a little like handmaidens – preparing large gaps in fences for her to ease her huge girth through. They climbed too – or, as they said, perhaps bumbled is the word. 1966 began in traditional style at the Pen-y-Gwryd when Dorothea presided at the New Year Dinner Meet. It was good fun, but the weather was wild; those who celebrated New Year's Day by climbing a snow gully on the Glyders were rewarded by a blizzard at the top.

The February Dinner Meet fared no better for weather, but not even the heavy and incessant rain could dampen the cheerful atmosphere – heightened by the comfort and warmth of Sid and Jammy's hospitality, at the Old Dungeon Ghyll. Len Winthrop Young was the chief guest, and sixty-one members and guests sat down to the meal.

The Annual Meeting, held as usual on the Saturday afternoon, started on a sad note, for Biddy Wells, a founder who had done so much for the Club's climbing prowess, had died the previous autumn. However, she would have rejoiced in the Club just now, for the number of full members was increasing and Jo Fuller, the meets secretary, reported that the varied meets had attracted a number of young climbers. She stressed that one of the main considerations of the Pinnacle Club should be safety in climbing and to this end there was to be a course on mountain rescue to be held during the Whitsun and Anniversary meets.

Organising climbing meets required quite different talents from those of dinner organiser, and Jo was grateful when it was proposed that Sue Long should take over this latter duty.

Janet Rogers, the *Journal* editor, was very keen that the Club should not have an old fashioned image and suggested an alteration to the cover design. This was approved, the illustration was discarded and the list of contents removed to the page succeeding the title; the cover was plain and uncluttered, designed by Marjorie Wood. Janet produced two journals published in 1966 and 1968 in worthy succession to the earlier editions.

Nine new associate members joined between February 1966 and February 1967: M Picken, A Grier, S Washington, R Lee, K Hoskins, G Cannon, J Ritchie, J Dilnot and B Burgum.

Mairet Picken, Vera's daughter, was already a keen visitor to club meets and at last old enough to join. She became a promising and enterprising climber. Tragically, she and her companion were lost on the Matterhorn in 1969.

Ray Lee had loved mountain walking since she was a child and had started rock climbing in 1962, first with Don Roscoe and later with her husband. She had led a few routes when she joined the Club and developed into a sound leader over the next few years, serving the Club well till prevented by family ties.

Kathleen Hoskins writes: "I started rock climbing at university (London) probably because I knew my mother wouldn't approve! Also it seemed the only way to get to know a particular student better (now my husband). Once we left university and both started work in London we spent most weekends in N Wales and occasional ones in the Lake District. We used to meet all the other London climbers in a pub in North London (The Crown) every Thursday night and arrange who was taking cars and giving lifts etc. We used to drink with Ken Wilson and he mentioned the Pinnacle Club to me and urged me to join – mainly I think so that he could find out more about it! He was fascinated by the idea of an all-women's climbing club and was curious about women in it.

"I went one weekend very nervously all by myself but was welcomed by Evelyn Leech to whom I am ever grateful. She really made me feel at ease and on the Saturday drove myself and her daughter Antonia to the Slabs and asked me to take Antonia up Ordinary Route – "just to see if I knew the ropes." There was a tremendous thunderstorm half way up which didn't help my nerves. I must have passed approval because Evelyn then went on to suggest I joined the Club. Until I got to know more members on other meets Evelyn was always so friendly and helpful. I remember once sitting forlornly in her old van and having to explain that I just didn't feel up to climbing at the moment as I had a bad period pain. She was so kind – she immediately produced a bottle of gin from the glove compartment and insisted I had a swig as she knew from past experience it was the best cure! She then took me off to the Pen-y-Gwryd for more medicinal alcohol. She kept in touch with me until she died even when we were out in Australia. Once in the club I was very pleased as for the first time it gave me a chance to climb 'in my own right'. Up to that time I had hardly done any leading but on club meets one was encouraged to take turns at leading and I found out how different it was to lead a climb – not just follow someone up it.

While Kathleen was in Australia she was something of a pioneer woman climber. The rock was warm, dry granite and her standard improved until she was leading VS. She and another English woman, Ann Dowlen, were probably the only women climbers in South Australia in 1969, but by 1972 there were plenty of them. Kathleen wrote an account of Australian climbing for the Jubilee *Journal*.

Jean Dilnot was at Bangor University, and like so many of the best people was a member of the mountaineering club. However, her real love was mountain walking and it was not for many years that this developed into a desire to rock-climb. She and Biddy Burgum both became teachers, lived near one another and went on holiday together. They did a lot of fell walking in many different areas: Derbyshire, the Lake District, Ireland, North Wales, and in particular along the ridges in Scotland. Jean says she supposes it was by recognising that they had to deviate from routes requiring a rope that they developed, late in the day, an interest in climbing. Biddy, as a trained gymnast, liked applying her skill to rock.

Jean writes: "We were invited to the Annual Dinner, held at the ODG in 1964 – Gravina was President and made us feel incredibly welcome ... so we took steps to become eligible for membership by taking an MA course in Llanberis. It was a great week, and ended with an ascent of Lliwedd.

"One of our warmest memories is of dear old Dorothy Lee and her splendid catering and organisation. On one meet we had driven up to the Hut mostly overnight at the end of a heavy week at school and as soon as we arrived she organised us to set off for Blaenau Ffestiniog!" Just before joining the Club Jean and Biddy went on a Mountain Leadership Course in the Cairngorms. They have also sampled orienteering in Wales, for fun and to help with their map reading skills. Most summers they went light weight camping in Scotland. They have walked and climbed in the Zermatt region and latterly have skied regularly in Austria and Italy each spring.

Gill Cannon, now Gill Fuller, writes: "I started climbing in my last year at school when my older sister joined the Sheffield University Mountaineering Club. I then joined the Manchester University Women's Mountaineering Club and became its president in 1961. During my university vacations I worked as a Voluntary Instructor at Plas y Brenin and climbed with various people including John Cleare who were active down there at that time. I got to know of, rather than know, Jo Scarr and Barbara Spark, but was not interested in joining the P.C. as I was happy leading easy climbs in my duties as an instructress but in my free time I preferred to second harder routes with various men.

"It was in 1966 when I returned from 18 months in the Falkland Islands that I felt the need to play a more responsible part in my climbing activities. Through a mutual friend I met Janet Rogers who invited me to come and meet the P.C. Since I married of course I've climbed mainly with Brian and become more of a mountaineer and ski-mountaineer rather than a climber."

Articles by Gill appear from time to time in *High* as well as in the Pinnacle Club Journals. She was journal editor for the Jubilee *Journal* and a member of the committee.

Easter 1966 was Angela Faller's first hut meet and there was nobody there when she arrived on the Friday so she went off to the Wenallt and climbed with friends on Carol Crack, Oxo, Bovine and Shake – all superb VS climbs on perfect rock, so the rather small meet in rainy weather with Evelyn Leech, Penny Storey and her guest, and Marjorie Tanner the only members was rather a comedown. Angela wondered where all the hard young climbers were and retreated to Tremadog for the Saturday. She did not understand Evelyn at all and interpreted her worried sense of responsibility as heavy disapproval, but she was very impressed by Marjorie Tanner. On the Sunday she went to climb on Lliwedd with another prospective member, Jancis Harris, who turned up later as Jancis Gay and joined for six years, and they had to traverse off after 90 feet in a hail-and-thunderstorm.

Angela Soper on Cave Arch, Stanage.
International Women's Meet 1984, Photo: Ian Smith.

The write-up in the Hut Book was by Antonia Leech, who appears to have enjoyed herself very much, especially at meal times!

One reason for the small meet was an unofficial one in Cornwall where Nea, Margaret Darvall, Sue Long, Frances Tanner, Alwine and Pat Wood and guests enjoyed glorious sunshine and climbed innumerable routes.

To make up for Easter, the Whit meet at the hut was blessed with warm sunshine. Margaret Darvall and Dorothy Lee should have been the first to arrive, but their car ran out of petrol short of Capel Curig so they spent a rather cramped night in it and reached the hut next morning to find their guest, Elizabeth Hallett, already encamped. While they spent the Friday at Cwm Silyn, others arrived. Ian and I came and camped with Timothy, nearly three, and Adrian two months old. We all made for the Moelwyns on Saturday – carricot included, for Adrian had to be near his milk supply – and Barbara James came over from Ogwen Cottage to climb with the Club and make our acquaintance, for we were due at Ogwen the next day for our mountain rescue course.

Angela Faller turned up that evening, also camping, and raring to go up to Cloggy, but Evelyn said we could not make special arrangements for a course and then fail to turn up, however nice the weather. At Ogwen Cottage we had a lecture first, then practical demonstrations of first aid and stretcher work. After lunch we tried everything out for ourselves, finishing with an orgy of abseils before going to climb on the Gribin. The following day we went to the Moelwyns again and Jean Dilnot remembers struggling to follow Angela up a climb, herself fully clad in breeches etc. and Angela, having floated up in a bikini, singing, perched on the next ledge. Angela was climbing barefoot in a bikini, hoping that her heroine, Gwen Moffat, would turn up – but she didn't. Angela had been reading the past journals at Cwm Dyli and was really keen to join – couldn't wait to get enough meets in and submit her application form.

Several people stayed on after the meet. At last Angela reached Clogwyn Du'r Arddu and climbed with Christopher Mitchell: Llithrig, Vember, led through on Longland's, Great Slab and Birthday Crack. Then they climbed Crucible on Cwm Silyn and The Grooves on Cyrn Las. Four of the climbs were in the Extreme grade and the rest Very Severe.

This was the last Welsh meet before the summer, and the hut was given over to students and family parties once more.

This summer there was a joint Pinnacle Club and Ladies' Alpine Club meet at Saas Fee, led by Eileen Healey who was expecting a baby soon and staying at a hotel with her husband, Tim. Angela joined them after climbing with friends in Chamonix and the first people she saw were Alwine Walford and Helen Goodburn. She learnt to her dismay that they would all have to share the cost of the guide. Angela nearly went back to Chamonix but decided to live on porridge and pancakes instead. She had given up her job at ICI when they wouldn't give her unpaid leave, so she was spending money carefully. When she met the guide, Guy Genoud, who was young, handsome and charming, she thought that at least he was worth paying for!

Helen writes: "It was a meet which had its difficulties, mostly concerned with personalities. I learnt that climbing ladies have fierce wills. There was Dorothea walking up to every hut, never using a lift (I didn't either, neither of us could afford to, but Dorothea also carried a tent and firewood and slept outside the hut). There was Alwine wearing all her rings because she couldn't afford to insure them and carrying drinking water in a large domestos bottle, which was rather disconcerting. There was Livia Gollancz in her highly individual home-made garments in strange combinations of colours. Angela came along and shocked everyone by wearing her bikini – even in the town if you please. The meet was great fun and we seemed to do a lot of climbing, nothing very hard but lots of variety, I loved it. I can't help feeling that the most dangerous part of the holiday was when I joined Dorothea in her car for a lift back to England. She would never stop, never admit to being tired. We were not allowed to camp overnight but crept into campsites after everyone was asleep and the gates locked. A short stretch out on a groundsheet and then out over the gate again before the warden was awake to demand any money." Janet Rogers had a similar experience, I believe. She spent the journey hidden under the rug on the back seat so that she couldn't see the road. Dorothea said she was really worried because Janet seemed ill.

Angela wrote a very detailed account of the meet, as she was learning to type at the time, and the following are a few extracts: "August 2nd. I was awake in time to go to early Mass in the new church ... Then it was time to prepare for three nights at the Weissmies hut. I took my tent down to save camp fees and as usual put the camping gaz stove in the sack for cooking at the hut ... The hut was warm, clean and comfortable.

"Helen and co. arrived last with Guy, having walked all the way from Saas Fee, and we all retired early in spite of the rain, with the Jägigrat in mind for the morrow.

"August 3rd. A surprisingly fine morning saw seven of us following Guy up the moraine at the back of the hut, making our way to the ridge under the dying stars. Guy knew the most interesting route onto the ridge, up a clean rock arête instead of a scree scramble. Joan and Christine (Sheard) tied on his rope, then went Dorothea and Helen with Lisbet between them and at the back I climbed with Alwine ... It was superb climbing, sometimes moving together, sometimes separately; always the exposure was considerable. There were several abseils from magnificent fixed rings and Guy would always wait to 'rassure' everyone with a spare rope and come down last himself ... The highest point on the ridge was gained early in the day and from there the route lost its height until it came to the spectacular final gendarme. This proved to be no harder than severe and there was a brand new peg in. I would have had this for my collection, but daredn't remove it under Dorothea's eagle eye."

The following day Angela climbed the North Ridge of the Weissmies with Dorothea leading, and Tim Healey. "Dorothea really took the bit between her teeth. She hardly faltered at any rocky section, and our route-finding was good considering the poor visibility, so we drew away from the others and soon lost sight of them ... We were very proud of Dorothea. I hoped that when I'm her age (63) I'll still be climbing as competently at that standard. We were still enjoying the rock when we gained the snow and half an hour's steady plodding brought us to the white-domed summit, at 1 p.m. We shook hands and congratulated each other on one of the best Alpine routes we had ever done."

Angela was there for the second week only, and Margaret Darvall had been there for the first week before joining the Gebbies and Grizel Paterson on the Atlas Mountains in Morocco. Other P.C. members were Mary Fulford, Livia Gollancz, Eveleigh Leith and Penny Storey. In all, the party achieved ten ascents.

They were lucky with the weather, for the season was a poor one. Janet and Nigel Rogers were rained out of Courmayeur and went once again to the Gran Paradiso. Here they warmed up on the North Face of the Ciaferon before tackling the North Face of the

Gran Paradiso itself by a variation on the 1935 Ademi route. Janet said they decided to name the new variant the Voie de l'Enceinte as she was by this time quite pregnant.

Pilley and I.A. Richards climbed in the Alps this year as usual, but the real excitement came at the end of their stay: Pilley called it one of the most surprising and exhilarating mountain episodes of their lives. Driven home by the weather, they decided to 'look in and wave to the Dent Blanche' (always their special mountain because of their first ascent of the North Ridge), before their final departure and discovered that the valley was organising centenary celebrations. The Dent Blanche had been ascended for the first time on July 18th, 1862, but "being four years late distressed no one. After all it takes a little while to reply to what they did last year at Zermatt."

The Richards were invited to take part in the celebrations and to go by air to the Rossier Hut with the cross which was destined for the summit. Of course they stayed and had a wonderful time, though the weather took charge of the situation. Pilley wrote about it for the LAC *Journal* of 1967 and PC Journal no.12.

With autumn approaching once more, Cynthia Agnew led another meet at Dale Bottom and Alison Adam led a 'Famous Names' meet in Swaledale: Lilian Bray, Mabel Jeffrey, Vera Picken, Trilby Wells, Chris Woods, Marjorie Wood and E.M. Clarke.

Chris Sheard led the Froggatt meet a fortnight later and new faces were Angela Kelly and Sandra Gamble. Sandra lived near to us in Leicester, and we gave her a lift. Others present were Margaret Darvall, who attended practically all meets during her presidency; Jo Fuller, Sally Westmacott, Pat Daley and Kath Hoskins and Angela Faller. Angela filled in her application form for the November Committee Meeting's approval, proposed and seconded by myself and Chris. She was a friendly person with a formidable list of hard climbs and we never imagined for one moment that anyone would have reservations. Indeed, Angela's name was one of several approved; but just as her name was being circulated to members, a BBC programme was broadcast which included an interview of Angela in the camp site at Chamonix the previous summer. This gave rise to a misunderstanding about Angela's opinion of other women climbers, and meant that Margaret Darvall, as President, had to write a most tactful letter asking for an explanation, not wishing to put her off.

Recently Margaret wrote, "She and Dorothea Gravina are the only current representatives of the flamboyant climbing character, which the PC used to specialise in – and they, like their forebears, have put a few backs up in their time. Angela is in direct descent from Lilian Bray, though much more decorative. What we want people to remember about her is the brilliance of her climbing and her personality."

Angela was very much a lone star when she joined the Club. For one reason or another, those who could match her ever-increasing abilities were unavailable or preoccupied with other things. Sylvia Yates and Jo Scarr were abroad and others such as Denise Wilson had young families. After the first meet or two she found plenty of willing seconds for hard routes, but there was a strong Pinnacle Club tradition that leaders should spend one day of a meet offering their services to anyone who wanted to climb and this, combined with the weather conditions, meant that most really hard climbs were done by private arrangement. Angela cannot help being a little envious of the surge of hard, young climbers who have recently joined the Club and are receiving every encouragement, on meets, to stretch their abilities to the limit. Jill Lawrence, for example, wrote on her application form, "Leading 6A,E4, hoping to improve" and almost immediately led E5!

Jill Lawrence on Cream. Photo: Ian Smith.

Putting envy aside, it will become apparent that Angela played no small part in ensuring that the Club continues to attract top women climbers, and her story seems to fit in naturally at this stage, even though she had to wait for entry until 1967.

"I started climbing while a Ph.D student at Leeds University. This followed from independent walking and Youth Hostelling from the age of 14 or so with my brother – very unsuitably equipped by today's standards but we knew how to use map and compass and never landed in trouble, even in snow ... Must have had some natural common sense. Yorks Dales first, then Lakes; Scotland when an undergraduate (Leeds, 1958-61) and Europe, hitching and Alpine walking. I never dreamed there was any chance of doing more.

"Anyway, while I was a research student at Leeds (late 1963) some friends from ice-skating invited me to join a new outdoor group that was being formed, as they wanted outdoor people. Rope technique was demonstrated and climbing at Almscliffe. I had no natural ability whatsoever on the boulders there; but when a shortage of leaders became apparent an extra voice was heard to volunteer – 'I'll try'. No one was more surprised than me that it was mine. So I started leading at an early stage and was hooked – evenings on gritstone, weekends in the Lakes. I discovered the Achille Ratti C.C. and used to hitch up to Bishop's Scale. From then on all holidays were for climbing and mountaineering, and I went through a fairly typical sequence of gaining all-round experience including a few minor epics. I never seconded any VSs, went straight onto leading them, and was happy leading at that standard in the Lakes. Gimmer Crack, Haste Not, Eliminate A – you'll remember the equipment we had then, and that no higher standard than VS had been defined. My standards on gritstone lagged behind, though in Derbyshire Severes were all right.

I learned about the Pinnacle Club from *Space Below My Feet*, which someone lent me. I still think it is one of the best ever climbing books. I wrote to Jo Fuller, the Meets Secretary, for details and went to the Dinner Meet at the Old Dungeon Ghyll in February 1966. Jo was most welcoming, and I met Chris Sheard. In wet miserable weather I plodged up Pike o'Blisco with Jo, Chris, Ray Lee and others, then sat in on the AGM. I remember looking around the assembled company trying to decide who looked likely climbing partners and whether it would be worth approaching anyone. I was working for ICI then – not much annual holiday."

It is fortunate that this was Angela's first meet and not the Easter meet already recorded, where Evelyn Leech gave the impression that the place for prospective members was not the sharp end and Angela felt she was saying wrong things without knowing why!

CHAPTER 28

1967 – 1969. Barbara Spark appointed to MLTB. New members. Meets. Helen and Chris in the Alps. Hard climbs and expeditions at home and abroad. Peuterey ridge. Janet Rogers President. Mairet and Ruth lost. A less serious accident.

1967 was seen in at the Pen-y-Gwryd, and it is reported that the committee would still have been in session at midnight if a shocked deputation from the bar had not called them out in time. It was a pleasant meet, with old and new members present and local members calling in.

The Annual Dinner Meet on February 18th-19th was also held at the Pen-y-Gwryd, in swirling snow and high winds. Five of us were staying at the hut, but regrouped after calling at the hotel. We were told that we must, repeat MUST, be back for two-thirty and the Annual General Meeting. Jean and Biddy joined Sandra and myself for a trip up Y Garn and round to the Devil's Kitchen from the Ogwen Valley and arrived back at the hotel breathless and weather beaten in the nick of time. To sustain members through the meeting there was a break for tea and hot buttered scones. Margaret Darvall was presiding.

The Secretary had to report the deaths of Lady Adrian in May 1966 and Lilian Bray in November. Hester Adrian's active climbing had been curtailed by an accident in which she lost her leg, but the indefatigable Bray had walked with others at the Yorkshire Meet a month before her death, aged ninety.

When it came to the election of officers the positions of treasurer and meets secretary were both up for consideration. Ada was the perfect treasurer and everyone trembled at the thought of losing her – "The President said that it would be advantageous to the Club for administration reasons to retain the services of Mrs A Shaw ..." – Yes, indeed! Likewise the Club was starting to reap the benefits of Jo Fuller's appointment to the new office of meets secretary, and she was asked to carry on. Helen Goodburn and Alwine Walford were the two new committee members.

During the very full BMC report came the information that Barbara Spark had been appointed to serve on the Mountain Leadership Training Board. "It has been a great source of satisfaction to obtain, in the first place, the acceptance in principle that there should be a woman on the M.L.T.B. and, in the second place, that the person should be Barbara Spark. I feel that this is putting the right person in the right place for she has practical experience of both sides of the question – firstly through her two years as instructor on the staff of Plas y Brenin and now in her job as Lecturer in Physical Education in the University of Bangor which brings her in close contact with young students. Many of these are interested in climbing and some are taking the M.L.T.B. certificate ..." wrote Nea Morin.

Up till now I had avoided dinner meets as offering little chance for climbing, but the magic of the occasion completely enthralled me. Barbara Spark welcomed guests in a lively speech which contained amusing personal digs at Ian McNaught-Davis; Elspet

MacKay for the LSCC, who was a long-term friend of many PC members, had a grand tale to tell of ancient rivalries, and Ian McNaught-Davis was in fine form. The lines of Margaret's speech were laid down by long tradition, as she responded to the Toast to the President and outlined the Club's activities during the year. I felt proud and excited to be part of it; so many members were there, representing every decade of the Club's history.

Members elected during the year were Angela Faller (Soper), Angela Kelly (Heppenstall), Jean Kitching, Sandra Gamble (Swindale), Barbara James and Jane Taylor, Avis Reynolds and Dorothy Wood. Dorothy Wood, a keen climber leading to VS standard, resigned from the club after ten years. The rest are still members.

Angela Kelly joined as a keen and experienced climber and mountain walker, having climbed extensively in mountain areas and on outcrops throughout the British Isles and abroad. She impressed Ken Wilson, first editor of *Mountain*, very much as having a figure not obviously athletic but raising her standard of leading to VS by sheer determination. He said, "By throwing herself at the rock." She has served the Club well on the committee, as business editor during the production of the Jubilee *Journal* in 1971 and as dinner organiser for four years (1977-80) at the same time as coping with her young family. Angela married Alan Heppenstall in 1971.

Jean Kitching became enthusiastic about mountains when she went to university in Grenoble for a year, then, in 1964, she went on a rock climbing course at Plas y Brenin. Jean joined the Pinnacle Club because she lived near Alwine and worked with Margaret Darvall at that oldest of women's rights organisations, the Fawcett Society, so could share transport. She climbed mainly at Swanage and was on one or two early ascents of new routes, but has rarely come to Wales. Recently she had a refresher weekend on one of Brede Arkless' women's climbing courses, which made her realize how out of date she was as regards equipment, but how much she would like to do more climbing.

Sandra is Ken Vickers' sister and was married to Derek Gamble when she joined the PInnacle Club. They were all members of the Leicester Association of Mountaineers and Sandra was on the committee. She had already been mountaineering for about five years – walking, camping, leading to about V diff. standard, and enjoying mixed routes in the Alps. She had also climbed in Norway, the Dolomites and Ireland.

Barbara James joined the Pinnacle Club with very impressive qualifications, having been a professional mountaineer since 1964. Her first hill experience was a course at Plas y Brenin while she was in the sixth form at school, then she joined the Chester Mountaineering Club. She was out every weekend from the Wirral when teaching there, with a dawn run back on Mondays in summer straight to the classroom, but she did not climb hard routes until she met Ron James and was taken up her first VS. After this she climbed with Ron but was going out with another chap till he was posted to Singapore. She married Ron in 1965.

Before her marriage, Barbara worked for a year at the Towers Outdoor Pursuits Centre as a climbing instructor, then moved to Ogwen Cottage where Ron was in charge. She was on the hill every day in term time and they spent Easter and Christmas holidays skiing and every summer in the Alps for five or six weeks until their money ran out. In the summer, after work, they were on the Glyders or Cloggy for evening climbing.

Barbara was at Plas y Brenin on the first Mountaineering Instructor Advanced Certificate course to be held. She had been professional for slightly less than five years so did not qualify for exemption, and qualified at the same time as others such as

Brailsford and Mortlock, who were in a similar situation. She had also, as a ski instructor, the British Association of Ski Instructors qualification, BASI 3 and took leave of absence for the 1968 season to train for her BASI 2. She worked as an instructor all season at Alpbach, and was skiing best ever and sure to pass when she broke her leg on the morning of the exam! She thinks that at that time she was the longest-serving full time woman mountaineering instructor, for Barbara Spark's activities were more varied.

At about the time Barbara James joined the Club, she led Barbara Spark on Cemetery Gates in the Pass. Again with Barbara, she led Mousetrap on Anglesey one hot summer day memorable for its atmosphere and her own pleasure, enhanced because they climbed in shorts and Ron was guiding on another crag somewhere nearby. In the Alps Barbara and Ron were working through the routes in Walter Pause's *In Extremen Fels* and had done eighteen of the routes up to the time of their divorce.

Jane Taylor, elegant, full of fun and a brilliant linguist, came to climbing from hill-walking in Scotland and had done a fair amount of rock-climbing when she joined the Club, leading to Severe and seconding harder routes. During her first season in the Alps she climbed the N Face of the Peigne, traversed the Courtes, did the Midi-Plan traverse and climbed the NNE route on the M. She became a committee member two years after joining the Pinnacle Club and was editor of the 1974 Journal. The tragic death of her husband, Colin, left her very tied, and she is unable to come on meets any more, but has translated several climbing books into English.

Avis Reynolds had been walking and rock-climbing for nine years when she finally filled in her application form. She led to about Severe standard in the Lake District and Wales – Tennis Shoe, Christmas Curry and a number of Kirkus' climbs, and was used to following harder routes with impatient leaders. In the end, she led them herself. Her husband likes fishing and doesn't climb at all. She still does a lot of climbing and has been the Club's representative on the BMC Committee for Wales for a number of years. She is also a gifted artist.

The Easter meet was held in Scotland in 1967, based in Glencoe Village and at the SMC hut, Lagangarbh. The weather was heavy rain, easing off then turning to snow, and although both groups were energetic, they never actually met. It was good weather for visiting, and four members were entertained to tea at the Grampian Club Hut by members of the Rucksack Club. The Lagangarbh contingent found the Gritstone Club there as well, and Angela Faller (now Soper) remembers, "Went up Ben Starav one day. Up Buchaille Etive Beag with Grits and everybody on a day not fit to be out at all. Great company. Weather improved after the weekend, when most people had left. Christine Sheard and I, with Pete Sugden, did Aonach Eagach in deep snow and glorious sunshine – she was 'topless' at one stage – a day we didn't want to end. Ditto on Bidean next day. Met Jack (Soper) with his field class on the top; they were using geological hammers for ice-axes."

The hut in Cwm Dyli was well used by a number of groups and families this spring, but the weather left much to be desired. Pat Wood, with two little boys who made themselves even wetter by falling into streams, was glad of the zoo at Colwyn Bay. They collected Denise Evans' boy, Chuck, on the way and were allowed to handle the python – a most successful visit.

For Barbara Spark's meet in July, the sun shone at last. Most people climbed, but one group managed to walk the Nantlle ridge without being shot at by farmers. Dorothy Lee didn't climb, but had the Saturday evening meal ready when everyone arrived back late and tired.

In the Lake District Angela Faller had been persuaded to try and lead Kipling Groove, the hardest route in the old guide to Langdale. She fell off at the end of the traverse, watched by Gwen Moffat and Janet Rogers, which embarrassed her very much. It had been described as a hand traverse, so she was doing her best to oblige. She writes: "Did K.G. the other week (1984), seconding one of the new prospective members who wanted to lead it – and stopped at the very place where I fell, to talk to her about it – could have stayed in balance for ages! Felt amazed that I could have fallen off from there."

That year she was climbing with Ken Wood and Allan Austin's team whenever she could tag on, but left for Kenya in mid-summer to join a geophysical team. She did what mountaineering could be fitted in and returned in April 1968. Ken and Dorothy Wood had a young family during these years and Angela climbed with each in turn. In April 1967 she did Shrike on Cloggy with Ken, on a very cold day, and somewhere around this time she led Cloggy Corner.

Helen Goodburn had started work in the Lake District in the autumn of 1966 and eventually managed to buy a car, so in the summer of 1967 she and Chris Sheard drove out to the Alps for six weeks, first to Zinal and then to the Badile area. Guy Genoud, the guide on the meet the year before, had told them there were a lot of mixed ridge routes around Zinal, of the sort they enjoyed and which would be well within their capabilities as a guideless team. Helen says it was a fantastic feeling setting out on their own. They were terribly slow on the first route, which involved a lot of step-cutting and when they returned the hut warden's son came bouncing out to tell them his father thought they must be dead! Every hut they went to they were met by stern-faced guides who didn't believe two girls could be competent. There always seemed to be one amongst them though, who had heard what they had done and was prepared to say they should be allowed to carry on. "Sometimes they deliberately took clients on the route we had chosen," says Helen, "and would manage to get in front of us because of their knowledge of the route. It became a matter of pride to beat them back to the hut.

"We wanted to do the N Ridge of the Weisshorn but were told it was too serious and difficult. We said we were going to do it and they implied they would prevent us. Eventually they gave in. There was a rock route in the nearby Val d'Arpette. If we managed to do this without mishap we were good enough to do the N Ridge. Off we went to this beautiful valley and camped by a stream where we found chamois footprints the next morning. It was an attractive little ridge with varied climbing. On the final col we met a guided party on the trade route and were applauded – Bravo Anglaises! We felt as if we were spied on.

"When we returned triumphant there was some surprise that we had done it. To our amazement one of the guides 'coincidentally' had a client who wanted to do the N Ridge. They still wouldn't let us out of their sight. In the event the weather stopped us instead."

I should like to see the guide that dared order Margaret Darvall and Alwine Walford about. Sometimes joined by Hugo, Alwine's husband, Margaret and Alwine were doing a number of guideless climbs in Corsica. Sue Gibson was also in the party but there was great confusion over meeting up because there were two hotels with the same name, so Sue climbed with Nea Morin, Micheline and some French friends. Nea and Micheline left a note in the Post Office, but the others didn't find it until Sue and Hugo had gone, so it was a diminished party who climbed together when they finally found each other.

Once more, Janet Rogers did a number of impressive routes in the Bregaglia, including a new route on the Punta Allievi, named Via Inglese, with Nigel and a friend. Penny Storey and her sister climbed Mount Olympus in Greece, but the bouquet for most adventurous traveller must go to Dorothea Gravina. To start with she hitch-hiked from South Africa to Egypt climbing Mount Kenya on the way; during the summer she went as a climbing leader to a Girl Guide based mountaineering holiday around the Zermatt area, leading such routes as the Wellenkuppe and Monte Rosa and climbing the Schalligrat – East Ridge Traverse of the Weisshorn on her own account. The high spot, both for her and for Sylvia Yates, was Mont Blanc by the Peuterey Ridge, made more exciting by bad weather.

The adventure started on July 18th and was the idea of Sidney Nowill, who climbed with Michel Vaucher as guide. Also in the party was a very favourite guide, Gilles Josserand, who led the LAC member, Elisabeth Parry. Dorothea and Sylvia climbed with an aspirant guide, Dominique Blanchet.

The fun started on the very complex and crevassed Frêney Glacier, which they chose in preference to the Col de l'Inominata. At one point the ice gave way beneath Sylvia's feet and swung her into a crevasse from which she was extricated by Dorothea and Gilles.

There is an exciting picture in the LAC *Journal* of some of the party in the couloir leading to the Brèche Nord des Dames Anglaises. The weather was still uncertain, but the hot sun made retreat impracticable, and by late afternoon they reached the southern end of the summit rocks of the Aiguille Blanche de Peuterey. They bivouacked here, for the heat had made the corniced ridge dangerous. By next morning, however, it had frozen and the arête went well, followed by a series of spectacular snow ridges – breathlessly fine and corniced. There were long abseils to the Col de Peuterey, and unpleasant stonefall, but fortunately nobody was seriously hurt. Dorothea was struck on the hip, which paralysed her leg for a time; nevertheless she and Sylvia had the brilliant idea of a brew-up and late-comers found the others ensconced in a snow dug-out complete with snowman and vast quantities of hot sweet coffee. By now the sky had clouded over and it started to snow, but any retreat was much more difficult than continuing the ascent. There were moments of fun, for Michel found that the way to tackle the snow of the Grand Pilier d'Aigle was on his hands and knees and the others all followed in this penitential attitude. At last they reached the ill-defined ridge leading to Mont Blanc de Courmayeur and found it shrouded in icy fog. Worse than that, they found the whole ridge covered in ice and the ascent took four hours. Dorothea said "This mountain has no top – we're cramponning straight to Paradise" ...

On reaching the top, they plunged into the teeth of a gale and it took two casts before they set off in the right direction for the summit of Mont Blanc. Unknowingly, they passed by two alpininsts whose bodies were found frozen to death later that day. If they had seen them they might have saved them. From the summit they fought straight down to the Vallot Hut and that sordid pigsty seemed like heaven when they reached it that evening. Elisabeth Parry wrote the account on which this summary is based.

Perhaps not in the mountaineering class was Dorothy Pilley Richards' ascent of Mount Sinai, but her article in the 1968 Fell and Rock *Journal* on this subject is full of delight.

The hut had been well used during the summer. Peggy Wild prepared for her Mountain Leadership Assessment Course ("Don't expect to pass" – but she did) and someone climbed Direct on Dinas Mot with Denise Evans, got her foot stuck in the top crack and had to take her PA off – "Not at all funny." Jean Dilnot and Biddy Burgum came for a wet week in August and found the causeway across Llyn Llydaw under water; Evelyn Leech recovered from moving house, Jo and Brian Fuller called in on their way back from Switzerland; Eveleigh climbed with Nancy Smith and there were family parties.

There were meets at Froggatt, Dent and Swanage, then a grand meeting of members at the hut for the November Meet. Saturday was a day of calm amidst the rain and hail. Several parties went to Tryfan and I climbed Pinnacle Rib with Dorothea. The occasion is impressed on my mind because she was swanking about being an old age pensioner and I was so pregnant (a useful excuse) that I couldn't keep up with her to the foot of the climb, so I let her carry the rope.

It was a lovely day to remember because widespread foot and mouth disease broke out soon afterwards and the fells were out of bounds until the following February. The New Year Meet had to be cancelled, and the last entry in the hut book for 1967 is on November 19th when Evelyn carefully made her way through a puddle of disinfectant to fix Foot and Mouth notices on the door and gate. Use of the hut was forbidden till the restrictions were lifted.

Fortunately the Annual Dinner Meet took place about a week after the outbreak ended, and sixty-seven members and guests attended the dinner at the Old Dungeon Ghyll. It should have been sixty-eight, but my third son came a fortnight early and arrived just as I would have been sitting down to the meal. The 1968 Dinner was a special occasion in more ways than one, though people did not realise it at the time, for Sid and Jammy Cross retired soon afterwards and went to live at Clappersgate – so it was the Club's final sample of their splendid hospitality.

Margaret Darvall presided once again at the Annual Meeting, which started on a sad note, for Mabel Jeffrey had died during the year. She had joined the Club in 1921, been president for the six years that included the war, and had attended meets to within a year of her death.

Membership now stood at 142, which was the highest point reached before the mid 1980s; after this peak it dropped to the 130s and remained constant for a number of years.

The outbreak of foot and mouth disease had meant a loss of revenue to the hut and many of the library books were mouldy through being in a damp, disused hut. Jo Fuller now had a house in Nant Peris and agreed it would be a good idea to keep some of the older and more valuable books there. During March Jo, with Christine Sheard, removed about thirty of them, listing them in the log book and drawing a careful map to show where Jo's house was. "People wanting to borrow these books, please call at any time – you will be most welcome."

There were some improvements to the hut as well: "A calor gas fire for use in the mornings or when the wind is in the smoky quarter; a bar light which pleases a large number of people because they can see to eat and read, but displeases some; heater lamps in the Dormitory that take off the chill nicely." The hut fund was growing steadily, and members of the Jagdula Expedition had donated a hundred pounds from their funds.

Nea Morin gave a very full BMC report, for there had been major reorganisation of the BMC itself and many other matters had been dealt with. Pinnacle Club members hoped that the Club could be represented on three area committees: Wales, Lakes and South East. The old Pen-y-Pass Hotel, remembered as a place of quiet carpeting and old leather where climbers were served pint mugs of tea while sitting in old fashioned comfort, had been bought by the Youth Hostels Association. They had promised to provide facilities for non-members, but provision of these, and in particular the plans of the proposed buildings, were to be watched with an eagle eye. For the first time the Annual Assembly of the Union Internationale d'Association d'Alpinism was to meet in Britain. Members from Eastern European countries had no foreign exchange facilities, so BMC clubs were asked to give a donation towards their expenses; the Pinnacle Club gave 5 guineas.

Margaret Darvall laid the foundations for a shortened meeting and one that could start later in the afternoon, by proposing that officers should prepare their reports in advance so that they could be circulated with the notice of the AGM. This turned out to be a brilliant piece of reform.

The spring meets included one in Patterdale, staying at Beetham Cottage. The Club used Fell and Rock huts so often that it is good to note that two parties of Fell and Rock ladies had an enjoyable stay at Cwm Dyli this year. Family parties at the hut included the Flews, Beards, Punnetts, and the usual Cooper-Poulton family gathering joined by Evelyn, Nea, Denise and Chuck.

Nea had been in Switzerland during May, when she represented the Ladies' Alpine Club at the Swiss Ladies' Alpine Club Jubilee, celebrating fifty years since their foundation. Margaret Darvall and Eileen Healey were there as well but obviously did not consider their ascent of the Titlis serious enough to deserve mention; a champagne party was held on the summit.

Later in the summer Margaret, with Mary Fulford, took part in a women's expedition to East Greenland with Joan Busby, Esme Speakman and Eilidh Nisbet, where they did as much exploration as possible, given transport problems and changeable weather, and achieved a first ascent.

Sally and Mike Westmacott were with a party climbing and exploring in the Hindu Kush, in the Chitral region, and upheld the party's honour by making the first ascent of a 19,000 foot peak. Bad weather prevented the second party's attempt and any further ascents.

I think this is the year that Jo Fuller and Gill Cannon drove up through Norway to the Arctic Circle, climbing and exploring. Jo says she does not keep records or take photos, but she wrote an article for the *Journal*; Mairet Picken, who had been to the Romsdal with friends, one of whom was Alison Lamb (Higham) wrote of their ascent of the Wall. Avis Reynolds went to Kandersteg for her first Alpine holiday, very successful, of which she also wrote in the *Journal*.

There were currency restrictions in 1967 and 68, so many people did not go abroad and the Froggatt meet in September was very heavily booked. Startled and full of consternation, Pinnaclers arriving at the hut found a large party of Climbers' Club members in residence. "This was no problem however, as over a glass of ale we soon came to an amicable arrangement, whereby the smaller men's party stayed in the women's bedroom, while the Pinnacle Club slept in the men's bedroom," wrote Gill Cannon in the report. Saturday and Stanage were rather wet, but a fine day and Froggatt cheered people on the Sunday.

There was an important committee meeting on the Saturday evening, for Barbara Spark had resigned as secretary, due to pressure of work. Kathleen Hoskins agreed to become acting secretary. One good result of this meeting was the decision to put members' phone numbers in the *Handbook*.

The Yorkshire meet was led as usual by Alison Adam and Chris Woods. It had developed into a meet for older members and the very young; one or two members brought young children and for several years Ada Shaw came with her husband and small son, Timothy, until the latter was well into his teens, no longer small, and had to spend the evenings doing his homework.

Alwine Walford led a Swanage meet based at the Square and Compass, a friendly little pub within walking distance of the cliffs, and the party climbed at Seacombe Bay. As usual, the Anniversary Meet in November was a great gathering of the Club; all the bunks were full and people camped round about or visited for the day. Tired of cold, wet climbs in the Pass, a large party went to Tremadog on the Sunday and Janet Rogers led Nea on One Step in the Clouds before leading Meshach (HVS) with Sheila Crispin. Angela Faller and Denise Evans were climbing together, and Gill Cannon with Kate Webb.

Students from Bangor University visited the hut four times in the next few weeks, finishing with a grand mixed party to celebrate the end of term by climbing day and night! – "John, Phil, Pete made midnight assault Lockwood's." Into the midst of this party came Angela Kelly, Jane Taylor and Gill Cannon who had made a snap decision to celebrate the end of term in the same way and in consequence found accommodation something of a problem. The result was a letter to the committee from Gill, backed by Janet Rogers, stating that it seemed unfair that while members could only invite husbands and brothers to stay at the hut, any number of men could be included in a block booking made by a member. Evelyn Leech had a few telling remarks to make about people who turned up without prior warning, but did concede that it might be possible to relax the rule if due notice was given. The committee agreed to discuss the matter.

Jean and Biddy came just before Christmas, to find the place cheerfully decked with holly; Evelyn came for a quick dust round – "NB. Sweeper will not pick up bits if it is already full up with dirt!" Pat Wood arrived that same evening with Nigel and Richard, now aged nine and eleven, and they chose an interesting route up Siabod next day, glissading down the NW side. Their party left on 22nd December and the hut was quiet for the brief spell before members gathered for the New Year Meet. This was Margaret Darvall's final "President's Meet" as she had nearly completed her three years in office and would be handing over to Janet Rogers, whom she had chosen as her successor, during the Annual Dinner Meet.

Janet was going through a very bad time just now, for her marriage had broken up, and she had written to Margaret in doubt as to whether she would still be a suitable person for the presidency. Margaret, of course, wrote back to reassure her, with the full approval of the committee.

Janet was very much in the mainstream of climbing at this time; two new routes climbed by Nigel and herself in the 1968 season were recorded in the first issue of Mountain. Mountain was first published in January 1969, rising from the ashes of Mountain Craft when the Mountaineering Association was taken over by the Youth Hostels Association. It was owned by the YHA and edited by Ken Wilson. Nigel and Janet, with Ian Roper and Kim Meldrum, had made first ascents of the South East face of the Punta Baroni and the SE ridge to the WSW summit of the Piz Zocca. Janet was seconding a number of routes on Anglesey, also climbing a lot with Jo Fuller – routes such as White Slab Direct, Integrity and Crack of Doom on Skye. Jo had her place in the first issue of *Mountain* as well; she wrote the review of Nea Morin's book, *A Woman's Reach*, doubtless because Brian Fuller was review editor.

Ken Wilson had been invited to the Annual Dinner this year, and it took place at the Pen-y-Gwryd Hotel on February 16th. The chief guest was Baronin Felicitas von Reznicek, author of *Von der Krinoline zum Sechtsen Grad*, who was a leading light in the foundation of the international association Rendez-vous Hautes Montagnes the previous year. It had been hoped that Charles and Denise Evans would be present, for Charles was President of the Alpine Club and Denise had been asked to propose the toast to the guests. However, Alwine Walford admirably performed the latter duty and Mike Ward, as vice-president of the Alpine Club, was able to attend. During the year Charles Evans received a knighthood for services to mountaineering, which gave Club members great pleasure on both his and Denise's account.

The dinner weekend was bright, cold and sharp, with mountains covered in deep, crisp snow, so the few skiers of Saturday were joined by many more on the Sunday with Barbara James lending them equipment and giving a number of them first rate instruction. Later on Sunday members were invited to Ogwen Cottage to see the Baroness' film of the international gathering of women climbers and a showing of "The Hazard."

It was a good weekend for entertainment, for Ken Wilson gave a slide show after the dinner on Saturday evening, illustrating with some wit his idea of women's place in the mountains – a brave man!

Despite Margaret Darvall's idea of having the reports circulated, the annual meeting went on so long that there was a scramble to finish it before guests arrived for the meal. Jo Fuller's report as meets secretary is of particular interest as being vital to the Club's survival:

"Despite good attendance ... there had been a marked lack of leaders. This had meant that large groups have been shepherded by the few willing to accept responsibility ...

"In order to perpetuate the traditions of the Club it is important that the really competent rock climbers not only instruct those who are beginners to the sport, but should also feel free to tackle routes more in keeping with their general standard.

"It is to be hoped that during the coming year general competence in the mountains and full participation in the responsibilities of a rope attempting a climb of any standard should be the most important aim of both Associate and Full Members attending meets."

Among the books given to the library were Nea Morin's *A Woman's Reach* and Gwen Moffat's *On My Home Ground*.

All official meets this year were recorded in the Jubilee *Journal*, and apart from a hut cleaning meet there were none before July, though the hut was well used, mainly by families. I had brought my family to the hut for Whitsun and made shameless use of the others as baby sitters on the Sunday when we went to the Wenallt, for I was keen to second Ian on Bovine. Mindful of the Meets Secretary's words, Jean and Biddy had led routes the previous day, but were very pleased for Ian to lead them on Oxo, which I think was their first VS climb.

Angela Faller was climbing more in the Lake District than in Wales: in June she climbed Deer Bield Buttress and North Crag Eliminate with Joe Tasker, and she writes of one particular route with Denise Wilson: "One highlight was July 20th, when Denise came from her cottage to join me in Langdale and we did Gimmer String. The new Red Guidebook was now published and HVS and Extreme grades had been defined. But I didn't tell Denise we were doing an Extreme and she didn't know till after. She didn't have any trouble, though. I was really pleased about that ascent."

The Alpine season started with a tragedy, although nobody suspected it until the middle of August. Mairet Picken and her friend, Ruth Speight had ten days of good climbing in Skye in June then, with brief calls at Vera Picken's and at Ruth's parents' they arrived in Chamonix on July 3rd. They acclimatised on the Brévent and the Nonne before being driven down by bad weather, then climbed the Aiguille du Purchelle, the NNE Ridge of the M and the Papillons Arête on the Peigne. Their letters conveyed their complete enjoyment of the climbing, and their desire to return for the Forbes Arête, which was out of condition. Meanwhile they went to Zermatt, leaving their car at St Niklaus and spending the night of 19th July at the Hörnli Hut in preparation for the Zmutt ridge of the Matterhorn. They left nothing in the hut, saying that they might go down the Italian ridge, so the guardian did not expect them back. They were not seen again.

Vera went to Andorra on July 18th for two weeks' climbing followed by another week with relatives, so she did not become seriously anxious till August 12th. The police were sympathetic but unhelpful, so Vera and Ruth's parents went to Chamonix to search on their own account. Finally they met Tut Braithwaite, who said he had spoken to them in the bar the evening before they left for Switzerland, so they set off for Zermatt and found Ruth's car.

Peter Gentil, Grant Jarvis and John Tooke were at the Bahnhof and made a thorough search in poor conditions because snow had fallen and was still falling; they also informed the Italian guides and police. It was almost certain there was no hope however. Vera says how good it was to see Nea, Margaret and Alwine in Zermatt the day before she left. Mairet was her youngest child, and the only one to share her enthusiasm for rock climbing.

Margaret Darvall had come to Zermatt after an exciting traverse of the Midi-Plan in new snow. Sally and Mike Westmacott had also come to the Zermatt area, after a good season in the Bernina; they went on the traverse of the Matterhorn by the Zmutt and Hörnli ridges and realised one of Sally's great ambitions by ascending the Breithorn Younggrat. The *Alpine Journal* was brought out in a new format in 1969 and had a section devoted to other organisations and clubs with a contribution from the Ladies' Alpine Club, so Sally's ascent was recorded there. Also recorded, in the British Isles section, was the ascent on Anglesey of Tyrannosaurus Rex (XS) by Ward-Drummond, Lawrie Holliwell, Pearce and Janet Rogers – "One of the best routes on Anglesey and maybe in Wales." Janet says she "had been on part of the first ascent by claiming to be a photographer." In August 1970 she took part in the TV spectacular on Anglesey, climbing Tyrannosaurus Rex with the Holliwell brothers.

Jane Taylor and Angela Kelly enjoyed the rock ridges of the Alpes Maritimes this year, and Ron and Barbara James climbed in the Vercors, the Dolomites and Chamonix, being especially delighted with the south face of the Chiarazzes – similar to the Comici on the Cima Grande, but freer; and satisfying a long ambition by climbing the north face of the Petit Clocher du Portalet.

I had done a number of climbs in the Lake District this summer and at the end of August managed to hold my brother-in-law when he fell from the second pitch of a rather damp Botterill's Slab. He had no runner in, so it was quite a long fall. We were helped by some Yorkshire climbers, who called out the rescue team and meanwhile wrapped John in a survival bag to keep him warm. They were very good and I wish I knew their names.

I went down and drove home as soon as the stretcher came, so that Ian could drive my sister-in-law to the hospital – they were at home looking after our combined families of six little children aged 0 – 6, so could not leave them until I returned. When they had gone I received two telephone calls; the first was from Ian telling me that John would be all right but that the press were nosing around; if they bothered me, I was to refer them to the Chairman of the Wasdale Mountain Rescue Team, Frank Monkhouse.

The second was from the press: "Ah, Mrs Angell," they said, "We hear that your daughter has been in a very brave rescue."

"Oh, yes?" I tried to sound like this daughter's clueless mother, "You'd better ask Mr Monkhouse about that!"

Fortunately the children were all asleep, for the private joke, coming on top of the relief that I hadn't disgraced myself and killed my brother-in-law, sent me sky high!

As autumn approached Annette Wilson came to the hut for a fortnight's walking and scrambling and there were the usual Froggatt and Yorkshire meets. The latter was more varied than usual for four Gritstone Club members guided Jo Fuller and Angela Faller potholing through the Lost John system and there was a good deal of climbing as well as walking.

In October the Club hut was used for the first time by my local club, the Wyndham Mountaineering Club from Egremont, (now re-named West Cumbria M.C.) They were a fairly new club, very active at that time in discovering new routes on the cliffs at St Bees Head.

The Anniversary Meet was crowded as usual and Evelyn Leech, who was catering, excelled herself by cooking an enormous and succulent roast of beef. The happy experience is vivid after fifteen years. It was fine enough to climb in the Pass and at Tremadog, and to do long climbs and scrambles on Snowdon and the Carneddau. The year had brought both success and tragedy, but the fellowship remained.

CHAPTER 29

1970. Whitsun at Cwm Dyli. Hard routes on Scafell and Pavey. British Women's Himalayan Expedition. Ron and Barbara James in the Dolomites. Barbara leads Cemetery Gates. Baptism of new rainwear.

1970 began in traditional manner with very snowy excursions and a good meal at the Pen-y-Gwryd, but for the Annual Dinner in February the Club had to break with tradition. The new owners of the Old Dungeon Ghyll were less than welcoming to climbers and members were sampling the Glenridding Hotel at Ullswater.

People whipped up appetites in wet, blustery weather and speakers at the Dinner were Angela Kelly, Brian Crofts of the Climbers' Club, and Janet Rogers.

On reviewing the year at the Annual Meeting it was obvious that the pattern of meets was changing – members had family commitments at Bank Holidays, so these would be planned in future as informal meets for groups of friends rather than the big affairs of the past. More frequent meets were arranged and Angela Faller took over from Jo Fuller as meets secretary. Kathleen Hoskins had gone to Australia shortly after her appointment as secretary and Pat Daley took her place in this key position.

Evelyn Leech was expecting to go into hospital for a major operation, so Peggy Wild became assistant hut secretary and later took charge. Alwine Walford, with her formidable organising powers, took over as dinner coordinator and new committee members were Nea Morin, Gwen Moffat and Shirley Angell. I was also made representative on the Lakes Committee of the BMC and was one of a group who were elected full members, so everything seemed to be happening at once for me.

Jancis Gay and Hilda Tyler, both very experienced climbers, were elected members during the year. Jancis was hardly seen again so it is not surprising that she was a member for just a few years.

Hilda wrote an article for the Jubilee *Journal* of how she and her husband, Ron, had started climbing; they went from strength to strength until his death in a tragic accident when he was electrocuted in 1969 and she joined the Club just as she was recovering from this blow. She led to VS standard with ease and confidence and regularly tutored police cadets in rock climbing at Ilkley during their Outward Bound courses. Always keen and lively, Hilda has been committee member and dinner organiser. After a few years she met Keith Young, who enjoys walking, and it was touching to see him carrying the rucksack and trying to keep up with the lightweight, dancing Hilda. Sadly Hilda left the Club when she married Keith, though members see them at Fell and Rock meets; however, I believe their main interest now is sailing.

It was May before many visitors used the hut, then Kate and Barry Webb brought their family, now numbering two, for an adventure holiday in the sun and some useful hut maintenance. The Angell family followed, camping, and were the constant element in the Spring Bank Holiday meet. Sandra Gamble and I did a seemingly endless route on Lliwedd; Sandra had a migraine and eventually confessed that she was in the midst of divorce proceedings and was 'sorry to behave like a wet lettuce.' A helicopter was buzzing around and we felt like being rescued by it, but fortunately it ignored our waves! Somehow Sandra got down to the hut and was looked after by Evelyn, who had come for the night.

Meanwhile Ian and our three little boys in their red wellies had brought up the coal and been on a fishing expedition, and Sheila Cormack arrived, looking full of health and beauty. She and her husband Alan had come from Manchester on their motor bike and he had dropped her off for the weekend. She and Ian went straight off to climb Gallop Step while Alwine and Hugo Walford, also newly arrived, from Hampshire, had a pleasant sunbathe and mug of China tea (Alwine's speciality) after their journey.

This sundrenched weekend was lazy climbing weather. We had a day at Cwm Silyn, returning to find that Jean and Biddy had arrived, so the following morning I had a route at Tremadog with them before heading for home and leaving the others, plus Alan Cormack, to further sunbathing and good routes.

This was Sheila Cormack's fourth meet and she was elected a member in July. She was already an experienced climber, leading to VS, with a good basic training on gritstone and three Alpine seasons behind her, also long walks such as the Lyke Wake. Her father was very keen, so climbing was in the family. She sets a punishing pace and strong men have been known to quail at the thought of a day on the hills with her. In April she had been on the meet at Malham with Angela Kelly, Jo Fuller and Christine Sheard when they did the Three Peaks walk.

This was a marvellous summer; at the Langdale meet in June Angela Faller and Angela Kelly walked to Scafell and climbed Chartreuse and Great Eastern with the Yellow Slab variation and the following day Angela Faller led Hilda Tyler and me up Stickle Grooves on Pavey. It was a splendid route on a perfect day, so I wrote an account for the magazine of our local climbing club and thenceforward was treated with a new respect! Whether or not my climbing technique was improving, this was the year in which I led my first complete VS climb, for I was leading through on Belle Vue Bastion with Joann Palmer and she didn't just fancy the second pitch, after which she said it was a shame for me not to lead the rest of it and have all the glory. In this casual fashion I achieved a milestone which pleased me very much.

Meanwhile members had already moved to the Alps or further afield. Janet Rogers went on the British Women's Himalayan Expedition to the Padar Himalaya, led by Niki Clough, and they had climbed two peaks and established Camp II on a third, more serious peak when the news of Ian Clough's death on Annapurna reached them and the attempt was abandoned. Other members of the expedition were Brede Arkless (now a P.C. member), Mary Anne Alburger, Audrey Whillans and the liaison officer, Mrs Shashi Kanla. Janet says she was planning another Himalayan trip with Niki when she died, in 1983.

Dorothea was climbing on Table Mountain, and Alwine Walford in Cyprus; nearer home were Angela Faller and Sheila Cormack in the Mont Blanc massif, climbing several routes including most of the Ryan-Lochmatter route on the Blaitière. With Robert West, Angela traversed the Aiguille de Charmoz, climbed Mont Blanc from the Italian side via the Dôme Glacier and, from the Torino Hut, the Géant by the normal route and the Petit Capucin by the East Face. Angela Kelly climbed with Alan Heppenstall, taking in the South West Arête on the Moine and the Zinalrothorn traverse, and Gill Cannon was discovering Central Switzerland as a good climbing area.

Barbara and Ron James were in the Dolomites continuing to clock up first British ascents: Mugoni Spitze by the Catinaccio – grade VI/A2 first female and first British, Furchetta north face (VI), Torre Giallo on the Pala – grade V+/A1 first female, Cima Grande by the Comici route – grade VI, Via Abram on Piz Ciavazes – grade VI-/A2 and five similar routes.

Barbara thinks two of these routes among the most memorable she has ever done. The Tre Cime were the first Dolomite rocks she ever saw, for Ron gathered her up from a package tour near Innsbruck and it was night as they drove up the stone and dirt track to camp near the Lavaredo hut. Next morning she looked out of the tent and saw Ron and his partner high up on the 2,000 ft grade 5 route opposite. This was in 1961 and when they walked below the North Face next day she was gripped on the path. What a contrast to actually climbing the face in 1970!

The road by now was wide and tarmacked with a toll gate at the bottom – no dirt track any longer. They had been waiting for decent weather and when it came they drove over to Cortina and camped at the foot of the road, prepared for a quick get away next morning and bedded early. By 4 a.m. they were off, with dry bread choking and tepid coffee thrown down throats. As they walked along the path under the face, they heard footsteps creeping up behind and increased speed. It was essential for safety's sake to be first on the route, so they soloed up the first few hundred feet of easy rock in the semi dark to get to the short grade 4 pitch, which Ron rushed up telling Barbara to take her time and hold up the two behind them – which she did – and give him time to get kitted up.

Eventually Barbara was up and the following party looked very doubtingly at the 'old' man and female! They waited on ledges to see if they'd make the first pitch. When they did, the others retired off the route and left them to it.

Barbara says: "There were seven hard, long, committing pitches. I'd heard so many stories of this face and route – Joe Brown nearly getting killed when abseiling off in a storm, another climber who'd been killed by lightning on the summit and of course, desperate stories of the epic traverse on the route after the main difficulties were over, and of another traverse at the top to reach the way off.

"The hard pitches went O.K. It's funny the things you remember, like the plastic right foot slip slop shoe suspended under an overhang by the thong for the big toe! Also the two Swiss lads on the very hard route on our left. It was so very incongruous to chat to them so near us, yet if either pair were in trouble, neither could help the other. I took a photo of them and it caught the atmosphere but it was left in a slide projector or something; lost for ever and so sad.

"As we sat on a big ledge after the seven main pitches, it was the first time I had stopped either paying out rope or actually climbing. We allowed ourselves twelve ginger nut biscuits per route and a litre bottle each of water and there on the ledge we sustained ourselves – at about lunchtime I think.

"I'd dreaded the steep corner then the long traverse left – the stories had sunk in, but all went O.K. But as the climbing eased, my arm strength disappeared in direct proportion making all seem like grade 6. The final straw was a storm flashing lightning in the distance coming nearer and nearer and the fear of drowning in the chimneys becoming very real – but I could move no faster. The little traverse at the top was a bit of a crawl but nothing like the awe inspiring epic I'd expected – what a relief. I'd been wondering what it was like all the route."

They were just off the rocky way off as darkness fell:

"From there it was back to the car, drive down and collapse in a cafe. All they'd got left was soup – tepid, not hot, with pasta letters floating in it. It didn't matter. Parched throats accepted it gratefully."

Barbara thinks she may have been the first woman to do this route, and it was just the two of them, with no back up team and nobody at the camp site to know if they were down.

A week earlier, on 14th August, the North Face of the Furchetta had proved another memorable route, as much for the background situation as for the route itself.

They were in the Dolomites and had agreed to meet a crowd of Welsh locals on a certain day at a certain time at the Bahnhof restaurant in Innsbruck. It meant a long drive from where they were climbing and the weather was just becoming settled, so Barbara was all for another route rather than driving to meet people they could see eleven months of the year, but Ron said a promise must be kept.

They reached the steamy valley after a sticky drive and the first pint of beer hardly touched the sides. Just as they were finishing it, their first friends arrived and they had another, and so on all afternoon until by 6 p.m. the party of very puddled Brits was finally complete. "The only sane thing to do was to get some food, so we all staggered towards Marie Therese Strasse and a restaurant." One member pretended to have a bad back and held up all the traffic while he crossed the road, straightening as he reached the pavement. The rest applauded the performance.

"It ended up with Ron driving away from the restaurant by 11 p.m. but before even the start of the Brenner Pass I took the driver's seat ... I drove down the Italian side of the Brenner and along the valley until it was time to turn off to the Vilnosstal, the home valley of the famous Reinhold Messner. Ron drove the last part and it was with relief when at 2 a.m. we blew up air beds, laid them beside the car and slept.

"At 6 a.m. we rose and the smell of the air squeezed from the air beds was evil – as was the sweat that poured from us up the 1,000 ft of loose scree to the foot of the route. I didn't remember ever sweating beer before!

"The first part of the route is only grade 4 so I carried the spare rope in my sack and was thankful when the difficulties proper began. It had been a hard morning after. The steep wall culminated in a famous chimney with a chockstone. Only after overcoming this section did one find the route book where we discovered that Messner had done the route a few weeks previously with the first woman to climb it. Consolation was that we were still the first British climbers on this great route.

"Once again there was a long walk off, and a storm approaching. We got to the hut as the first huge drops began to fall – we had not stopped even to stow away our gear properly. The guardian looked in wonder at the odd pair who arrived obviously straight off a route and so late after all the walkers. Had we taken so long on the normal route? On hearing we had completed the north face he looked very dubious and asked some "innocent" questions. Only after hearing our correct answers did he make us VERY welcome, free food and all we could manage. What a celebration. The only trouble was, as usual, we were so thirsty that forcing food down was lower in our priorities although politeness required a good demolition job on the food."

When Barbara came back to Britain she led Barbara Spark on Cemetery Gates, graded Extreme, and thinks of the whole season as her best ever.

The hut in Cwm Dyli, which had been a haven for families over the summer – Angells, Punnets, Coopers and Poultons; and the Albon family visiting after 13 years' absence – welcomed members back at the November Meet. Saturday was fine enough for good routes, but pouring rain put most people off on the Sunday. Seven of us went round to Capel, where I bought myself a new oilskin anorak. Of course we had to try it out, so we had a wet and slippery ascent of Pinnacle Rib, where Jo Palmer's big wooden wedge made us feel a lot safer than we might have done. It was great fun to look down at the road through the deluge and see groups of happy walkers striding along and keeping their spirits up by singing. Jo and I drove straight back to Cumberland after the climb, only stopping to strip and change into dry clothes in the doubtful privacy of Jo's van. My anorak was effective enough, but nothing could have stopped the water running up my arms when I climbed.

CHAPTER 30

1971 – Jubilee Year celebrations and Journal. New members. Alpine routes. Peru. Dorothea's travels. Evelyn Leech dies.

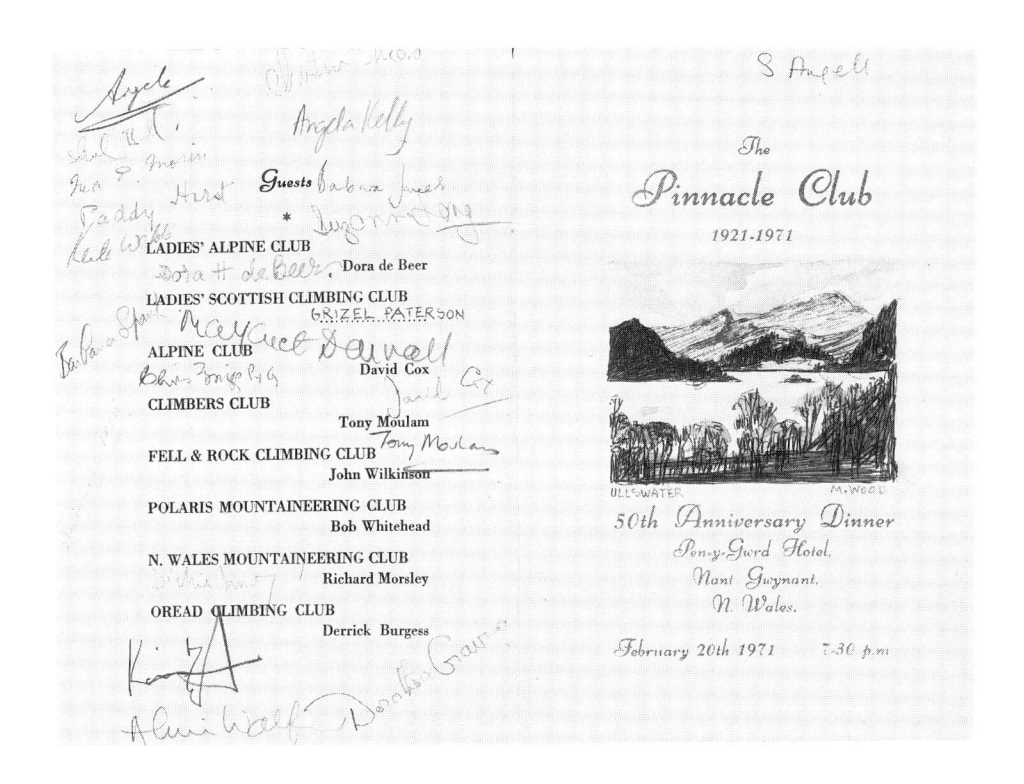

The Pinnacle Club 1921-1971

LADIES' ALPINE CLUB
Dora de Beer

LADIES' SCOTTISH CLIMBING CLUB
GRIZEL PATERSON

ALPINE CLUB
David Cox

CLIMBERS CLUB
Tony Moulam

FELL & ROCK CLIMBING CLUB
John Wilkinson

POLARIS MOUNTAINEERING CLUB
Bob Whitehead

N. WALES MOUNTAINEERING CLUB
Richard Morsley

OREAD CLIMBING CLUB
Derrick Burgess

50th Anniversary Dinner
Pen-y-Gwryd Hotel,
Nant Gwynant,
N. Wales.

February 20th 1971 7-30 p.m

1971 was a very special year for the Club, being the 50th anniversary of its foundation. The New Year meet was a cosy affair with about fifteen members present at some time or another but the big event was to be the Annual Dinner Meet in February.

Alwine Walford had carefully planned a menu which would be festive and a little different without taxing the ovens at the P-y-G beyond their limit, Chris Briggs was making a special effort to fit in as many people as possible, and all was going swimmingly when a postal strike put paid to all proper communication just at the crucial time. Marjorie Wood collected the special gold-printed menus and personally illustrated over sixty of them with her beautiful water colours because it was impossible for other artists to send their work. Minutes and annual reports could not be circulated to members, and it was very hard to tell just how many people were going to attend the Dinner.

Alwine Walford took it all in her stride, and the arrangements were an outstanding success. Special guests were Don and Audrey Whillans, Kevin Fitzgerald and H.M.

Kelly, and club representatives who were sharing in the celebrations included Dora de Beer, Grizel Paterson, David Cox, Tony Moulam, John Wilkinson, Bob Whitehead, Richard Morsley and Derrick Burgess. Three Original Members: Paddy Hirst, Trilby Wells and Len Winthrop Young were there.

Evelyn Leech proposed the toast to the guests; she had not fully recovered from her operation and ten weeks in hospital, but had been persuaded that she was the only Club speaker of sufficient stature available for the task on such an occasion. Some may have suspected that it would be our final chance to hear her skill; she died later in the year. The other star speaker was Kevin Fitzgerald, who had us weeping with laughter before he had spoken three words and kept us in this state of agonising delight for the all too brief duration of his speech.

Eighty people had filled the two rooms during the meal, and afterwards we all fitted into the games room to see Janet's slides and hear her entertaining account of the Padar Himalaya. I felt very honoured to be squashed comfortably onto a settee next to Kevin Fitzgerald, whom I had not met before. The P-y-G was very full indeed but Chris Briggs did us proud and managed to be both host and guest. Absent friends were Sid and Jammy Cross, whom we had hoped to honour on this occasion, but they were unable to come.

The Club did not forget its purpose and some members for whom it was half term managed three days' climbing at Tremadog; others preferred the enticing, snowy ridges and five of us climbed Central Trinity Gully on Snowdon on the Sunday, then back over Lliwedd before driving home.

The Annual Meeting on the Saturday had gone well. Evelyn reported that the table bought with Mabel Jeffrey's bequest was installed at last – in fact there were two: the long refectory table and a smaller one to be used separately or as an extension. These substantial, beautifully made tables had already been much admired.

Gill Cannon had hoped to have the Jubilee *Journal* published in time for the dinner meet but, as always happens, members had been slow to produce the goods. She had made an impassioned plea for articles on fringe activities and I had felt so sorry for her that I wrote one on sketching the routes for a climbing guide to St Bees Head. This led to an amusing incident; Gill said, very kindly, that it didn't quite fit in, but – what I have always thought so tactless as to be extremely funny – she handed it back to me in a large envelope, boldly marked "REJECTED MATERIAL"!

She felt keenly the responsibility of producing something worthy of a national club and, despite all the worries, she made a very good job of it. The inspired simplicity of Frances Tanner's cover design caught the eye and the contents included a balanced selection of historical articles, hard climbs and a range of activities. The only disaster was a printer's error in which Gwen Moffat's contribution was cut off in mid-sentence, leaving Gwen and her readers equally frustrated. Gill had had to shop around for photographs, but she found some very fine ones. The presidential photograph of Janet Rogers was a striking character study by John Cleare, showing her impish face framed by dark hair and a helmet.

Three new members were elected during the Dinner Meet: Joann Palmer (Greenhow), Stephanie Rowland and Anne Shepherd (Wheatcroft).

I met Joann through Colin Greenhow and we went out climbing together on summer evenings, then she came to Pinnacle Club meets and immediately found friends and climbing partners in such as Sheila Cormack. She joined as a good leader of Severe and selected VS climbs and was going from strength to strength when she fell off her motor bike and damaged her knee badly. She has a young son now but still climbs when she has free time.

Steph Rowland had enjoyed mountain walking since the age of ten, and had walked and scrambled in the Alps for six seasons, climbing to grade IV in Central Switzerland. In rock climbing she was a very experienced second but did not do any leading until she joined the Club. She is a strong person in the mountains and, with her husband, Clive, has taken part in a number of first ascents, both summer and winter, on Skye and in northern Scotland. She says that many of the routes remain unrecorded, but one example of a winter route on Liathach is Footless Gully, grade IV, on Coire Dubh Beag in 1977. Summer routes on Skye include Resolution, VS, 1974, and The Rent, VS, 1980, on Sgurr an Fheadain. Another interesting experience was taking part in the first ascent of an unclimbed mountain in Arctic Norway. Anne first heard of the Pinnacle Club through Climbing Days, showing the power of Dorothy Pilley's book forty years after she wrote it. Anne writes: "I had just moved back to Manchester from London and was looking for someone to climb with, having been in the Rockhoppers when based in London. I had originally started climbing when on a Leeds University expedition to the Atlas in 1968, but found it difficult to make much progress when in London. The move to Manchester and regular weekends away, often with the Pinnacle Club, or members, was the major factor."

Anne developed into a sound leader on rock climbs to VS standard, and a strong leader on Alpine routes, amongst which she counts as best the Nadelgrat from the Dom Hut, the Eisengrat on Piz Roseg and the traverse of Piz Palu to Pt Zupo in the Bernina. She thinks the Skye ridge in 1981 was quite a special event, and the completion of the Munros in 1981. "Serious Munro-bagging went on for about 4-5 years, so quite successful from south of the Thames.

"The other episode that I will never forget is the Wind Rivers trip in 1983. We had a very successful two weeks, climbing Gannet, Frémont etc. before the accident."

She and her husband changed base to climb Mount Hooker, little knowing how important their self-rescue and survival techniques were to prove during the next few days.

Anne writes: "We had just climbed the mountain (about 12,500ft) and were traversing down a ridge when a large block came away with me attached. I fell about 20-30ft and sustained a fractured skull, broken leg and wrist (all on the left side). Apparently I was not properly conscious for about half an hour but then have clear memory. Robert helped me down the first steep part of the ridge and I was then able to progress crab-wise over slabs to a col at about 11,000ft. This took about 6 hours. Robert left me on the second half of the descent to get our tent, which was a further 2,000ft lower. He pitched this on the col and I arrived just as it started to rain. "There was bad weather all night and Robert left at first light to walk to the road end (a journey which took 8 hours on the walk-in but which he did in about 4 on the return). As the warden's station was unmanned he then drove about 60 miles to the nearest telephone, but the weather was too bad to send a helicopter until mid afternoon.

"I was then taken to Pinedale, where it was decided I needed an air-ambulance to Salt Lake City. I arrived there about midnight, some 36 hours after the accident.

"This all sounds rather worse than it was at the time for me – if not for Robert.

"I have done little serious climbing since then, partly because my wrist has not completely recovered, partly because I doubt my ability to progress further, and get less out of repeating previous climbs. Last year the best days were spent in remote Scottish areas, Knoydart, Appin, etc."

When Anne wrote they had just returned to Surrey from Scotland, hoped to go again within a fortnight and were off to Austria the following month. This gives some indication of their lifestyle. Anne has been a committee member, edited the 1976 *Journal* and had had a double term as meets secretary. She is Hon. Auditor at present.

When Pat Daley had the *Handbook* printed she arranged for it to have a celebration gold cover; most members heartily approved, but some thought it a little ostentatious. This just underlined the fact that it is impossible to please everybody, especially a strong-willed group of women climbers; sometimes I am astonished that we are, in fact, such a supportive and harmonious group!

In contrast to the Dinner Meet, just one aspirant member turned up to climb with Janet Rogers at Easter. It was Alison Lamb's first meet and they climbed Main Wall on Cyrn Las on the Saturday. Evelyn Leech was writing her final entries in the Log Book at about this time. Despite her increasing illness she called in on May 6th with materials for the spring cleaning meet, did a little decorating and cemented up two rat holes. Her next entry reads: "May 8-9. Spring Cleaning Party: Janet Rogers, Helen Jones, Angela Kelly, Sheila Cormack and – ...

Evelyn Leech spent Saturday afternoon doing odd jobs within her capabilities and admiring the energetic work of the party. Plans to climb on Sunday which I hope come true – .

"May 19th. Looked in, and did upstairs windowsills and took away second big curtain for washing. E.W.L."

Her last recorded visit was at the Whit meet on May 29th, when she and Nea Morin visited for the day. She died in September.

Gwen Moffat was also a day visitor, suffering the fate of an author who was rapidly becoming established but couldn't afford a secretary; she had a frozen shoulder through typing too much. This put me in the happy position of proving a useful climbing partner for her and one day we had a very pleasant time on Canyon Rib in the Aberglaslyn Pass, not realising that it had been put out of bounds due to the danger of rocks falling on the footpath below.

On 10th July Alwine Walford brought a small LAC group to the hut, including Meena Agrawal on her first visit. Alwine had called in to see Evelyn and found her too unwell to come to the Pinnacle Club meet the following weekend. Alwine was leading this meet and the party had a morale boosting day in the hot sunshine, climbing routes in the Moelwyns which the guide book graded VS. The following day the group divided its attentions between Glyder Fach and Cwm Silyn and the same grades gave a greater sense of achievement!

There was now a substantial group of members leading to this standard, and there had been a most successful Wasdale meet in June. The Club was swinging quite rapidly from having a few rather overworked leaders on meets to having plenty of leaders willing to climb routes of various standards, so the best climbers felt more free to develop their skills. Some members felt that the Club's great tradition of being helpful and caring to each member of a meet was slipping a little, and it is certainly a tradition which must be jealously guarded.

Adventures in the Alps and further afield this summer were well documented in the next *Journal*. Ron and Barbara James did two first British ascents and Barbara was the first British woman to climb four more, two of which she led throughout: the Funffingerspitze traverse (IV), and the Via Franceschi (VI/A1) on the Torre Grande de Avernau in the Cinque Torri.

Barbara Spark and Molly Porter, with three other young women, spent the summer in Peru and climbed eight peaks, of which five were first ascents. (An article was published in the 1972 AJ).

Nea Morin and Margaret Darvall, Sue Long and Alwine Walford joined the Rendezvous Haute Montagne in Jugoslavia, and Joann and Colin Greenhow were climbing a number of routes in Central Switzerland, grades III to VI, following Ron and Barbara James up the Graue Wand (VI) of the Gletschhorn and probably making the first British ascent of the Feldschijen West Ridge (V). They led through on all these routes.

Dorothea Gravina spent the summer travelling by bus to India then spent three months in Nepal, walking to Everest Base Camp and then to Pokhara. She walked past Annapurna and Daulagiri to Tukucha, and climbed Dambusch Peak (nearly 20,000ft). She continued to South India, mostly by bus, then to the Seychelles and by cargo boat to Mombasa. On her way to Capetown she visited Tanzania, Zambia, Victoria Falls, Rhodesia, then did some climbing on and around Table Mountan. She arrived in Europe in July 1972 and set off for the Alps: the Dolomites for the LAC meet, Zermatt and finally Chamonix, where she soloed the Ordinary Route on Mont Blanc. She said now her family were grown up and didn't need her any more she could please herself what adventures she had – she always did them on a shoestring so that the money would spin out for as many as she wanted, and also because it was more fun.

The gritstone, Yorkshire and Dorset meets were now firm favourites for the autumn. Not until the Anniversary Meet did members fully realise the gap left by Evelyn's death. Her daughter, Antonia, and her future husband came for a short ceremony on the Saturday in which her ashes were buried near her old home at Pont-y-Pant. Lying on the ground were little acorns sprouting shoots and some of us took one or two to plant in her memory. Nea wrote a full appreciation of Evelyn and a little about her life for the 1973 Journal. Some Pinnacle Club members, including Nea and myself had been able to attend the memorial service to Evelyn in her Parish Church on Anglesey on October 3rd. It had been easy for me to attend as our local Wyndham Mountaineering Club had booked the hut for the weekend (their third consecutive year of glorious sunshine) so the whole family came down and Ian looked after the boys on the Sunday morning.

Several people made long journeys to do honour to Evelyn – she was a very special person.

CHAPTER 31

1972 - 73. Denise Wilson President. New members. Climbs and meets. A night ascent of Snowdon.

It is surprising how often annual dinners are a time of crisis. In February 1972 the country was in the throes of power cuts and members arriving at the Skiddaw Hotel, Keswick, on the Friday evening found the place lit by Bluet gas lights. We had grave fears for the dinner, but the management had things well under control and 57 sat down to a splendid feast on the Saturday night. Jane Taylor introduced the guests. She had looked breathtakingly elegant on the ski slopes that day, and now she was even more so as she gave a witty and charming speech to which John Wilkinson, President of the Fell and Rock replied. Sid Cross was so impressed by Jane's speech that he suggested her for a speaker at the next FRCC dinner, where she had equal success. This year, at long last, Sid and Jammy Cross were the Club's special guests in thanks for their tremendous hospitality to all members. In spite of this, Sid was asked to propose the health of the Club and President, which he did admirably; kindly and humourous, he had done plenty of research and had a special memory of Evelyn Leech. Janet Rogers' reply should probably be in the Guinness Book of Records as the shortest ever known – she said it was out of kindness to her successor, Denise Wilson, who was taking over the presidency, and could hardly fail to make a better speech next year! For the entertainment afterwards, Angela Faller showed her slides of the Haute Route from Chamonix to Zermatt – a tremendous achievement for a beginner on skis, and told with humour and modesty which made the account thoroughly enjoyable.

Saturday had been such a lovely day that several people were late for the AGM. The Secretary reported that, as usual, several members had represented the Pinnacle Club at the dinners of other clubs. I had attended the LSCC Dinner, held at the St Enoch Hotel, Glasgow – the last one to be held in the Victorian splendour of this gracious building with its enormous rooms and high ceilings. It was no longer economic to run and was pulled down shortly afterwards to make way for modern development. I was very much impressed by Scottish hospitality and the inspired home entertainment. Mr and Mrs Gold made me welcome for the night and I was collected next day for a walk over the hills – filled with so much breakfast and with such a large packed lunch that it was hard work keeping up with the others!

Gwen Moffat's BMC North Wales report told of the proposed pumped storage schemes, the explorations of Rio Tinto Zinc and access worries due to the selling of farms on the Vaynol estates. A major concern of the Lake District area committee was the upgrading of the A66 into a trunk road to the west coast.

With tenure of the hut uncertain, members were united in wanting a permanent, but movable, memorial to Evelyn Leech. Antonia said her mother had often said she would like the hut to have new bookshelves so that the books would keep in better condition. An

Evelyn Leech Memorial Fund was opened immediately and had soon reached a hundred pounds.

Alison Lamb and Antonia Leech became members at this meeting; Antonia for her mother's sake as much as anything, for rock climbing came a poor second to horses with her, but she had many friends in the Club, and many happy memories.

Alison Lamb had been a friend and climbing companion of Mairet Picken and was with her on her Norwegian trip. As a child she lived half way up Helsby Hill, so did plenty of scrambling at an early age, then in her early teens her parents introduced the family to the Lake District and hillwalking.

"Every year," writes Alison, "Dad and I used to try and get one day on our own away from younger brothers and sisters and do some interesting things such as Striding Edge. Much of my inspiration for bigger things came from listening to Mairet Picken and her family, first on a trip to Switzerland with them in 1962 and later on European cycling trips with Mairet." Alison was in Holland at this time but came back in 1966 and had her first Scottish trip with Mairet, who persuaded her to join a club. Alison was studying at Kingston upon Thames so joined the students' club there and one of the friends she made was Fiona Green (now Longstaff).

Mairet was now at Dundee University and Alison joined her for a rock climbing holiday, first in Glencoe, where the exposure terrified her, but she regained confidence on the Aonach Eagach ridge. Then came Ben Nevis and Tower Ridge, which really thrilled her although the weather was damp and cloudy. During the following week of perfect weather on Skye their skill and confidence rose by leaps and bounds. Next year came Norway, then 1969 when Mairet and Ruth (a friend of Alison's from the Helsby Hill days) were killed. Friends helped Alison over the shock and when she went to Hull University she enjoyed being a member of the climbing club. She was a committee member when she made contact with the Pinnacle Club.

"I instantly felt a home with the P.C. and made many good friends. At this stage I also met John Higham and of course did lots of climbing with him, some to quite a high standard, but I have always been happier being an equal on the rope rather than just a good second even if this meant dropping the standard a bit."

A prospective member whom Margaret Darvall had under her wing at the Dinner Meet was Vida Strasek. An architect from Ljubljana, Yugoslavia, and unable to bring money out of that country, she was having an initial struggle to learn the language and pay her way in Britain. Everyone liked her immediately and admired her spirit and she was offered the hut to live in for a month at the end of March. While she was there Annis and some friends, including ten young people descended upon the hut and Annis wrote to Pat Daley, the Secretary: "She took the arrival very calmly! We all liked her a lot. I didn't see her climb but was impressed by her independence and competence in the wintry Welsh hills."

Earlier in the month Dorothy Wood had brought Cynthia Heap to the hut and they had enjoyed leading through on several routes at Tremadog. Cynthia had been climbing for three years, seconding a number of hard routes as well as leading to VS, and was very keen. She joined the Club in 1973, later married Ed Grindley, and resigned when she moved to Scotland, where she is a member of the LSCC and, at the time of writing, custodian of Black Rock Cottage and district nurse in Glencoe.

During the month that Vida spent in Cwm Dyli she was out almost every day, not counting three days "in the bed (caught could)." Her English was improving by leaps and bounds but not yet perfect. A prospective member, Julia Knight, joined her over Easter and they went out together, then came Annis Flew's party.

Annis left a bottle of Benedictine for the spring cleaning meet the following weekend, and Vida waited for them to arrive but the only person to come was Nea, who went for a walk with her. The Benedictine was not wasted, however, for Jo Fuller and some friends came a week later and, with Vida, had a great hut-tidying session before the arrival of a Gritstone Club meet. Vida stayed with Antonia for the weekend.

When members came for the Spring Holiday Meet they found both Vida and Jo Fuller in residence. Jo was taking things easy after being ill with bronchitis, and wrote a kind note in the hut book which pleased my boys: "Many thanks to Ian Angell and the boys who collected lots of wood, brought up most of the coal from the dump, and guided me up the pipeline to Llyn Llydaw – I could almost keep up with Stephen aged $4^1/_2$ but when he ran up the last steep section I was left panting in the rear of the party!"

Jean Dilnot and Biddy Burgum were the other members on this very rainy meet; Julia and I took Vida to Dinas Bach, still in the rain, and she did her first British climb!

Joann Greenhow led the next meet, and her report is a masterpiece:

Langdale Meet at Rawhead Cottage, 17th-18th June.

Veil upon veil, layer upon layer, cloud drifted over the setting sun. Dry Lakeland stone, out-thrust, bare, awaited impatiently the ritual – the weekend bath. In harmony with the deteriorating scene, I took to bed – ill. Aspirant member Dawn Haigh, welcomed members, served tea and mouseproofed the food.

The scene was set and like a prophecy foretold, a steady downpour greeted Saturday.

Two parties left in disgust for a stomp ... Meanwhile the rockhoppers, saving Raven for a rainy day, made a mass assault on Castle Rock, Thirlmere. The overhanging north face provided just the sport to dispel Angela Faller's blues and whet Shirley Angell's appetite with Overhanging Bastion and Zig Zag. Via Media and Barbican succumbed to Jo and Dawn.

A wet Sunday – with wet knickers – too much! More coins into the Drying Room meter. A brave six left for a wet Raven Crag . .

The burping, male lunch-time beer-wallowers rubbed eyes in horror to see Raven garlanded thus – a case of one too many? B Hannan, K Webb – Evening Wall, Revelation; S Cormack, A Shepherd - Original/Holly Tree, Evening Wall; S Cormack, A Shepherd – Original/Holly Tree, Evening Wall, Centipede. J.G.

Gwen Moffat brought her friend Adelaide Cotchin to the July meet at the Club hut and other prospective members were Barbara Hannan, Jean Roberts, Vida Strasek and Dorothy Wright. The leaders, Hilda Tyler and Denise Wilson, concocted yet another entertaining meet report. The main party had a ridge walk in increasingly bad weather, so came back to the hut early:

"About eight in the evening an astonishing figure came into the hut – it wore an anorak, black lace pants and climbing boots! Angela, returning from Llanberis via Snowdon, explained that the causeway over Llydaw was flooded and she had waded across.

"An immaculate Anne Shepherd appeared on Sunday with early morning tea. No-one would have guessed she had spent Saturday doing the fourteen peaks! A splendid achievement, carried out in spite of inclement weather."

Sunday was fine enough to do hard routes in the Pass. The hut was impressively clean and tidy, for Margaret Darvall and Alwine Walford had used a wet weekend to do extra cleaning and repairs. They had not come to this meet as it was the weekend before the joint PC and LAC Dolomite Meet.

The Dolomite meet was based on the Refugio Passo Sella and nine of the members belonged to the Pinnacle Club out of a total of twelve (several being members of both clubs) plus ten friends. Barbara James had organised it and Ron James and Dave Bland came as guides. The only sad thing about the holiday was Barbara's leg, which she had damaged shortly before coming away and was in plaster to the thigh. We all (except Barbara) walked or climbed routes every day in the Sella area and on the Cinque Torri, up to Grade V, and they are written up in the *Journal* and *Handbook*. The most notable occasion was Nea and Dorothea's traverse of the Funffingerspitze with Ron. When they reached the end, Dorothea handed Nea her stick, which she had been carrying for her in her rucksack, and all the tourists who had been watching from the hut gave them a tremendous welcome. Alwine Walford and I were on the route as well, but none of the onlookers realised that Alwine also was a grandmother! Margaret Darvall and Meena Agrawal climbed the route the following day and had the unwelcome excitement of an electric storm near the summit, but it was a most interesting and varied route.

This was the holiday on which I shared a room with Livia Gollancz; she usually partnered Eveleigh Leith and would probably say that their best climb was the grade III S.E. Face of the Torre Inglese on the Cinque Torri. Ron and I climbed the Via Miriam, V, of which Miriam Underhill and Margaret Helburn had made the first tourist ascent in 1927 with the Dimai brothers and Angelo Dibona – not only were we steeped in history but also soaked with rain when we reached the top! We romped up it and I earmarked it as a future lead, but I have never been back.

Joann and Colin Greenhow proceeded to the Dolomites after a bad experience on the Lamsenspitze, Schwarser Riss (V): "Wonderful scenery but desperate, vertically stacked shale on N. Face routes. The 'Bergwatch' graded all routes at VI+, and laughed like a drain at the guidebook description, 'some loose rock'. The retort to 'Do many folk get hurt?' was, 'No, no, just dead.'"

In the Dolomites they climbed the Cima Piccolissima, Preuss Cracks (V) in boots and duvets, "Just like Glencoe in February," then the Cima Grande, Comici N Face (VI), Yellow Edge (V+), Cima Piccolissima Little Cassin (VI) and Punta Fiamma (V).

Angela Faller was in the French Alps this summer and found various strong partners with whom to climb the N Ridge of the Peigne, Contamine route on the Moine, Cordier route on the Courtes, Mer de Glace face of the Grépon, Old Brenva, Frendo Spur, and, in the Dauphiné, the NNE Pillar of Les Bans. She also soloed the Midi-Plan traverse, went ski-touring at Easter and climbed the Ebnefluh, and sailed round the Western Isles of Scotland. A good year.

Barbara Spark was in the Bernina Alps with John Cheesemond. They did eight routes, including the Eisnase on the Piz Scherzen and the N ridge of the E peak of Piz Palu, then they went to Chamonix for the Old Brenva and the Forbes Arête. Stephanie Rowland and her husband Clive also climbed the Forbes Arête before going to the Otztal, Anne Shepherd was in the Dauphiné, Jane and Colin Taylor found good climbing in the Pyrenees, and Denise Wilson and Peggy Foster, with their respective families, found the Alpes Maritimes an ideal climbing centre for both adult and family outings.

Back home the Poulton-Cooper contingent were finding their ideal centre, as usual, at the hut. Pleasant autumn meets followed, and the wet November meet was enlivened by Alwine's catering and provision of wine followed by slide shows of the Dolomites Meet, Sue Long's and Antonia Leech's weddings, and Dorothea's Himalayan trek. It was sad that Annette Wilson would never more sleep in her place by the fire; she had died in May, soon after writing an appreciation of Evelyn for the *Journal*, so her own obituary appeared in the same issue, published in 1973.

The frosted snow sparkled in the moonlight as members drove to Wales for the Annual Dinner in February 1973. Jo Greenhow and I with two guests, Royanne Lavender and Dawn Haigh, piled out of the car staggering from a long drive after a long day's teaching and at almost the same time Denise Wilson arrived with our chief guest, Myrtle Simpson of Arctic fame. Somehow we all took on a new lease of life and, with Kate Webb, Sheila Cormack and Steph Rowland, we set off for Snowdon. When we reached the summit I was so tired that I just had to lie down in the snow – which worried the others! – however, five minutes sufficed, and as we made our way down to the Pen-y-Pass and back to the hut, a perfect dawn was just breaking. This was Myrtle Simpson's first taste of Snowdonia – and a memorable one I think.

Alwine spent most of Saturday organising things for the Dinner – to some purpose, for sixty members and guests fitted comfortably into the dining room at the Pen-y-Gwryd. The speakers were Angela Faller introducing the guests, Myrtle Simpson, Trevor Jones and Denise Wilson as President. Myrtle and Denise seemed enlivened if anything by their midnight trip. Myrtle gave an invigorating message that it is possible to have adventures and a family at the same time, but Ray Lee said to me afterwards that it was virtually impossible unless you were in certain professions or had spare money, and Myrtle was a little airy in saying that anyone could do it if they had the will.

Eileen Healey and her family were back from a stay in Kamala and after the meal she showed slides of wildlife in the game reserves of Uganda, Kenya and Tanzania, also of a trip to the hills to climb Kadam. Her son, John, aged 8, was one of the party which climbed the North Ridge of Tryfan next day.

The Annual Meeting on the Saturday afternoon considered a proposal from Peggy Foster and Bertha Rostron that there should be one grade of membership: full. "Some of the Associate Members have been in the Club for 20-30 years, surely ample qualification for full membership, and amongst recent associate members there are mountaineers and rock climbers of a very high standard, many of them active members of the Club. With one rate of subscription there should be one grade of membership."

This was discussed very fully but it was thought that some were happy to join as associate members and improve their leading abilities to qualify for full membership later. The Club did not wish to discourage such members and at the same time felt that they would like the standard for full membership to remain high. It was pointed out that associate members were reviewed regularly and transfers to full membership made.

This year Pat Daley had completed her three years as secretary and I took over the office, with Joann Greenhow taking my place on the BMC Lake District Committee. The next month was a busy and exciting one for me, for with plenty of help from Pat Daley, I was plunged straight into the secretary's job and produced the 1973 *Handbook*. There were all the kindred clubs to write to, to check that their information was still correct, then the whole thing to check and set up neatly, ready for the printers. My father had retired and come to live with us, so we had a pleasant trip to Ambleside to Lakeland Printers, then the proofs to read a week or two later. At long last the printers mailed the handbooks to members and I made sure that copies went to all interested friends and clubs and two copies to the Records Office. This, and preparations for the Annual General Meeting are the secretary's busiest times, but there is a steady stream of interesting letters and enquiries throughout the year. I think every secretary of the Club has found the work very rewarding.

There was a double booking at the hut on the weekend after the Dinner: Annis Flew and a large family party were confronted by an even larger group of Barbara Spark and her Bangor students – beds were found for 26, including one on the table!

By contrast there were far too few at the hut maintenance meet. Anne Shepherd, Angela Faller and Gwen Moffat painted themselves to a standstill in beautiful weather, so felt extra virtuous: "All you other slackers with guilty consciences (well, you should have) please note jobs still to be done ...

"On back of crockery cupboard we found a note from Antony Flew (husband of Hut Secretary) in 1959 who records that he painted that cupboard and put formica top on – all by himself without help from women!" Annis was the next visitor and wrote: "Yes, I well remember the glee with which he wrote this and fixed it on!!"

Cynthia Heap and Vida Strasek have already been mentioned as joining the Club in 1973; others were Barbara Hannan, Adelaide Cotchin, Dorothy Wright, Dawn Haigh and Meena Agrawal.

Barbara Hannan had had two years' walking and rock climbing experience and was very keen – living in Middlesex but with experience in N Wales, the Peak District, Lake District, Glencoe and Skye, also three weeks in Zermatt. She led to VS standard. She is now Barbara Prince and lives in New Zealand.

Adelaide Cotchin was a mature and delightful person, a veterinary surgeon married to Professor Ernest Cotchin, a leading veterinary pathologist; with their family of four almost grown up and off her hands she engaged Gwen Moffat as a guide, thinking herself too old, at 54, for a group course. She was a natural climber to whom everything was an adventure and after the first week she often stayed with Gwen and they climbed together as friends. Adelaide had loved mountain walking since her student days and it was Alpine routes which made her think she would enjoy rock climbing, in particular, the Riffelhorn. Gwen introduced her to the Pinnacle Club and she was able to manage two or three meets a year, but she had many interests and abilities and was in turn both secretary and president of the Society of Women Veterinary Surgeons during the 1970s. She fell after completing a climb with Gwen on Glyder Fach in 1978 and died three days later. They were on easy, broken ground at the bottom of the climb and had been looking up at other climbers, which Gwen thinks must have caused a moment's disorientation when Adelaide looked down once more; also her first slip must have stunned her, for she made no attempt to save herself. It took Gwen a long time to recover from the loss of her friend through this senseless accident, and the tragedy which it brought to Adelaide's family.

Dorothy Wright is another member who joined the Club at a mature age, but she had been rock climbing since she was twenty. She and Bernard, her husband, were both at Manchester University in 1945 when they started climbing together and she was soon introduced to all the Diff. and V.diff. classic routes of Wales and the Lake District. They had their first experience of Scottish winter climbing in the cold Easter of 1947.

In 1951 they joined the Karabiner Mountaineering Club in Manchester, with whom Dorothy and her friend Betty had been out on several occasions already (Betty Whitehead joined the Pinnacle Club in 1975). Bernard was outdoor meets secretary of the Karabiner Club for many years.

They were greatly influenced by Plum and Robbie Worrall, who taught the whole club to ski and extolled the delights of Austria as a climbing area. Dorothy and Bernard soon discovered the Otztal, Zillertal and Gross Glockner for themselves.

They often visited the club hut at Coniston and gradually Dorothy became prepared to lead the climbs she knew well. Dorothy writes: "Don Brown of the K.M.C. was a big influence about this time and as he had more holiday than Bernard I accompanied him to the Lakes and Scotland. He would always try to make me lead the easier pitches and we did some interesting routes together.

"The K.M.C. was always friendly with the Rock and Ice and the Rucksack Club, so we came to know many famous names in the climbing world and watch them climbing, and heard stories of first ascents of climbs in the Pass and Cloggy at first hand. Denise Shortall was friendly with the Rock and Ice about this time, and one of the main subjects of conversation was what Denise had led the previous weekend. I remember her leading Rie up Longland's (which was my first VS) and also watching her climb confidently and rapidly on Kirkus' on Cwm Silyn."

Through their friendship with Geoff and Anne Sutton, Dorothy had her first sight of wet weather climbing; they met Nea and Denise in Wales and all walked up into a Cwm where the Morins donned socks over their gym shoes and were off up some difficult route in the rain. The others did not join in.

On a joint meet with the Yorkshire M.C. they met Ron and Hilda Tyler. Ron and Bernard climbed at about the same standard and they made a trio on a number of hard routes. When Ron died Hilda became a fearless leader. She often took Bernard up difficult routes and Dorothy was sometimes a little anxious – it was almost as if she had a death wish, and they gave her one or two frights by getting into difficulties. Hilda took Dorothy to one or two Pinnacle Club meets and kept asking her to join, but Dorothy didn't consider herself up to the climbing standard, so it was not until 1973, when Denise Wilson was president and asked Dorothy once more that she thought Why not? as long as her love of mountaineering and past experience could count and not her present performance.

Although Denise is much younger than Dorothy, they had their families at about the same time and in equal number. Dorothy writes: "I had been determined not to give up climbing and Bernard was soon trained into changing nappies, etc, and very cooperatively gave up either alternate weekends or one day of each weekend. There were several young mothers in the Karabiner Club and we used to take carry cots and all the paraphernalia up to the crag and take turns babysitting. The invention of the papoose was a godsend but this did not happen until my third child was talking and could say "no". My fourth loved it and was four and a half before he would give it up and even then scrounged piggy backs from his older sister.

"Holidays on the continent were now out, we spent most Munroing in Scotland as the children loved camping and whoever was minding them could drive the car to "the other end"; thus we could traverse long ridges and I got used to walking on my own. Unlike many women I seem to meet nowadays I have never been frightened of being alone in the mountains and this may be the reason."

Before the children came, Dorothy and Bernard spent every holiday in the Alps or Norway. They climbed at Turtagro and were on a crossing of the Alfotbree – an exciting adventure since the maps were very old and the glaciers had receded. Robbie and Dorothy were the first non-Norwegian women to get up a certain route on the Romsdalhorn – only about V diff but they had their names in the local paper. "Then we went to the Dolomites," writes Dorothy, "Camped at Sella Pass and hired a guide – Johann Demetz, whose son had come to our K.M.C. dinner once. We climbed with the guide alternate days to save money, and to pick his brains of knowledge of the route we wanted to try ourselves next day. We never actually got to the top of any of our routes, but that was because it snowed or rained and our guide book was in Italian. I remember puzzling over what a "mezza luna" was and how we could reach it (on the Langkofel) while the rain poured into the top of my anorak and out at the bottom."

Dawn Haigh, now Dawn Hopkinson, started climbing through coming to work in the Lake District teaching at Wyndham School and writes: " ... a stark contrast from my previous year touring the country working in children's theatre! Naturally enough teaching P.E. brought me in contact with Don Greenop, Tony Baldwin and Colin Greenhow – they bullied me up and down the climbing tower – and gradually Tony (my first husband) and I linked up with Colin and Jo Greenhow. My first meet was one being 'led' by Joann in June 1972. She picked me up from work – it turned out that she had a migraine and I was full of anxieties about meeting these climbing ladies! When we got to the hut she disappeared to bed, leaving me to mouseproof all the food before sitting and waiting for the arrival of the members!

The dinner meet was Dawn's first introduction to the hut; she was horrified enough at humping her gear across the little bridge up to this strange place without being confronted with plans for a midnight ascent of Snowdon. She remembers grimly trudging along and visions of Sheila, all health and fitness, disappearing into the night – "I found my first ascent of a snow covered Snowdon by moonlight quite an experience. We took a leisurely way back and somehow it was morning and sunshine as we sat on the hillside overlooking Pen-y-Pass. My next ambition was to meet Gwen Moffat – I was full of inspiration from reading her book *Space Below my Feet*, and spent all day bothering Jo to let me know when we saw her. That evening we got changed in someone's room before dinner – there was a pleasant lady in a blouse and tights chatting to me – imagine my surprise when I discovered she was THE Gwen Moffat and she had talked to me!

"Good routes I have done – the two Alpine ones that I remember most are the Brenva Face of Mont Blanc – arriving on the summit as Dawn broke (which one, she asks!) and the Whymper couloir on the Verte – we raced up in fine style and time receiving congratulations from a guide on the route and the guardian at the hut when we returned.

"I am still thriving and climbing, still trying to feel confident on 4Cs, running the odd marathon and have also learnt to ski – life gets more active as I get older, not less. Went to Roaches last weekend and saw a wallaby – makes the jamming scars worthwhile!"

Meena Agrawal and I travelled out to the Dolomites Meet together in 1972. As Meena had an Indian passport, she had to get visas for every country she passed through on the train, which meant hours wasted calling at embassies. Unfortunately she had omitted Belgium and our boat went to Ostend, but the minor trials and tribulations that followed made me think what an extraordinarily nice person she was and we got on really well. She is small, slight and a vegetarian with a very small appetite so where does she find the energy to practise surgery and go up Himalayan peaks? She said she hoped I got appendicitis, as she was all prepared; another of her talents is to write poems to suit all occasions. In 1985 she wrote down details of her life for me. She says:

"It is always difficult to write about oneself. I started climbing in India; climbing was very much in its infancy there, especially for ladies. I heard about it and applied for the Ladies' Mountaineering Course at the Himalayan Mountaineering Institute, Darjeeling in 1962. This was the basic course and I enjoyed it immensely, and subsequently went on to do the Advanced Course the following year. After that I helped to organise some and participated in other Himalayan expeditions. Obviously this was expensive and the Himalayas are miles away from Bombay and one couldn't go on expeditions every year. In between times I used to go trekking and climbed in the Western Ghats, nearer Bombay.

"I came to U.K. in 1972 for surgical training and subsequently did my F.R.C.S. in general surgery. I have since branched out into paediatric surgery and am a paediatric surgeon at present.

"Last year I was doctor and member of the Indian Everest Expedition 1984. We got 5 people on the summit, including one girl, Bachendri Pal, who became the 5th lady in the world to summit Everest.

"I am leaving with an Indo-British team in 2 weeks for an expedition to the Eastern Karakorums. We are going to the Siachen Glacier and will hopefully attempt some peaks in that area. it should be interesting as this area has only recently been opened up for climbing and I have never been to that part of the Himalayas. Not much is known about the area either.

"It was while I was working at Leicester that I met Sandra Gamble (now Swindale) and she introduced me to the Pinnacle Club.

"I won't start on reminiscences as they would fill a book! I have fallen into crevasses, been swept down in an avalanche in the Himalayas, helped to rescue people and treat injuries and illnesses on the mountains, met many fascinating people and made wonderful long-standing friendships on the mountains and also sadly lost a few friends on them too."

In 1966 Meena was deputy leader and doctor on the Indian Women's Expedition to Kokthang, Sikkim Himalayas and climbed a subsidiary summit.

In 1968 she was member and doctor to the Indo-Japanese Ladies Expedition to Kailash, which she climbed.

In 1970 she was leader of the Ladies Trisul Expedition and climbed Trisul (23,360ft).

Since living in Britain she had frequently been called back to lead expeditions or as expedition doctor; she was on the Indo-New Zealand Ladies Expedition to Hardeol in 1974; led the Indo-Japanese Ladies Expedition to Kamet and Abiganin on which the latter peak, 23,130ft, was climbed in 1976; led the successful Indian Women's Expedition to Kamet, 25,447ft, in 1977; led an Indo-Japanese expedition to Japan in 1981, when they climbed several peaks in the Japanese Alps; and was a member of the Indian pre-Everest expedition to Mana peak in the Garhwal Himalayas in 1983.

After this, climbs in Britain and Europe sound small fry! She is a member of the Pinnacle Club, Alpine Club, Climbers'Club Bombay, Himalayan Club India and the Indian Mountaineeriing Foundation.

There was a prospective member at the next meet, which was a joint one with the ladies of the Lancashire Caving and Climbing Club using their hut in Torver. The weather was cold and unsettled so we spent Saturday at low crags on Wallowbarrow and I offered to climb with the guest, Ann Redman. A slim young thing who looked like Peter Pan, she obviously had a tremendous respect for me as secretary of the club; she summed up the route with an experienced eye, then flowed up it without a pause, looking down in puzzled surprise when it gave me food for thought. A brilliant climber, she joined the club in 1974 and earned international acclaim on hard rock routes. After her marriage (she became Ann Storry) she was very ill for many months and so far has never regained her enthusiasm.

The weather was unsettled during the early summer, but perfect in July, which was just as well, for the strong-sounding line-up was feeling very weak kneed:

"The meet was attended by Denise Wilson, Shirley Angell, Christine Sheard, Helen Jones, Hilda Tyler, Kate Webb (camping with her family), Anne Shepherd, Joann Palmer, Angela Heppenstall and Royanne Lavender (guest).

"Saturday dawned fine but we got up at a leisurely pace with no mention of climbing until breakfast was over. Enquiries about suggestions for the day's activities brought forth a stream of "excuses". The Club seemed to be showing signs of becoming an "invalids' society". However we set out intrepidly to the Moelwyns where superb rock and hot sunshine restored lost confidence. Routes included Slick, Slack, Kirkus, Orangoutang, Pinky with everyone taking their share of the leading – for some it was a return to the "sharp end" after long periods of enforced abstinence." I think this is an occasion when we would all have been content to second routes if we had been in a mixed party – which would have resulted, at least in my case, in a sense of depression and lack of achievement rather than one of pleasure and well-being.

I had had a heavy year due to my father's retiring and coming to live with us then becoming very ill. My sister gave my father and the family a holiday so that Ian and I could go to Arolla and we did some fine routes but even I was surprised at my state of exhaustion. We had read in the February *Climber and Rambler* of the Pigne/Cheilon Traverse, described as one of the classic Alpine traverses, full of interest and variety, so tackled it as our second route and enjoyed it very much; however, on our way down, as I wrote in my diary, "The Ruinette, which was our objective for the next day, was looking gorgeous on our left, but I was so shattered that the thought of climbing it made me cry and I had to be comforted with sweets"! We saved the Dent Blanche for the climax of our holiday. Jo and Colin Greenhow came to Arolla while we were there and enjoyed the same two routes, amongst others, before taking charge of a guided party.

Several Pinnacle Club members were on the LAC meet in the Alpes Maritimes led by Ron and Barbara James, and Nea Morin wrote an account for the Ladies' Alpine Club *Journal*. Margaret Darvall was the leader and other members were Meena, Suzanne, and Sandra Gamble.

Not only did Ron and Barbara James make three first British ascents this year, but they were also involved in making a series of educational films on rock climbing for the BBC which were shown as the series ROCKFACE in the spring of 1974. They were filming in Derbyshire in September and the gritstone meet called in to have a look after wearing themselves out on Burbage Edge on the Sunday.

The hut had been used by family parties and visitors all summer and Ann Redman and Alison Lamb came for a few days in October. Ann led Shake on the Wenallt one evening and two days later they went to Carreg Alltrem: "Great day – good weather – Lavaredo, Lightning Visit + Ordinary Route." Lavaredo was a route with a considerable reputation at that time.

Anne Shepherd led the November meet, at which there was further considerable climbing activity by the 23 members who all came back ravenous – to enormous quantities of Anne's delicious chocolate cake spread deep with butter icing – and this was only to keep us happy while the evening meal was prepared!

The committee meeting was a long one, for Colin Greenhow had undertaken to make the book cupboard in memory of Evelyn Leech and had sent designs and queries as to the members' requirements; also, organising an annual dinner is a serious business – Ian used to read the minutes despite my protestations that they were private and laugh at the details I recorded on menu, cost and timing!

There was a petrol shortage all winter, which led to small or cancelled meets; but for the first time since the Morins and Evans the Hut was used for a proper family Christmas: "Kate and Barry Webb and family spent a beautifully quiet Christmas, complete with paper chains and Christmas tree."

Anniversary Meet 1985. Dorothea Gravina and Gwen Moffat. Photo Dorothy Wright.

CHAPTER 32

1974 – 1975. Annual Dinner Meets. Cromlech Boulders. Meets and members. Evelyn Leech's memorial. Good routes abroad.

The 1974 Annual Dinner was held once more at the Skiddaw Hotel, Keswick in the middle of February. One of the committee's decisions in November had been that nobody should have to miss time on the hills for the sake of a meeting and that no annual meeting should take longer than an hour, so we arranged for afternoon tea at 4.30, as dusk was approaching, and the meeting at 5, then the dinner at 7 for 7.30. It was a bold move, but it paid off! and the approximate timing has been adhered to ever since.

After the meal the four speakers – Barbara James, Dennis Kemp, Fred Piggott and Denise Wilson – provided pleasant entertainment, the star turn being Dennis who realised the value of visual aids and produced a number of most fetching hats from various parts of the world as his speech progressed, finally presenting the Club with the gift of a pictorial tea towel for the hut. The puzzling question of how to provide the entertainment demanded by some and also to allow time for talking to friends, was solved by my giving a lightning show of members' activities, accompanied by protests that I was pushing the slides through too fast. It was a very good weekend, ably organised by Hilda Tyler.

At the Annual Meeting Kate Webb took over as Hut Secretary and a booking fee of a pound was ratified for catered meets. Gwen Moffat alerted members to Caernarvonshire County Council's proposal to blow up part of the Cromlech Boulders, much loved by climbers and mentioned in George Borrow's Wild Wales, no less, in order to widen the road up the Llanberis Pass. This was a battle while it lasted – the workmen even got as far as drilling holes for dynamite but were driven off by climbers who filled in the holes with concrete, so the press reported. Ann Redman was elected a member at this meeting, also Jean Roberts, an experienced climber who lived near Sandra Gamble in Leicester and joined the Club for five years. Later in the year Pat Downes and Royanne Lavender became members. Pat Downes was also a member for only five years, which was very sad indeed, for she was a competent and charming person. She married David Danson in September 1974 and they went out to Australia almost immediately, where they climbed in the Blue Mountains of New South Wales, skied on the Snowy Mountains, and explored both these areas by bush walking. When the time came for them to return to the British Isles three or four years later they trekked their way through S.E. Asia to Nepal on their way home. They both came to the following dinner meet, but Pat resigned her membership soon afterwards.

Royanne Lavender lived and climbed in West Cumbria and took some persuading to come on a Pinnacle Club meet as she had plenty of climbing partners, in particular Bob Bennett with whom she had put up a new route on Scafell Pinnacle in 1972, Leftovers (VS), "A good little climb to the left of Left Edge." She writes: "I started climbing when I went to college in Ambleside and met some lads from the Phoenix Club in Huddersfield

– they were really great and willingly took me with them – at that time I just lived for weekends. I bought my own rope a few months later." Royanne's first independent route was Rake End Chimney on Pavey Ark with Kathy Murgatroyd – now a member of the LSCC. She says, "I started a climbing club at college but we didn't do anything spectacular. The hardest route I've ever led (not the hardest route according to the book) was Botterill's Slab, which I did with Kathy some years later."

At the time she joined the Pinnacle Club Royanne was out every weekend and in summer during the week as well. She married Ian Wilding in 1976, and says, "Since I married, other activities have occupied my time (boat building, windsurfing, having babies etc) but the club has kept me in touch with the climbing world. – I personally think that people without children fail to realise how much they tend to cramp one's style (Myrtle Simpson apart). I don't like taking small children on walks they don't want to go on – the quavering 'Mummy, is it time to go home yet?' starts after the first 10 minutes! Sarah, my eldest, is now asking to be taken for walks, so this must be the time to start her – probably in a few years we'll be climbing together.

"The first meet I attended was the dinner meet at which Myrtle Simpson was guest speaker. This meet was memorable for two things – she was a very good speaker, but the main thing was the wonderful moonlit walk from Cwm Dyli, up the pipe-line and so to the Snowdon summit. There was a fair amount of snow around – we were thankful for our axes in one or two places.

"The following year, at the dinner at the Skiddaw Hotel, when I still knew hardly anybody I casually suggested a trip to Iceland, which is how I met Alison Higham and we did go to Iceland that summer although nothing of mountaineering merit was tackled – two was too small a number for the seriousness of the terrain."

Royanne joined the Ribblehead meet in March, staying at the cosy little Gritstone Club hut and making a 27 mile round trip of the Three Peaks Walk in the thought-provoking company of Alex White's small daughter, Tabitha, and Denise Wilson's 7-year-old Richard. Several members were mentioning their offspring with justifiable pride, and Kate Webb wrote: "Being burned off by an asthmatic 4 year old on Crib Goch was quite mortifying." However, she and Barry, "full of red wine and enthusiasm, rushed off and did Gallop Step. A sobering experience."

Several family groups used the hut during the summer and the well-used Elsan brought a joke from some bright spark: "What gets higher and higher and nearer the bottom?"

Other family parties were in the Alps. The Angells were in the Dolomites with Peter and Hilary Moffat of the Fell and Rock with their two girls. They traversed the Vajolet Towers followed next day by two grand family crocodiles up the Catinaccio d'Antermoia; then we joined the joint PC/LAC meet in San Martino which was already in full swing. Ron and Barbara James were in charge of climbing and Alwine Walford was leader. Jean Punnet wrote about it in the final Ladies' Alpine Club *Journal*; the Alpine Club had opened its ranks to women in May and as the main reason for the formation of the LAC was the exclusion of women from the AC, a merger was agreed. The decision prompted H.M. Kelly to write to me as Pinnacle Club Secretary, trusting that the Pinnacle Club "would resist the blandishments of the Climbers' Club," some of whose members had been pressing for the inclusion of women for the past seven years. Harry Kelly knew only too well the fragile confidence of many women climbers and how easily their independence could be swamped.

1974-75

When autumn came, Jo and Colin Greenhow came to the Hut with a beautiful Alpine style book cupboard Colin had made for Evelyn Leech's memorial. Colin had charged Guides fees, not those of a carpenter, as being cheaper and more appropriate. Kate Webb and her family were there to welcome them and they spent a day in assembling it and mounting it on the wall. The first of the Alpine style bunks was put in at about the same time, ready for the Anniversary Meet. Dorothy Wright and her friend Betty Whitehead catered for this very full meet. It poured with rain and the hut smelt powerfully of Rentokil, for woodworm had reappeared and the damaged timbers were being replaced under guarantee. The work was completed by December and the Webb family put the hut together again before settling down to Christmas festivities once more.

1975 started with the smallest meet possible when Maud Godward and Winifred Jackson met for the New Year Dinner at the Pen-y-Gwryd. They did not go to the hut, still awaiting another visit from the Webbs for sanding and varnishing purposes. This was done just in time for a booking from the Yorkshire Mountaineering Club on 6th February: "Some hairy YMC members invaded these chaste portals at 11.30 p.m. Friday to find Anne Shepherd already in residence. Our surprise was no greater that hers – ("Honest, lidy, we 'ave booked it, honest ...")." In fact the group included such old friends as Danny Helliwell and Alan and Josie Medlock, so there was no problem at all.

The following weekend was the Dinner Meet and there *was* a problem about this for Ian McNaught-Davis was one of the speakers. He had been invited many months in advance and since then an article of his had been published in *Mountain* which had upset several Pinnacle Club members. He was a regular contributor and both irreverent and satirical – with a special eye for women as I realised when he described "round hipped girls from a P.E. college ... sad and discouraged as a well-muscled regular ... climbs round them without appearing to notice either the climb or their thighs." On this latter occasion he had a dig at all single-sex clubs with a reasonably actionable summing up of the membership of the Pinnacle Club. (He was wittily answered by a letter from Barbara James in September).

Personally, I thought he was showing his usual McNaughtiness and thereby obscuring one or two thoughts worth pondering, in particular the expectation that women will achieve less than men – thereby leading to "patronising dishonesty."

We wondered whether to advise Ian not to come, but decided to let things stand. As it was, he arrived to a sense of unease, not helped by the fact that the dinner was an hour late. I was hosting him, so kept him supplied with pints of beer and made innocent conversation about how much we had enjoyed his speech last time. Later I realised the power of the spoken word for, whatever Ian had planned to talk about, he changed it to a discourse on the law of diminishing returns! Nea had guided his young feet in their first steps at Harrison's and he was further demoralised by her refusal to speak to him – vainly he protested that he had been trying to do women climbers a service. The meet report was most carefully worded: "Our guests were introduced very competently by Anne Shepherd. Ian McNaught-Davis replied with *a speech as amusing as his articles*. (Italics mine). The toast to the Club was given by Ron James, his pleasant manner so free and easy raised plenty of laughs." Hidden daggers ...

This was Denise Wilson's last meet as President and at the AGM she was warmly thanked for the happy atmosphere she had maintained in the Club. Alwine Walford was elected in her place.

Alex White, Betty Whitehead and Jane Stedman joined the Club this year. Betty came as Dorothy Wright's friend and has much the same background; one of her earliest memories of a meet is that she was one of the snugly bedded ones listening to preparations for the midnight ascent of Snowdon in which Myrtle Simpson took part. She had compassionate thoughts for Myrtle who, with her reputation as an arctic explorer had little choice but to appear enthusiastic. "To my horror," writes Betty, "Dorothy showed every sign of being persuaded to join them, but I was determined not to spend my time groping around Snowdon in the dark and then being shattered for a good day on the Saturday. The ironic thing is I can remember little of what we did the next day, but I am sure those who did go will have very clear memories of it even if they did spend half the morning in bed!"

Alex White's first meet was when she and her ten-year-old daughter walked the Three Peaks. She came as a strong outdoor person, interested in walking, climbing and cycling. The Pinnacle Club had obvious attractions for her and she is a sound VS leader who has also taken part in fell racing, skiing, and climbed good Alpine routes. She became a committee member within a year of her election.

When Jane Stedman first came on meets she was still at college; full of eagerness and inclined to puppy fat, she attacked climbs to about mild severe standard so it was with some surprise that I suddenly found her leading me on a VS – a slimmer, confident Jane. She often climbed with Dave Biggs, and they married and spent their honeymoon climbing routes from their tent on the Sella Pass. Dave was a major ingredient in Jane's success as Hut Secretary in the early 1980s. Jane has kept her maiden name, which makes one wonder how to address the envelope when one sends them Christmas cards. Now their daughter is growing up, Jane hopes to make a comeback in the climbing world.

Royanne Lavender vividly remembers the first meet to be held after the Dinner. It was the first meet she had led and was based at the Yorkshire MC hut above Coniston, a venue not well known to members. Only careful map reading enabled her to drive up to the front of the hut. She writes: "Sheila Cormack arrived at the bottom of the track in the dark – walked all the way up with her gear only to find our car at the top. She was furious and absolutely blasted me – I was nervous enough about leading a meet as it was and almost decided never to come again! – we are the best of friends now by the way!"

On the Saturday the weather looked unsettled but the climbing was really good and Dorothy Wright and I reached the Sun Inn at Coniston just before closing time after a long day doing climbs up the valley and ending on Dow. We had half a pint of shandy each to help us on our way and floated back to the hut in an intoxicated haze – a living warning not to drink on an empty stomach!

The previous year a joint meet with the Ladies' Scottish had resulted in fine climbing on the Etive Slabs; this year the clubs met for climbing on Arran followed by a farewell gathering with the almost-translated LAC in Dorset. At the Lakes meet in June we discovered Scrubby Crag and Grendel – "The crag's all over old women!" shouted one callow youth to his mate, and laughter spiced our pleasure in the climb. Wales was very rainy by comparison but brave souls climbed Tryfan North Buttress and Belle Vue Bastion and wise ones went to Anglesey – Ann Redman, Sheila Cormack, Jo Greenhow and Denise Wilson found fine weather at Gogarth and climbed Simulator and Bezel, both worthy of respect.

Soon it was time for lucky people to go to the Alps. Ian and I linked once more with the Moffats and their children and the holiday was divided into the three-day cycles familiar to climbing parents: a climb with the families, a climb for one pair of adults while the others have a family expedition, then the other adults have their turn. We found Central Switzerland ideal and routes I did with Ian were S.E. Pillar of Bergsigen (V A2); S Wall to point 3252 of Galenstock, Grade V in mist and drizzle; and the S wall of the Kl. Buelenhorn, grade VI. It rained on the way up and we had hail at the top; quite exciting and it was a first British ascent.

Angela Faller and Ann Redman were doing similar routes in the same area and Angela also climbed the N Ridge of the Badile, the Zmutt ridge of the Matterhorn and the Eiger-Monch traverse. Ann Redman had represented Britain at the UIAA meeting in Chamonix in the autumn of 1974. Margaret Darvall was in the Kulu Himalaya in 1975 and climbed Ladakhi (18,300ft). Anne Shepherd in Zermatt discovered that her injured ankle did not let her down on long Alpine traverses, and she led the Rotgrat Ridge of the Alphubel, the Allalinhorn and the Nadelgrat traverse. She wrote an account of the last named for the *Journal* and Meena wrote a most moving account of her 1975 Himalayan expedition.

The Webbs used the hut intermittently all summer to recover from various sailing marathons – a 22 hour struggle back from the Isle of Man amongst them, and there were other family and group visits. The Anniversary Meet had fine weather and attacked some of the old guide book 'Extremes' in the Pass. Dorothy Pilley Richards had been unable to come but called in at the hut a few weeks later for old times' sake. This autumn the gritstone meet saw a great lead of Valkyrie by Angela Faller and I had a day off from the Yorkshire meet to attend the opening of the George Starkey hut in Patterdale, meeting once again Bishop Williams and Bim, always so friendly to Leicester climbers.

Once more the year ended with the Webbs having a quiet Christmas at the hut.

CHAPTER 33

1976 -1977. Meets. A secretary's post bag. Everest ascent. New members. Meet at High Moss. Scottish skiing meet.

1976 started in Glencoe with a most successful joint meet with the Rucksack Club: members skied, climbed gullies and traversed the tops in perfect weather – two fiercely independent single-sex clubs enjoying each other's company!

A month later the weather was a disappointment at the Annual Dinner, but nothing else was. The Langdales Hotel made the Club very welcome, Alwine Walford, in her first year as President had everything completely under control with her usual blend of charm, decisiveness and attention to detail and the speeches were very good indeed. The Club discovered that Ray Lee had a masterly line in dry humour, worthy to introduce Sir Jack Longland, who replied for the guests. Sir Jack was a topical figure, at odds with the Hunt Report as to the management of his special brain child, the Mountain Leadership Training Board. Chris Briggs of the Pen-y-Gwryd had recently been awarded the MBE so was given the honour of proposing the health of the Club and President – which he did in a lighthearted manner with many amusing memories.

There were several changes in the officers and committee at the Annual Meeting. Kate Webb was going to Bolivia so her position as Hut Secretary was taken over by Annabelle Barker and Anthea Evans and, as in Kate Webb's case, by their husbands as well! My final year as secretary had been a busy one, with a questionnaire on a proposed BMC insurance scheme, a letter from a German publisher wanting to include information about the Pinnacle Club in a climbing encyclopaedia, a Czechoslovakian climber wanting a copy of Cecely Williams' *Women on the Rope* (which Cecely very kindly supplied, free, as there was a currency problem), and, after Junko Tabei, the Japanese woman's ascent of Everest, a phone call from a woman journalist attached to the Daily Mirror asking why women from Britain hadn't reached the summit first. To the last I replied that one needed time and money as well as ambition and that speaking personally as the mother of a young family, if I had the chance of a Himalayan holiday I'd choose an area with more variety. This was most unwise, as the journalist wrote an article about British women being sensibly concerned with bringing up their families. I could see myself being thrown out of the Club, but fortunately the Mirror editor threw the article out, so it was never published!

Anyway, it was time I went, and Sheila Cormack made a splendid job of Secretary for the next six years. Angela Heppenstall (Kelly) brought her friend Fran O'Connor to meets and she joined this year. Others joining were Sue Smith, Anne Fildes, and Anthea Evans.

Sue Smith had been a committee member of her university mountaineering club and very keen on both British and Alpine climbing. Now she had a young family and her husband would have been unhappy about her joining a mixed club, so the Pinnacle Club fulfilled a real need for her.

Anthea had considerable rock-climbing experience and came as Annabelle Barker's friend. She joined just in time to assist her as Hut Secretary!

Anne Fildes, (now McMillan), had climbed top-grade routes, usually with her husband. She says: "I was sitting on a rock stance, tied on with a sling, part way up a rock climb, somewhere in Wales. I was waiting for a hard man to get up the next pitch. This gave me plenty of time to watch two other climbers on the cliff. The climbers were both women, I think one may have been Annabelle Barker. They were on an easier climb, but were leading through and working together in this way meant that they were moving faster and having much more fun than I was. The idea of becoming a Pinnacler myself occurred to me." The joint meet with the Rucksack Club was Anne's first. "I thought the girls looked very hard and opted to walk up to the skiing ground with the Rucksack Club the next day." – Thus casually Anne throws out her comparative impressions of Pinnacle Club and Rucksack Club! – "It was Sheila Cormack who organised the meet and that evening I had only to mention that the route I really wanted to do was the Aonach Eagach Ridge and Sheila had it arranged that we would do it the following day. We had a splendid day with sun, snow and good views. However, I also found that I could hold my own as a Pinnacler."

In June I completed the 46 miles of the Ramblers' Association Lake District Four Three Thousand Peaks Marathon Walk. Ian rags me and says I like picking up certificates, but the back-up and organisation were useful. The snag was the lack of sleep and 2 a.m. start after a hard day's teaching. Fortunately the generous time allowance meant I could have a doze at each refreshment area and an extra one half way up Scafell. It rained off and on with hail storms on Helvellyn, but I enjoyed all except the last mile through Keswick.

Except for Pinnacle Club meets, the remainder of 1976 was a very dry year – however, the impression remains of compass reading in the mist and rain and the ascent of unseen Munros. Scotland relented in August, and Club members enjoyed routes shortly to appear in Ken Wilson's Classic Rock. By a cruel irony the gritstone meet had to be cancelled due to restricted access to crags during the drought so the meet moved to Wales – where the hut was ankle deep in water as rain poured down!

Ann Redman was the first Pinnacle Club member to go to the USA expressly to spend a holiday in Yosemite, which she found much to her taste. Others have followed her example and come back with technique and confidence greatly improved. Other areas, notably the Tetons, have been popular as well in recent years.

Autumn saw a new venue at Bryn Hafod, the Mountain Club (of Stafford) hut in Cwm Cowarch. In spite of storms and heavy rain, members so much enjoyed the hut and its surroundings that they seized the chance to book it again for the following year. The caving centre, Whernside Manor, was another new departure for the Yorkshire Meet. The party included two husbands, four sons and an Austrian girl and we went over the fells on this occasion rather than under them; later the centre provided a most successful caving meet for the Club. The centre supplied packed lunches which included a home made biscuit full of fruit, fudge and chocolate. When members raided the kitchen for the recipe they were shown a whole book full of sustaining goodies for hungry cavers and spent the evening copying them out.

At the invitation of the Rucksack Club, the Pinnacle Club joined members and some of their wives for a meet at High Moss, their hut in Dunnerdale, at the beginning of December; it was so successful that it became an annual event with each club taking it in turns to provide a slap-up meal on the Saturday night followed by an informal showing of slides by any who happened to bring them – sociable occasions with a warmly glowing fire and much fun and laughter. This year there was snow and a hard frost to tempt members to great ridge walks and a descent by moonlight; others found the moonlight itself so tempting that they climbed Scafell by its light and bivvied near the summit to greet the dawn.

This was the last meet of the year, but Jane Stedman brought a guest to the hut just before Christmas and the hills were already extremely beautiful in their Christmas finery of snow.

The New Year meet, once so popular, had become an annual pilgrimage for Maud Godward at which she met one or two members. This year her companion was Penny Storey and they welcomed 1977 with quiet festivity.

The Annual Dinner Meet at the end of January was at the Waterloo Hotel, Betws-y-Coed, which had quoted a very reasonable price for rooms in the annexe.

In spite of the good weather, most people were in time for the Annual Meeting. The Journal edited by Anne Wheatcroft had recently been published and was well received; it had cost £280. Notice was given that the annual subscription would be raised to £3.50 to cover rising costs.

A fair proportion of the meeting was taken up with BMC business. In the Lake District area there had been parking and access problems and an enquiry into the proposed 10mph speed limit on Coniston, Ullswater and Derwentwater. The Club had been fortunate in having Ruth Hargreaves to speak on behalf of the Pinnacle Club, for it entailed her attending the hearing every day for two weeks. The noise and danger of fast boats on these waters was a trial to those on the surrounding hills as well as other users of the lakes, but those wishing to water ski felt victimised, so the battle raged fiercely.

Avis Reynolds reported on the first year of the newly formed Committee for Wales. Their concerns were pumped storage, road widening schemes and the proposed Cambrian Way. Even nearer home, the effect of the feared closure of Cwm Dyli Power Station was considered: the hut could be in danger of floods when the dam was lowered and would almost certainly be left without electricity. Fortunately it would probably be worth while for them to keep the power station operating – as has proved to be the case.

That evening, when the time came for speeches, Denise Wilson introduced the guests, for the original speaker was unable to be there. Denise had become Vice-President when Alwine succeeded her as President, so Alwine had no hesitation in telling her that this was an occasion on which she earned her right to the title. Welcome guest speakers were Alan Blackshaw and Harry Sales.

Jenny Hyslop and Jean Drummond were elected members in 1977. Jenny's first meet was in Langdale in April. She lived near Coniston and had started climbing with her brother about a year previously. He was already making a name for himself by discovering new routes and Jenny, wanting to branch out on her own account, had been on an Austrian Alpine Club Rock and Ice course and was looking for a chance to improve her leading. She was a member of the local rescue team as well. We all liked her and she led a delightful meet in Coniston but resigned after two years. As she said, we always climbed in a crowd and she loved mountains for their solitude so there seemed no point in being a member, though she still climbs with individual members of the Club.

Jean Drummond had always wanted to climb, probably because her father forbade whistling and climbing trees as unladylike. He also forbade hitch hiking, so when she was eighteen she and a friend hitched round the Lake District staying at Youth Hostels. They had their first taste of climbing on Seathwaite Slabs when they were given a lift by two young men who took a fancy to them and were running a course based at Glaramara in Borrowdale. Jean is not surprised that the course members were less than enthusiastic in their welcome for two extra girls getting free instruction. The men lent the two young innocents a tent and came round for payment that evening!

Jean was a keen cyclist, so the urge to climb remained in the background for many years, though she had her first sight of the Matterhorn when on a cycling holiday, and vowed to climb it. Eventually she fulfilled a desire to live in Canada, where she roamed the Rockies – still one of her favourite places.

When she returned to England she went on a course with Geoff Arkless, based in the Llanberis Pass. "I turned up the first morning to find I was the only course member, other than two aspirant guides," writes Jean. "I was to be the guinea pig! What a wonderful week I had! I remember falling off Dinas Mot and swinging pendulum-like across the face. Flying Buttress I thought great and at the top of Spiral Stairs had kisses all round. Of course I fell for one of the Guides and a good time was had by all – but ships that pass in the night – I often wonder what happened to him!

"I then tried going to my nearest climbing club, but after a couple of winter evenings where I received not one word of welcome, I did not persist. I managed three or four visits to Wales with an acquaintance, on one of which I did one VD route on Glyder Fach in socks in the pouring rain. My mother was horrified that my new walking boots had let in to such an extent! I ventured to the Alps one summer and bought my first ice axe."

Soon Jean went to live in Canada once more, returning to England in the late sixties. She says, "I started doing a lot of walking and camping and eventually met my husband – who climbed! Our courting years were spent climbing and walking. We had our first season in the Alps – seven peaks including the Matterhorn.

"We climbed in the Lake District regularly, doing all the easy classics. I remember vividly the elation on completing Tophet Wall on Gable, especially as I was doing alternate leads with Tony. I still think that the best severe in the Lake District.

"Then, married and living in the Lakes, a chance conversation in the staff room at work led to Tony and me making some very dear friends and skiing the High Level Route – a great adventure in itself." Two of the party were Sheila Cormack and Joann Greenhow and they persuaded Jean to join the Pinnacle Club, bringing her along to the meet with the Rucksack Club in Dunnerdale. She remembers: "I was thoroughly nervous by the time I reached the Duddon Valley. Would I be able to keep up? Would the hut have mud floors? be cold etc. etc? My first shock was entering the beautiful stone built hut to see everyone sitting around a roaring log fire. There were books in a corner and pictures on the walls. My bed was a single bunk with a Dunlopillo mattress and Sheila Cormack brought me tea in bed – I never looked back."

This was true. Jean determinedly pushes her standard of leading up – very cross with herself if ever she fails to meet her target – and her love of adventure has taken her to the United States, Africa and the Himalayas, not to mention ski touring and countries nearer home. She has served on the committee, as dinner organiser and as secretary, which is not a bad record for someone who says she is not a 'club' person.

A fortnight after the dinner came the Club's first skiing meet based at the Cairngorm

Club hut near Braemar. It is a well-appointed hut and the radiators were so hot that they scorched my best nightie but seemed to make no impression on the icy-cold bedrooms. I had taken my three boys with their home-made skis and Alison Higham most kindly helped keep track of them in the thick, snow-laden mist at Glenshee. The others were able to ski tour on the Sunday, which had better weather.

This was a great year for family meets at the hut. Faithful users such as the Coopers, Poultons and Flews were augmented by Angela Heppenstall with her toddler and baby being introduced to "the cottage in the mountains" and the Beard family came twice. No less than four families came to the maintenance meet in March: Denise Wilson and family, Annabelle and Bill Barker and family, Alex White and Tabitha, Anthea and Alan Evans and family. Alan and Bill made the new Alpine-type bed while the children had a marvellous time burning up the old infested wood and rubbish and members did the spring cleaning and maintenance.

Highspots of the year were the Borrowdale meet in June when the fourteen members with at least a 40-year age span all climbed, totting up at least 14,000 feet of rock between them, followed by the July meet in Wales on which a strong Yorkshire contingent climbed on Craig yr Ysfa: Mur y Niwl, Pinnacle Wall, the Grimmett and Amphitheatre Buttress. Small successes paled beside the achievement of the Czech girl, Dina Sterbova, who soloed Noshaq (24,581ft) in the Hindu Kush.

The Anniversary Meet was so wet that some members retreated to the amenities of the leisure centre on Anglesey. Whatever the weather, it was a great gathering of old friends: Nancy Smith came for her first meet for some time and Peggy Wild was able to spare a day away from the Adventure School. The wild weather forced Dorothea Gravina to retreat from her tent and join us in the none-too-dry hut. Our most impressive guests were from the Irish M.C.: Ingrid Masterson and Bairbre Sheridan who arrived mid-morning on a light motor bike which was almost submerged by them and their equipment. Fortifying themselves with a late breakfast after their all night journey from Dublin they made their way (in the rain) to the Watkin Path.

Ingrid was all set to join the Pinnacle Club in 1977, having brought up her family, but a most unexpected baby in 1979 delayed her application till 1982. Bairbre, much younger, was also keen but is now married with three little children.

Ingrid has Irish tales to tell and thinks the following worth including as quite peculiarly Irish. In January 1961, shortly after her marriage, a pregnant Ingrid, her husband Noel and a friend decided to traverse the Ridge of the Reeks in Kerry and camp overnight in the snow on the summit of Carrauntuohil. On the first day all except the weather went according to plan: the temperature rose, the wind freshened and the rain came down to melt the snow. As this is an Irish tale, the borrowed shelter was of course a *desert* tent complete with fly netting but not constructed with mountain tops in mind. Fortunately it was pitched before the wind reached its full force.

"However," says Ingrid, "We got no sleep that night." The wind rose to 90mph and all three of them spent their time in holding the tent pole upright; meanwhile their friend, a solicitor, kept them amused all night with witty tales of law practice in rural Ireland. At one stage Noel had to crawl out on all fours to collect rocks – fortunately in plentiful supply – to hold down the sides of the tent, but morning came at last and the three strode forward through the thick mist, ready for more Irish adventures. Today nothing went to plan at all. Their half-inch map, the most detailed available, was inaccurate and they went down an unmarked spur instead of the north ridge – wondering at the incredible steepness of the cwm. Too late to turn back, they realised where they were and slogged out the Hag's Glen miles over rivers in spate to reach a farm and beg a lift round to their car. They've had many a winter camp since this memorable epic, and in bad weather too – but with equipment more suited to the mountains!

Ingrid writes: "My first exploit on a mountain solo was at the age of 19 when I went up Muckish in Donegal by a rather scrambly route and got caught out in thick mist – I was terrified, as before that I had only been on treks with, the Irish Youth Hostels Association. Soon after I bumped into some rock climbers belonging to the Irish Mountaineering Club and promptly joined the club.

"However my early years' mountaineering activities were rather frustrating as I had started nursing training and the hours were desperate, so I mostly got out by myself.

"My first real Alpine trip was in August '64 after I'd had two babies, with the Mountaineering Association. Walt Unsworth was the tutor; I learnt a lot and we did some good routes. I led one rope with another girl. I have recently discovered I have been immortalised from that trip: on the cover of *Peaks Passes and Glaciers* by Walt Unsworth there is a picture of our group that year on the traverse of the Leiterspitzen; I am the figure (no lid) in the red shirt sitting beside the girl in the white helmet at the bottom of the pinnacle."

Most of Ingrid's trips for the next ten years were with parties of guided groups as she wasn't keen on sticking her neck out too far with small children to bring up. She climbed in Austria, Switzerland and the Dolomites, also ski toured with her husband including a traverse of the Bernese Oberland. In 1973 she really went to town with the High Level Route in April and the Rendezvous Haute Montagne when she climbed with Sylvia Yates in the Urner Alps. From now on she felt free to lead parties and climb with friends and had three very good seasons in the Dauphiné Alps including ascents of Pelvoux, Meije traverse, Sialouse traverse, and an attempt on the Ecrins traverse abandoned in icy conditions. Ingrid says, "The third trip to the Dauphiné was a free bonus – I was sent by A.F.A.S. (The Irish equivalent of Outward Bound) as an assistant and interpreter with a group of novice Irish alpinists. It was very good from a climbing point of view and I learnt some novel new techniques from the French as well."

In 1982 Ingrid enjoyed routes in the Bregaglia with 3 other Irish MC members, including the N Ridge of the Badile.

Ingrid had often felt the lack of other women her own age and approximate standard to climb with, and her enjoyment of PC meets is borne out by the lengths she goes to to attend them. I think a piquancy is added when she has to judge the number of routes she can fit in before making a dash for the Irish boat.

CHAPTER 34

1978 and 1979. New members. The duties of a president. Expeditions. Annapurna and death of Alison Chadwick. Caving. Camping.

The end of January 1978 saw the club in the very cradle of Lakeland mountaineering for its Annual Dinner, at the Wasdale Head Hotel.

John Wyatt was one of the speakers; his tales of life as a Lake District warden were due for publication and his speech was good publicity for his book, being full of humour and memorable events. Christine Sheard introduced the guests and Charles Pickles of the F&RCC, who had known many of the older members well and said that Trilby Wells taught him to climb, kindly spoke a few words. Not only did Alwine Walford round off her presidency with an excellent speech but she augmented a donation from Dorothy Pilley Richards to provide everyone with port to accompany their coffee.

One of Alwine's first acts as president had been to ask me whether I would be her successor when she retired in three years' time. She was working out a long-term strategy for the Club and soon dropped hints as to who should be president after myself – fortunately our minds were working along the same lines! This weekend I was duly elected president and new committee members were Alison Adam and Helen Jones. Another decision at the Annual Meeting was to adopt the area round the Club hut and up the pipe line and keep it free from litter. Also, from now on meet leaders catered only for the Saturday evening meal, where necessary. Eliminating communal breakfasts would make shopping easier for the meet leader, make it easier for early risers to get out quickly, and cut down on initial outlay.

Jenny Beale, Jane Hillmann and Wendy Aldred joined the Club this year.

Jenny writes: "Unlike some Pinnaclers, I was not brought up to climb. I grew up on the Sussex coast and spent my childhood in and on and around the water, learning to sail at a young age. My first real hillwalk was an ascent of Snowdon with two student friends. The following year, 1974, I worked in Dundee, where I met some LSCC members, including Sheila Cormack. I was tremendously excited by Scotland and longed to explore the hills. I remember my first attempt at rock climbing – an evening on a crag near Edinburgh – and thinking that this was the most exhilarating thing I had done since planing a sailing dinghy in a stiff breeze! Some hillwalking followed, and I discovered many other similarities between sailing and mountaineering: the need to be in tune with the weather and the pleasure of achieving what one sets out to do in wild and beautiful places, not to mention the need to cope with being wet, cold and wind-battered much of the time!

"For me, the Pinnacle Club was somewhere where I felt at home, in that it was such a relief to be among other women who took physical things for granted, and who expected to be at the front end instead of tagging along behind men. I never found an equally compatible crowd in sailing, so that when I moved back to Scotland from London I more or less gave up sailing and took to the hills instead. I must in particular mention Sheila Cormack's endless encouragement and support, which I valued a great deal."

Jenny wrote this from Ireland when recently married and expecting her first child. She had explored the hills, taken up windsurfing and was looking forward to six months in Zimbabwe and the chance to explore parts of Africa.

Jane Hillmann's story starts in Africa, so she could probably give Jenny ideas about good climbing areas. She writes: "I started climbing in 1971 whilst in Uganda. The desire to travel first led me to Africa, then to join the Uganda mountaineering club. I soon found myself not only travelling around the country but up rock faces. Discovering that I quite enjoyed climbing led me impetuously, 4 months later, to take part in an expedition to the Ruwenzoris. This 2 week 'holiday' awakened a love of both mountains and climbing which, I hope, will never die. Quite why, I don't know. It rained for most of the 14 days we spent there and despite climbing Mount Stanley, Alexandra and Baker I had only one summit view which lasted at least 30 seconds.

"Thereafter I climbed on numerous rock outcrops in Uganda and twice on Mount Kenya, reaching the Nelion summit on one trip, happily in perfect weather.

"A 2 year stay in Ethiopia followed where little good rock was to be found. However a very memorable trip to the Simien mountains was made which involved climbing Ras Dashan, Ethiopia's highest mountain.

"A return to Britain via the Alps, plus two years in Scotland took me back into climbing on a regular basis. It was in Scotland that I met Alison Higham and Sheila Cormack and thus came to hear of the Pinnacle Club.

"A move down to Basingstoke propelled me into the Club at great speed as I supposed, quite rightly, that there would not be many women climbers in that area."

Wendy Aldred writes: "In my teens I did a lot of climbing with Dad, including a few trips to the Alps and also climbing with friends. When I began work I found it difficult as a female to find partners and so looked around for a club. I wrote to the Fell and Rock and the Pinnacle. The F&R were not very helpful but I got a very nice letter from Sheila Cormack so I decided to attend a meet in December 1977 in Patterdale. I had heard all sorts of stories about cigar smoking ladies! Anne Fildes, the meet leader, told me not to be too concerned about the Club's reputation so immediately I started to worry and wonder if everyone was a really hard climber. I arrived an hour too early and so sat in a pub for ages. Eventually everyone arrived and seemed really friendly tho' I was concerned when next morning I discovered one member – Jane Stedman – had walked from Windermere during the night.

"Saturday brought a cold and dry day with gale force winds but off we set for what turned out to be a superb day in the snow on Striding Edge, on to Raise and down Sticks Pass. "In the evening I was let off assisting with the meal as that's what I did at work all day and so spent the time by the fire listening to endless stories.

"The following day we went up High Street which was equally enjoyable, via Three Tarns to the Knot, Stony Cove Pike and down by Hartsop Dod ... and so ended the first of many meets.

"After a good day on the hills I like nothing better than to sit by the fire at Cwm Dyli, mug of wine or tea by my side listening to older members with their talk of early days. One of my hobbies is collecting old mountaineering books and the day I got my set of PC *Journals* from Dorothea Gravina I was overjoyed.

"I joined a national club because with me moving around so much I don't have to join another club. Belonging to an all women club prevents problems with men not wanting to climb with women unless the men can lead etc. – tho' the problems aren't so bad as they were eight years ago. When I joined there weren't many young members; since then there has been an influx."

Wendy started climbing on gritstone with her father and had her first trip to the Alps when she was 14. When she found friends to climb with, her father sent her on a course to Plas y Brenin to make sure her rope techniques were sound and when she was 18 she invested in proper rock boots. That same year came one of her most memorable experiences; she and her father went to the Bernese Oberland and set off for the Strahlegg hut with heavy sacks. Wendy says: "Half way was a hut which was as far as the day trippers went, as a large rock face with spikes and ladders put them off.

"As we reached the top of this the snow began to fall and the mist came down obscuring all the red markings and tracks across the glacier. Being our first day I was pretty tired and the never-ending glacier and mist didn't inspire me. We stopped for chocolate and words of encouragement from Dad – you know the sort – it's just over the next hill, not much further. The snow came down faster but a small breeze sprang up and I looked up to see the mist swirl and lift enough to see the roof of the hut. We had to pass the outside toilet first which was sparkling new, the old one having been carried away by an avalanche. The guardian, who was mending a window which had suffered a similar fate, looked quite disappointed. We were the only people in the hut and I think he had wanted a night on his own. It felt odd to be just us up there in the mountains – no one around – the silence disturbed only by the seracs crashing below on the glacier.

Next day the weather was worse and so we abandoned our ideas and returned to the valley. As we reached the glacier the mist lifted and we were able to see the huge seracs we had passed the day before. I was in the lead trying to hurry the pace to get past them but my father insisted on taking photos. The noise of the stream passing underneath was tremendous and I kept peering round to make sure it wasn't an avalanche – but no, all stayed in place whilst we were there.

"Since our trip the hut has been destroyed by an avalanche and not replaced."

1978 was a year of well attended meets. The Anniversary Meet, catered for by Alwine, and the joint meet with the Rucksack Club were full to overflowing. A highlight for me was one of the Scottish meets on which we spent a day on the Etive Slabs then went swimming in the loch.

I discovered that one of the president's tasks, that of inviting people to speak at the Annual Dinner is both frustrating and rewarding. The Pinnacle Club speaker was no problem as Gwen Moffat, who had been able to attend a number of meets this year, promised to introduce the guests. This was very good of her as, although she speaks with flair and style she feels she lacks the charismatic brilliance of a natural orator and therefore much prefers to stick to writing. Perhaps many writers feel like this: I wrote to Eric Newby, the author of the hilarious *Short Walk in the Hindu Kush* and he wrote with relief that he would be in China: "It is lucky for me that I have this cast iron alibi as the thought ... throws me into such as state of panic that I have to leave my food untouched. I'm sure you wouldn't want this to happen at your dinner." His note paper was headed with a charming sketch of his house and out of a top window issued a balloon containing the words, "You can come back from China, Eric, the dinner's over!"

With a regretful chuckle I started writing a persuasive epistle to the Lake District writer and climbing historian, Alan Hankinson, whom we had hoped to invite the following year to our Lakeland dinner. The invitation caused him equal anguish but he bravely accepted: "Your letter came as a horrible surprise and has caused me many sleepless nights but you put the matter so persuasively and the honour of being asked is so great and the whole thing so irresistibly intriguing that I can only accept and say thankyou. No doubt I shall live to regret the decision."

I hope he did not regret it, for his speech went very successfully and, after reading some of his books, members were delighted to meet him in person.

The most outstanding achievement by women mountaineers during the year was the ascent of Annapurna I (26,504ft) the first eight thousand metre peak to be climbed by an all female expedition. Irene Miller and Vera Komarkova reached the summit, but two days later Vera Watson and Alison Chadwick-Oniskiewiez were killed somewhere between the top camp and the summit. Alison Chadwick, who had married a Polish climber, was the top British woman mountaineer and her father launched a special fund to be administered by the Mount Everest Foundation, to encourage British women mountaineers to plan expeditions. The Pinnacle Club Lahaul Expedition in 1980 was the first to benefit from this fund.

This is not to say that there were no Pinnacle Club members in the Himalayas in 1978. Dorothea Gravina wanted to reach Annapurna and did so by using local buses from Istanbul to Nepal before starting her trek. Most of the excitements came on the journey, with trouble in Tehran, Kabul and Delhi but, as she said, it was so much more amusing than flying.

Ann Redman went to Pakistan with Brede Arkless and Marion Wintringham and climbed their objective, Bakhor Das, an unclimbed twenty-thousander. Brede was to be the second guest speaker at the 1979 Dinner; unlike the men, she had expressed no qualms, but she had now been on two expeditions which included Pinnacle Club members so it was reasonable to suppose that she knew something about us.

Angela Faller spent a different summer, climbing and sailing round the Scottish Islands, and came back married to Jack Soper. She wore her wedding ring at the Gritstone meet in September, and eventually Jean noticed. Needless to say, we were delighted for both of them.

1979 started with a snowy meet in Langdale, but all my thoughts were geared to the Dinner at the Waterloo Hotel, Betws-y-Coed, at the beginning of February. Tony Drummond drove Jean and myself down on the Friday evening. My mind was in a whirl with the thought of the Annual General Meeting, my speech at the Dinner and the certainty that I would forget everyone's name, but on Saturday morning Angela Heppenstall firmly took me to the North Ridge of Tryfan saying the snow would be perfect and it would be a nice short day. When we returned there was a phone call from Brede to say that she had suddenly had to go into hospital so couldn't give her speech! Tony Drummond had jokingly said in the car coming down that he could always oblige if somebody dropped out, so I turned to him in my hour of need and he nobly came up with the goods.

I did not discover Brede's story till later, but this astonishing woman had slightly miscalculated the arrival of her eighth child, who was born that evening (while Ann Redman looked after the rest of the family).

Stella Adams on Mesach, Tremadog, 1984. Photo: Ian Smith.

Brede first made an impression on the climbing scene in the 1950s as Brede Boyle, and she became a tutor for the Mountaineering Association. In the 1960s and 70s she became a British Mountain Guide, married Geoff Arkless and had eight children while remaining a top class climber, guide, leader of expeditions and organising her family – all this by the time she was in her middle thirties. Of late years she has become increasingly interested in helping women to realise their full potential as climbers, and she runs courses specially for women as well as general courses. She joined the Pinnacle Club in 1984.

Everybody was very hungry that evening, for although the meal was delicious the hotel had misguidedly thought that a women's club would not eat potatoes. Many were forced to go down to the bar for cheese and biscuits before watching Alison Higham's excellent slides of explorations and routes on Baffin Island. Sunday saw a traditional ascent of Moel Siabod followed for some by tea with Denise Evans at her home in Capel Curig.

Jane Stedman's friend Tanya Gregson became a member at this meet. Others joining during the year were Sandra Corbett who has climbed hard but is now more interested in mountain marathons and Alwine Walford's daughter, Elizabeth Scott who has a young family and lives in Thanet, which makes transport difficult. The other five are well known names on meets: Teresa Hughes, Margaret Clennett, Fiona Slator (Longstaff), Stella Adams and Jacqueline (Jay) Turner.

Stella Adams, whose husband John has put up many new routes, is a small, slim person whose standard of leading is well into the E grades and continues to rise. Even more valuable to the Club is her readiness to offer encouragement to people, whatever their climbing standard. Her advice on suitable routes for prospective leaders is invaluable, from V diff to E grades. This is not all, for she is now a most efficient treasurer – when Ada Shaw had been treasurer for 24 years we began to be afraid that there would be nobody who had learnt her skills, so she spent a year handing her job over to Stella and the club relaxed once more.

Jay Turner, also a strong climber and more recently a keen ski mountaineer as well, was on the committee within a year of joining and became secretary the following year. Fiona Longstaff has been meets secretary and Margaret Clennett librarian.

Margaret seconded severes when she joined the club. Her man had a climbing partner and her standard was not conducive to finding other partners so she wrote to the BMC for the address of the PC secretary. She had heard it was a 'hard' club so was most reassured to find climbers of her own standard as well. Her first meet was camping at the Gower and she travelled up with the Wheatcrofts and climbed with Alex White. Being used to a local club, it took her a long time to get used to all the travelling she had to do to join a meet, but she decided it was worth it. In 1984 one of her most memorable climbing days was with Sheila Cormack on the Lakes meet: they went to Scafell and climbed Mickledore Grooves, Great Eastern, Botterill's and Jones' Route. The weather was so good it was a shame to go down, so they walked back over the tops and reached the car about 10.30 p.m. after a 14 hour day.

Memorable Alpine trips started in 1980 in Zermatt with Belinda Swift, followed in 1981 by the Bernina with Jay, Steph Rowlands and Jean Drummond. One of their routes was the traverse of the Piz Palu, going up with the hordes but leaving them on the summit as they weren't doing the traverse. Going down the Fortezza ridge Steph had a shouting match with a guide, who made his party overtake them on a fixed rope.

Pinnacle Club members were planning a Himalayan expedition for 1980 which I was keen to go on but meanwhile Alwine Walford asked if I would like to go to Kashmir in 1979. Ian and the boys said they would cope very well without me, so I jumped at the opportunity and was even more glad that I had gone when circumstances made it impossible the following year.

The plan was to spend a week in each of four different climbing areas and report on their suitability for a more serious expedition. We did this and had the holiday of a lifetime, climbing Mahadeo by two routes, then climbing further peaks in the Thajwas area, and from Gulmarg and Aru.

It was a kind of Royal Tour, for Alwine and her family were remembered with affection and esteem. As Nea Morin and Margaret Darvall were members, my husband called it the Golden Oldies Expedition. Other members were Sue Gibson, Katherine and Alastair Gebbie and Sally, an American friend of Katherine's. The age range was 37 – 73, which was rather neat.

Other people were abroad in 1979; Gwen Moffat was following the Californian Trail from Omaha to San Francisco, collecting time off to climb now and again; and Jenny Beale travelled four thousand miles and back on the Trans Siberian Railway to have a look at the Great Wall of China.

At home there were all the favourite meets and in November five Pinnacle Club and Ladies' Scottish members went apprehensively to Whernside Manor for a caving course. They had a warm welcome on arrival but as they listened to the pouring rain and thought of the melt water from the previous week's snow filling up the cold, wet and uncomfortable caves they wondered why they hadn't stuck to climbing!

"We were kept very busy learning new techniques, seeing slides, going to lectures, being fitted out with equipment and of course actually going down potholes. We began with an easy cave – Borrans – just to get accustomed to grovelling in the mud and squeezing through narrow slots. Then we went into Long Churn Entrance to Alum Pot which was full of exciting moments like trying to get through the "cheese press" which was a horizontal maze through a gap only a foot thick. Finally after practising SRT (single rope technique) in the rain up a tree we were taken to Bull Pot which goes vertically down for several hundred feet. The abseiling down was fun but the climbing back up was hard work and if you can use SRT up a waterfall whilst swinging around in pitch darkness then prussicking out of a crevasse must be child's play!"

Ben Lyon was the instructor, and they had a thoroughly enjoyable weekend, so it was sad to read soon afterwards that the centre was underused and in financial difficulties.

I was fast learning how philosophical one has to become when planning the annual dinner. Angela Heppenstall went to endless trouble to arrange a venue in the Lake District which suddenly decided it couldn't accommodate us, so the 1980 Dinner was held at the Royal Hotel, Bowness on Windermere, which rescued the situation at the last minute. Another last minute change had to be made, for with the forthcoming expedition applying for funds we had invited as speaker an old friend who was also Secretary of the Mount Everest Foundation, David Edmundson. It was a great shock when he died in December 1979. I had to suppress some superstitious qualms about my effect on the people I invited to speak at dinners before approaching our stalwart friend, Sid Cross. Our other speaker, Denise Wilson's husband, Chris, had fine tales to tell of being allowed to carry Denise's rucksack when he first met her as Denise Shortall. For the second year I was supported by a Drummond, for Jean introduced the guests.

New members during the year were Julia Haston, a sound leader with winter and Alpine experience; Gwen Joy, daughter of one of the Seth-Hughes sisters famous in the thirties; Pat James, who joined via a Plas y Brenin course and Reading Mountaineering Club; and Sally Keir, very experienced and a VS leader "sometimes" who was coming back to climbing now her family was grown up. She did not receive a proper welcome on her first meet, but fortunately for the Club, she persevered. She is a valuable member with many talents and is currently Meets Secretary.

There were some good meets this year. The spring ones had all the excitement of anticipating the Himalayan expedition, and one breezy evening in April saw a large number of us on the rather sloping ground outside Coppermines Cottages, pitching and inspecting the expedition tents. The following month there was a proper camping meet in Langdale, a climbing meet par excellence with even the high crags warm and welcoming. Hut bookings were becoming increasingly expensive, with many clubs demanding full payment when the booking was confirmed, so as not to lose revenue. This led to the Pinnacle Club arranging many more camping meets with the added advantage that plans could be more flexible and the venue changed according to the weather.

With members climbing in America, Canada, the European Alps and elsewhere, summer meets at home were poorly attended.

Undoubtedly the major event was the Pinnacle Club Expedition to Lahaul in which eight members took part. They had been heralded in the May edition of *Climber and Rambler* as "Sheila and her Magnificent Seven," and they deserve a chapter to themselves.

CHAPTER 35

1980 Lahaul Expedition.

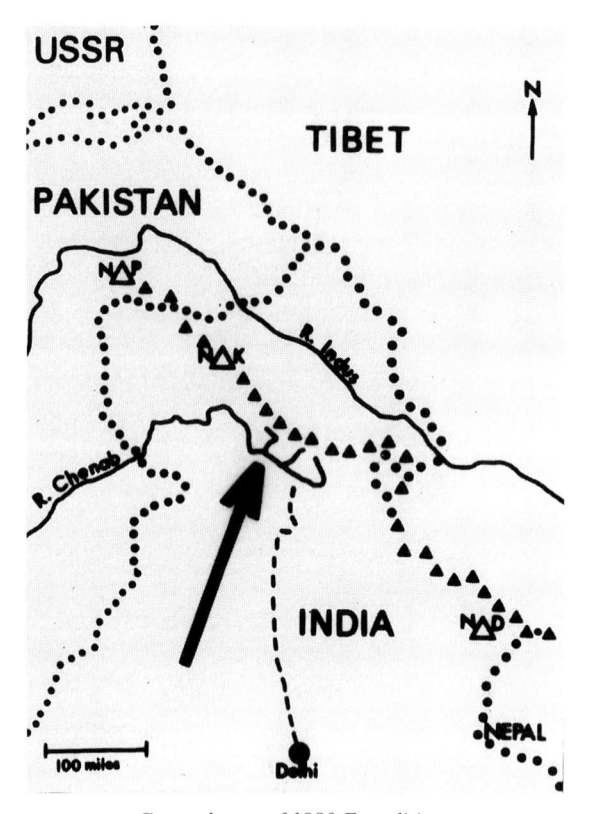

General area of 1980 Expedition.

Everyone agreed that there should be another Pinnacle Club Expedition, and there it rested. Sheila Cormack soon realised that the only sure way of having one was to start organising it herself, so she wrote to Steph Rowland who replied eagerly. This was in the summer of 1979, and by December the team was formed: Sheila, Steph, Jean Drummond, Sheila Crispin, Stella Adams, Angela Soper, Jay Turner and Denise Wilson. All but Jay were teachers of some description, free only in July and August, so areas affected by the monsoon had to be avoided.

Kashmir had been suggested originally, but was dismissed as too accessible and well-explored. Sheila writes:

We eventually fixed on a valley in the Lahaul district of North India which seemed to offer plenty of virgin climbing at a reasonably easy technical standard. Jean organised food, Sheila Crispin got the medical supplies, Steph equipped us and Jay persuaded British Airways to fly us to Delhi. I was left to make the official application, apply for various grants and do the detailed planning."

Some of the latter work was shared by all members of the expedition, and Pinnacle Club meets throughout the spring were enlivened by their discussions.

The final plan was to book with the Indian Mountaineering Federation a high peak in the upper Miyar Nala, a virtually unclimbed area which had only recently been opened to foreign expeditions. The only other climbing party in the area had been the King's School, Ely, 1978 Expedition, led by Dave Challis, who was able to indicate the area's potential. They could reach Udaipur by bus and walk in in three days to the Gumba Nala, a side valley running NE from the Miyar Nala. The IMF peak having been booked and paid for would give them freedom to climb lower peaks in the area as well.

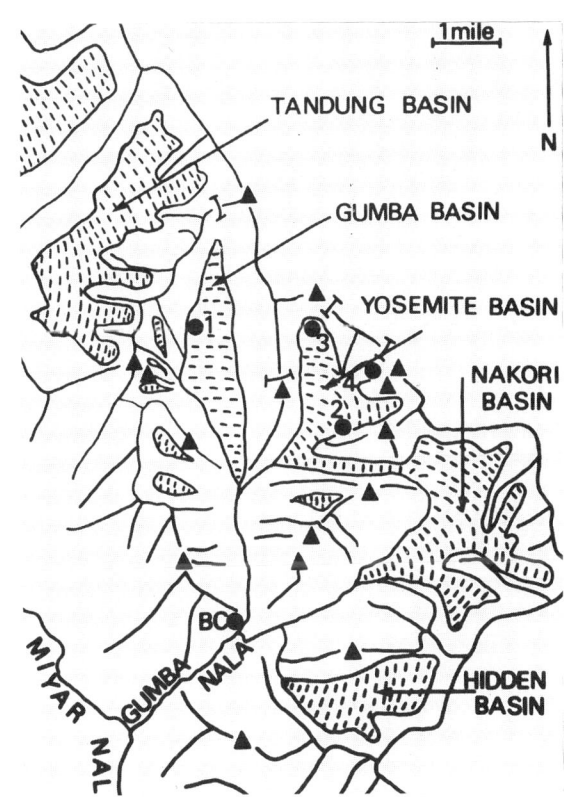

Area explored by 1980 Expedition.

To start with everything went wonderfully smoothly; three members travelled out a fortnight early with the expedition supplies wrapped in bright pink polythene and, with the help of British Airways staff, Delhi customs was cleared within about three hours. Joined by a fourth member, they were able to spend the rest of the fortnight in Kashmir, where they joined Alison and John Higham and baby Richard on holiday from the Far East.

Back in Delhi, they linked with the other four members and their liaison officer, Sushama Mahajan, who at 24 was the youngest by two years. She writes: "We proceeded to the airport where I met the other members of the expedition and a galaxy of pink boxes. I don't know which intimidated me more."

The private coach was loaded up and a night journey to Manali confidently expected, but the party had reckoned without puncture stops and the journey took 24 hours. This was only a foretaste of frustrations, however, for when they drove over the Rhotang Pass to Ruding the following day they found that heavy rain had washed away a bridge and destroyed sections of road between Ruding and Udaipur. The coach driver thankfully dumped the expedition 25 miles short of the usual roadhead.

Sushama writes: "That's when the porter-induced migraines started (as did the mash and tinned ham)." Because of a shortage of ponies and porters it took four days to get all the expedition gear to Udaipur, after which thirty porters were hired for the four day carry (doing seven or eight miles a day) to base camp, and the five expedition members who remained with the baggage tried to stifle their frustration at being nearly a week later than expected and enjoy the beautiful valley and easy days to the full.

Steph, Sheila Crispin and Jay went on ahead to find a place for base camp. They were anxious to see the terrain they had chosen so carefully from the old Indian Survey maps and, overjoyed at finding a perfect site for base camp a couple of miles up the Nala, they pressed on to have a look at their IMF peak "20,537ft."

Jay writes: "Very shortly after leaving the Base Camp site it came into view, towering up in a startling and menacing fashion." They went back to base with mixed feelings, realising that the peak was probably beyond the range of the expedition but appreciating the numerous peaks which they could turn their attention towards.

In fact the peak "20,537ft" caused some agonising, and differences of opinion. The face of the mountain falling to the Gumba Glacier was very steep and about 5,000ft high with icefalls, avalanche tracks and steep rock ridges, but a route could perhaps have been

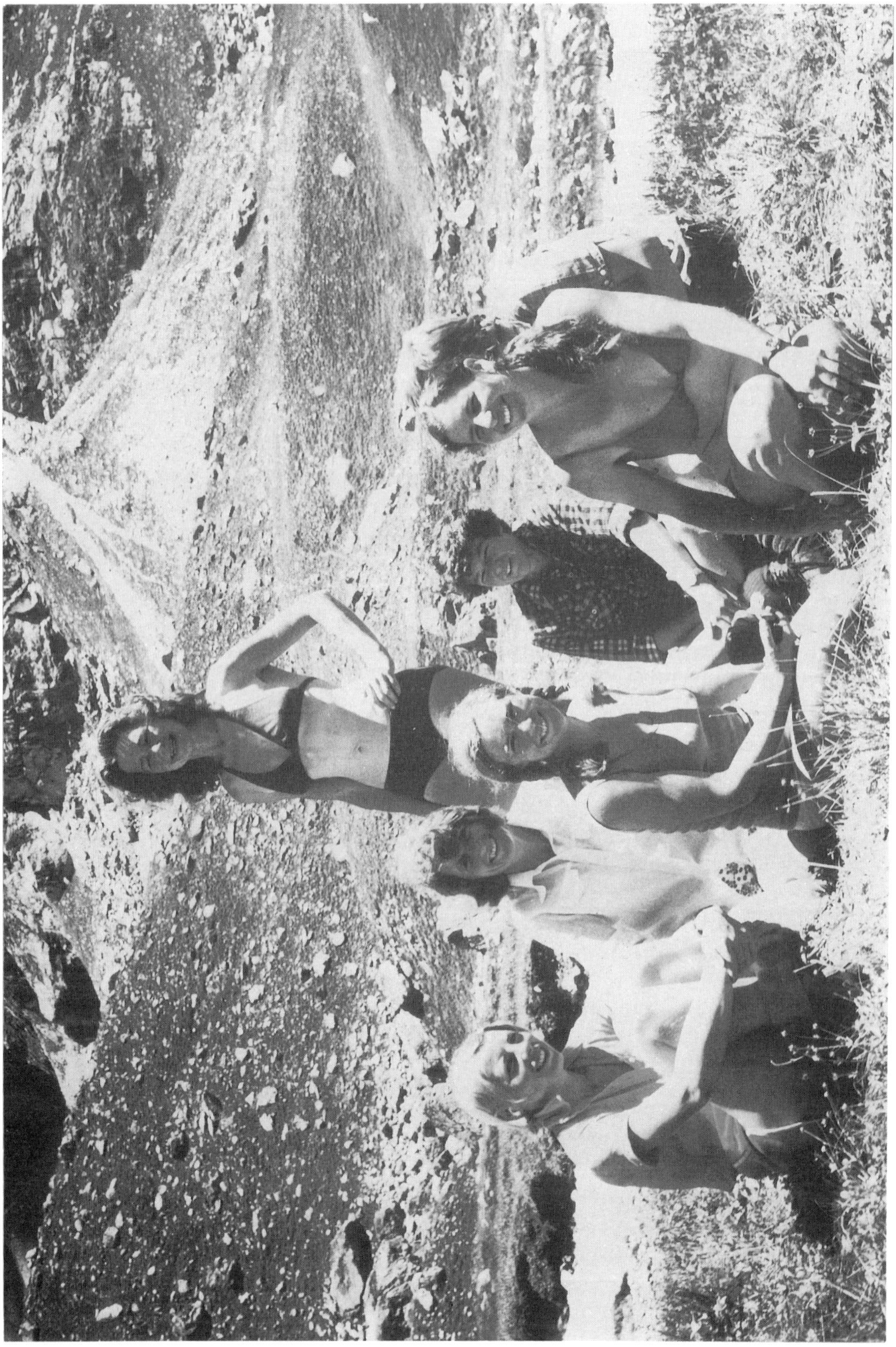

forced from the Gumba Col. It would have led with some difficulty over a subsidiary peak and the ground beyond was not visible. The group decided that they were not prepared to employ siege tactics and were further deterred by the unsettled weather and heavy snowfall during their first fortnight in the mountains. All energies were concentrated on enjoying the other peaks available.

Base camp was situated at just over 13,000ft, at the upper level of the local shepherds' summer pastures, and the nearby peaks offered very pleasant climbing and scrambling to a height of between sixteen and eighteen thousand feet. Everyone enjoyed the feeling of acclimatisation and the thrill of accomplishing first ascents. When the rain set in in earnest they went on a four day exploratory trip up the Miyar Nala. As this party returned on 2nd August another group went to bivouac up the Nakori Nala and despite a wet night and misty morning climbed two fine peaks just under 18,000 ft in height – a continuation of the imposing rock peak, Deception Point, which two of them had climbed on the first day. They believe the higher of these two peaks had been climbed by the party from Ely, but this was the only one which was not a first ascent.

Just as the weather was improving, Steph Rowland and Sheila Crispin had to return to Britain and, to add insult to injury, arrived home with Shigella flexneri dysentery. Steph's condition was so serious that she was taken off the plane on a stretcher and had a week in a London hospital. Happily, both members fully recovered. Unaware of these events, the six remaining members established a camp on the Gumba Glacier at 15,800 ft and attempted a fine mountain much admired by Steph when she first saw it, so they named it Steph's Peak. The first attempt was by Stella's Ridge, a narrow rock route of about AD standard which gave excellent climbing to about 17,900ft, when Sheila and Stella ran out of time. The following day Denise, Jean and Jay set out to see whether they could push the route further. Denise writes: "We had to cross the right hand snow basin to reach the ridge; the snow was firm and it looked temptingly easy to climb straight up to a gully which led direct to the col. We decided to try that route and descend by the rock ridge.

"Once in the gully the angle was steep and there were icy patches, but enjoyable though calf-screaming front pointing, led us easily up to the col by midday ... It was still early and the top seemed close enough to touch, with an obvious snow couloir slanting off left and leading up to the summit ridge. Let's just nip up there before lunch. Was it euphoria or altitude? Jay was doubtful and opted to look after the food whilst her elders, who perhaps should have known better, roped up and jauntily set off up the snow, only to be brought to an abrupt halt after a few feet."

The snow was abandoned for rock leading to an ice-festooned gully; clouds swirled around and Denise and Jean made moves which would be difficult to reverse; also, they wanted to get to the top.

Hampered by soft, deep snow, they reached the summit at 5 p.m., tried to find a rake which would lead them back to the col, Jay and the food, but had to settle for a gully from which they might be able to break out left. Darkness caught them in a little niche in the ice and they set about making it home for the night.

The morning brought falling snow, and Denise tells an exciting tale of the return to the col and descent to an unfamiliar white valley. "Surely it must be the Gumba? Then all doubts and fears were resolved. Waving and shouting, a tiny figure appeared on the moraine far below. What a marvellous reunion with Sheila, who brought warm clothes and Mars Bars." With Angela carrying their gear, they plodded up the moraine to camp, warm sleeping bags and hot soup.

Steph's Peak was the highest and most exciting ascent on the expedition, but the mountains surrounding the next glacier to the east were so shapely and beautiful that the party named it Yosemite Valley. In particular there was the beautifully proportioned Half Dome, 19,100ft, guarded by its steep rock face 4,000ft high. Stella and Sheila were the ones to discover a way to its summit. Scarcely less high was Pinnacle Peak, climbed by Angela and Denise, and the party had easier ascents of two more peaks; the Keep and the Castle, as well as several cols.

Meanwhile Sushama had arranged porters for the return trip. The walkout was more speedy, buses ran from Udaipur, and there was time to visit Triloknath Temple on the day of the summer fair and to spend a day at the Taj Mahal. They flew to London on 28th August, filled with the happiness of their achievement: new to the Himalayas and entirely on their own they had climbed 14 peaks between them between 16,000 and 19,000ft, all but one of which they believed to be a first ascent. Five of the peaks had a second ascent by different members of the party. They also reached several high cols and explored the Gumba system of valleys and glaciers and the upper Miyar Nala. If they were ready to rest on their laurels they found this was not to be: there were reports to write up, articles for magazines, maps to draw and slides to show. I remember the thrill of seeing the slides for the first time one evening on a gritstone meet that was based at Angela's house near Leeds – we all basked in the happiness and success of the Club's own Himalayan meet.

CHAPTER 36

1981 and 1982. Sixtieth Anniversary Dinner. Skye Ridge. International Climbing Meets. Fiftieth Anniversary of Emily Kelly Hut.

Thus the Club became sixty years old and we celebrated the anniversary at the Annual Dinner Meet at the end of January. It was held at the Royal Goat, Beddgelert, which has a large and splendid dining room, and we invited Brede Arkless and John Barry as our special guest speakers. It was my final dinner as president, so I crossed my fingers, but to no avail – shortly before the weekend John Barry phoned to say he was snowed up in the Zermatt valley. (We took this with a pinch of salt, thinking where our own preference would lie, but John later said it was frustratingly true – he was marooned at a hut and could move neither up nor down). I could only pray that Brede wouldn't have another baby.

Saturday was cold, but fine enough for climbing so Angela Soper, President Elect, Jean Drummond, Dinner Organiser and myself as Retiring President climbed Craig Dhu Wall at Tremadog and were back in good time to gather our wits for the annual general meeting.

With Sheila Cormack as secretary things were well prepared and went very smoothly and I thought how lucky I had been not to change secretaries in mid office, as usually happens to presidents. I still had a pitfall to overcome however, for I was waiting for the dinner guests when I saw this attractive person with bright hair look in enquiringly and then depart; she looked in again and I knew it was Brede so I welcomed her and apologised, saying I expected someone with dark hair. Fortunately Brede accepted this remark with her usual bubbling humour; she made a good speech too, when the time came. Sheila Cormack introduced the guests and Len Winthrop Young, our very special Original Member and First President inspired us all with the speech which sparked off the writing of this history. It was a very special celebration.

As the year progressed, the value of having a really inspired climber as president became obvious. I had felt strongly that to be truly helpful to women climbers, the Club had to support and encourage the stars as well as those of more modest ability, and the most I had ever been able to do in this respect was act as second to Angela. Now Angela herself was climbing with such people as Brede Arkless and Jill Lawrence, and later on, when the Pinnacle Club helped host the International Women's Meets she, as President, could meet the guests as an equal, ably supported by other members such as Stella Adams. Angela took part in the first of these international meets in 1980.

Members joining during the year were all experienced rock climbers and mountaineers, but it is good to note that those who admitted to leading pleasant severes on their application forms are now leading much harder routes. Sheila McKemmie's experience included the Polish Tatras and Kenya's Point Lenana. Mary Loukes (now Waters) is a lively member of the Yorkshire Mountaineering Club, is keen on photography and has 165 parachute jumps to her credit; she has also run the London Marathon. Lynda Dean had twice completed the latter event and was also keen on caving and potholing; she brought the skills of joiner and carpenter to the Club and is one of the few women with a Heavy Goods Vehicles Licence. Felicity Andrew's other activities include orienteering, skiing and ski touring.

Two of the new members had already made a name for themselves in a wider sense: Belinda Swift Howe and Ingrid Masterson. Ingrid, who has had many articles published in the Irish MC Journal, had been introduced already.

I had read Belinda's article, "First 6000m Peak" in the July 1980 edition of *Climber and Rambler*, which was about a climbing trip to Peru she had made with another woman, Anne Pendlebury. She had already spent five weeks in the Annapurna region of Nepal, going through much snow to the Thorung La at 17,500ft during February and March, with two other women. In Peru she had climbed Pisang, 18,700ft and Nevade da Copa Norte, 20,300ft. She has written a book of her adventures from Teheran to Kathmandu, under that title, and published it herself for the fun of it.

Belinda writes: "I started climbing when I was 27 – having always been a mountain walker with my father from the age of six. I longed to climb but thought I was too old, and didn't like to lumber the 'hard' men in the club with my modest efforts on rock. Alpine climbing was different – introduced to me by the Austrian Alpine Club and two courses in the Zillertal and Stubai. On the second – the so called Advanced Rock and Ice Course – Peter Habeler was the guide for the five of us who turned up. A memorable holiday watching his 'ballet on rock' and 'skiing' down thousand foot snow gullies as though he was wearing skis. I had always realised that there were pianists who performed on a level way above one I could ever reach and now here was someone whose expertise in mountain terrain was on another plane to that of ordinary mortals. This was before he had climbed Everest or was much known outside Mayrhofen.

"I met Anne Wheatcroft through the AAC and over a number of years she repeated, "You ought to join the Pinnacle Club." I think I was finally spurred on to make the effort because of having returned with my friends Pat and Marion from our three month trip from Teheran to Kathmandu. I felt that to have the time and money for such a venture was one thing but to know two like-minded women who were free at the same time is another. The Pinnacle Club is clearly full of like-minded people."

There was no Club meet outside Europe this year, though one could have called it a mini-meet in Yosemite and members visited Peru, Pakistan, Crete, Corsica, Cyprus and several different areas of the United States. The most eventful meet of the year was at the Loch Coruisk Hut, Skye, at the end of May. Eight members and four guests either walked in, came from Elgol by Mr MacKinnon's boat, or arrived in style from Arisaig on the President's yacht, Alba. All the main summits had at least two ascents, several corries and tricky sections of the ridge were explored and as a highlight to the week a large party set out at 4 a.m. on the Wednesday to attempt the whole ridge. Angela Soper took a mere seven hours to complete a solo traverse from Garsbheinn to Gillean but Jay Turner, Denise Wilson and her son, Richard needed twice as long so had to contend with a hailstorm and a dusk descent.

Jean Drummond, Kate Webb and Felicity Andrew were also making a bid for the traverse when they were literally swept off their feet by a party ahead of them on Bidean. The last man dislodged a huge block which took him, Kate and Felicity down the mountain, luckily stopping in a jumbled mass of scree at the very lip of an enormous drop.

Fortunately they escaped lightly and Jean was able to organise a highly efficient rescue, although it is to be doubted whether Felicity considered that a helicopter ride and three free nights on the National Health made up for her damaged ankle and cancelled holiday in Iceland.

Alpine forays this year included everything from ski touring to climbing on the Handegg Walls (the 'in' place in Central Switzerland) and at home Alex White competed successfully in the Derwent Horseshoe and other fell-running events while Anne Wheatcroft completed the Scottish Munros and Sheila Cormack completed both Munros and Tops. Sheila's friends could have been forgiven for thinking that her eagerness for climbing Munros whenever the weather was too bad for rock climbing might be dampened. Not so.

Sheila had been Club secretary for six years now, and in 1982 she handed over to Jay Turner. Angela's first Dinner Meet as President was a great success, the guest being Bill Peascod who had recently returned to England after 25 years in Australia and did not have far to come from his Lake District home to the Glenridding Hotel. Jane Hillmann introduced the guests in fine style and Angela's account of Pinnacle Club activities was both entertaining and impressive. The non-stop sound of conversation and laughter continued well into the small hours of Sunday morning. When I asked Bill Peascod to autograph my menu card he drew a small sketch of a lake and mountains – a reminder, if one were needed, that he returned from Australia as a successful artist.

In 1982 there was a meet at Cwm Dyli at the same time as the Welsh part of the BMC International Women's Meet. Angela, Sheila and Stella were climbing with the latter and

Members of the International Meet at Cwm Dyli.
L-R: Mandy Glanville, Rosie Andrews, Nicole Niquille, Christine Jambort. Photo Ian Smith.

Club members were invited to Plas y Brenin in the evening to take part in the buffet and disco and to meet the guests. Lively, attractive girls with fine muscles and broad shoulders were the focus of attention in all directions. I was glad to keep my shoulders covered up.

This year, with all its usual and unusual activities, was working towards the climax of the fiftieth anniversary of the opening of the Emily Kelly Hut in November 1932. Two weeks before the event there was a maintenance meet and the hut was painted and scrubbed and bookshelves put up on the new partition wall, built to keep out the draught from the door. The area was scoured for dead trees and branches to provide fuel for the Anniversary bonfire. It poured with rain, and as the wood was stacked behind the hut it was hard to imagine it would ever be dry enough to burn, let alone be ready in a fortnight.

Over thirty guests had been invited from all over Britain, along lines similar to those who had been invited fifty years before. Representing the Rucksack Club were Brian Rhodes and Brian and Joyce Cosby; Harry and Ruth Ironfield were able to represent the Fell and Rock Club; Bonnie Masson came from the Climbers' Club; Yorkshire MC sent Danny Halliwell, Edgar Davis and Peter Stott, and the Oread Pete Scott, Dave Owen and Gill Male. Of course our sister club, the Ladies' Scottish came, in the persons of Maureen Brocklehurst and Edna Stewart.

Cwm Dyli Power Station was represented by Salisbury Roberts and Mr and Mrs Dewi Thomas, and Chris Briggs was invited from the Pen-y-Gwryd Hotel. Finally there were the friends, husbands of members, who had helped with the hut: Bill Barker, Dave Biggs, Colin Greenhow, Barry Webb and Chris Wilson. Great lists were drawn up giving detailed arrangements and times. The only item not given a time because completely incalculable was "Last guests depart."

Being realistic, nobody was expected to stay at home all day getting ready for a party, so chores commenced at 5 p.m. on Saturday although one item was a small exhibition, which I had prepared from material sent to me by members and was able to put up on the Friday night.

It was a rainy weekend but miraculously the rain ceased for the Saturday evening and the night was warm and dry. Club members were given a hearty meal at 6 p.m. (for obvious reasons) then the tables were cleared and rearranged with a delicious variety of buffet dishes prepared by members. Betty and Dorothy cut up dozens of lemons and busied themselves with the mulled wine. The lighting of the bonfire was by no means left to skill in woodcraft, and the initial blaze ensured that any subsequent fuel would burn furiously, however damp it was. Soon the glow revealed members and guests as they gathered round its warmth, paper cups filled to overflowing with the comforting beverage, greeting old friends and meeting new ones.

With the aid of a torch, Angela and I gave our speeches – mine a short history of the hut and Angela's one of welcome. It was a rewarding atmosphere in which to speak, with everyone in the audience basking happily in the warmth, the wine and the sense of occasion and more or less determined to be pleased! The final event outside was a magnificent firework display, followed by a companionable crush inside the hut as people made for the buffet.

Who knows what time we went to sleep that night? It was a time to look back and a time to surge forward. Angela was thinking of new ways for the Club to fulfil its purpose, and Sheila Cormack, the succeeding president, continued the trend. The Club which for sixty years had gained membership by introduction and word of mouth, has reverted to the original way in which it was advertised in the press, and there are regular advertisements in climbing magazines about the "Women's Rock-Climbing Club." Membership has risen to 150 with about 50 more women eager for details of meets. Even with the changing times, many girls and women still feel the desire to develop their own independent skills in a women's club and enjoy the companionship and support of other members. May we be true to our founders and continue as pioneers into the unknown, pushing back frontiers at whatever standard each individual has reached.

Most of all, let us enjoy the sport and each other's company.

Mulled wine by the bonfire.

SUBSCRIBERS

1. Joan Cochrane
2. Lynda Dean
3. Jean Drummond
4. Denise Wilson
5. Stephanie Rowland
6. Frances Tanner
7. Fiona Wilson
8. Ada Shaw
9. Belinda Swift-Howe
10. Sue Gibson
11. Winifred Jackson
12. Sally Keir
13. Angela Soper
14. Wendy Aldred
15. Suzanne Pearson
16. Fern Levy
17. Stella Adams
18. Margaret Darvall
19. Mary Bailey
20. Maud Godward
21. J E Beard
22. Jane Stedman
23. Jacqueline Turner
24. Mandy Glanvill
25. Barbara James
26. Pat Henry
27. Avis Reynolds
28. Margaret Turner
29. Anne Wheatcroft
30. A C Perry
31. Sheila Crispin
32. Isabel Taylor
33. Alison Cairns
34. Mary Waters
35. Sheila Lockhart
36. Sheila McKemmie
37. Mary D Glynne
38. Annabelle Barker
39. Sheila Cormack
40. Jo Polak
41. Vera Picken
42. Joan Cochrane
43. Dorothy Wright
44. Judith Huskins
45. Jean Brazier
46. Kay Hewins
47. Graham Willison
48. Noel Williams
49. Eileen Bunt
50. Peter H Hodgkiss
51. Anne P Wood
52. Sheila Hennebry
53. Penny Storey
54. Pamela Glanville
55. Anne McMillan
56. Pat Daley
57. Nancy Smith
58. Kate Harper
59. R J Hopkinson
60. Angela Soper
61. Eileen Healey
62. Susan M Smith
63. Molly Johnstone
64. Oliver Turnbull
65. Janet Davies
66. Cecily Haussmann
67. F Paul French
68. Susan Logan
69. Pamela Holt
70. Gwen Moffat
71. Jean Dilnot
72. Biddy Burgum
73. Alison Higham
74. Fern Levy
75. Jenny Beale
76. Royanne Wilding
77. Margaret Clennett
78. Gladys-Jean Punnett
79. Beryl May
80. David Campbell
81. Alison M Adam
82. Honor Smith
83. Heather Doyle
84. Mary Fulford
85. Dorothy Wright
86. Maggie Dudley
87. Sally Rawcliffe
88. West Cumbria Mountaineering Club
89. E M Bennett
90. Shirley P Bull
91. Heather M Monie
92. Fiona M Longstaff
93. Rosalind Hill
94. Rosalind Hill and Gwen Chambers in memory of Christina Barratt.
95. Alwine Walford
96. Freda Bean
97. Kathleen Hoskins
98. Marjorie Wood
99. Jean Bollom
100. Betty Whitehead
101. Rosemary Scott
102. Eleanor Winthrop Young
103. Janet Miller
104. Caroline Marsh
105. Teresa Hughes
106. Brenda Whisker
107. Sally MacIntyre
108. M H Dew
109. Joan Dally
110. June Ginger
111. Annis Flew
112. Joann Greenhow
113. Phyllis Jackson
114. Marjorie Heys-Jones
115. Ruth Edwards
116. Sylvia Yates
117. Angela Kalisch
118. R M Beadle
119. Daloni Cooper
120. Dorothy Wright
121. Ladies' Scottish Climbing Club
122. Coral Richards
123. Jean Kitching
124. Meena Agrawal

INDEX of PEOPLE

Abraham, Ashley, 142
Adam, Alison, 29, 34, 36, 39, 46, 50-58, 60, 77, 79, 80, 133, 139, 180, 186, 196, 232
Adam Smith, Janet (Mrs Michael Roberts), 27, 102, 133
Adams, Stella, 237, 240-44, 245, 248
Adrian, Dr., 26
Adrian, Hester, 26, 189
Agnew, Cynthia, 169, 180
Agnew, Mollie, 137, 139, 140, 141, 145
Agrawal, Meena, 208, 213, 215, 217-9, 225
Albon family (Bloomfield), 204
Alexander, Constance, 47-9, 55, 169
Allaun, Miss R, 47, 53, 56
Allison, Dr. Sheila, see Dr. Hennebry.
Angell, Ian, 178-80, 184, 197, 201, 212, 219, 222, 224-5
Angell, Shirley, 178-80, 184, 194, 197, 198-201, 204, 209, 210, 212, 214, 219, 222, 224-5, 226, 227, 230, 232, 234, 238, 245, 249
Angell family, 178-9, 184, 200-1, 204, 212, 222, 224-5, 230
Anthony, Miss, 21
Albon family, 204
Alburger, Mary Anne, 201
Andrew, Felicity, 246-7
Andrews, Berta, see Gough.
Arkless, Brede, 201, 235-7, 245
Arning, Dorothy, 25, 28. 29, 34, 50, 66, 67, 74, 96, 100, 119, 134, 139, 149, 156
Appleyard, Mr., 81
Aston, Beryl, see Jennings.
Atchuk, 153-5
Atu, 61

Banon, Major, 153
Baldwin, Muriel, 111, 138-140, 144
Barclay, Riona, 79
Barford, John, 77, 82
Barker, Annabelle (Harrison), 171, 226, 230
Barker family, 230
Barker, Dr. Mabel, 44, 51, 57
Barnard, O., 118
Barratt, Christina, 42-3, 48, 67, 72, 130
Barratt, Geoffrey, 43, 48
Barry, John, 245
Baxter, 52
Beale, Jenny, 232-3, 238
Beard family (Joyce Taylor), 172, 195, 230
Beattie, Joan, 133

Belfield, Sally, 171
Bell, Ilsa, 11, 20-21, 22, 38, 58
Bennell, P. (Holt), 89
Bennett, Edith, 44
Biggs, Dave, 213
Biener, Carl, 83
Biner, Bernard, 179
Binns, Mrs A.H., 8
Bishop, Millicent, 140
Biven, Peter, 127-8
Blackhurst, Frances, 140, 147
Blackshaw, Alan, 228
Blaikie, Iris, 58, 78
Bland, Dave, 213
Blandy, Nigella, 114
Bonington, Chris, 118, 173, 179
Boucher, Kay (Hewins), 105-6, 111, 112-3
Bower, G.S., 9
Burgess, Derrick, 206
Bradley, M.G., Major Godfrey, 49, 57, 73
Bray, Lilian, 4, 6, 7, 9-14, 16, 22, 23, 25, 27-29, 31, 32, 34, 36, 37, 43, 46, 50, 65, 71, 74, 80, 81, 86, 101, 111, 130, 134, 139, 146, 147, 176, 186, 189
Bray, V., 132
Brazier, Jean (McCann), 87-8, 96, 118
Bridge, Alf, 48
Briggs, Chris, 111, 147, 205, 206, 226
Brook, Richard, 118
Brown, Barbara (Mrs Dawkins), 70
Brown, Don, 216
Brown, Joe, 114, 169, 173
Bryan, Mrs Helen, 42, 44, 49, 50, 58, 60, 65, 72, 80, 89, 94, 111, 128, 175
Bryan, Philippa, 60
Bull, Shirley, 98, 99-101, 146, 147, 155
Bulman, Mr, 69
Burgum, Biddy, 181, 182, 189, 194, 196, 197, 201, 212
Burnett, T.R., 71
Burnham Smith, Mrs 4
Burton, Mrs E., 76
Busby, Joan, 104, 195
Byrom, Jessie, 94

Cain, Ginger, 132
Cairney, Maud, 33
Cameron, Jim, 103, 167
Camrass, Evelyn, 117
Cannon, Gill, (Fuller), 181, 182, 195, 196, 201, 206

Carpenter, Nancy, see Ridyard.
Carr, Evelyn, 34, 48, 49
Carr, Herbert, 7, 10, 13, 34, 48
Carswell, Jack 51
Chadwick, Alison, 235
Chandra Ram, 61, 64
Chandra Singh, 61, 63
Cheney, Mrs, 66
Chevalier, Pierre, 35
Chorley, Professor R.S.T., 8, 9, 54
Chorley, Katharine, 31, 54
Clarke, Ann, see Sutton.
Clarke, E.M. (Lynn) 38, 56, 80, 139, 186
Clegg, John, 125-6
Clennett, Margaret, 137
Clough, Ian, 173, 201
Clough, Niki, 132, 201
Clune, Dorothy, 47, 49, 50
Coates, Beryl, 102, 129
Coates, H., 17, 18
Coates, Joyce, 82, 84
Cobham, J.M., 47, 90
Cochrane, Joan, 59-60, 66-68, 70, 75, 77, 78, 82, 83, 96, 167
College, Ray, 145
Collie, Ida, 49
Collingwood, Sylvia, 42
Collins, Miss, 18
Cook, John, 142
Cook, Lawson, 31, 55, 88
Cooper, Alastair, 55
Cooper, Catherine B.R., 82, 84
Cooper family (D. Seth Hughes),151, 173, 204, 214, 230
Corbett, Dr. Katie (Catherine), 9-11, 15, 18, 21, 22, 27, 29, 31, 32, 34, 36-39, 41, 46, 50, 51, 66-7, 69, 74, 75, 80, 82, 86, 97, 101, 146
Corbett, Rooke, 31
Corbett, Sandra, 237
Cormack, Sheila, 201, 208, 212, 214, 224, 226-7, 229, 233, 237, 240-44, 245, 247, 248, 249
Cotchin, Adelaide, 212, 215
Cox, David, 206
Cox, Janet, see Davies.
Coxhead, Elizabeth, 103, 104
Crispin, Sheila, 155, 156, 175, 196
Crofts, Brian, 200
Cross, Jammy (Mary Nelson), 51, 55, 58, 194, 210
Cross, Sid, 51, 55, 58, 72, 90, 194, 210, 238
Cumming, Violet, 51
Cunningham, Philip 121
Curtis, Janette, 138

Dack, Sheelagh, 131

Daffern, Tony,
Daley, Pat, 128, 129, 200, 208, 214
Damesme, Alice, 27, 35
Daniell, Emily (E.H. Young) 6, 8, 21, 85
Danson, Pat (Downes), 221
Darvall, Margaret, 103, 110-113, 119, 121, 122, 127, 128, 133, 134, 135, 137, 145, 146, 152, 168, 173, 175, 180, 184, 189, 192, 198, 209, 213, 219, 225, 238
Davidson, g, 38
Davies, Janet, (Cox, Rogers), 104, 120, 131, 132, 134, 145, 152, ˙164, 169, 173, 176, 181, 185-6, 193, 195, 196, 198, 200, 201, ˙206, 208, 210
Dawson, Dora, 38-9, 56
Dean, Lynda, 245-6
de Beer, Dora, 206
Debenham, Virginia, 131
Deed, Biddy, 46, 47, 53, 56, 57, 60, 68
Delany, Frances, 121
Demetz, Johann, 130, 217
Denny, F, 80
Dew, Margaret (Moggy), 89, 128-9
Diamond, Jack, 55
Dilnot, Jean, 181, 182, 189, 194, 196, 197, 201, 212
Disley, John, 127
Donnison, Annis, see Flew.
Dorje, Phu 138,
Doughty, J.H., 4, 9, 17, 49
Dowlen, Ann, 181
Downes, Bob, 164
Downes, Pat, see Danson
Drummond, Jean, 228-9, 235, 239, 240-44, 245, 246
Drummond, Tony, 229, 235
Duerden, John, 82, 91
Duerden, Pat, see Whinnerah.
Dunsheath, Joyce, 121
Dutton, Miss, 4, 8, 11, 22
Dwyer, George (Scotty), 103, 113
Dydynski, Mrs, 11

Eden-Smith, B. (Gabriel), 4, 5, 8, 11, 18, 20-24, 26, 29, 36, 39, 43, 45, 46, 49, 50, 51, 55, 58, 65, 80, 104, 167
Eden-Smith, Mr., 8
Eden-Smith, Jock and Waddy, 8, 21, 24
Edmundson, David, 238
Edwards, Menlove, 49, 60, 88
Elliott, Miss Agnes 49
Elliott, Mr. and Mrs. Claude, 15
Emery, Betty, 113
Evans, Anthea, Alan and family, 226, 230
Evans, Charles, 121, 125, 132, 133, 164, 172, 197

Evans, Denise, see Denise Morin.
Evans family (Chuck, Robin), 139, 172
Evans, Dr., 10, 17, 19, 23
Evans, Mrs, 4, 5, 10, 19, 23

Faller, Angela, see Soper.
Feruseth, 24
Fildes, Anne, see McMillan.
Fitzgerald, Geraldine, 38
Fitzgerald, Kevin, 205, 206
Fitzgibbon, Molly, 44, 46, 48, 50, 58, 88
Flew, Annis, (Donnison), 89, 109, 110, 115, 118, 124, 132, 133, 139, 144, 146, 150, 151, 152, 164, 172, 212, 215
Flew, A.G.N. (Tony), 139,
Flew family, 215, 230
Food, Rev. Frank, 180
Forsyth, Nancy, 47, 49, 50, 52, 58, 71
Foster, Peggy, 174, 213, 214
Franco, Jeanne, 138
Frazer, George, 137
Fulford, Mary, 168, 169, 185, 195
Fuller, Brian, 153, 182,
Fuller, Gill, see Cannon.
Fuller, Jo, 153, 155-6, 167, 168, 176, 180, 194-7, 201, 212

Garner, Madge (Mrs Gillespie), 82
Gay, Jancis, 182, 200
Gebbie, Katharine, 168, 171-2, 238
Geddes, Sir Patrick, 44
Gentil, Peter, 178, 198
Georges, Antoine, 25, 32, 37
Georges, Joseph, 21, 23, 25, 27, 32-3, 34-5, 38, 46, 48
Gibson, Suzanne, 95-6, 100, 109, 111, 114, 118, 130, 146, 152, 168, 180, 184, 192, 209, 214, 219, 238,
Ginger, June (Hunt), 157, 164, 165, 167-8
Glynne, Mary, 47, 52, 113, 114, 142, 169
Glynne Jones, Owen, 47, 142
Godward, Maud, 102, 103, 109, 110, 119, 122-3, 133-4, 145-6, 152, 223, 228
Gollancz, Livia, 168-9, 170, 173, 185, 213
Goodburn, Helen, see Jones.
Goodchild, Lt. Col., 116
Gold, Mr & Mrs, 210
Gordon, Philip, 128
Gotch, M.S., 85
Gough, Berta (Andrews), 47-50, 53-60, 65-70
Grace, W.G., 85
Gravina, Christopher, 121
Gravina, Count, 120

Gravina, Dorothea, 116, 119, 120-1, 123-4, 127, 132-5, 137, 139, 145, 150-3, 158-62, 166, 168, 171-2, 175-6, 184-5, 193-4, 201, 209, 213-4, 230, 235
Gravina, Michael, 121
Gravina, Tim, 121 153
Gray, Dennis, 175
Gray, Dorothy, 66, 69, 70, 77
Greenhow, Colin, 206, 209, 217, 220, 223
Greenhow, Joann, 201, 204, 206-7, 209, 212-4, 217, 219, 223, 224, 229
Greenwood, Sylvia, 105, 127, 130
Gregory, Eileen (Healey), 74, 79-60, 88, 90, 98, 102, 109, 110, 113, 115, 118, 121-2, 125-8, 130, 133-5, 137, 140, 146, 152, 184, 214
Gregson, Tanya 237
Grieg, Eileen, 28
Grier, A, 181
Griffin, Elizabeth, 53
Griffiths, Jean, 111, 112, 149
Griffiths, Miss, 43
Grindley, Cynthia (Heap), 211
Grutter, Marie, 59, 67, 82, 131, 149
Grosvenor, Mary, 47
Grosvenor, Mr., 49
Guinness, Maurice, 175
Gunther, Mr., 121

Hadfield, Miss, 24
Haigh, Dawn, see Hopkinson.
Hale, Ruth, 43, 46, 50, 51-4, 56
Hall, Miss E.N. (Sam), 25, 27, 31, 33
Hall, Judith, see Huskins.
Hall, Kate, see Webb.
Hallett, Elizabeth, 184
Hankinson, Alan, 235
Hannan, Barbara, see Prince.
Hargreaves, A.B., 47, 49, 99
Hargreaves, A.T., 49, 51, 54, 55, 58, 118
Hargreaves, Ruth (Heap), 42-3, 46, 49, 51, 55, 58, 80, 228
Harland, Miss E.F., (Mrs J.C. Appleyard), 8, 11, 20
Harper, Susan, 36-8, 39, 42, 46, 51, 52, 58, 66-8
Harris, Mike, 137
Harrison, Annabelle, see Barker.
Haston, Julia, 239
Healey, Eileen, see Gregory.
Healey, John, 214
Healey, Tim, 134, 152
Heap, Cynthia, see Grindley
Helburn, Margaret, 213
Helliwell, Danny, 223
Henderson, R.B., 6, 21, 85

Hennebry, Dr. Sheila, 94
Henry, Pat (Wood), 135, 136, 139, 140, 144, 150, 153, 158-62, 168, 171-2, 177, 184, 191, 196
Henson, Jack, 103
Heppenstall, Angela (Kelly), 186, 190, 196, 198, 200, 201, 208, 219, 226, 230, 235, 238
Heppenstall family, 230
Herbert, Rie, see Leggett.
Hey, Wilson, 52
Heys-Jones, Marjorie, 36-8, 39, 42, 46, 52, 70, 72, 77, 81
Higgs, Dorothea, 56, 60, 69
Higham, Alison (Lamb), 195, 208, 211, 219, 230, 233, 237, 241
Hill, Rosalind, 72
Hillmann, Jane, 232-3, 247
Hilton, Miss, 18, 36
Hirst, John, 10, 13, 15, 21, 52, 55, 76-7, 99
Hirst, Joyce, 55
Hirst, Paddy (Annie Wells), 2-4, 8, 10, 11-14, 21-2, 24-8, 52, 55, 76-7, 147, 206
Hobkinson, Miss, 38, 43
Hodladay, Percy, 48
Hopkinson brothers, 54
Hopkinson, Dawn (Haigh), 212, 214-5, 217
Horsford, Ann, 111, 112
Hoskins, Kathleen, 181, 195, 200
Howarth, Jill, 146
Huddleston, Miss A., 8
Hughes, Joyce (Tombs), 95, 109, 132
Hughes, Teresa, 237
Hunt, June, see Ginger.
Huskins, Judith (Hall), 125-7, 128, 130, 132, 147
Hutson, Cicely, 58
Hyslop, Jenny, 228

Imberty, Pierre, 109
Inglis Clarke, Charles, 56
Innes, M, 88
Isherwood, Mrs, 17, 18, 26

Jackson, Eileen, 42
Jackson, John, 175
Jackson, Monica, 117, 132, 175
Jackson, Phyl, see Raven.
Jackson, Winifred, 70, 72-3, 74, 79, 82, 103, 127, 128, 140, 147, 165, 223
James, Barbara, 184, 190-1, 197-8, 202-3, 209, 213, 219, 221-3.
James, Pat, 239
James, Ron, 202-3, 209, 213, 219, 222
Jeffrey, Mabel, 27, 56, 57, 59, 60, 65, 67, 69, 70, 72, 79, 80, 81, 87, 89, 110, 134, 186, 194, 206
Jennings, Beryl (Aston), 97, 109, 110, 118, 122

Jennings, Eunice, 44
Jigmet, 153-5
Johns, M, 79
Johnson, Mrs, 8
Jones, Emlyn, 137
Jones, Helen (Goodburn), 132, 175, 180, 184, 189, 192, 208, 219, 232
Jones, Trevor, 214
Josserand, Gilles, 145, 193
Joy, Gwen, 239
Joyce, J.E., 53

Kain, Conrad, 46
Kanla, Shashi, 201
Keatinge, Bridget, 133, 140
Keay, Miss, 43
Keir, Sally, 239
Kellett, Brian, 71
Kellett, M., 118
Kelly, Angela, see Heppenstall
Kelly, Emily (Pat), 1-9, 11, 14, 15, 16, 18-19, 39, 69
Kelly, H.M., 3, 4, 7, 9, 11, 17, 18-19, 20, 23, 24, 26-7, 31, 49, 50, 54, 55, 88, 205, 222
Kemp, Dennis, 111, 221
Kerr, Fay, 152
Kershaw, Jim, 146
Kershaw, Mary, 150-1, 155, 164
Kenyon, J.A., 71
Kidd, Diana, 82-3
Kilshaw, J.B., 26
Kindleysides, Ada, see Shaw
King, Dora, 75, 77, 80, 82-3, 90, 97, 102, 110, 118, 127, 146
Kirby, Mr., 94
Kirkus, Colin, 48
Kitkat, Betty, 165
Kitching, Jean, 190
Knight, Julia, 212
Kogan, Claude, 137-8
Komarkova, Vera, 235

Lamb, Alison, see Higham
Lamb, Mr., 23
Lambert, Georges, 109, 115
Lambrick, Lucy (Mrs Parry), 47, 54, 69
Lancaster, Constance, 55, 58
Lavender, Royanne, see Wilding.
Lawrence, Jill, 186, 245
Lawrie, Mrs Ursula, 46
Lawton, Isabel, 138
Lawton, N., 102
Lear, Miss, 39, 46
Lee, Dorothy, 135-6, 138, 150, 191-2

Lee, Rae, 181, 214, 226
Leech, Antonia, 73, 88, 102, 105, 127, 144, 184, 209-12, 214
Leech, Ben, 38, 66, 73
Leech, Evelyn W. (Lowe), 34, 37, 39-42, 46, 49, 50-53, 55, 57, 61, 65-68, 70-75, 77, 79-84, 86, 88, 91, 100, 105, 111, 118, 131, 144, 148, 166, 175, 181, 196, 199, 200, 206, 208-9
Lees, John, 92-4, 109, 121, 124, 132
Leggett, Rie (Herbert), 94-5, 109, 110, 114, 115, 118, 123, 128, 172, 216
Leith, Eveleigh, 140-1, 152, 168, 173, 185, 194, 213
Lemar, Iris, 130
Linnell, Maurice, 48
Littledale, Miss, 53
Littlejohn, Anne, 43, 116, 119, 120, 129, 130, 139, 144, 145, 147, 152, 162, 164, 165, 168-72
Lockwood, 2, 96
Long, J.V.T., 17,18
Long, Suzanne, see Gibson
Longland, Jack, 94, 118, 225
Longstaff, Fiona (Slator), 237
Longstaff, Miss V., 53, 61, 65
Loukes, Mary, see Waters.
Low, Gladys (Jean Punnett), 49, 52, 58, 61, 128, 204, 222
Lowe, Evelyn, see Leech.

McAndrew, Miss, 49, 52
McCall, Patricia, 82, 84
Macdonald, Sheila, 33
McGuinness, Tommy, 142, 143
Machin, Cyril, 76, 87, 112
MacInnes, Hamish, 132
MacKay, Elspet, 190
McKemmie, Sheila, 245
McMillan, Anne (Fildes), 226-7, 233
McNair, C., 79
McNaught-Davis, Ian, 92, 169, 189, 223
MacRae, Susannah, 119, 133
Magri, Stella, 75, 78, 79
Mahajan, Sushama, 241, 244
_Mallory, 15, 44
Manison, Harold, 146
Mann, Ella (Standring), 23, 31, 36, 51, 52
Marples, Miss Winifred (Jo), 25, 35, 78, 82
Marriott, Charles, 92
Masterson, Ingrid, 155, 230-1, 246
Maxwell, Eric, 77
Medlock, Alan and Josie, 223
Mendus, Ieuan, 51
Michaelson, Miss B.L., 4, 5, 8, 9, 11, 21
Middleton, Nan, 39

Miller, Irene, 235
Milner-Brown, Dorothy, 47
Mingma, 161
Minor, Olive, 9, 11
Moffat, Gwen, 80, 81, 90-1, 92-4, 102, 103, 109, 115, 116, 121, 124, 132, 133, 135, 138, 144, 152-3, 197, 200, 206, 208, 210, 212, 215, 217, 221, 234, 238
Moffat, Hilary, Peter and family, 222, 224-5
Moffat, Sheena, 92, 136, 144
Monie, Heather, 101, 146, 147
Montague, C.E., 15
Moore, Miss Jocelyn, 87, 102
Morin, Denise (Evans), 75, 77, 82, 88, 90, 92, 98, 102, 111, 115, 118, 121, 122, 125-8, 130, 132, 133, 139, 144, 145, 148-50, 158-62, 164-6, 175-7, 180, 193, 216, 237
Morin, Ian, 77, 90, 92, 102, 115, 118, 133, 151
Morin, Jean, 35
Morin, Micheline, 27, 132, 151, 192
Morin, Nea, 27, 31, 35, 65-6, 68, 71, 75, 77, 79, 84, 86, 88-90, 92, 94, 95, 97, 100, 102, 104, 111, 113-115, 118, 121, 125-6, 127-8, 131-3, 135, 137, 139, 144, 151, 155, 164, 174, 176, 184, 192, 194-7, 200, 208, 209, 212, 213, 216, 219, 238
Morley Wood, 11
Morsley, Richard, 206
Moseley, Ronnie, 114
Moulam, Tony, 84, 88, 90, 127, 206
Munday, Mrs Don, 33, 148
Murgatroyd, Kathy, 222

Naylor, Mrs, 86
Nelson, Mary, see Jammy Cross
Newby, Eric, 234
Newby, J., 102
Nisbet, Eilidh, 195
Norbu, Pemba, 161
Norman, Sylvia, 34
Nowill, Sidney, 114, 193

O'Brian, Miriam, 33, 35, 38
O'Connor, Fran, 226
Oldham, Mabel, 150-1, 155, 164-5
Oliver, Maud, 82, 84, 87, 88
O'Malley, Mrs, 4
Ormiston Chant, Mrs T.C., 8
_Orr Ewing, Jean, 42-3, 46, 52, 71

Pacolaski, 'Taddy', 50
Pal, Bachendri, 218
Palmer, Joann, see Greenhow.
Papworth, Julia, 147
Parkinson, Peggy, 109, 122

Parsons, Patricia, 128
Parry, Elisabeth, 193
Parry, J., 89
Paryski, Witold, 50, 52, 53-4
Paterson, Grizel, 206
Patey, Tom, 173, 175
Paxton, John Hall, 23
Peascod, Bill, 247
Peck, Trevor, 127
Perramon, Louis, 109-10
Perren, Bernard, 102, 104
Perren, Gottlieb, 104
Picken, Mairet, 150, 181, 195, 198, 211
Picken, Vera (Unicombe), 47, 48, 69, 70, 136, 146, 150, 153, 155, 165, 186
Pickles, Charles, 232
Pigott, Mr, 58
Piggott, Fred, 221
Pillar, Judith, 171
Pilley, Miss D.E., (Mrs I.A. Richards) 4, 7, 8, 10, 11-13, 21-25, 28, 31, 32-3, 43, 46, 48, 50, 51, 54, 58, 60, 77, 80, 82, 90, 91, 98, 100, 102, 109, 115-6, 120, 130, 133, 140, 146, 186, 193, 225, 232
Pilley, John, 21
Pilley, Violet, 24-5
Pirie, Miss Evelyn, 42, 44, 50, 51, 58, 60, 65, 80, 94, 175
Porter, John, 146
Porter, 15
Porter, Mollie (Taplin), 134-5, 140, 145, 146, 209
Poulton, Penelope, see Seth Hughes.
Poulton family, 151, 172, 204, 214, 230
Prince, Barbara (Hannan), 212, 215
Prince Philip, 130
Pritchard, R.E.W., 9, 24
Proctor, Rosalind, 47, 49
Punnett family, 204
Punnett, Jean, see Gladys Low.
Pyatt, Edward, 73
Pyatt, Eileen, 71, 73-4, 89, 97, 109, 118

HM Queen Elizabeth, 75
HM Queen Elizabeth II, 130

Radcliffe, Miss, 22, 67
Rambaud, Micheline, 138
Ratcliffe, Mrs J., 67, 70
Rathbone, Miss C., 4, 5, 8
_Raven, Joan, 65
Raven, Phyllis (Jackson), 51, 65, 66, 67, 70, 71, 73, 74, 79, 82-3, 109
Redman, Ann, 219, 221, 224, 225, 227, 235
Reece, Peggy, 152
Reid, Hilda, 121

Reynolds, A.B., 31
Reynolds, Avis, 190, 191, 195, 228
Reznicek, Baronin F. von, 197
Richards, I.A., 7, 21, 23, 25, 28, 31, 32-3, 46, 49, 58, 60, 90
Ridyard, Nancy (Carpenter), 47, 50, 58, 71, 80
Ritchie, Brenda, 34, 43, 46, 48, 49, 54, 57, 58, 60, 65, 72, 110, 130, 132, 149
Ritchie, Jean, 181
Roberts, Mrs Cicely, see Wood.
Roberts, David, 66, 98
Roberts, Geoff, 94, 118
Roberts, Janet, see Janet Adam Smith.
Roberts, Jean, 212, 221
Roberts, Mr. & Mrs., 73
Robinson, Jill, 128
Rogers, Janet, see Davies.
Rogers, Nigel, 152, 173
Roscoe, Barbara (Spark) 148, 150, 153-5, 158-62, 164, 172, 189, 191, 195, 203, 209, 213, 215
Rostron, Bertha, 131, 138, 152, 214
Rowland, Steph, 206, 207, 213, 214, 240-44
Rowlands, Megan, 118, 119
Ruck, Ruth, 94, 118, 156
Russenberge, Vicki, 90-1
Rylatt, Freda, 68, 70, 73-5, 79-80, 82-3, 84, 85, 94

Sales, Harry, 228
Scalet, Giacomo, 132
Scarr, Jo, 131-2, 133, 138, 144, 148, 150, 153-5, 158-62, 164
Schaaning, 24
Schjelderup, Fru, 14
Schroeder, Mary, 37
Scott, Doug, 179
Scott, Elizabeth, 237
Scott, Gladys, 51
Scott, H.E., 49
Scott Johnson, Marjorie, 42
Seth Hughes, Daloni (Mrs Cooper), 42, 46, 49, 50, 51, 55, 151, 204
Seth Hughes, Jennet, 49, 50, 52, 53, 55, 65, 74
Seth Hughes, Penelope (Mrs Poulton), 42, 49, 50, 51, 52, 55, 61, 65, 66, 74, 151, 155, 204
Shaw, Ada (Kindleysides, Moss), 81, 84, 89, 97, 114, 128, 131, 135, 145, 146, 152, 189, 196, 237
Sheard, Christine, 174, 180, 185, 186, 192, 194, 201, 219, 232
Shepherd, Anne, see Wheatcroft.
Sheridan, Bairbre, 230
Shortall, Denise, see Wilson.
Simpson, Jim, 125-6
Simpson, Myrtle, 214, 222
Sims, Eve, 134

Sims, N., 57
Sladen, Geraldine, 56-7, 58, 60, 61, 65
Slator, Fiona, see Longstaff.
Slingsby, Cecil, 1, 2, 14
Smith, Annette and Janet, 58
Smith, Cym, 142-3
Smith, Dorothy, 74
Smith, Miss G.M., 49
Smith, Nancy, 102, 113, 118, 140, 141-4, 145, 149, 150, 153, 158-62, 164, 168, 172, 173, 177, 230
Smith, Sue, 226
Somervell, L.W., 71
Somervell, Mrs., 24
Somervell, Dr. T. Howard, 78
Soper, Angela (Faller), 32, 182, 184-5, 186-7, 190, 191, 192, 197, 200, 201, 210, 212, 213, 215, 225, 235, 240-44, 245, 246, 248, 249
Spark, Barbara, see Roscoe.
Speaker, G. R., 34
Speakman, Esme, 96, 119, 195
Speight, Ruth, 198, 211
Spilsbury, Harry, 99
Stanley, Miss, 4
Stark, Betty, 117
Stedman, Jane, 224, 228
Sterbova, Dina, 230
Stewart, Mary, 173
Stewart, Midge, 57
Storey, Penny, 104, 114, 119, 122, 133, 134, 145, 185, 193, 228
Strasek, Vida, 211-2
Stuart, Catherine, 47
Styles, Showell, 126
Summersgill, Mrs., 20
Supersaxo, Heinrich, 83
Sutcliffe, Anne, see Wood.
Sutton, Ann, 111, 128, 129, 216
Sutton, Geoffrey, 92, 216
Swift, Belinda, 237, 246
Swindale, Sandra (Vickers), 186, 189, 190, 200-1, 218, 219
Sykes, Kathleen, 68, 77

Tabei, Junko, 226
Tanner, Frances, 145, 148-9, 150, 164, 173, 177
Tanner, Marjorie, 155, 156, 164, 168, 182
Taplin, Mollie, see Porter.
Tarbuck, Ken, 148
Taugwalder, Alexander, 83
Taugwalder, Otto, 38, 83
Taylor, Isabel, 119-20, 121, 145
Taylor, Jane, 190, 191, 196, 198, 210, 213
Taylor, Joyce, 72-3, 88, 89
Taylor, Dr. M., 26, 32, 39, 46, 50, 53, 149

Teague, E., 82
Tebbutt, Joan, 71, 75
Temba, Ang, 161
Tensing, Dawa. 137, 159-60, 176, 177
Tharby, Doreen, 73, 88, 89, 94, 109, 115, 168
Thomas, Eustace, 31
Thomas, Margaret, see Turner.
Thompson, Dorothy, 21, 23, 25, 27, 33, 34-5, 38
Thompson, P., 92-4
Thompson, Phyllis, 142
Till, Mollie, 142
Todd, Miss H.M., 8
Tomasak, Miss Anna, 159
Tombs family, 132
Tombs, Joyce, see Hughes.
Tonsberg, 26
Trench, Bill, 94
Turner, Harriet, 4, 9, 18, 21, 27, 66-70, 80, 84, 171
Turner, Jay, 237, 240-44, 246, 247
Turner, John, 116
Turner, Margaret, 94
Turner, Muriel, 25
Tyler, Hilda, 200, 201, 212, 216, 219, 221
Tyson, John, 159

Underhill, Miriam, 213
Unicombe, Vera, see Picken.

Van der Straaten, Claudine, 138
Vaucher, Michel, 193
Vaughan Thomas, 85
Vickers, Sandra, see Swindale.
Viney, Dick, 92

Walford, Alwine, 164, 168, 174-5, 184-5, 189, 192, 196, 197, 198, 200, 201, 205, 208, 209, 213, 214, 222, 223, 225, 228, 232, 234, 238
Walford, Hugo, 174-5, 192
Walker, M., 57
Wallbank, F., 17
Wallbank, Mrs F., 4
Walton, Kathryn, 171
Wangyal, 153-5
Ward, Miss K.,4
Ward, MIke, 197
Warren, Miss L.A., 54, 65, 67
Washington, Sybil, 164, 181
Waters, Mary (Loukes), 245
Watson, Miss R. M., 53, 56
Watson, Vera, 235
Webb, Kate (Hall), 172, 175, 179, 200, 214, 219, 220-3, 225, 226, 246
Webb family, 219, 220, 222, 225
Welchman, Miss, 91

Wells, Annie, see Paddy Hirst.
Wells, Biddy, 2, 3, 9, 10, 11, 19, 21, 24, 28, 31, 33, 34, 52, 53, 57, 65, 68, 69, 76, 80, 81, 86, 97, 138, 147, 149
Wells, Trilby, 2, 9, 10, 11, 18, 19, 23, 26, 27, 31, 32, 34, 51, '52, 53, 57, 65, 66-7, 68, 69, 76, 80, 81, 86, 97, 138, 147, 149, 186, 206
Westmacott, Sally. 129, 155, 156, 162, 168-9, 173-4, 195, 198
Wheatcroft, Anne(Shepherd), 206, 207-8, 212, 213, 215, 219, 220, 223, 225, 228, 247
Whillans, Audrey, 201, 205
Whillans, Don, 114, 169, 179, 205
Whinnerah, Pat (Duerden), 82, 91
White, Alex, 16, 222, 224, 230, 247
White, Hester, 57, 59, 65, 79
White, Tabitha, 222, 230
Whitehead, Betty, 216, 223, 224, 248
Whitehead, Bob, 206
Whittaker, J., 144
Whymper, Ethel (Mrs Blandy), 38
Wigner, Mrs., 4
Wild, Miss, 4
Wild, Peggy, 78-9, 80, 86, 88, 89, 94, 109, 115, 168, 178, 193, '200, 230
Wilding, Royanne (Lavender), 214, 219, 221-2, 224
Wilkinson, Freda, 131, 138
Wilkinson, John, 206, 210
Williams, Bishop Ronald, 180, 225
Williams, Cicely (Bim), 225, 226
Williams, Mr. & Mrs.(Power Station), 70, 73
Willink, Hester, 150
Wilson, Alicia, 51, 56, 65, 68
Wilson, Annette, 44, 45, 48, 49, 50, 53-56, 59, 66-70, 80, 82, 83, 84, 86, 87, 96, 97, 100, 105, 109, 124, 146, 156, 175, 214
Wilson, Chris, 238
Wilson, Denise (Shortall), 94-5, 114-5, 119, 123-4, 133, 152, 168, 176, 197, 210, 212, 214, 216, 219, 221-4, 228, 230, 240-44, 246
Wilson family, 222, 230, 246
Wilson, Graham, 24
Winter, Horatia, 80, 82-3
Wilson, Ken, 197
Winthrop Young, Eleanor (Len), 1-8, 11, 14-16, 18, 20-21, 22, 23, 24, 26, 27, 29, 60, 71, 180, 206, 245
Winthrop Young, Geoffrey, 1, 2, 16, 33, 70
Winthrop Young, Jocelyn, 60
Wintringham, Marion, 235
Wood, Anne (Sutcliffe), 140
Wood, Cicely (Roberts), 57, 60, 65, 66, 98
Wood, Lucy, 74, 84

Wood, Marjorie, 28, 31, 38, 39, 46, 51, 53, 56, 58, 65, 79, 80, 86, 97, 133, 134, 138, 148, 181, 186, 205
Wood, Pat, see Henry.
Wood, Sidney, 52
Woods, Chris, 89, 103, 127, 133, 138, 196
Work, Beryl, 194
Worrall, Plum, 216-7
Worrall, Robbie, 216-7
Wright, Dorothy, 190, 192, 211, 248
Wright, J.E.B., 31, 103
Wyatt, John, 232

Yates, Sylvia, 153, 155, 162, 164, 165, 168, 171-3, 193, 231
Young, Gladys, 6